Regional Planning: A Comprehensive View

Regional Planning: A Comprehensive View

JEREMY ALDEN and ROBERT MORGAN

LEONARD HILL BOOKS an Intertext Publisher

Published by
Leonard Hill Books
a division of
International Textbook Company Limited
Kingswood House, Heath & Reach nr Leighton Buzzard, Beds LU7 0AZ

First published 1974

ISBN 0 249 44137 3

Printed in Great Britain by Pitman Press, Bath

Contents

Preface   *vii*

1   Introduction to Regional Planning   1

2   The Development of Regional Planning   9

3   Regional Planning Theory   57

4   National Regional Policy and Regional Planning   83

5   Regional Planning Institutions   123

6   The Regional Planning Process   167

7   Analytical Techniques for Regional Planning   211

8   Procedural Techniques for Regional Planning   259

9   Problems and Prospects of Regional Planning   309

Appendix 1   Regional Differentials in Economic and Social Performance
             in Britain and EEC Countries 1968   323

Appendix 2   A Summary Bibliography on Regional Planning Techniques   327

Appendix 3   An Introduction to Published Sources Containing Regional
             Data on Regular Time Series   337

Index   356

Preface

Regional planning is to us a potentially very valuable social tool. That is why it is important to further debate about its nature and to encourage its development. At this moment it is still a very new form of planning and there is no doubt a long road to travel and mistakes to be made before it becomes a finely tuned and effective tool. The subsequent pages will no doubt make some of those mistakes, but the sustaining hope has been that they will too help it a little further along the road.

The difficulties have been greater because the organizing idea has been the concern to produce a comprehensive statement of the subject as a whole. As far as we are aware this has not been attempted before. This doubled the challenge we took up and also demonstrated the urgency and importance of that challenge.

In addition to setting out the nature of regional planning as we see it, a central commitment has been a concern critically to assess its current state and to search and suggest lines of improvement and development. Indeed the work is much more an attempt to develop and to encourage the development of the subject than an attempt to define, charactize and thus to freeze what it is. In this sense it is a presentation which asks for active use by the reader, for challenge and refutation.

It follows that our market is anyone interested in and concerned about regional planning—students of all forms of planning primarily perhaps, administrators and practitioners, but hopefully other groups and interests as well.

We would like to thank Mrs. Myrtle Robins for her patience and hard work in typing the manuscript. For reading parts or the whole of the manuscript we would also like to express our thanks to Owen Hooker, Roy Walker and Trevor MacMurray, and to Donald Harris for this and other things. All responsibility for what follows remains with us.

1 Introduction to Regional Planning

Introduction

The work presented here is concerned with the nature of regional planning as a particular form of planning action. Its concern is to clarify and elaborate this nature and to provide a basis for its improvement and development. In order to do this much information has been brought together and tentatively synthesized. In particular, consideration is given to the definition of this form of action, its particular role and contribution, its knowledge base, its methods and its techniques. But the motivating concern is not so much to transmit this information and knowledge but rather to contribute to its active growth and development; it is more concerned to suggest than to assert, to stimulate rather than prematurely to confirm and mould. The substance of the subject as it has been assembled and structured here is not a package to be passively accepted but a package to be broken up, reassembled and discarded with the development of the subject. The task set is difficult and demanding but the current and potential significance of regional planning also makes it exciting, relevant and worth while.

The Nature of Regional Planning

It is simplistic but nevertheless helpful to explain the difficulty of clearly defining the nature of regional planning as a product of vagueness and ambiguity in the two component terms — region and planning. In other words, planning as an activity, and regions as areas within which this activity is pursued, are both rich yet imprecise concepts. Accordingly, the brief interpretation of these concepts offered at this stage simply serves as an aid to a preliminary definition of the field of interest. Both concepts are elaborated later.

Planning may be viewed as a highly disciplined and formalized activity through which a society induces change in itself. It involves the application of scientific knowledge in order to solve the problems and achieve the goals of a social system. Any social system therefore which has adopted planning, whether it be a firm, family, town or region, may hope to determine its own future. Further, in evaluating the steps taken to reach this future, it may learn, and through learning it may engage in a continual process of self realization.

Within the context of this broad perspective of planning, it is possible to recognize a number of different forms of planning, and the most significant of these is the division into private planning and public planning. Private planning is concerned with planning within the micro social systems of society and has developed furthest in the context of the firm. Public planning on the other hand is concerned with societies and major sub systems, such as sectors of the economy, towns and regions, within society. Public planning is undertaken by institutions accessible to and responsible to the public. It is as such imbued with a very different ethic and style of operation to private planning. An attempt has been made in the succeeding chapters to locate regional planning within the context of this emerging concept of public planning and more generally within the context of the planning discipline.

The problem of defining what is meant by the term 'region' has absorbed a very great deal of interest and debate, particularly amongst geographers. However, not all of this energy has been fruitful and there is now a remarkable but potentially disconcerting variety of meanings associated with the term, so much so that, as Perloff has pointed out, this has not unnaturally led to scepticism regarding the validity of regional planning.[1] However, recently and from within the planning world a simple but suggestive approach has been adopted of viewing regions as spaces which are larger than any single urban area, that is, as supra urban space.[2] At the same time a region is contained within a nation and is thus a sub national space.

It could be argued in defence of this very broad definition that rather than conferring on regional planning vagueness and ambiguity it endows it with a valuable territorial flexibility, a flexibility unique amongst all of the various forms of public planning.

This is an issue which is returned to later. At this stage it is possible to draw together the interpretations that have been outlined above and thus to define regional planning as a particular type of structural solution to the problem of societal self articulation. In other words, in order to overcome the problems it is experiencing or to realize the goals it has set for itself, society or groups within society may institutionalize the planning of supra urban spaces.

The Rationale for Regional Planning

The questions immediately arise: What are the specific reasons which explain why society may resort to a regional planning form of action? What is its specific and distinctive contribution to the process of societal self articulation?

In the first place regional planning may be institutionalized because of its particular ability directly to engage certain types of problems experienced by groups and individuals within society. The list of problems is varied and endless but by way of illustration it includes: the problem of inadequate employment opportunities on declining coalfields; the problem of adequately exploiting a fertile coastal plain or of overcoming limitations on agriculture in some harsh highland area through use of the most advanced technology; the problem of improving access to and the distribution of the higher order types of social facilities; the problem of insecurity in some newly acquired territorial addition to the state; the problem of groups experiencing social economic or political disadvantages in some area of the nation state and of others experiencing physical discomfort through overcrowding and congestion.

Generalizing, regional planning is particularly fitted for dealing with those problems which arise with regard to those large homogeneous areas of the earth's surface to which the geographer first gave the term 'region'. Included here are the river valleys, highland areas and coastal plains that provide the platform for so much human activity. However regional planning is infinitely more flexible and subtle than this in terms of the nature and range of the space to which it can be applied. Homogeneity is by no means a necessary pre-condition. Regional planning may also be developed for dealing with problems which arise with regard to those spaces occupied by an increasingly mobile population. These are spaces which are polarized around one or more nodes of intense social and economic activity and which achieve their definition not through homogeneity but functional interaction and interdependence. Journey to work and journey to shop flows are two important expressions of this interaction and interdependence.

However, the strength of regional planning and a major reason why it is so important is because it is not constrained in its application by ultimately limited concepts of homogeneous or polarized spaces. Regional planning may be deployed to deal with any issue which arises within supra urban space which society wishes to engage. Any such space can be given administrative definition and planned accordingly. Thus a region may be defined which embraces two homogeneous regions in order to solve their distinctive problems through complementary action. Or a region may be defined which embraces two markedly separate polarized nodes in order to fulfil their potential. Or a space may be defined which covers only a certain portion of a given homogeneous problem area because of limitations on resources to solve all its problems. The crucial point is that a region may be defined as part of the process of planning, of society determining its future. It is not necessarily defined first with reference to criteria of homogeneity or functional interaction and then planned afterwards. In short it can be defined in prescriptive as well as descriptive terms.[3]

Summarizing, regional planning is able to focus planning resources on a very wide but specified range of planning problems. Through embracing these problems it can tackle them more directly and thus potentially more adequately than other forms of planning. This is the first, the most obvious and the most basic rationale for regional planning.

The second reason which explains why society may institutionalize regional planning is the value of this form of planning in helping the operation of other forms of planning. Regional planning is a superior form of planning to others, including, for example, local and national planning in its ability to tackle certain issues and problems more directly than them. It is also a logical complement to these others in so far as it may aid their functioning and improve their performance.

At this stage in its historical development regional planning has been seen to be of particular utility to two forms of planning: national economic and local physical planning. It has been increasingly realized in a very large number of countries that the achievement of national economic goals such as full employment and maximum rate of economic growth cannot be realized adequately through national planning alone. In brief, national governments have introduced a spatial dimension into their decision making through regional policy making. This introduces a spatial dimension into what has previously been largely a sectoral approach to national economic planning. As such regional policy is a component of national planning concerned to allocate resources between regions. However, the point is that regional policy leads on to a concern to develop regional planning. This is so because, if resources are to be most effectively allocated, then there is a need not simply to allocate them between regions but also within regions, by regional planning undertaken as part of the process of national planning. Similarly if resources are to be most effectively articulated then there is a need for regional as well as national action.

The need for regional planning has also been increasingly appreciated by local physical planning agencies. Increasing mobility of the population has played an important role in this respect. The increasing volume of traffic has brought about a realization that schemes devised for a local area are of little value unless related to a much wider solution for traffic flows, and simultaneously that mobility may make nonsense of land-use allocations. Regional planning has consequently come to be seen as a means for providing a framework of reference for the local land-use transportation planning process.

National economic planning and local physical planning are the two main forms of planning that have so far stimulated the development of regional planning. It remains to be seen whether other forms, for example social planning, add to or subtract from the need for regional planning. Whatever the case, the point remains that regional planning may make a contribution not only through directly solving a regional problem but also through aiding the functioning of other forms of planning.

The third and final rationale that is distinguished here is briefly and simply that a society may choose for a variety of reasons to create some form of regional government, and this government may wish to plan, and thus regional planning is institutionalized. The ultimate rationale for regional planning in this case is the rationale for planning in general, namely that it is deemed to be a superior way of ordering societal affairs than non planning.

The Development of Regional Planning

It follows from the above discussion that regional planning is viewed as a particular form of planning action which may be invoked for a variety of different reasons and purposes. It also follows, by implication, that regional planning is not and cannot be characterized as being economic or social or physical planning; it cuts through and may embrace all such forms of planning. It is contended that the characteristics of regional planning which give it identity and form derive not from the problems which it tackles, whether these are described as being economic or social or political or of transport, but from its structural characteristics; the fact for example that it is sub national in the power it deploys; that it is supra urban and therefore concerned to treat with more local, spatially circumscribed and usually powerful governments; that it deals with spatially extensive issues which may require a considerable degree of abstraction and generalization. It is characteristics such as these which give regional planning its identity and which serve to differentiate it from other forms of public planning action.

In other words, despite the variety of the ways in which regional planning gains expression, whether as a fire fighting exercise to solve some spatially extensive problem, as a functional aid to national planning, or as a service to regional government, it is a part of the sustaining thesis underpinning this work that there is sufficient unity between all of these to permit an identifiable form of planning to be distinguished. Further than that the thesis is that this form of planning is sufficiently distinctive from other forms of planning to require the elaboration of its own knowledge methods and procedures, and that its significance is such that these do in fact require development and improvement.

In summary the subsequent work is committed to seeking an explication of the distinctive characteristics of regional planning; to seeking ways and means for the improvement and development of regional planning and thus to the creation of a significant tool through which societies may choose to improve their well being.

It must be contended that the underlying thesis is problematical, the intention somewhat grandiloquent. Regional planning is a very newly developed form of action, explicating its characteristics from past limited experience is difficult; it has for example until now been used more to address economic rather than social problems and has been more the work of *ad hoc* institutions than regional governments. Further the number of institutions capable of regional action are few and their capability not always fully developed so that the base for learning and developing from live processes is still limited both in Great Britain and other parts of the world. In all this the challenge is to elucidate and foster the development of the subject in a way which does not attempt prematurely to fix and then rigidly to mould its nature but in a way which is open and problematical. Finally in so far as commitments are necessary to this process then these may be grand so long as they are not imperialistic, insensitive and dogmatic commitments seeking at all costs to implant regional planning into societies.

The Approach in Outline

Given these perspectives and commitments the broad outline of approach is as follows. Chapter 2 is concerned with the historical development of regional planning. This development is considered not with the objective of trying to establish the identity of regional planning through examining its evolution but with the objective of appreciating the type of problems and opportunities which it has been seen to be capable of responding to and resolving, and which have induced its development. Its history is examined too in order better to appreciate the current state of regional planning, and the chapter ends with a stocktaking of its position in different parts of the world.

In Chapter 3, the focus of concern is the field of knowledge which the regional planner draws upon in making policies and plans. Although the whole universe of human knowledge is potentially applicable, it is suggested that there is a particular core of knowledge upon which the regional planner is especially reliant. It follows from previous statements that the regional planner is concerned with society as a whole rather than say the economic system or social system; however it has also been suggested that regional planning is concerned with society in supra urban space; it follows that the regional planner's distinctive concern is with the effect of supra urban space on society; in other words with the effect of the way in which society distributes itself in supra urban space on total societal performance. It must be emphasized that this is not the sole sphere of knowledge of interest to the regional planner but it is the sphere of knowledge which is drawn upon in giving expression to those actions which are quintessentially regional planning actions. The objective of Chapter 3 is to order and review the state of this sphere of knowledge.

Regional planning is quite frequently confused with the term regional policy and vice versa; in Chapter 4 a clear distinction is drawn between them, a task essential to clarifying the identity of regional planning. Regional policy is basically central government policy making for the regions, whereas regional planning concerns policy making at the regional level. An understanding of regional policy is critical to regional planning because it may often induce or constrain regional planning and because it may complement or partly substitute for it. The core of the chapter is therefore concerned with the nature of regional policy as a form of action, with an assessment and evaluation of its capabilities in the light of British experience, and deriving from this an appreciation of the need for and the role of regional planning action.

One of the advantages of regional policy is that it can be generated and sustained by an established strong institution, namely central government, whereas it is frequently the case that planning institutions capable of generating and sustaining regional actions are often non existent or more generally are often regarded as weak. In Chapter 5 the main alternative regional institutional formulas are identified and assessed, with particular reference to Great Britain. A main conclusion that emerges is the view that regional planning may be quite unlike local and national planning because more usually than not the existence of a form of government comparable to these levels will be absent; this throws the emphasis in regional planning towards a more outward bridge building inter-institutional form of planning and decision making.

This leads on to a fuller consideration of the nature of the regional planning process in Chapter 6. It is only comparatively recently that attempts have been made to investigate the nature of the public planning process and to consider alternative styles or methodologies for ordering this process. The core of the chapter is concerned with the identification and assessment of these alternative approaches or methodologies of planning. In the final part of the chapter a tentative attempt is made to identify the outlines of a theory of the regional planning process which is seen to hinge on the relationship between alternative planning methodologies and the distinctive structural character of the regional environment.

Whatever methodology is chosen, techniques, which are more finite and defined sequences of operations, are an essential part of the total regional planning operation. In Chapter 7 techniques for analysing regional problems and issues, for developing an understanding of the way in which these are likely to change, and for predicting the consequences of alternative actions are identified and assessed.

In Chapter 8 the focus is on the issue of choice, an issue central to all planning methodologies. A range of techniques are considered which can aid the process of evaluation and decision between alternative regional plans; the relative merits of these techniques are assessed and possible ways of combining them in order to exploit their respective characteristics, are identified.

Finally in Chapter 9 an overall assessment of regional planning is made, lines of synthesis drawn, critical problems are identified and discussed, and challenges, opportunities and prospects for the future are speculated upon.

References

1   Perloff, H., 'Key Features of Regional Planning', *AIP*, May 1968.

2   Friedmann, J., 'Regional Planning as a Field of Study', *AIP*, August 1963.

3   For a more abstract and extended consideration of homogeneous, polarized and administrative spaces, see for example, Boudeville, J. R., *Problems of Regional Economic Planning* (Edinburgh University Press, 1966).

2　The Development of Regional Planning

Introduction

The purpose of this chapter is to examine the development of regional planning as a form of planning action. Its development is analysed both as a means of appreciating the pressures and issues that have given rise to this form of planning action and as a means of appreciating its present practice.

The development of regional planning in Britain, and other countries, provides evidence to show that this form of planning action is able to provide solutions to a wide range of problems and issues in contemporary society and that its use is being extended in a variety of ways. The evolution and development of regional planning has consisted of a number of quite separate attempts by planners to cope with specific societal problems. While the use of regional planning to tackle a particular problem can be easily identified, it is only when the multi-purpose usefulness of this form of planning action is examined that a really convincing case begins to emerge for regional planning. Because the individual uses to which regional planning may be applied have not been articulated and meshed together into a coherent corpus of thought and action, a situation exists where regional planning means different things to different people.

The societal problems which have initiated regional planning can be identified as social, economic, political, administrative, physical and cultural; they have been articulated at varying levels of abstraction with varying degrees of adequacy of perception to the needs of the individual in society. Quite naturally, a range of skills can be identified which have developed over a period of time, to meet these varied societal needs.

The Social Context of Regional Planning

The development of regional planning has been a movement to seek solutions to problems experienced at the level of everyday living: problems of income; the cost of living; of unemployment; of changing jobs; of overcrowding and long daily journeys to work; of inefficiency and inequality in the provision of services, especially for transport, housing, health and social services, water, and recreation.

These problems have all been conceptualized by administrators, professional planners, and academics, into a number of problem areas, some of long standing but others quite recent in origin. The long standing problems focus on those of the depressed areas, the physical city, and the administration of services. More recently, regional planning has developed in relation to the problems of growth, equality, autonomy and self fulfilment. While the problem of the administration of services is a long standing one, it has gathered pace and received increasing attention in recent years. The development of regional planning, based on the more recently expressed problems, has been made with specific regard to some fundamental values held by society. These newer societal problems have not been conceptualized with such specificity as have the older, and perhaps more tangible problems.

It is conceivable that many problems suited to action at the regional level will be seen as soluble in some other form of action, for example at the urban or national level. Much depends upon the nature of the problem and the understanding of those articulating the process. However, with the establishment of regional planning as a recognizable and widely known level of action, it may be expected that groups in society may come to see it as relevant to the particular problem or issue with which they are concerned. At the same time, those with an interest in the field will be concerned to demonstrate its relevance to a range of problems and issues in society.

After looking at some early developments in regional planning this chapter concentrates on the problems and issues identified above as being the main motivating forces behind the development of regional planning in Britain to the present time. The development of regional planning in Britain is followed by a brief consideration of the development of this form of planning activity in the developing countries and other developed nations; the chapter concludes with some overall assessment of the current practice of regional planning in contemporary society.

Some Early Developments in Regional Planning

It is important to remember that regional planning is not an innovation of the 1960s and 1970s, although it has been in recent years that its method and technique have become more scientific and sophisticated, and hopefully more effective. As Hufschmidt has observed in his assessment of the development of regional planning in the United States,[1] this activity today seems far removed from the regional planning philosophy of the 1920s, although many of the ideas and concepts developed by Geddes, Mackaye and Stein are relevant today.

The current activity of regional planning is more comprehensive in scope and content than the land-use/ecological approach that typified the movement in the 1920s, particularly in the United States, but also in Britain. Hufschmidt has identified five main phases through which regional planning, in both theory and practice, passed in the United States. Firstly, the natural resource orientation of the 1930s and early 1940s, typified by the Tennessee Valley Authority, and the regional planning studies of the National Resources Planning Board;[2] secondly, the cultural regionalism approach of the Southern school of sociologists, typified by H. Odum and R. Vance of the University of North Carolina;[3] thirdly, the regional science school, typified by Walter Isard and the Regional Science Association;[4] fourthly, the regional economic development approach applicable to both developing countries and to depressed or underdeveloped regions of developed nations; and fifthly, the approach that emphasizes the urban–metropolitan nature of regional problems and issues developed by John Friedmann.[5] Hufschmidt stresses that while regional planning in the United States today can be thought of as an amalgam of the regional science, regional economic development, and urban–metropolitan focus approaches, there is no adequate synthesis, and any attempt to define a body of theory and practice for regional planning encounters this difficulty. While it is not suggested that the development of regional planning in Britain follows this pattern, Hufschmidt's observations on the development of regional planning in the United States do offer an interesting comparison for consideration and debate about its development in this country.

Some early examples of regional planning in Britain during the 1920s are illustrated by the South Wales Regional Survey (1920) and the Doncaster Regional Planning Scheme (1922). While historical accounts of regional planning experiences are considered within the appropriate substantive context later in this chapter, some mention should be made of the Doncaster plan, as this was to some extent a forerunner of regional planning in this country. A conference of local authorities was convened by the Ministry of Health on the subject of industrial development in the South Yorkshire Coalfield, and this was held in Doncaster on January 16th 1920. The conference resolved to prepare a regional planning scheme for the whole area comprising the coalfields surrounding Doncaster. The eight local authorities concerned, covering an area of 108,000 acres with a population of 140,000, formed a Joint Town Planning Committee for the Doncaster Region which held its first meeting in May 1920. Professor Patrick Abercrombie (Liverpool University) and Mr. T.H. Johnson (Doncaster

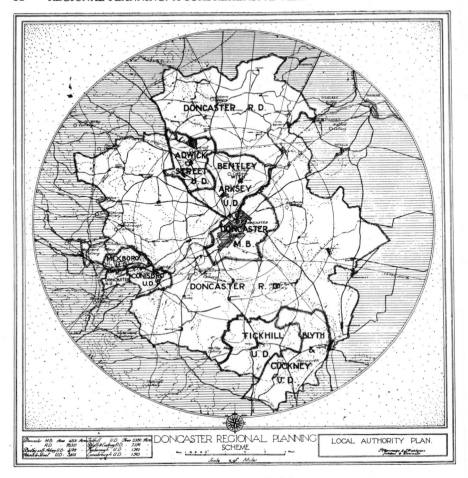

Fig. 2.1   Study area of Doncaster Regional Planning Scheme, 1922.
            Source: *Doncaster Regional Planning Scheme* (University of Liverpool
            Press, 1922) Plate II.

architect and surveyor) were instructed to prepare an outline Plan and Report
for the area, (see Figure 2.1). As the Report emphasized,[6] this was the first
Regional Planning Scheme to be prepared in Britain, and was different from the
1920 South Wales Regional Survey,[7] in that in the latter case, no actual
development plan was prepared. In addition the South Wales planning study had
been the work of a large committee with extensive resources comprising local
authorities, central government, industry, and the trade unions. The Doncaster
plan noted with some pride 'The authors of the Doncaster Regional Scheme have
plunged boldly into concrete proposals affecting in definite ways the future
growth of every local authority in the district.'[8] The Report was approved by
the Joint Committee in July 1922 and subsequently published.

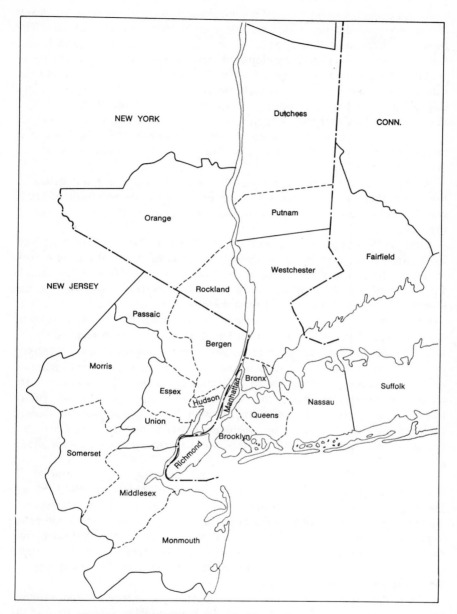

Fig. 2.2   The New York Metropolitan region.
Source: Reproduced from Yeates, M. and Garner, B., *The North American City* (Harper and Row, 1970) Figure 17.2.

In many ways, current regional planning recognizes, perhaps belatedly, many of the problems and issues that were in essence identified 50 years ago. The Doncaster Regional Scheme grappled with problems of urban growth and transportation, of industrial development, and of self fulfilment. A number of growth strategies were envisaged for the 'metropolis' of Doncaster, and the nature of the task was similar to that now facing many of the vast city regions throughout the world. The strategy to concentrate the whole of the growth of the region in Doncaster itself was rejected in favour of a strategy based on a ring of satellite towns or urban communities, mainly taking existing villages for their nuclei, but some involving new centres. These small communities were seen as 'foyers of social life'.

At the same time as the early regional plans were being prepared in Britain in the 1920s, there were significant developments being made elsewhere, of which two examples deserve a mention in any assessment of the development of regional planning.

First, in 1922, a private organization, the Regional Plan Association of New York, was set up to study the social and economic problems of the New York region. Several authors[9] have remarked on how today, over 50 years later, this is still the only public or private body seriously concerned with studying the planning problems of America's largest metropolitan region (see Figure 2.2). It covers an area of nearly 7,000 square miles embracing 22 counties in parts of three states, and in 1960 had a population of over 16 million. A regional plan[10] was prepared for New York in 1927, the sponsors of the project having observed the need for a plan of physical improvement, in relation to the principal economic activities. With the rise of the motor car in the 1920s as an important means of urban transport, the regional plan also focused on future transportation patterns and population growth. The regional plan was heavily criticized by a number of people, including Lewis Mumford, a member of the Regional Plan Association of America, for its assumptions of future urban growth.

Another major development in regional planning, which occurred in Germany, focused on the Ruhr, with the establishment in 1920 of the Siedlungsverband Ruhrkohlenbezirk (SVR). This was the first major regional planning agency of its kind in the world, and has continued to function as an important and integral part of the current planning system; the SVR celebrated its fiftieth anniversary in 1970 by holding an international conference at its headquarters in Essen on the role of regional planning in the new European Economic Community.

The founding of the SVR by a special Prussian law of May 1920 gave formal recognition that the acute problems of the Ruhr could no longer be met by individual towns, but rather that action on a regional scale was required. Under the law the local authorities, or Gemeinden, transferred to the Verband those

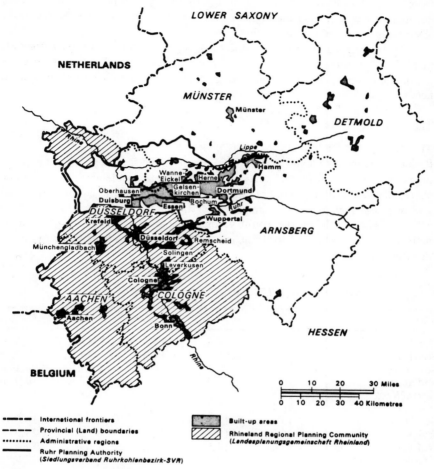

Fig. 2.3   The Ruhr Region.
Source: Hall P., *The World's Cities,* p. 125.

powers necessary for the development of the region. These included co-operation in the preparation of town plans, transportation planning, and financial assistance to individual local authorities. Since the early years of its development the SVR has become one of the best known *ad hoc* innovative regional planning institutions. With a population of over ten million people, the Rhine–Ruhr region dominates Federal Germany; the extent of the SVR areas is shown in Figure 2.3. Faced with environmental problems caused by rapid and uncontrolled industrial expansion in the nineteenth century and economic problems by the decline of this industrial structure (mainly the coal industry from the mid 1950s), much of the energy of the SVR in recent years has been devoted to strengthening the region's economic base by stressing the economic advantages of locations in the Ruhr.

It is clearly apparent from this brief assessment of some early developments in regional planning that this form of planning action has been used for some considerable time, in an attempt to grapple with a number of vital societal needs.[11]

The Development of Regional Planning in Britain

THE PROBLEM OF THE DEPRESSED AREAS
Probably the most fundamental factor in initiating the first steps toward regional planning, and one of the most formative factors in determining its basic characteristics until the present day, was the development in the 1920s and 1930s of the high rates of unemployment in the older industrial areas of the country. The whole of the country, including to a lesser degree prosperous metropolitan areas, shared the basic problem of unemployment. This situation is illustrated in Table 2.1.

Table 2.1   Unemployment in 1920s and 1930s Percentages

Area	1925	1929	1932	1934	1938
London	6.7	5.6	13.5	9.2	7.8
South East	4.5	5.6	14.3	8.7	7.7
South West	7.2	8.1	18.1	13.1	8.1
Midlands	10.8	9.3	20.1	12.9	10.0
North West	11.5	13.3	25.8	20.8	17.7
North East	16.5	13.7	28.5	22.1	12.9
Scotland	15.6	12.1	27.7	23.1	16.8
Wales	16.2	19.3	36.5	32.3	25.9
N. Ireland	N/A	14.8	27.2	23.4	24.4
United Kingdom		10.4	22.1	16.7	12.9

Sources: Department of Employment and McCrone, G., *Regional Policy in Britain*, 1969 Table 11, p.100.

It was partly for this reason that the development of action of a regionally orientated nature was slow in developing. It was not until well after the peak of unemployment in the country as a whole had been passed and when the overall national position began to improve much more rapidly than in the depressed areas that action was forthcoming. In the event, action came from central government in the form of a national regional policy rather than regional initiatives and action. The high level of unemployment in the depressed areas was associated with a dependence on a declining industrial structure, which was highly specialized and concentrated in a small number of industries, throughout the nation, with the exception of the South East of England. The problem was by its very nature regional in scale. The relative position of the depressed areas became weaker as the more prosperous areas, unfettered by government restrictions of any kind (e.g. planning legislation of the 1940s), enjoyed increased prosperity.

The movement for regional planning to cope with the problem of depressed areas was essentially concerned with providing jobs, not at all for purposes of economic growth, but to give unemployed men work for social reasons. The social aspect of regional policy is still as important a concept today as it was in the depression years of the 1930s. Economic growth itself, while providing greater resources for society's future use, has necessitated unemployment, for decline in particular industrial sectors or parts of national space is a natural accompaniment to economic development. However, the movement for regional planning has been largely a response by society to safeguard its security and well being from the social cost of economic growth.

The lethargic response of national government to the depressed area problem has already been commented upon. Although the severity of the problem led few to doubt that it was one requiring national action, it was not until 1931 that selected universities in the regions were requested to undertake studies into their respective regional situations. No action followed the publication of these studies until 1934 when government investigators were sent to the four depressed areas of S. Wales, Central Scotland, West Cumberland and the North East Coast to gain further knowledge of the situation (Figure 2.4). Then, in 1934, the Special Areas (Development and Improvement) Act was passed. This Act represented the first official attempt by central government to solve the immediate problem of providing unemployed men in the depressed regions with jobs, and the first attempt to influence the spatial distribution of economic activity.

To implement the Act, two Commissioners were appointed, one for England and Wales, and the other for Scotland. The Commissioners were appointed for 'the initiation, organisation, prosecution and assistance of measures designed to facilitate the economic development and social improvement'[12] of the Special Areas. The Commissioners were intended to have wide powers, and be free of traditional government departments. The Chancellor of the Exchequer indicated during the course of the Bill that 'they must not be afraid of making experiments even if these experiments fail'.[13] In practice, however, the Commissioners' powers were limited; they had no powers, for example, to grant aid where a specific grant was already being administered by a government department. Much of the early work of the Commissioners was devoted to grants for improvements to infrastructure. The influence of the Commissioners was further constrained in the sense that the Act limited the areas to those taken by

Glasgow
Linlithgow
Kilmarnock
Holtwhistle
Newcastle Upon Tyne
South Shields
Hartlepool
Alston in Carrigill
Pembroke

Fig. 2.4   The pre-war special areas.
Source: McCrone, G., *Regional Policy in Britain,* 1969, p. 94.

the government investigators, and by no means were all of the depressed areas, in terms of heavy unemployment, included. However, it was argued that the knowledge and experience gained in the Special Areas could later be applied over a broader field.[14] Experience and appreciation of the nature of the problem did in fact lead to some early and radical changes in policy.

In 1937 the work of the Commissioners developed more in the direction of directly attracting industry following the Special Areas (Amendment) Act. The Act authorized the Treasury to make loans to industrialists, and the

Commissioners to let factories, and to offer contributions towards rents, rates and taxation.

It was probably in the promotion of trading estates that the Commissioners achieved their most obvious and immediate effect on the Special Areas. The extension of their activity into the field of industrial development reflected a better diagnosis of the basic problem. It was realized that regional economies had collapsed and could not be expected to revive without influence over the national distribution of industry. The early work on the depressed areas touched upon here[15] was undoubtedly an interesting experiment and innovation, and despite its limitations it sharpened national perception of the problem, and established a tradition of differential action within the nation. Because of the severity of the problem, national government involvement in its solution was established, and at the same time it developed a conviction that regional planning was essentially concerned with the problem areas and more especially with the solution of unemployment in these areas.

Amongst the most significant contributions of the Commissioner for England and Wales, were those made in his Third Report.[16] The Commissioner, Sir Malcolm Stewart, pointed out that little reduction in unemployment had been achieved, and suggested that excessive growth in the congested areas particularly London, should be controlled to alleviate problems in the Special Areas.

The government immediately responded to these suggestions in first of all passing the Special Areas (Amendment) Act, and secondly in establishing a Royal Commission in June 1938 to inquire into the causes of the distribution of the industrial population, the disadvantages attendant upon concentration either in large towns or certain areas of the country, and to consider appropriate remedial measures if so required. The subsequently published Barlow Report[17] is one of the most important milestones in the development of regional planning in Britain, and is considered further later.

Central government's regional policy has still not achieved one of its basic aims established now for forty years, namely, to reduce regional differentials in rates of unemployment.[18] Unemployment today remains a central problem; in 1971 the level of unemployment reached over one million people. The social aspects of unemployment are as important as the economic ones of potential output not being achieved. To the individual employee and his family, unemployment can be anything from a temporary inconvenience to a crisis. In its mildest form unemployment may represent a delay of a week; at the other extreme, unemployment may mean absence from the labour force for more than a year.[19]

In recent years the whole structure of unemployment has changed. It seems that from the end of the 1960s economies have, and will continue to, run at a higher level of unemployment than before. The reasons why people, when out of work, need not seek a job immediately include higher wage levels, whereby people can draw upon saving to finance unemployment, the tendency for female labour activity rates to rise whereby if the husband loses his job one income is still being earned, the social legislation of the Redundancy Payments Scheme of 1965, and the introduction of earnings related benefit for unemployment in 1966. However, while a higher rate of unemployment may be expected, significant regional variations will continue to conflict with social values.

Thus, despite the inclusion of other variables in addition to unemployment, such as migration, activity rates, incomes, employment growth, rateable values, personal health and welfare etc., in assessing the vitality of different areas in the country, unemployment has retained a prominent place, and the reduction of unemployment in the depressed areas is an integral element of the government's current regional policy as embodied in the 1972 White Paper and subsequent Industry Act.[20]

The contribution of the depressed area problem to the initiation, development and current state of regional planning would be difficult to overestimate. Here it is sufficient to note that it has established very firmly in the national consciousness that the prosperous and depressed areas of the country are indeed dissimilar, and that regionally orientated national government policies and actions are required to deal with these dissimilar areas.

THE PROBLEM OF ECONOMIC GROWTH

The problem of economic growth has made a more powerful and influential impact on the development of regional planning than even the problem of the depressed areas. In particular, the problem of economic growth has induced the view of regional planning as an integral component of comprehensive national planning.

The development of regional planning up to the 1960s had not been a movement for greater economic growth, and it was not until the early 1960s that the question of economic growth received an increasing amount of attention in relation to the problem of depressed areas. One of the most important reasons for the increasing awareness of the importance of economic growth was the extent to which regions varied in their level and growth of prosperity. The extent and persistence of regional differential in those variables which are used to measure economic success became firmly established as 'the regional problem'.

In the achievement of full employment the emphasis has been placed on the concept of growth rather than the former concept of reducing unemployment. In the 1960s the development of regional policy by central government took place with explicit regard to economic growth as the motivating factor. Economic growth provides an opportunity for society to increase the quantity and quality of resources available for future uses in addition to present needs. The development of regional planning in relation to the issue of economic growth has become increasingly articulated at national level since the publication of a document 'Conditions Favourable for Faster Growth' by the National Economic Development Council in 1963. Since that statement the regions and their resources have been looked at rather differently than hitherto. In the first place it has been realized that unemployment and low activity rates are economically wasteful and need to be utilized; in the second place, it has been realized that there is a need for a comprehensive system of regions within which resources may be managed and articulated.

Concern with the poor level of economic performance of the country as a whole has been expressed to a large extent in the desire for a more rapid and stable rate of economic growth,[21] The poor economic performance of Britain has been measured in relation to that achieved by other Western European countries. This situation is illustrated in Table 2.2. Additional emphasis was placed on economic growth because of the series of balance of payments deficits from 1964 to 1968 which illustrated dramatically the extent to which internal economic policy is constrained by the nation's external position.

Table 2.2 Growth of Gross National Product Per Head at 1963 Market Prices, 1958-67

EEC countries		Average annual percentage increase EFTA countries	
Germany	3.7	UK	2.5
France	3.9	Sweden	3.8
Italy	4.8	Norway	4.0
Belgium	3.8	Denmark	4.2
Luxembourg	N.A.	Austria	3.7
Netherlands	3.7	Switzerland	3.1
		Portugal	3.2

Source: Britain and the European Communities An Economic Assessment, Cmnd. 4289, February 1970.

Although national and regional differences in rates of growth of Gross National Product may appear to be small, perhaps only one percentage point, it is important to recognize the cumulative nature of economic growth. Economic growth grows in a compound and not a simple arithmetic progression; this phenomenon is illustrated in Table 2.3.

Not only is growth cumulative, and therefore one half per cent change important, but the size of the GNP is significant. A half per cent change in GNP is equivalent to an extra £250M of resources for society's use.

The demand for faster economic growth has not only been made at national level but also at sub national level. Numerous agencies have been established to

Table 2.3 Effect of Different Growth Rates in a National or Regional Economy

Year	Percentage growth rate			
	1	*2*	*3*	*5*
0	100	100	100	100
10	110	122	134	163
30	135	181	243	432
50	164	269	438	1147
70	201	400	792	3043
100	271	724	1922	13150

N.B. Income in Year 0 = 100
Source: Extract from *An Introduction to Positive Economics,* R. Lipsey, Chapter 56, p.802, 2nd Edition, 1966.

improve, *inter alia,* the economic performance of their area; for example, the Highlands and Islands Development Board in Scotland, the North East Development Council, the Scottish Council for Development and Industry, the Merseyside Development Association, and the Mid-Wales Industrial Development Association, to name but a few. In addition, individual local governments have not been idle in seeking ways of achieving faster economic growth rather than waiting for central government policy to be effective.

The concern of central government with the issue of economic growth was expressed in the Local Employment Act of 1960, the Budget and Local Employment Act of 1963, and the measures undertaken by the Labour government 1964-70. A fourth phase began in October 1970 with the publication of a White Paper[22] outlining the newly elected Conservative government's approach to a regional policy.

In the early 1960s the problems of economic performance and accommodation of population growth were examined in a number of reports, including the Report of the Inquiry into the Scottish Economy,[23] the Report of the National Economic Development Council on Conditions Favourable to Faster Growth,[24] the White Papers on the North East,[25] and Central Scotland,[26] and the South East Study.

When the Labour government took office in 1964 the contribution which regional planning could make towards the development of the nation as a whole, and individual regions, was recognized by the establishment of the regional planning machinery with REPCs and REPBs, and the publication of the National Plan[27] in 1965. The emphasis was clearly placed on the issue of economic growth, with the establishment of 'Economic' Planning Regions, Regional 'Economic' Planning Councils and Regional 'Economic' Planning Boards, and a National Plan which was essentially an 'economic' plan. The role of the Department of Economic Affairs, established in 1964 as a completely new department in central government, having responsibility for the new regional

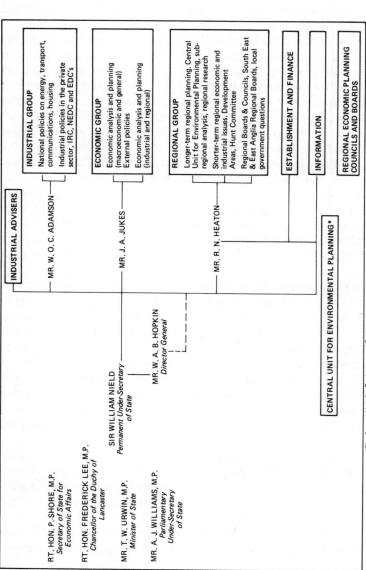

INDUSTRIAL ADVISERS

INDUSTRIAL GROUP
National policies on energy, transport, communications, housing
Industrial policies in the private sector, IRC, NEDC and EDC's

MR. W. O. C. ADAMSON

ECONOMIC GROUP
Economic analysis and planning (macroeconomic and general)
External policies
Economic analysis and planning (industrial and regional)

MR. J. A. JUKES

REGIONAL GROUP
Longer-term regional planning. Central Unit for Environmental Planning, sub-regional analysis, regional research
Shorter-term regional economic and industrial issues. Development Areas, Hunt Committee
Regional Boards & Councils, South East & East Anglia Regional Boards, local government questions

MR. R. N. HEATON

ESTABLISHMENT AND FINANCE

INFORMATION

REGIONAL ECONOMIC PLANNING COUNCILS AND BOARDS

RT. HON. P. SHORE, M.P.
Secretary of State for Economic Affairs

RT. HON. FREDERICK LEE, M.P.
Chancellor of the Duchy of Lancaster

MR. T. W. URWIN, M.P.
Minister of State

MR. A. J. WILLIAMS, M.P.
Parliamentary Under-Secretary of State

SIR WILLIAM NIELD
Permanent Under-Secretary of State

MR. W. A. B. HOPKIN
Director General

CENTRAL UNIT FOR ENVIRONMENTAL PLANNING*

*The Central Unit for Environmental Planning is an inter-departmental team based on DEA
Source: DEA Progress Report. No. 50. March 1969

Fig. 2.5   The Structure of the DEA.
Source: DEA Progress Report, no. 50, March 1969.

planning machinery and national economic planning, warrants particular attention as it had a marked impact on planning activity in the mid 1960s and subsequent years.

The main task of the Department of Economic Affairs was seen[28] as the co-ordination of the activities of the economic departments of government so that their decisions were consistent with the achievement of a faster growth while avoiding inflationary pressures. Within the context of a large balance of payments deficit in 1964, it was not surprising that the government's planning machinery focused upon the issue of economic growth. The DEA was organized in three main interrelated groups as illustrated in Figure 2.5: Economic Planning Group; Industrial, Prices and Incomes Group; and Regional Planning Group. The Central Unit for Environmental Planning, an interdepartmental team, was also based in the DEA. The Regional Planning Group was responsible for economic planning in the regions, including regional implications of national policies. In addition, of course, economic planning machinery had been set up in the regions during 1965, and early 1966. Regional planning was clearly seen as an integral part of central government's national planning with its economic orientation. One whole chapter (Chapter 8) in the National Plan was devoted to regional planning.

Subsequent planning documents published by central government were far less specific on the role of regional planning. The document *The Task Ahead* published in February 1969, succeeded the National Plan as a statement of the government's national economic planning. Chapter 9 of the document was devoted to regional strategy. *The Task Ahead* was succeeded by the revised strategy *Economic Prospects to 1972,* published by the Treasury in 1970, in which regional policies were covered by just two paragraphs (44 and 45). The government's comprehensive view towards regional planning in the latter 1960s changed to a narrower one which focused upon the role of regional policy as an aid to national economic development, and this view has persisted through the 1970s.

While the reorganization of central government by the Labour government in October 1969 abolished the DEA, the Scottish Office and Welsh Office remained unchanged, and responsibility for the regional planning machinery in England was transferred to the Ministry of Housing and Local Government, now within the Department of the Environment.

The problem of economic growth has stimulated the development of a knowledge base and clearly above all else an institutional structure for regional planning.

THE PROBLEM OF THE PHYSICAL CITY
In sharp contrast to the previous problem of the depressed areas, the problem of the physical city really arose as a consequence of economic success; the advantages of highly concentrated forms of settlement for engendering economic

growth brought resultant difficulties for accommodating the resultant activity. Rising incomes associated with this economic success at the same time allowed the articulation of life styles requiring more space and different contexts to those traditionally offered by the city. As a consequence one had, as soon as technology allowed and better communications developed, the spread and flood of suburban expansion, particularly by those most able to capitalize on the new technology.

Fundamental problems of overcrowding and congestion however remained, particularly in the largest metropolitan area of London. In their report[29] published in 1940, the Royal Commission on the Distribution of the Industrial Population drew attention to the worldwide development of intensive urbanization, which in Britain had already presented certain distinctive features. The report emphasized first, that the acreage of Britain in comparison with other Western countries is very limited in relation to the size of population, and secondly, expressed concern at the rapid growth of population in London and South East England (see paras. 33 and 39 of the Barlow Report). Part III of the Barlow Report considered what social and economic advantages and disadvantages arise from the concentration of jobs or people in large towns in particular areas of the country.

The main feature, however, of the Barlow Report was that it brought together Town and Country Planning policy (based on population growth) and Distribution of Industry (based on jobs) policy for the first time. The report was the first official recognition that the congestion problems of some cities and the unemployment of the depressed areas were different aspects of the same problems. In particular, it was envisaged that the problem of the exploding metropolis could help to solve the problem of the depressed areas. The methodology contained within the Barlow Report had an immense impact on the approach to regional planning during the next 30 years, and it is only in recent years that some of the concepts contained within the Report have been challenged.

The Barlow Report recommended the creation of a national authority (National Industrial Board) for purposes of regional planning, Also, the NIB had the option to establish divisional or regional bodies if required. Three members of the Commission dissented in a Minority Report and went further to recommend the creation of a new government department to control regional planning with a definite system of regional bodies. As is the fate of Royal Commissions, neither the majority nor minority recommendations were adopted. However, the Barlow Report saw the first official movement towards the need for reform of central government to achieve the opportunities available by planning on a regional scale.

Prior to Barlow, planning was largely a local affair generally unconcerned with the distribution of population between one locality and another. The recommendations of the Barlow Report therefore marked a very considerable extension of the then existing activity of planning. Nevertheless, at the time of the Barlow Report the concepts and techniques of physical planning were beginning to gain momentum. Motivated by anti-urban ideologies and led forward by the inventive work of Howard, physical planners began to see the solution to the problem in the form of new towns and expanded towns set down beyond the constraining green belt and located in a wider regional context. The development of regional planning to meet the problem of city or urban region was motivated largely in social terms to eradicate congested and blighted living conditions in the big cities. In the early post-war period the concepts of new towns, green belts and city regions, plus industrial development certificates, became framed into a new and more sophisticated strategy for physical planning. It became better equipped than at the time of Barlow to deal with the problem created by the expanding metropolis.

However, the relationships of these proposed solutions to the everyday experience of the individual in the metropolitan areas was, and is, in many ways non existent because they failed to touch vital social and economic issues. Whereas the unemployed steelworker or miner in the depressed areas could clearly see the solution to his problem in terms of more work, it was much more difficult for the Londoner to see the relationship between his inadequate living conditions and a master plan for the whole of the London metropolis—a plan simultaneously ordering a vast range of variables and where internal logic and balance were not therefore to be tampered with.

One witnesses here the crucial role played by academics and professionals in translating an everyday problem into a coherent solution. The role of the physical planner has been especially powerful in this regard, and for this reason the relationship between individual experiences and a coherent solution is a tenuous one. The need for the solution appears to be more grounded in professional thinking than in the articulation of immediate experiences of ordinary people.

The net result was nevertheless a realization of the need to develop strategies for metropolitan areas on an enlarged spatial scale. That scale is now usually termed city region; and although it is misleading and no longer tenable to discuss the problems of the physical city, it would nevertheless appear to be the case that behaviour patterns are now occurring in a wide spatial scale of regional dimensions. The demand for regional planning has arisen in recognition of this spatial explosion in patterns of human behaviour which are increasingly being expressed on this regional scale. Social planning and community development have begun to focus on 'regional man' as well as urban, suburban and rural man. One striking example of this is Young and Willmott's *The Symmetrical Family*. This book extends their original studies of local communities, notably Bethnal Green, to examine human activity in the whole London region.[30]

The extent of the metropolitan explosion in terms of growth and its resultant problems has been examined by Hall[31] in the major metropolitan regions throughout the world, covering London, Paris, Randstad Holland, Rhine-Ruhr, Moscow, New York, and Tokyo. In Britain, the first major attempts by central government to plan on a regional scale to tackle problems of urban growth were made in the mid 1940s, particularly with the preparation of the Greater London Plan in 1944, and Clyde Valley Regional Plan in 1946 by Sir Patrick Abercrombie. Other regional plans included the South Wales Plan of 1947 by A. Lloyd and H. Jackson, and the North East Development Area Outline Plan by G. Pepler and P.W. Macfarlane in 1949, both prepared for the Ministry of Town and Country Planning. These advisory strategy plans were to have provided useful guidelines for the local planning authorities established under the 1947 Act.

These early attempts at preparing regional plans were unsuccessful in the sense that they were purely advisory and no administrative system was established to implement the proposals. In addition, the techniques of regional planning were inadequate to deal with the complex task of preparing plans for the use of land on such a large scale. In the early post-war years the planning process remained basically unscientific.

Some mention must be made of the Clyde Valley Regional Plan and that for the North East of England. The regional plans for London and South East England are considered in greater depth in the following pages. The 1946 Clyde Valley Regional Plan was a report prepared for the Clyde Valley Regional Planning Committee by Sir P. Abercrombie and R.H. Matthew, and published in 1949. The aim of the Clyde Valley study, as stated in the preamble to the Report was 'to lay down, in broad terms, an outline plan for the development of the Clyde Valley Region'.[32] The Clyde Valley Region was one of three areas for which plans were then being prepared, the others being the Central and South Eastern Region and the Eastern Region. In extent, the Clyde Valley Region covered the counties of Dumbarton, Lanark, Renfrew, a large part of Ayr, and part of the county of Stirling.

The regional planning staff on the project represented a range of skills including a sociologist and economist as well as physical planners, and were concerned with the economic and social structure of the region as well as its physical structure. The Clyde Valley Regional Plan was perhaps the first of its kind to state explicitly that 'physical planning to be fully effective should go hand in hand with economic and social planning'; indeed, this was the first of the Report's 76 conclusions and recommendations.[33] While the regional planners were concerned with the distribution of population and location of industry, the desperate housing conditions were also well known at the time and the necessity for immediate action was recognized.

The Clyde Valley Regional Plan is an important document for both the substantive issues it covered and the approach to regional planning which it adopted. The injection of economic and social planning into the regional plan was made in a way which many regional planning studies of recent years have failed to do. For the regional planner, the Clyde Valley Regional Plan must rank as an outstanding piece of work which still has relevance for current regional planning.

The North East Development Area Outline Plan[34] was essentially a physical planning exercise rather than an economic one. The plan recognized that some areas in the North East were unlikely to attract industry and that other areas that did have such potential would need to be selected. This led to an acceptance of population decline in some areas, and New Towns as growth points in other areas. The approach adopted in this 1949 document contained the main ingredients of later regional planning studies (e.g. the White Paper on the North East 1963). While the Plan was relatively well argued and thorough in physical and economic terms, its social content was weak. An example of the relevance of the 1949 Plan to current regional planning may be drawn from policies pursued by Durham County Council; these policies have remained in sympathy with the approach first put forward in the 1949 Plan, namely a planned approach to urban growth and decline, through a process of selection.

The 1968 Town and Country Planning Act illustrates the recognition given to the need for land-use planning to be undertaken on a regional scale in order to accommodate the economic and social demands of society. The 1968 Act was foreshadowed by the report of the Planning Advisory Group published in 1965.[35] The role of local planning authorities in the planning process was emphasized in the report (para. 1.44), particularly 'the need to ensure that their development plans give effect to the intentions of the regional plan'.

Improvements in the preparation of strategy plans prepared in the latter 1960s and early 1970s for the development of regions have been largely due first, to the improvement of regional planning techniques, especially those used for plan selection, and secondly, to the improvement in the administrative system whereby some form of regional planning machinery has been established to provide a linkage between central and local government. This regional planning machinery has partly been established by central government in the form of Regional Economic Planning Councils and Boards, and partly by the initiative of local government in the form of Standing Conferences on regional planning in the regions. The 1970 Strategic Plan for the South East was prepared by the South East Joint Planning Team which comprised the SEEPC, the government chiefly through the MHLG, and the local planning authorities via the Standing Conference on London and South East Regional Planning.

The pressures on making decisions for future land-use through the preparation of regional strategy plans are well illustrated in the attempts made by government over the past 30 years to provide guidelines for the use of land in the South East of England.

Fig. 2.6   The Greater London plan.
Source: 1944 Greater London Plan, Chapter 1.

The Abercrombie plans for the London Region[36] were the first major attempt to assess the future demands on land-use in a region dominated by the metropolis (see Figure 2.6). The 1944 Greater London Plan was comprehensive in both substance and techniques given the state of planning at that time. The role of the plan was outlined in the preamble to the report: 'Not only the necessity for some plan of action became obvious; the opportunity presented itself to locate population and industry more logically, to improve transport radically, and to determine a proper use of land. Finally, the ultimate size of London was inescapably involved.' (Preamble to 1944 Greater London Plan, Page 1).

Unfortunately the 1944 Plan was based on two false assumptions, which illustrate the relevance, yet also the difficulties, of forecasting future land-use. In the first instance the plan accepted the recommendation in the Barlow Report that no new industry should be admitted to London and the Home Counties except in special cases. The first false assumption was that employment growth would be restricted by control over industrial development—an assumption of the 1943 County of London Plan. In fact employment grew rapidly through unrestricted office development (no control was imposed on the expansion of offices in London until the mid 1960s). Secondly, it was estimated that the population of the South East would be stabilized or even reduced. This was in keeping with the Barlow recommendations and the then national trends. In fact, the population increased because of the increase in the birth rate in the 1950s and the influx of overseas immigrants.

The central theme of the 1944 plan was clearly focused on decentralization of people and jobs to, in the words of the plan, 'improve housing conditions in those areas which are overcrowded, and to reduce the concentration of industry in the London area which has caused an expansion of the metropolis to a size which has become quite unmanageable, and one which has made of Londoners a race of straphangers.'[37]

The Greater London Plan shows in a marked way the extent to which the relevance of a planning strategy depends upon the validity of the assumptions used. In the face of heavy pressures for development in and around existing settlements within and beyond the green belt, and the continuing problems of congestion and inadequate housing in London, the local planning authorities in London and the Home Counties decided that their mutual interests would best be served by a joint organization through which they could work together on regional planning issues. This led to the establishment of the Standing Conference on London Regional Planning in 1962, representing all the local planning authorities in the area covered by the Abercrombie Plans. Subsequently the membership was extended, and now, as the Standing Conference on London and South East Regional Planning, it covers the whole South East region; similar developments have been made in other regions of Britain with local authorities making a joint attempt to tackle common problems by establishing Standing Conferences on regional planning.

In a White Paper *London – Employment: Housing: Land* (February 1963),[38] the government recognized that 'the need to match jobs, land, transport and housing over the next 20 years called for a regional plan'. Subsequently, to provide some guidelines for the future use of land, a second major attempt to accommodate future development in the South East region through the preparation of a planning strategy was made in 1964 with the publication of the South East Study which assessed land-use needs up to 1981. The report proposed a second generation of New Towns and major town expansions in the region. Improvements in the preparation of plans were sought throughout the latter 1960s and in 1966 the South East Economic Planning Council was established, principally to be concerned with regional economic planning, but also, in conjunction with Ministry of Housing and Local Government, to prepare a regional strategy plan to accommodate future growth (or decline) in the region. The SEEPC published a *Strategy for the South East* in 1967 looking

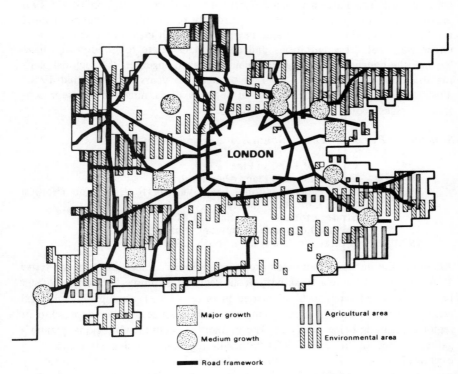

Fig. 2.7   Regional planning strategy for South East England 1970.
Source: *Strategic Plan for the South East 1970,* map 35.

ahead beyond 1981 to 2000, and this was succeeded by *A Strategic Plan for the South East* in June 1970, which adopted a similar role in setting out future growth patterns for the region, as shown in Figure 2.7.

An important feature of the planning strategy prepared by the SEJPT was that the implications of the regional strategy for 33 planning authorities in the region were considered in some depth. Any planning authority in the South East could assess the effect of development in the region for the respective authority. Unfortunately, the remaining weakness, unsolved since the 1940s, has been that no regional planning agency exists to implement the proposed plan. However, the strategic planning approach adopted for the South East of England by a joint team of the planning agencies involved, has been extended to other regions.

Finally, in relation to South East England, some mention must be made of the 1969 Greater London Development Plan and the public inquiries of 1970. In a background paper[39] to the GLDP, the planners emphasized the extent to which London is a regional city (see Figure 2.8). 'Its social and economic relationships are so strong in areas outside its boundary that we cannot really conceive of South Eastern England except in connection with London.'[40] Two major developments in the region are currently proposed: the Channel Tunnel and the construction of the major new town of Milton Keynes, which is well under way. All these ambitious and costly plans relate to London and have become the concern of the regional planner. Taken together, the regional plans for the London region over a period of some 30 years from the mid 1940s illustrate vividly the task and potential of regional planning and the main substantive issues upon which it has been based.

Sequence of Regional Plans for South East England

1943	County of London Plan
1944	Greater London Plan (Abercrombie)
1963	White Paper 'London — Employment: Housing: Land' (HMSO)
1964	South East Study (MHLG)
1967	Strategy for the South East (SEEPC)
1969	Greater London Development Plan (GLC)
1970	A Strategic Plan for the South East (SEJPT)

Alongside the movement towards preparing regional strategy plans in the latter 1960s developed the related activity of sub regional planning. The activity of sub regional planning needs to be identified in so far as it may comprise an integral element of an overall regional plan, and is in essence another expression of regional planning being practised. The momentum behind sub regional planning gathered pace in the mid 1960s with sub regional planning strategies being organized by both local authorities and central government. Local authority groups had responsibility for, for example, the Leicester and Leicestershire Study[41] and for the Nottinghamshire and Derbyshire Study.[42] In many cases

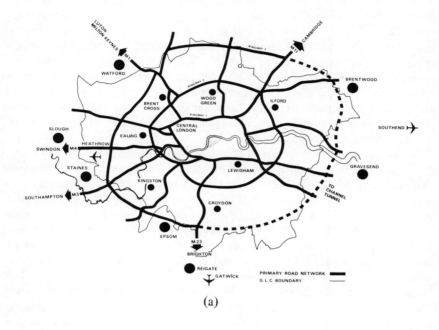

(a)

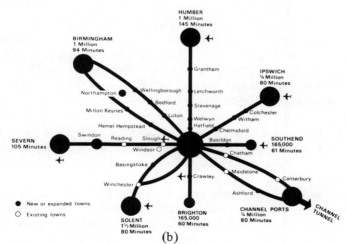

(b)

Fig. 2.8   The London city region.
(a) London region.
(b) Regional Links.
Source: *Tomorrow's London,* p. 127 (GLC, 1969).

local governments considered it desirable to join together in order properly to embrace some problem or realize some common goal. Central government has been responsible for major studies of Humberside, Tayside and Severnside, and consultants employed by government have prepared schemes for, amongst others, the Teesside Survey and Plan, for South Hampshire, the expansion of Ipswich, and Central Lancashire.[43] Most of these studies were undertaken in the latter 1960s at a time when central government was concerned with coping with an envisaged population increase of substantial proportions. Subsequently lower population forecasts resulted in less urgency being attached to the problem of accommodating future urban growth.

It has been illustrated that the problem of the physical city arose as a consequence of economic success; this problem, so fundamentally different from that of the Development Areas, has continued to be of central relevance in the movement for regional planning. The relationship of the accommodation of population growth and the growth of urban areas remains one of the basic issues in planning; this has already been seen in relation to the regional plans for the South East of England; it was the population problem which eventually dominated the Advisory Committee and the planners on the 1946 Clyde Valley Regional Plan. In his book *Urban Development in Britain: 1964-2004*, P.A. Stone emphasizes the accommodation of population growth as one of the key planning problems of our time. Forecasts of expected population have been an integral part of the conceptualized problem of the city or urban region. Although official population projections by the Registrars General have fallen from a 20 million increase by the end of the century on 1965 based projections[45] to an increase by 2000 of 11 million on the 1970 based projections[46] for Great Britian, it is clear that decisions will have to be taken now on the siting, size and shape of urban development in 30 years time. Although current[47] population projections based on 1972 data forecast a much slower growth, only 6 million, from 54 to 60 millions, by 2001, than was projected at the height of the rising birth rate in 1964 (the 1972 projection is some 11 million fewer by 2001), it is still a considerable increase. In addition, it has been estimated[48] that approximately nine million people need to be accommodated in new locations due to the need to replace the worn out parts of the existing urban stock.

The Barlow Report estimated that the population of Great Britian, at 46 million in 1940, would rise to only 47 million by 1961, and then decline to 46 million by 1971. Although the assumptions underlying the Barlow Report's forecasts proved to be invalid, so too may the present view held by many planners of the 'population explosion' to be faced in this country. Since 1964 the birth rate has taken a sudden and continued down turn which will affect long term estimates of urban growth; with this continued fall in fertility, and as death rates have decreased only marginally, instead of predicted continued growth, it is feasible to envisage a decreasing population in the future, or at least a population that is not growing. While the annual number of births in England and Wales increased by 11 per cent in the five years 1959-64, the rate fell by 10 per cent in 1964-69. The excess of births over deaths in these three years were:

1959	220,850
1964	341,235
1969	219,500

This trend has continued in the 1970s and the excess of births over deaths in 1972 was only 131,000, and if it continues at the present rate then the excess of births over deaths could disappear before the end of the 1970s. In addition the immigration Acts of the 1960s have reduced drastically the gain to population by overseas migration; the number of Commonwealth citizens admitted for settlement to Britain fell to 30,000 in 1970. The 1971 Immigration Act might be expected to strengthen this process.

THE PROBLEM OF EFFICIENCY IN ADMINISTRATION
The development of regional planning in Britain has been conceptualized largely as two active movements concerned with tackling two different kinds of problem, namely those of the depressed areas and of the city or urban region. However, a third major movement for regional planning has arisen concerning the difficulties of administering a complex society. These difficulties have been identified and experienced in the form of expensive and inadequate services in both quality and quantity, and this has been translated by the administrator into the general problem of efficiency. Basically, the administrator, like the physical planner, has conceptualized the problem in terms meaningful and understandable to him. This has involved increasing criticism of a great deal of the administrative machine in the light of its inability to deal with an increasing number and complexity of services. A number of solutions, both implemented and proposed, have pointed towards a regional level of decision making. For present purposes it will be sufficient to consider some of the main services which are now being administered on a regional basis; in particular, attention is focused upon health, transport, water and recreation. The regionalization of administration and government for a wide range of issues is considered in Chapter 5 on regional institutions. However, before looking at some current developments in the regional provision of services, it might be helpful to consider these in the context of past developments in the movement for regionalism.

While the reform of administration and government at central and local level is considered in Chapter 5, as has already been shown, regionalism is not a new idea of the 1960s and 1970s, but rather a revival of interest from that shown in the first decade of this century. Regionalism was first advocated, by academics, as a solution to local government problems based on a system of relatively large regions. In 1904 the Fabian Society advocated the reform of local government on a regional basis, and this was followed by a report published in 1905, 'Municipalisation by Provinces', which recommended the establishment of a heptarchy of seven or eight provinces.

The need for larger sized areas not only in spatial scope but in terms of population thresholds has been a constant theme in many schemes for administrative reform. The work of the Fabian Society was followed by that of P. Geddes *Cities in Evolution* in 1915,[49] emphasizing the need for a regional approach to local government to meet the needs of a city-region style of life. In 1916 C.B. Fawcett published *Provinces of England*[50] recommending reform of local government and devolution of central government functions to provide a system of federal government with twelve provincial parliaments replacing the county system. The movement towards regionalism was given further impetus by the work of G.D.H. Cole in *The Future of Local Government* published in 1921,[51] in which he advocated dividing England into nine regions.

In the 1930s greater attention was given to the role which regionalism might play in the organization of central government, in addition to the need for reform of local government. From the 1930s the development of regionalism was pursued mainly by central government. Indeed, the 1930s was an important decade for the involvement of government in, and commitment to, planning at the regional level. During the war regional Commissioners were appointed to co-ordinate the work of local authorities, and in the economic sector, in 1940, Regional Boards were created in order to co-ordinate industrial production. After the war the regional organization was dismantled. Both the regional Commissioners, and the Commissioners for Special Areas, were ended. The Regional Boards became the Regional Boards for Industry in 1945, with functions of purely an advisory nature, but membership drawn from both government departments and industry. The establishment of the RBI followed very closely the recommendations of the Minority Report of the Barlow Commission. The RBI, in turn, were disbanded in 1964, and replaced by the new regional planning machinery in the form of Regional Economic Planning Councils (non civil servants appointed for their interest in the region) and Regional Economic Planning Boards (government officials). This action strengthened the linkage between central and local government's administrative functions, and provided the first major step towards achieving a more meaningful institutional framework for regional planning.

Questions about the effectiveness of the present administrative organization assume the continuance of the existing pattern of central and local government. However, government organization is at present undergoing change, both at local and national level, with increasing emphasis being placed on the appropriate framework required for regional planning.

Provision of services on a regional basis

The Local Government Act of 1972 brought about fundamental changes in the organization of local government, with many services now being provided by new authorities which may be described as regional in their scale of operations. In addition to this general provision of services[52] by a reorganized local government structure some important services have recently opted for a regional administration.

Health services   The reorganization of the National Health Service was outlined in a White Paper of August 1972 for England,[53] with comparable documents being issued for Scotland and Wales. In a foreword to the English White Paper, the Secretary of State for Social Services, Sir Keith Joseph, emphasized that a reform of the NHS administration was being made 'solely in order to improve the health care of the public'. The government decided that effective organization of the health services in England requires two levels, regional and area, in addition to the central Department. Since each area health authority will serve the same population within the same boundaries as its matching local authority, the purpose will be that formal divisions between the health, the education, and personal social services will be bridged by the arrangements for collaboration. As far as Wales is concerned, the whole area has been designated a region with one board, subdivided into area authorities (see Figure 2.9).

Under the current arrangements, there will be central strategic planning and monitoring by the DHSS; regional planning and general supervision of operations (as well as some direct executive functions) by regional authorities; and area planning and operational control by area authorities co-ordinated with local authorities sharing common boundaries. The regional health authority (RHA) will have a regional planning responsibility which will include settling priorities when there are competing claims between areas. This is an example of a regional agency being an allocator of resources rather than the central Department.

Transport services   As the Buchanan Report 'Traffic in Towns' in 1963 illustrated,[54] everyone is conscious of 'the traffic problem' and that it is increasing in scale and complexity. The report also emphasized the need for regional transportation planning with the designation of urban regions in an attempt to cope with the problems posed by the growth of motor traffic. As the report pointed out,[55] however, the existing administrative machinery was not designed to carry through the programme which was required.

The early 1960s saw the preparation of a number of regional transportation studies focused mainly on metropolitan regions. Two particular studies, those of the SELNEC (South East Lancashire North East Cheshire) Transportation Study and the West Midlands Transport Study, were representative of attempts being made by regional planners to tackle transport problems.

In October 1963 the then Minister of Transport invited Manchester

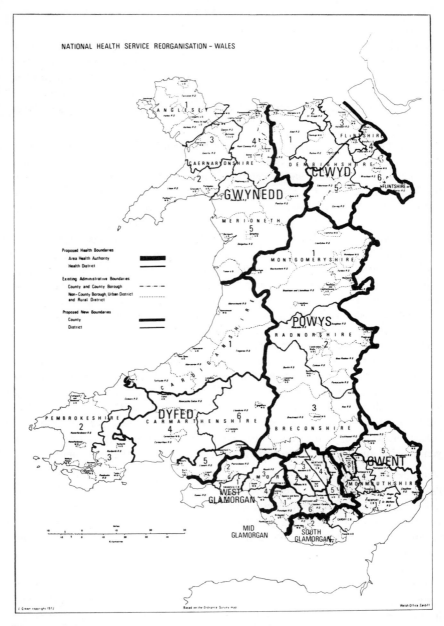

Fig. 2.9   National Health Service reorganization — Wales.
Source: *Management Arrangements for the Reorganised NHS in Wales* (HMSO, 1972).

Fig. 2.10   The SELNEC transportation study.
Source: *SELNEC Transportation Study*, p. 9, 1972.

Corporation to convene a conference with other major local authorities in the
SELNEC area to consider the establishment of a Transportation Study. At a
conference held in the November of 1963 agreement was reached as to the need
for a comprehensive Transportation Study to be carried out in the conurbation.
In the Autumn of 1969 the assets of the municipal bus undertakings in the area
were vested in the SELNEC PTE (Passenger Transport Executive) and the
representatives on the Steering Committee of the Study were replaced by
representatives of the SELNEC PTA (Passenger Traffic Authority) and of the
PTE. Both the PTA and PTE had been established under the 1968 Transport

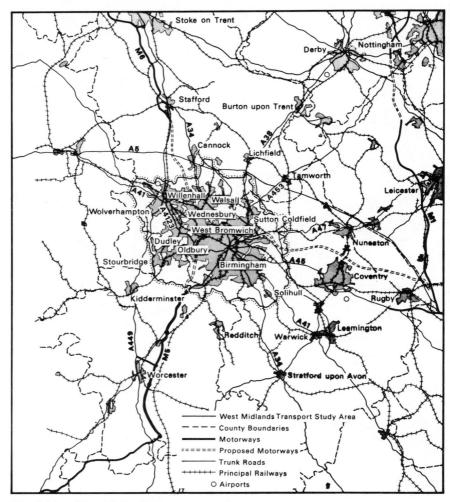

Fig. 2.11   West Midlands transport study.
            Source: *West Midlands Transport Study*, Vol. 1, Preface (HMSO,
            1968).

Act, which is considered further later in this section. The Study's main aim was
to produce a recommended highway and public transport system for the study
area (see Figure 2.10) with the view to implementation by 1981, this date being
subsequently revised to 1984. After the evaluation of alternative transport
systems had been completed, a Broad Transportation Plan,[56] comprising
complementary highway and public transport networks for 1984 was selected.

A decision to establish the West Midlands Transport Study (see Figure 2.11)
was taken in December 1963 in circumstances similar to that of SELNEC, at a
conference between the Ministry of Transport and local authorities. As with the

SELNEC Study the organization of the West Midlands Study comprised both a Steering Committee and a Technical Committee. The Study was undertaken by consultants (Freeman, Fox, Wilbur Smith and Associates) under the direction of the Technical Committee. The terms of reference of the West Midlands Transport Study included 'a comprehensive survey of all forms of transport in the West Midlands Conurbation and to analyse its relationship to all types of land use and to other factors affecting the demand for the movement of transport; and to make forward projections with the aim of providing guidance on the desirable future pattern of road development and public transport facilities'.[57]

The West Midlands Transport Study was only the second major land-use/transportation study to be undertaken in Britain, and the techniques used were developed from those used in the London Traffic Survey and other studies in America.

While the idea of regional transportation planning has existed for some time, it has manifested itself in various ways. In Britain, the nearest example of a regional organization for transportation planning are the PTAs and PTEs established under the 1968 Transport Act. The Act enabled the Minister of Transport, if he 'considers it expedient', i.e. an optional clause, to establish the new machinery 'for the purpose of securing the provision of a properly integrated and efficient (a key word in the drive for regionalism in administration) system of public passenger transport to meet the needs of that area'.[58] The PTA/PTE machinery covered the conurbations of West Midlands, Merseyside, SELNEC, and Tyneside. Under the 1972 Local Government Act the PTA/PTE machinery became automatic, with each metropolitan county becoming a passenger transport area, and the PTA is the county council;[59] in addition West Yorkshire and South Yorkshire were added to the PTA list. In the case of London, of course, special arrangements exist with the GLC and the London Transport Board.

Under the 1972 Local Government Act, non metropolitan areas have a responsibility to 'develop policies which will promote the provision of a co-ordinated and efficient system of public passenger transport to meet the needs of the county'.[60] While a new opportunity exists for many authorities to involve themselves with regional transportation planning, a strong case exists for a more comprehensive regional entity. The difficulties of introducing regional transportation planning have been analysed in some depth by Gakenheimer in his study of the American position.[61] The idea of establishing regional transportation planning entities has been considered for some time in America, and Bills have been submitted to Congress to establish regional transport authorities for the whole country. There are, as might be expected, however, a number of difficulties with the operation of regional transportation planning, including the definition of boundaries for regions, conflict with national policies, new powers required on finance, etc.

Water services   The government reorganized, again from April 1974, water services in England and Wales by establishing 10 regional water authorities, shown in Figure 2.12, to take over the existing functions of river authorities.[62] In fact, there are nine RWAs in England and a Welsh National Water Development Authority, and these replace 1,600 authorities administering the water services in England and Wales at the present time.

The new regionalized water industry is substantial, employing 75,000 staff, with an annual revenue of £350 million, and an investment budget of £300 million a year. To administer this large undertaking a comprehensive management structure has been implemented based on the Report of the Ogden Committee.[63] The structure of a large RWA is illustrated in Figure 2.13; the diagram emphasizes the comprehensive and powerful nature of the RWA's management structure.

The government's policy in implementing the new RWAs has been designed to meet the following needs; sufficient quantity and quality of water given increasing household and industrial use; disposal of waste without damage to the environment; adequate provision for drainage of land and flood protection; development of freshwater fisheries; navigation needs on rivers and inland waterways; and amenity aspects which must be developed in a way compatible with other needs.

Recreation and sports services   A considerable amount of literature has been published in recent years of the need to plan for the demand for all forms of leisure activity which will increase at an unprecedented pace during the next 30 years.[64] While the direction of the movement towards increased leisure seems fairly clear, there has been insufficient research on the nature and pace of this movement. With the recent proposals for more flexible working hours and the prospect of a four day working week,[65] the future of leisure time has entered a critical phase. In the past, the movement towards shorter hours has been influenced by a number of factors, including increases in productivity, the value workers place on shorter hours rather than larger earning, the needs of employers, and changes in the occupational and industrial structure. While the breakthrough from a five day to four day week may not yet be imminent, that of rearranged workweeks and more flexible working hours has already gained in practice in Britain recently.

To help meet the increased demands of more leisure time in relation to sporting activities the government established, by Royal Charter, the Sports Council, an independent body with executive power, operative from April 1st 1972. Exchequer aid is given to the Sports Council through the Department of the Environment, and independent organizations have been established for Scotland and Wales. The Great Britain Sports Council meets only to consider

Map 2

PROPOSED REGIONAL WATER AUTHORITIES

Areas in England within Welsh
National Water Development Authority

Areas in Wales within
Severn – Trent Water Authority

NORTH EAST WATER AUTHORITY

NORTH WEST WATER AUTHORITY

YORKSHIRE WATER AUTHORITY

WELSH NATIONAL WATER DEVELOPMENT AUTHORITY

SEVERN – TRENT WATER AUTHORITY

EAST ANGLIA WATER AUTHORITY

THAMES WATER AUTHORITY

WESSEX WATER AUTHORITY

SOUTH WEST WATER AUTHORITY

SOUTHERN WATER AUTHORITY

MILES
10 0 10 20 30 40 50

0 20 40 60 80
KILOMETRES

© Crown copyright 1973

DOE December 1972

Fig. 2.12   The new regional water authorities.
Source: *A Background to Water Reorganisation in England and Wales*, map 2 (HMSO, 1973).

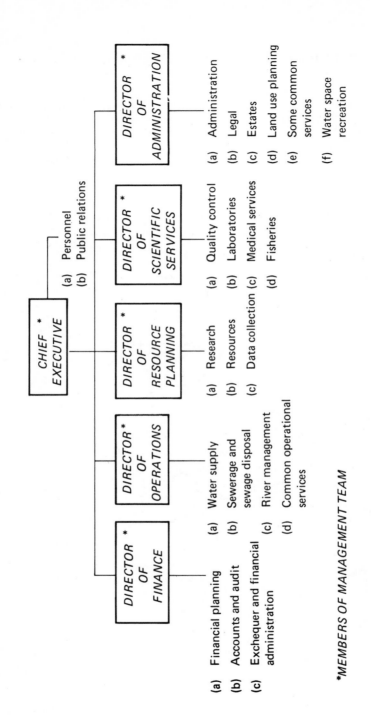

Fig. 2.13   Regional corporate management team — large authority.
Source: *The New Water Industry Management and Structure*, Fig. 2,
p. 33 (HMSO, 1973).

national issues, otherwise decisions are made individually by the bodies for England, Scotland and Wales. The English Sports Council is organized on a regional basis itself with six constituent regions.

The Sports Council's functions include the provision of appropriate grants for sporting organizations, activities and projects; assistance to British representative teams competing in international sports activities; the provision and management of national sports centres and forging closer sporting links with, and among, local authorities. The administration of recreation and sports services has already become a major item in the overall provision of services which are required for contemporary life styles, and might be expected to increase in both quantity and quality quite rapidly in the future.

Conclusion: efficiency in administration
Many difficulties arise in the administration of services in a complex society. Increasingly in recent years, these difficulties have been met by introducing a regional structure of administration and decision making. At the present time this movement towards regionalism in administration and government is extremely strong, and has certainly been seen as providing the means to meet the challenge of service provision in a variety of fields.

THE PROBLEMS OF EQUALITY, AUTONOMY AND SELF FULFILMENT
The problem of equality is a relatively new one in terms of its impact and implications for regional planning; however, it has been a significant force in the development of regional planning to the present day. This issue has focused on a greater awareness, stimulated by social research and political parties, of very considerable diversity in the quantity and quality of services, especially social services, between different areas of the country. If such disparities can be eliminated the equality of life chances may be increased; the reorganization of the National Health Services and local government services on a regional scale might be expected to help achieve this end.

The emergence of autonomy as an issue in society represents the crystallization of the previous issues and problems. The problem of representation and control is intimately related to the problem of administrative reform; and then to the problem of equality; it is also related to the problem of economic growth in so far as regional economic policies may in part at least stem from our attempt to articulate social potential of the regions; it is related to the problem of equality in the sense that initiative and participation are intimately related to autonomy. The problem of autonomy like many others expresses itself at many different points in society, but it may be expected to express itself at the regional level as this, for other reasons, becomes the centre of important decisions. It has already expressed itself at this level where strong regional identities and cultures are involved. In Wales, the Welsh Nationalist Party, Plaid Cymru, have argued strongly for an Elected Assembly similar to that promised for Scotland. Plaid Cymru[66] has stressed the inability of Welsh people to gain access to decision making; the Welsh Council is nominated by the Secretary of State and has only advisory powers; the Secretary of State is responsible to Parliament in Westminster; and the Welsh Office itself is not responsible to any representative body of Welsh opinion. The problem of autonomy has become more, rather than less, dominant in recent years as a pressure for regional planning. Indeed, the pressures of regionalism might be expected to intensify, with growing regional consciousness in England as well as Scotland and Wales; the European context of the EEC with extra pressure of work on Whitehall and demand for separate regional representation at Brussels, particularly in relation to access to the regional development fund; and the general problem of remoteness of government from the governed. Also, in recent years, there has been an exploration[67] of new forms of politics and government centred upon the need to put the community first. The problem of autonomy has in part focused upon the need for action at the regional level. This reappraisal of fundamental societal values may be expected to play a dominant role in the future development of regional planning.

As indicated at the beginning of this chapter, the problems of self fulfilment, growth, equality and autonomy are relatively new ones, and represent a more abstract stream of thinking in the development of the demand for regional planning than the older established problems of the depressed areas, the physical city, and the administration of services. They have developed more out of the consideration of explicit goals than out of consideration of urgent problems. Nevertheless, they do, and indeed must, relate back to the individual, his problems, needs and values. The problem of self fulfilment is all embracing; it is relevant to all the problems identified in this chapter. The most fundamental value underlying the demand for regional planning has been this desire for self fulfilment. Regional planning offers a new channel of articulation and a new form of action. Through this the individual may hope to achieve greater control and influence over society's future and over his own future in such a way as better to realize himself whether through greater control of government or through a more secure and favourable social and economic environment.

Regional Planning in Developing Countries

Of necessity, this look at the development of regional planning in developing countries, and later, in other industrial countries, must be brief. It is perhaps sufficient, however, to recognize that regional planning as a form of planning action has been used fairly extensively in developing countries. Perloff has given the view[68] that regional planning in the less developed countries today, with only few exceptions, is much more promise than reality. While it is true that regional planning has a very long way to go to be truly meaningful, a number of noteworthy regional programmes in a few countries have actually got under way. The different and as yet emerging forms which regional planning has taken in its evolution in Great Britain have been mirrored to a marked extent in the countries of the Third World. Thus Waterston's threefold classification of forms of regional planning in these countries is evocative of the British experience.[69] In the first place Waterston distinguishes planning for the city region or a depressed part of a country. In this situation, very often, a special authority may be created to formulate a plan and implement programmes. Some examples in the developing countries include the Superintendencia do Desenvolvimento do Nordeste (SUDENE) in the North East of Brazil,[70] the Corporacion Autonimadel Valle del Canca (CVC) in the Canca Valley of Colombia, and the Corporacion Venezolana de Guyana (CVG) developing a new city in the interior of Venezuela, called Ciudad Guyana. This example in Venezuela has become the subject of a great deal of interest by a number of regional planners including John Friedmann and Lloyd Rodwin.[71] Regional planning has also been recognized as an instrument of planning with many developing countries in Africa, including Ghana[72] and Nigeria. Nigeria particularly has an acute problem in coping with the rapid rate of urbanization with limited resources. Nigeria has shown a remarkable growth in population since the end of the second World War, focused mainly on a few large towns; the 1952 population of 33 million had grown to 55 million by 1962, and 61 million by 1968, i.e. a million people per year—a dramatic expansion of the physical city. Lagos, with a 1962 population of 665,000 reached 1.5 million by 1971; towns like Ibadan, Port Harcourt, Kano and Kaduna have growth rates of from 7.6 to 11.5 per cent per annum.

Secondly, sub national regional planning may refer to the preparation of a series of regional plans covering an entire country as part of the process of preparing a national plan. Nigeria, India and Pakistan[73] are good examples of this type of regional planning.

Thirdly, regional planning may refer to the fitting of projects under a national plan to enhance economic development of depressed regions. In Yugoslavia the Investment Bank allocates its resources to regions with special need of economic development. In general however, this form of regional planning has been taken furthest by the older industrialized countries.

The organizational problems of metropolitan and regional planning in developing countries have been analysed by Kutty,[74] where attention necessarily focuses upon the implications of rapid population growth and the crucial role of economic development as population growth in metropolitan areas far outstrips growth of employment. Kutty sees the most effective location for metropolitan planning with regional government, but notes that even in the more developed countries this form of government has yet to take firm roots, and only a beginning has been recently made with cities like London and Toronto. At least in this respect, the developing countries face a regional planning organization problem similar to that in the developed countries, i.e. regional forms of government for tackling problems which can be solved only on a supra urban basis.

Regional Planning in Industrialized Countries

Regional planning has been used in industrialized countries as a form of planning action in ways similar to those in Britain. Examples can be found of regional planning being used to cope with the problems of the depressed areas (either older industrial areas or underdeveloped rural areas), the physical city, economic growth, and administration of services.

Italy is quoted as a classic case of most aspects of the 'regional problem', and in particular that of dualism between the backward, mainly agricultural South and the more advanced industrial North. The Cassa per il Mezzogiorno (development fund for southern Italy) was established in 1950 to promote the modernization of infrastructure, agriculture and industry. The role of the fund has been examined in some depth by Watson in relation to regional development policy and administration in Italy.[75] The Cassa per il Mezzogiorno has become one of the major *ad hoc* regional planning agencies in the world. Other examples of regional planning being used to cope with the depressed area problem can be cited. In the United States, legislation for lagging regions has included the Area Redevelopment Act of 1961, the Appalachian Regional Development Act of 1965, and the Public Works and Economic Development Act of 1965, which created five new multistate regions and the Economic Development Administration to promote economic growth in depressed areas.

During the past two decades France has developed a comprehensive system of regional planning; Hansen has claimed[76] that it is the most comprehensive in Europe. The implementation of regional planning in France is carried out by agencies at both the national and regional levels (see Figure 2.14). France illustrates in a dramatic way the dual problem of the depressed areas and rapid urban growth in the Paris region. While permits are required for development in the Paris and Lyons areas, there are decentralization grants available to firms moving out of Paris. A range of incentives are offered by the government national regional policy to encourage investment in the development areas in the south and west. A detailed report on the regional problems in the EEC countries has been prepared by the Commission of the European Communities, as a next step in the development of a Community Regional Policy.[77]

The use of regional planning to cope with the metropolitan explosion can be seen in many countries; Hall has examined the major city regions of the

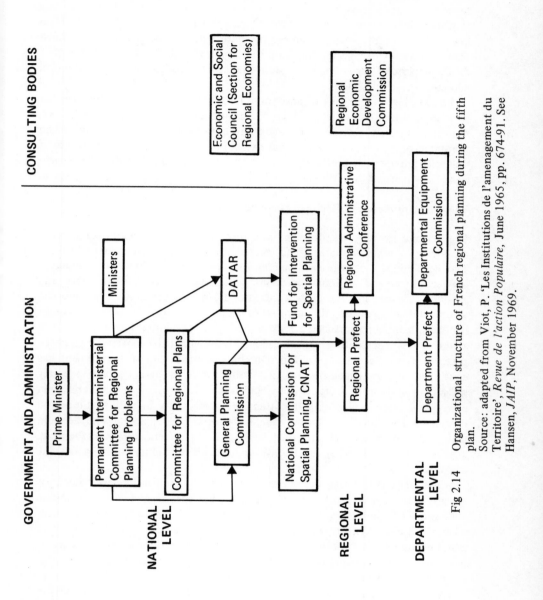

GOVERNMENT AND ADMINISTRATION

CONSULTING BODIES

Prime Minister

Ministers

Permanent Interministerial Committee for Regional Planning Problems

Committee for Regional Plans

General Planning Commission

DATAR

National Commission for Spatial Planning, CNAT

Fund for Intervention for Spatial Planning

Economic and Social Council (Section for Regional Economies)

Regional Economic Development Commission

Regional Prefect

Regional Administrative Conference

Department Prefect

Departmental Equipment Commission

NATIONAL LEVEL

REGIONAL LEVEL

DEPARTMENTAL LEVEL

Fig 2.14   Organizational structure of French regional planning during the fifth plan.
Source: adapted from Viot, P. 'Les Institutions de l'amenagement du Territoire', *Revue de l'action Populaire*, June 1965, pp. 674-91. See Hansen, *JAIP*, November 1969.

world,[78] not only in Western Europe but also Russia and Japan with case studies on Moscow and Tokyo. In Poland there is a special network of regional long term planning centres and a centre for spatial aspects of the long term development of the whole country. In additon to a basic goal of the socialist planned economy being to 'eliminate irrational extremes in the development of different parts of the country',[79] attention has been focused on the distribution and costs of urban growth.

Finally, just as the issue of autonomy has been an expression of the need for regional planning and regional decision making in Britain, so too has this been the case elsewhere. Regionalism is very strong in Spain, and also in Italy. When the Italian government chose the rival city of Catanzoro as the regional capital of Calabria province in October 1970, there were weeks of rioting in Reggio Calabria which felt that it was the first choice.

The Current Practice of Regional Planning

The demand for regional planning has evolved from society seeking solutions to a number of urgent problems and the realization of some fundamental values. The development of regional planning has, quite clearly, involved interaction between local and national problems, and issues of a physical, social and economic nature, and within the context of a debate concerning the appropriate administrative structure of coping with these problems. The development of regional planning has reached a critical stage since the initial impetus was given at the turn of the century, and the momentum behind the movement gathered pace after the Second World War. On the one hand, central government has continued and extended its regional policy, established a regional planning machinery with an advisory capacity, and taken a leading role in the preparation of regional strategy plans. On the other hand, and partly induced by the action of central government, a strong case has emerged for planning and decision making to be made at the regional level itself. At present, however, the weak institutional framework for regional planning is a hallmark of its current practice.

While regional planning was started as an activity to plan the development of specific regions which had to solve important but specific and *ad hoc* economic and social problems, as Kuklinski has observed,[80] we have seen in most countries a clear trend to widen the scope and systematic nature of this form of planning action. In addition to a body of experience to draw upon, recent years have witnessed a growing belief in the ability of regional planning to cope with problems of everyday living.[81]

The role of the regional planner, and education for regional planning, in the overall system of planning, has received attention only in recent years. Planning education in university and polytechnic planning schools now places considerable emphasis on the methods and techniques of planning on a regional basis. However, the success or failure of regional planning in a given country not only depends upon the quality of the education, the planning institutes and their staff, but on improving the understanding of the basic issues of regional planning in a contemporary society. As a particular form of planning action it is undoubtedly true to say that regional planning has begun to establish its identity in a forceful manner, although much remains to be done.

The present practice of regional planning in many countries is closely linked to the operation of national regional policies by central governments. Regional planning agencies throughout the world have become involved with the problems of the depressed areas, and their linkage with national regional policies of central governments have become a feature of regional planning. Nowhere has this been more the case than in Britain, where planning agencies have operated within the context of a national regional policy which has been pursued for some 40 years. This relationship is of central importance to regional planning, for national regional policies may impose constraints on the one hand, or even induce regional planning on the other. An understanding of the linkage between regional policy and regional planning is necessary to clarify the role of regional policy in so far as it might be seen as a substitute for regional planning and vice versa. This aspect of regional planning has received less attention than it deserves, and has given rise to much confusion over the operation of these two forms of action. With UK membership of the EEC a great deal of emphasis has been placed on the need for a common regional policy for the Community; in this context, the activity of regional planning has taken a secondary place.

Given the onset of a number of institutional reforms the region might be expected to increase in relevance and importance, with local government reform; the reorganization of central government administration; and the search for common social, economic and environmental policies in the EEC which is essentially a community of regions having both specific and general needs.

The acceptance and use of regional planning as a form of planning action will only increase if it is found to be relevant in meeting changing societal needs. Although considerable developments have been made in planning at regional level, regional planning has not yet fully discovered itself either in terms of content or approach, nor in achieving an institutional arrangement suited to that discovery. It is to these fundamental issues that the succeeding chapters focus their attention.

References

1   Hufschmidt, M.M. (ed), *Regional Planning: Challenge and Prospects* (Praeger, F. 1969). See especially Chapter 2, 'A New Look at Regional Planning', by the editor.

2   During the years 1936-43 the National Resources Planning Board published a series of thirteen regional planning reports covering regions as diverse as New England, Alaska, the Arkansas Valley, and the St. Louis metropolitan region.

3   Odum, H.W. and Moore, E., *American Regionalism: A Cultural Historical Approach to National Integration* (Henry Holt & Co., 1938); and Vance, R., 'The Regional Concept as a Tool for Social Research', in Merrill Jensen (ed), *Regionalism in America* (University of Wisconsin Press, 1952).

4   See Regional Science Association, Papers and Proceedings; also Walter Isard, *Methods of Regional Analysis: An Introduction to Regional Science* (John Wiley & Sons Inc., 1960).

5   See, for example, Friedmann, J. and Alonso, W. (eds), *Regional Development and Planning* (MIT Press, 1964).

6   *The Doncaster Regional Planning Scheme,* Report prepared for the Joint Committee by Abercrombie, P. and Johnson, T.H. (The University of Liverpool Press, 1922).

7   *Report of South Wales Regional Survey* (Ministry of Health, 1920).

8   Op. cit. page 3.

9   Yeates, M.H. and Garner, B.J., *The North American City* (Harper & Row, 1971).

10   *Regional Survey of New York and its Environs 1927,* Vol. 1, by Committee on Regional Planning of New York and its Environs.

11   For a further description of the role of regional planning in the metropolitan regions of New York and the Ruhr, see Hall, P., *The World Cities,* 2nd ed. (World University Press, 1967).

12   *First Report of the Commissioner for the Special Areas (England and Wales),* Ministry of Labour, Cmnd. 4957 (HMSO, 1935).

13   Above cit.

14   Denison, S.R., *The Location of Industry and the Depressed Areas,* p. 127 (Oxford University Press, 1939).

15   For a more detailed analysis of the problems of the depressed areas, see McCrone, G.M., *Regional Policy in Britain* (Allen & Unwin, 1969).

16   *Third Report of the Commissioner for England & Wales,* Ministry of Labour, Cmnd. 5303 (HMSO, 1936).

17   Barlow Report, January 1940, *Report of the Royal Commission on the Distribution of the Industrial Population,* Cmnd. 6153 (HMSO, 1940).

18   The Regional Employment Premium, for example, established by the Labour government in 1967, and a guaranteed life until 1974, was aimed primarily at reducing regional differentials in unemployment. See *The Development Areas: A Proposal for a REP,* p.10, para 22 (HMSO, 1967).

19   See report on the probability of remaining unemployed, Research Series No. 1, DEP (HMSO, 1968).

20   White Paper, *Industrial and Regional Development,* Cmnd. 4942. March 1972, and *Industry Act 1972* (HMSO, 1972).

21   Many people, however, including economists, have stressed the costs of economic growth, and challenged 'growthmania' as a prerequisite for an advanced 20th century society. See, for example, Mishan, E.J., *The Cost of Economic Growth* (Penguin, 1969).

22   *Investment Incentives,* Cmnd. 4156 (HMSO, 1970).

23   Toothill Report 1961 (HMSO, 1961).

24   April 1963, HMSO.

25   Cmnd. 2206 (HMSO, 1963).

26   Cmnd. 2188 (HMSO, 1963).

27   *The National Plan,* Cmnd. 2764 (HMSO, 1965).

28   See lecture by Sir Eric Roll to the Royal Institute of Public Administration on The Role of the Department of Economic Affairs, November 1965.

29   Barlow Report, op. cit.

30   Young, M. and Willmott, P., *The Symmetrical Family* (Routledge, & Kegan Paul, 1973)..

31   Hall, P., op. cit.

32   *The Clyde Valley Regional Plan, 1946,* page 1 (HMSO, 1949).

33   op. cit. Chapter 13, pages 340-344.

34   *The North East Development Area Outline Plan* (HMSO, 1949).

35   The Future of Development Plans, Report by Planning Advisory Group.

36   *Greater London Plan 1944*, Abercrombie, P. (HMSO, 1945).

37   above cit. Chapter 3, 'Decentralisation', page 30.

38   Cmnd. 1952.

39   *Tomorrow's London – A Background Paper to the Greater London Development Plan* (GLC, 1969).

40   above cit, Chapter 2, 'London: Regional and World City' page 13.

41   Published jointly by the City and County Councils, March 1969.

42   Published jointly by both City and County Councils, 1969.

43   For a more extensive coverage of sub regional planning studies undertaken in the 1960s, see *Proceedings of the Nottingham Symposium on Sub-Regional Studies September 1968* (Regional Studies Association, 1969).

44   Stone, P.A., *Urban Development in Britain: Standards, Costs and Resources 1964–2004* (Cambridge University Press, 1970).

45   See *The National Plan*, Cmnd. 2764 (HMSO, 1965).

46   Thompson, J., *The Growth of Population to the End of the Century. Social Trends*, No. 1 (HMSO, 1970), and *Monthly Digest of Statistics* (HMSO, 1970).

47   Registrar General's population projections: 1972 based.

48   Stone, P.A., op. cit.

49   Geddes, P., *Cities in Evolution*, (new and revised edition) (Benn, 1968).

50   Fawcett, C.B., *The Provinces of England*, (new edition) (Hutchinson, 1960).

51   Cole, G.D.H., *The Future of Local Government* (Cassell & Co., 1947).

52   See *Local Government Act 1972*, Chapter 70, especially Part IX, Functions (HMSO, 1972).

53   *National Health Service Reorganisation, England*, August 1972, Cmnd. 5055 (HMSO, 1972).

54   *Traffic in Towns:* Buchanan Report, (HMSO, 1963).

55   Buchanan Report, Above cit, para 48, Report of Steering Group.

56   SELNEC Transportation Study. Report of the Technical Control Team. A Broad Transportation Plan for 1984, March 1972.

57   West Midlands Transport Study, 1968, p. 2, Vol. 1.

58   *1968 Transport Act*, Part II, Clause 9.

59   *Local Government Act 1972*, Part IX. Section 202.

60   above cit. Section 203.

61   Gakenheimer, R., 'Regional Transportation Planning Experience in the United States: A Critical Review of Selected Cases', in *Perspectives on Regional Transportation Planning*, De Salvo, J.S. (ed) (Lexington Books, 1973).

62   *A Background to Water Reorganisation in England and Wales* (HMSO, 1973).

63   *The New Water Industry Management and Structure*, Report of Committee Chaired by Sir. G. Ogden (HMSO, 1973).

64   See, for example, Cullingworth, J.B., 'Planning for Leisure' *Urban Studies*, May, 1964: and Dower, M., *Fourth Wave – The Challenge of Leisure*, A Civic Trust Survey, January, 1965.

65   The extent to which the 4 day work week has caught the imagination of the American public is described by Janice Hedges in 'A Look at the 4 day Work Week' in *Monthly Labor Review*, US Department of Labor, October, 1971.

66   *Plaid Cymru, An Elected Assembly for Wales*, 1973.

67   See, for example, Slesser, M., *The Politics of Environment: A Guide to Scottish Thought and Action* (Allen & Unwin, 1972).

68   Perloff, H.S., 'Education for Regional Planning in Less Developed Countries', Chapter 1, in *Issues in Regional Planning*, Dunham, D.D. and Hilhorst, J.G.M. (eds) (Mouton, 1971).

69   Waterston, A., *Development Planning* (Johns Hopkins Press, 1965).

70   Haddad, P.R., 'Problems and Policies of Regional Planning in Brazil', Chapter 4 in *Issues in Regional Planning*, above cit.

71   See Friedmann, J., *Regional Development Policy – A Case Study of Venezuela*, (MIT Press, 1966), and *Planning Urban Growth and Regional Development*, L. Rodwin & Associates, (MIT Press, 1969).

72   Bannerman, J.E., 'Problems and Policies of Regional Planning in Ghana', Chapter 6, *Issues in Regional Planning*, above cit.

73   Shibli, K., 'Regional Planning and Development in Pakistan', Chapter 5, above cit.; also M. Datta-Chaudhuri, Regional Planning in India, Chapter 9.

74   Kutty, M.G., Metropolitan and Regional Planning Problems of Organisation, Symposium on Urbanisation in Developing Countries, held by International Union of Local Authorities in December 1967 at Noordwijk in the Netherlands.

75   Watson, M.M., *Regional Development Policy and Administration in Italy* (Longman, 1970).

76   Hansen, N.M., 'French Regional Planning Experience', *JAIP*, November, 1969.

77   Report on the Regional Problems in the Enlarged Community, Commission of the European Communities, Brussels, 3 May 1973.

78   Hall, above cit.

79   Malisz, B., 'Urban Planning Theory: Methods and Results', in *City and Regional Planning in Poland*, J. Fisher (ed) (Cornell University Press, 1966).

80   Kuklinski, A.R., 'Education for Regional Planning', Chapter 2 in *Issues in Regional Planning*, above cit.

81   At the 1973 annual conference of the Association of Municipal Corporations, many members argued strongly how regional planning and regional government would answer many of the problems discussed at the conference, i.e. problems of everyday living.

3 Regional Planning Theory

Introduction

It has been suggested and also increasingly recognized that planning theory may be broken down into two distinct components, substantive theory and procedural theory.[1] Procedural theory seeks to elucidate the procedures or methodologies of planning and the appropriate use of these, whereas substantive theory is concerned with knowledge of the substance, of that segment of reality which is the focus of planning action. Although a simple division, it is considered to be a convenient and helpful one for structuring this introduction to regional planning. Accordingly this chapter focuses on substantive regional planning theory and Chapter 6 is concerned with procedural regional planning theory. In discussing substantive theory an attempt is made first of all to define that particular realm of substantive knowledge with which regional planning is concerned. The second aim is to offer a comprehensive outline of this field of knowledge. The intention is to present an overview of the subject and thus to help promote a synthesis of what is still a highly disparate field.

The previous chapter traced how a variety of pressures and issues in British society, but also elsewhere, have crystallized out in a concern to develop some form of public planning action at a regional scale. These issues have also induced in turn the development of a body of thought concerned to understand them. This particularly applies to the issue of economic growth which has led to the development of a significant and potentially very fruitful set of concepts and propositions regarding the influence of the locational dimension of society at a regional scale on economic development. Much of this work evolved through the 1950s and 1960s in the context of Third World countries.

Other issues have been less fruitful in realizing the development of a body of theory as yet; the social (equity) and political (autonomy) issues are recent. The physical problem has been long standing and powerful but no attempt has been made to conceptualize what a body of physical development theory might be about.

What however has become quickly established, is the view that the distinctive nature of regional planning is its concern to understand both physical and economic issues, to respond to these and mutually accommodate them through a unique integration of economic and physical planning skills.[2] This view has been bolstered by the simplistic and mechanistic idea that physical planning decreases in importance and economic planning increases in importance from the local to the national level of planning, thus at the regional level both are of equal importance.[3] But clearly the range of issues which regional planning can be expected to confront are not necessarily either physical or economic, or even social, political or administrative. Regional planning is a particular type of planning structure for inducing public action and ultimately its most fundamental characteristics stem from the nature of this structure rather than a given set of current issues which it happens to be confronting. It has already been contended that the defining characteristic of this structural arrangement is that it is supra urban in focus; accordingly it is concerned with supra urban issues, or more fundamentally with society in supra urban space, and more particularly with the effect of supra urban space on the working and performance of society. This is the defining core of substantive regional planning theory.

This then is a definition of that portion of the universe of human knowledge which is particularly relevant and necessary to regional planning. It is not a sphere of knowledge to which regional planners lay exclusive claim, it is not a sphere of knowledge which it is their mission to improve *per se*, it is not the only body of knowledge they draw upon, but it is the sphere of knowledge upon which they are especially reliant in recommending those courses of action which are the particular responsibility of the regional planner.

These courses of action need an understanding of the way in which resources come to be distributed within the societal spatial system, and with the way in which they can be redistributed; with the way in which space acts as a friction on the use of allocated resources and with the way in which resources allocated to one group may be appropriated by another. They are courses of action which seek to develop institutional and spatial strategies which serve to guide the flow of resources in a way which maximizes their intended and minimizes their unintended effect on the societal system at the supra urban scale.

Society and Supra Urban Space

It has been suggested that regional planning theory is concerned with the relationship between spatial structure, that is the way in which society distributes itself in space, and the behaviour or performance of society. At this stage in its development the body of propositions within regional planning is, however, not only relatively fragmented, but also relatively untested. This makes it necessary to discuss the relationship between society and supra urban space in compartmentalized rather than synthetic terms. It also means that the discussions and statements that are offered below need to be treated with a very great deal of care and with sensitivity regarding their as yet insecure basis. Although the discussion is therefore tentative and somewhat disjointed, one theme does emerge to knit it together, and this theme concerns the spatially concentrated nature of human activity. Observations, explanations and implications of this phenomenon form the core of the chapter. In order to provide some direction through the succeeding discussion, it is worth noting one important implication in advance. If the propositions incorporated in the body of this chapter are verified, then it follows that regional planning focuses on nodes of concentration, on towns and cities. It treats either a node and its hinterland, the city region, or a larger space typically polarized into several nodes; and it is the control of the size, relative location and institutional relationships between these which is a crucial element in regional planning decisions.

Economic Activity and Supra Urban Space

Economics has traditionally been a non spatial discipline, but the recent realization of the importance of the 'where?' aspect in economic development issues is now rapidly changing that tradition. Economics in consequence has now made more of a contribution to the understanding of society and supra urban space than any other social science apart from geography. Geographers have played an important part in describing and thus drawing attention to the distribution of economic activity over the land surface. Ullman, for example, in his seminal paper, drew attention to the strong concentration of economic activity in the North East of the USA. This is an area covering 7 per cent of the land surface of the USA, yet containing 43 per cent of that country's population and 70 per cent of its industry. Moreover, concentration, Ullman suggests, would appear to be the rule[4] (Figure 3.1).

Ullman's findings are presented in regional terms largely because of the availability of data, but it is important to recognize in moving towards an explanation of the phenomenon of concentration that the dominance of the north east region is articulated through the urban and metropolitan areas contained within it. The reporting unit is the region, the urban area the generator of the data recorded by this unit. This point is also relevant in considering the issue of concentration in Great Britain. Here a great deal of attention has focused on the regional differences between the north and the south of the country, with the consequence that the more fundamental division between the metropolitan area of London and the rest of the country has at times been ignored.

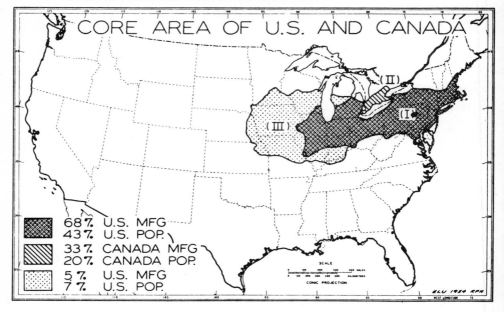

Fig. 3.1   Core areas of the USA and Canada.
Area 1 7.7% area, 52% income, 70% population
Areas I and II combine (%USA plus Canada) 3.7%, area, 41.2%
population, 65.9% industrial employment.
Source: Ullman, E., 'Regional Development and Concentration'.
Papers and Proceedings of the Regional Science Association, vol. IV,
1958.

An historical approach to the phenomenon of concentration is helpful
because it offers insight into and poses questions about the actual process
through which a concentrated pattern has developed. Lampard in his survey of
the growth of cities finds the process of economic development inevitably
accompanied by a process of concentration; that nowhere amongst the advanced
nations of the world has concentration consequently failed to appear.[5]

Lampard suggests that this process of concentration or urbanization (the
process of population concentration in urban areas) is not so much a passive
index of the process of economic development but rather an active ingredient;
the means through which an increasingly specialized economy evolves as well as
the product of that process. More particularly cities are seen as providing an
essential means through which the increasingly specialized and thus dependent
parts of an economic system may achieve integration.

The city clearly minimizes the cost attached to overcoming the friction of
space; interdependent activities can here interact readily. At the same time
economies of a wider nature may be gained in the context of the concentrated
pattern; the availability of these external economies in the form of specialized
labour, public overhead capital, transport services and so on may be regarded as
crucial in allowing new units to evolve and develop.

A part of the total concept of the external economies evolved by Marshall included the atmosphere of invention that pervades industrial towns. In other words, the entrepreneur existing and potential may here enjoy the ready circulation of ideas and information, and by cross fertilizing and synthesizing these, arrive at significant new insights or inventions with experimentation on these, further encouraged by that atmosphere. It is, perhaps, here that the really crucial and creative role of the urban and metropolitan area in economic development begins to emerge; it is here with the process of invention and innovation that one can detect the heart of the process of economic development. For these reasons much of the succeeding discussion focuses on the spatial setting of invention.

This is the key process focused on by Pred in his analysis of urban growth in the United States in the nineteenth century.[6] Pred argues that invention was inevitably concentrated in these settings because here the density of interpersonal information exchange was highest and therefore too the probability of realizing a synthesis of an inventive nature. A more systematic and formal attempt to incorporate the concepts and proposition presented above into a general theory of urbanization has been outlined by Friedmann.[7] In his information model of urbanization, Friedmann argues that the majority of traditional reasons for explaining the growth of cities can be synthesized around the concept of the city as a high access social system. Cities provide the highest probabilities of potential interaction, and since all interaction is a form of communication, it can be said that they provide the highest potential point for information exchange; cities have grown and multiplied because people seek conditions of more rather than less potential for information exchange. This potential may be seen to vary over a given settled space in terms of the two variables of mass and distance, whilst the degree to which information may be sought also varies with the type of decision making unit. This gives a basis for understanding the manner in which a given space is structured or sifted out between different types of decision makers. This model and its central concepts are undoubtedly abstract, but it offers the basis of several rich propositions, all of which deserve to be translated into hypotheses and tested, and several of which help to inform the later sections of this chapter.

More incisive and more influential propositions have at this stage derived not from attempts to explain the general phenomenon of urbanization but from work on the process of economic development. Paramount here is the work of Perroux which lies at the core of current regional planning thought and which informs a very considerable proportion of regional planning action. Perroux starts from a basic concern for the phenomenon of economic development and with the process of structural change that accompanies this phenomenon.[8] Following on from Schumpeter, Perroux envisaged this structural change in terms of the rise and fall of industry and the diffusion of the effects of these changing industries on others within the economy. In a frequently quoted statement Perroux suggested that 'Growth does not appear everywhere at the same time; it manifests itself in points or 'poles' of growth with variable intensities; it spreads by different channels and with variable terminal effects for the economy as a whole.'[9] The process is one then characterized by a sequence of structural differentiation.

Central in this process of differentiation is the propellent industry. These are simply industries with output growth rates higher than the average; but they do in their growth affect other industries and the total output of the economy. The basic mechanism through which these effects are induced are important in the overall model. The role of external economies is stressed for example, in changing the profits of a firm; it is argued that over and above any decision it may have taken to maximize profits through taking into account its own purchases and sales, that the actions of other firms may induce profits through changing the level of purchase prices and sales. It is also argued that the propellent industry may affect the total output of the economy by changing the climate of a period, upsetting the horizons of entrepreneurs and generally exercising a destabilizing effect. The propellent industry through its successful innovation may increase the inequalities between entrepreneurs intensifying their relative desire for gain.

Here then one has the general image of a dynamic innovative industry moving ahead of others but inducing change in those related to it, the whole acting as a vector of forces or a pole, and this pole and the propellent industry within it exercising a turbulent and potentially further creative effect on other entrepreneurs within the economy. The pole described is entirely economic and occurs in economic space; the latter being an abstract concept having nothing to do with the space of traditional geography. It is a space defining and embracing a specified set of interrelationships.

It is with the concept of the industrial complex and its key industry that Perroux's work begins to take on locational or spatial implications of special relevance to regional planning. The key industry is an industry which when it expands is capable of inducing the expansion of either one or several other industries. This property is seen to exist in varying degrees between all industries, but a key industry is one where the inducement effect is particularly large; larger than the average propellent industry. The key industry is envisaged as part of a complex of industries; it is engaged in interaction and communication with several industries, and this whole complex is seen to take a territorially or locationally concentrated form; it is a geographical pole. The phenomenon of territorial clustering is viewed as intensifying the activity of the complex. Consumers with varied and progressive consumption patterns, the satisfaction of collective needs such as transport and housing all stimulate the complex. It follows that in parallel with the process of structural differentiation, and as a product of the changes entailed in this, Perroux envisages an economy also developing through a process of spatial differentiation. This joint sectoral and spatial differentiation consists of innovative active thrusts leaving behind but also impelling and inducing change in more passive dependent areas of the economy.

Perroux's contribution undoubtedly owes a great deal to long established concepts and formulations. In particular the concept of external economies and industrial interdependencies together with Schumpeter's theory form the main base of his work. Perhaps the most appropriate way in which to view his contribution is in the terms expressed by Lasuen.[10] Lasuen suggests that Perroux essentially translated Schumpeter into spatial terms and thus the geographical pole as developed by Perroux is the geographical image of the newly innovated industry and its linked industries as developed by Schumpeter. Because of the incisive and creative thrusts which Perroux made his work has attracted very considerable comment. A not inconsiderable proportion of this has however failed either to critically test or to extend his work and it has become engulfed in terminological issues. This in part at least is a reflection of vagueness and ambiguities in his formulations. Many of the concepts are inadequately defined and many of the mechanisms poorly elaborated.

The first major critical issue in Perroux's work concerns the nature of the relationship between poles in economic space and poles in geographical space. Hansen and other critics have pinpointed empirical examples which expose weaknesses in the hinge between developments in economic space and developments in geographic space.[11] By way of example, reference may be made to the frequently quoted case at Lacq in France where exploitation of a natural gas deposit corresponded to Perroux's description of a propellent industry yet it failed to fulfil expectations regarding the attraction of an industrial complex.[12] Because of the availability of superior external economies elsewhere, it has been more economical to transport the gas to already industrialized areas than to create new industrial development at Lacq. This and other examples, however, merely serve to underline a point which is evident in Perroux's writings, namely that the relationship between the two types of polarization is ambiguous, a propellent industry may or may not become a key industry. It could be argued of course that this denies Perroux's formulation the status of a theory.

Perroux has also been subject to criticism because his formulation fails to offer any explanation regarding the actual location of his geographical poles, that it cannot in consequence claim to be a theory of the spatial distribution of economic activity.[13] It is true that Perroux's work fails to explain the actual geographic location of industry, but it does not attempt to do so, it is not a location theory in classic location of industry terms. There is, however, a more serious criticism underlying these points and this is the neglect of the role of external agglomeration economies in explaining the eruption into society of the propulsive industry. The existence of pre-existing geographic poles containing these economies is ignored. In other words the spatial structure of economic activity may play a crucial role in the evolution of propulsive industries, and is not necessarily a passive reflection of their location.[14] It is evident from these two initial criticisms that Perroux has not adequately articulated the economic and geographical dimensions.

The recent contribution of Lasuen pays careful attention to clarifying Perroux's concepts and to testing the core of his propositional system rigorously.[15] Lasuen addresses his empirical work to the key question regarding the necessity for development to be polarized in all spaces. At least with regard to geographic space Lasuen presents evidence to suggest that development is becoming decreasingly polarized. Basically Lasuen's work points to an increasing stability in the relative size and rank of cities, whereas following Perroux's argument, increasing rates of innovation should lead to increasing rates of city growth and decay. Lasuen suggests that increasingly, polarizations over economic space distribute themselves over the system of cities in such a way that a relatively stable growth in that system is permitted. This he argues reflects the emergence of a multi-product/multi-plant/multi-city type of organization replacing the original one product/one plant/one city type. Innovations are now adopted and diffused through a highly flexible organizational structure so that no firm is overwhelmingly committed to one innovation in one area which could be expected to rise and fall with the product.

Lasuen's work has considerable policy implications, suffice here to note that it points to the importance of the organizational structure of firms in regional planning. More generally it indicates the potential of acting in one type of topological space, for example, modifying organizational relationships between firms in order to realize goals in another topological space; for example, reducing geographic inequalities in economic prosperity. This in turn underlines the need to avoid a myopic concern for spatial action in regional planning and to grasp the potential of action on the aspatial structure of society in order to eliminate spatial and non spatial inequalities. Lasuen stresses that the basic concept here of related topological spaces is derived from Perroux, and further that his work rather than negating Perroux's shows how useful Perroux is in understanding current trends. One might add that over and above this, Perroux's writings remain a fertile source of ideas.

At this stage some consideration has been given to a central issue in Perroux's work, namely the relationship between economic and geographic poles. A second issue concerns the nature of the relationship between the poles and the remainder of the space under consideration. Space outside the pole is seen as passive and dependent, yet at the same time capable of being uplifted and transformed under inducement effects from the pole; space outside the pole thus experiences both its favourable and unfavourable effects. Translated into geographical terms it is clearly important to appreciate the factors influencing the incidence of these two effects; in the process it becomes possible to obtain a more synoptic view of the working of an economy in the spatial dimension than that obtained by simply focusing on the pole. The issue is taken up in the succeeding section.

Growth Poles in Supra Urban Space

It has already been indicated that Perroux suggested that both sectoral and geographical space are made up of two contrasting elements, the first active and propulsive, the second passive and dependent on the propulsive part. The passive is at one and the same time left behind but also potentially stimulated by the propulsive pole. The relative strength of these two opposed influences of the pole on the remainder of a given space is clearly crucial for the long run performance of that space; at the same time the manner or mechanisms through which these influences are expressed is of equal significance in characterizing the ongoing processes and actual working of the economy in its spatial dimension. For these reasons these influences and the manner of their working are given some attention here.

In an effort to bring some order to the terminology in this area of regional planning theory, Friedmann has suggested the adoption of the terms 'core' and 'periphery' to describe the two elements indicated above. Core thus replaces concepts such as metropolitan areas, centres, growth poles and growth centres, and periphery replaces concepts such as the hinterland or fringe area. The division of geographical space into these two elements basically reflects Perroux's work, although the conceptualization of such a model has also been developed by other economists.[16] In essence then, Friedmann suggests that any geographical system contains two spatial sub systems, a core which is the dynamic propulsive heart of the system, and a periphery which is simply the remainder of a system existing in a state of dependence upon and subservience to the core. The initial recognition of such a division was of course made at the national scale. Friedmann, however, is able to garner evidence to suggest that such a division may equally be valid at the regional continental and world scales.[17]

It is within this context that attention can be paid to the central problem of the mechanism through which the core stimulates and stagnates the periphery. Central here are the contributions of Myrdal[18] and Hirschman.[19] Both these authors implicitly use a core—periphery model and both, although working independently, developed very similar conceptualizations of the mechanisms relating these sub systems. Both Myrdal and Hirschman distinguish two types of transmission effects from the core to the periphery, the one favourable the other unfavourable.

The favourable effects consist of the flow of investment activities by the core in the periphery; for example, in raw materials necessary for its industry or recreational outlets for its population. It includes too the purchase of peripheral products. These favourable flows are termed spread effects by Myrdal and trickling down effects by Hirschman, and they clearly give rise to new core regions in the periphery. This is in keeping with Perroux who argued that poles being centres of accumulation and concentration of resources naturally give birth to similar centres.

The unfavourable effects consist of the flow of people out of the periphery and also the flow of capital seeking higher, more secure returns in the core, the depression of the periphery's activities where they are in competition with those of the core, and psychological effects such as the imprinting of apathy and resignation into the culture and the rejection of the values of the core regardless of their crucial significance in stimulating economic development. Myrdal termed these effects backwash and Hirschman termed them polarization.

The key issue clearly concerns the relative balance between these two effects. Where backwash dominates, the periphery may be reduced to a very weak state tenuously related to the core. Where spread dominates, then an integrated and relatively homogeneous spatial system may evolve and the periphery accordingly disappears.

As Hilhorst indicates, to the degree that the core has to rely on the output of the periphery for further growth, then trickling down can be expected to dominate.[20] This is the view which Hirschman tends to take arguing that sooner or later the core will have to reduce congestion in itself, overcome supply difficulties and increase the size of the home market. Thus Hirschman sees deliberate economic policy intervention as an aspect of trickling down in the later phases of his model. Myrdal does not include government intervention as part of his model, and holding to his theory of circular and cumulative causation, argues that the core will continue to experience a circular upward re-enforcing cycle of favourable effects, and the periphery the very reverse. As far as Myrdal is concerned, government intervention is outside the model but should, he would argue, be invoked as early as possible to counteract the circular and cumulative effects of the core.

It would appear that, excluding government intervention, Myrdal's view would suggest increasing divergence of regional per capita incomes and Hirschman's increasing convergence. However, given that Hirschman argues that government intervention to increase spread is inevitable, that Myrdal argues that such intervention ought to be taken and can be undertaken as a nation prospers, then both arguments would suggest that convergence increases with the development of national economies; Williamson has provided some evidence to suggest that this might indeed be so.[21]

Consideration of the flows of backwash and spread are considered in more detail at a later stage, before this is possible it is necessary to inquire further into the actual structure of geographic space.

The System of Cities and Economic Development

At this stage the theoretical contributions outlined above would suggest that any given national space is resolved into one or more growth poles. However, empirical observation, much of it ordered in a vast quantity of geographical literature, indicates that settlement within this space is regularly ordered in both size and function and distribution. This system of cities or central places clearly poses issues regarding the relationship between Perroux's growth poles and these central places. In particular the question is raised whether all settlement nodes are growth poles. The more general issue regarding the role and implication of a system of central places for the process of economic development is also raised.

Central place theory originated with the attempts by Christaller in 1933 to explain the size, number and distribution of towns, and the work he generated focuses basically on the relationship between settlement nodes and the area these nodes serve. Centralistic principles he argued were basic to community life with the town acting as a centre of the regional community mediating its commerce and acting as its central place. The latter was seen to vary in importance dominating regions of different size and arranged in a hierarchy of several size types in such a way that the total distance moved by residents within a given space for goods and services of varying cost and frequency of need were minimized.

Although an attempt to produce a general theory of settlement it is based exclusively on the servicing activities of settlements, and for this reason and other simplifying assumptions, the pattern of the real world differs markedly from the theory. Central place theory has nevertheless claimed some validity as a theory of service activity location and has continued to be developed and extended. It contains a number of vitally important concepts such as the interdependence between town and region and the hierarchical arrangement of functions and centres which appear to be highly relevant to understanding the performance of society in supra urban space. The work of Friedmann in particular has been very suggestive regarding the relationship between central place systems and national economic development.[22] Friedmann has developed a simple but appealing model which suggests the stages of spatial organization a national economy moves through in its progress from a primitive pre-industrial position to industrial maturity. The model is open to a very considerable number of criticisms but is such a fertile source of ideas about the relationships between economic development and spatial structure at the supra urban scale that it is worthy of considered attention (Figure 3.2).

In stage 1 of the model a spatial pattern of separate cities is depicted each

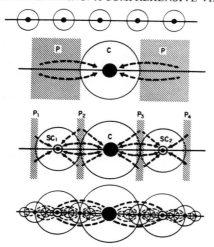

Fig. 3.2   Spatial structure and national economic development.
(a) Independent local centres—no hierarchy.
(b) A single strong centre.
(c) A single national centre, strong peripheral sub centres.
(d) A functionally interdependent system of cities.
Source: Friedmann, J., *Regional Development Policy* (MIT Press, 1966).

existing in an enclave quite isolated from the others. Stage 2 depicts the pattern at a time of incipient industrialization. The pattern is dominated by a single strong centre or core surrounded by a periphery. It is thus basically a primate city situation that is a situation where the largest city is several times the population of the one second in rank. Friedmann resorts to the influence of external forces especially colonial ones in explaining the evolution between stages 1 and 2.

Stage 3 witnesses the gradual transformation of the core—periphery situation, a single national centre with strong peripheral sub centres emerges. Intermetropolitan peripheries now replace the previous national periphery; the sub centres within the periphery bring resources into the national economy with the result that the growth potential of the national economy is enhanced. In the final stage, stage 4, a functionally interdependent system of cities is depicted, the intermetropolitan periphery is completely absorbed and full integration of the economy achieved, thus minimizing interregional imbalances and maximizing the nation's growth potential. In this stage high communication potentials become diffused over the national space; the different communication demands of families and firms which had structured space into a hierarchy of places offering different information exchange probabilities can now more readily be met amongst all possible locations. At the same time inventiveness as a function of the probabilities of information exchange becomes diffused over the national surface and astronomical inventive capacity is realized.[23]

Friedmann thus advances the proposition that where economic growth is sustained over long periods its incidence works towards a progressive integration of the space economy.[24] The model is particularly suggestive bringing out the role of the hinterland phenomenon of cities and the importance of a developed system of cities in achieving an integrated space economy. The city, its immediate relationship with its hinterland and its relationships with other cities are not simply reflections of a process of economic growth, but also appear to be the means through which that growth is realized. There are some very important points of substance within the model and the argument presented here. These will be considered first before giving criticism to the model as a whole.

In the discussion of Perroux's work the inventive and thus the de-stabilizing role of cities acting as growth poles was stressed. In the wider geographical view presented in central place theory and Friedmann's model it is interesting to note that the role of the city as an integrative and thus stabilizing influence is stressed. Two aspects may be distinguished in discussing this integrative role of the city. In the first place an upward process of resource mobilization may be recognized and in the second a 'downward' process of innovation diffusion.

In Friedmann's model the placement of a city in the periphery in stage 2 and the reduction of the intermetropolitan periphery in stage 3 pinpoint vividly the upward process of resource mobilization. The resources of the nation are articulated into the national economy through the city; place bound resources may be released; the horizons of people changed; the plans of entrepreneurs de-stabilized; new opportunities and choices are presented; channels of social mobility opened up. In this way the city mobilizes and harnesses the resources of a national space.

This at least would appear to be the unstated assumptions behind Friedmann's argument. But they are clearly assumptions which require rigorous examination. The possible dangers of a policy based upon these arguments are illustrated in Shachar's evaluation of Israel's development policy.[25] Here the creation by the core of a coherent system of central places has by the process of its implementation created a dependent and thus fragile system of settlements. The placement of cities in the periphery may be a superimposition which fails to articulate its resources, precisely because it is a superimposition.

A linked mechanism in the mobilization of resources is the ability of the city immediately to influence its surrounding hinterland; it can bring its channels of articulation to a significant area around and about it but with decreasing effectiveness with distance; a point emphasized in the proposition by Friedmann that the spatial incidence of economic growth is a function of distance from a central city.[26] Berry and Neils thus show clearly how a range of economic variables form well marked gradients along transverses between metropolitan areas in the USA.[27] Moseley in a study of the impact of Rennes in France concludes that towns even lower than the 25,000 population limit defined by Berry and Neils may have a significant spatial impact on the economic standing of their commuting hinterlands.[28]

Quite clearly here the existence of a complete and coherent system of central places is seen as a prerequisite for the proper articulation of resources of a national economy. This self same system may be equally crucial to the rapid and effective diffusion of innovations within a nation space. Following Hagerstrand,[29] Friedmann proposes that economic impulses are transmitted in order from higher to lower cities in the urban hierarchy, that the primary city generates inventions and lesser cities diffuse these in the form of innovations. This is a proposition of potentially very considerable significance, holding out a powerful insight into the way in which an economy works and evolves in the spatial dimension. It is thus worth noting a parallel proposition from Thompson.[30] Thompson has advanced a filtering down theory of industrial location. Very briefly, he argues that cores that invent and first develop a new industry enjoy very rapid growth rates characteristic of the early stages of an industry's life cycle together with the high incomes which go along with the specialized skills needed to develop the new product. As production becomes rationalized and routine, however, the high skill and income requirements become costly and unnecessary; the industry thus spins off to lower order cores which gain an industry not only growing less rapidly but which is also less demanding in its skill requirements and therefore it does little to upgrade the incomes or education of the recipient labour force.

Although both Hagerstrand[31] and Berry and Neils[32] have produced evidence in support of Friedmann's proposition, there are very considerable data problems in initiating such a test. It might well be questioned, however, whether the largest city is necessarily the greatest generator of inventions and whether size is the main determinant influencing adaption of these inventions. These would appear to be somewhat mechanistic assumptions.

The concept of a cascade of impulses down through the hierarchy of settlements does perhaps indicate in finer detail the two crucial spatial flows discussed earlier, namely backwash and spread. Both may operate in the form outlined here. It must be acknowledged, however, that a proportion and perhaps even a vast proportion of the impulses generated by the primary city will exercise an indeterminate effect on the welfare of the periphery. They will be changes generated and diffused out without conscious awareness of their effect on the periphery and at the same time they may elicit different responses according to the circumstances into which they are diffused.

Here then a regular and coherent system of cities would, according to the propositions being advanced, aid the speedy development of an economy and at the same time enhance its integration along the line of the breakthrough, helping to ensure that no parts of the national space are left behind and out of touch with the innovation. Misra, for example, highlights the issue by suggesting that in India the process of 'trickling down' is halted because a particular level in the hierarchy of growth foci is missing.[33]

Finally, consideration is devoted to an overall criticism of the model advanced by Friedmann. Friedmann's model is of undoubted value in depicting and highlighting a number of central issues and propositions in regional planning, and some of the more important of these have been described above. However, there are a number of problems associated with the model. Limited testing has failed to substantiate the main motivating idea behind it, namely that an integrated system of cities is intimately related as both cause and effect to the process of economic development; Berry's work has demonstrated a lack of such a relationship.[34]

Over and above this far from extensive testing, it might be noted that the model has, as has been indicated, a certain mechanistic bias and in addition to this has a major fault of being deterministic. It is presented as the almost inevitable unilinear sequence through which nations must evolve. Both the mechanistic and deterministic features of the model stem perhaps from an over regard for economic variables and a lack of concern for goals other than economic growth and development.

In highlighting the role of spatial structure the model underplays the significance of aspatial action. Shachar's evaluation commented upon earlier illustrates the possible need to articulate a nation's potential, not through inducing spatial change from the core, but through organizational and institutional change in the structure of society which will enable the periphery to articulate itself. To the extent that the model directly implies spatial action it may be far from appropriate.

Three major issues of substance emerge from the discussion: the concept of growth poles, of backwash and spread, of a hierarchy of central places. Each can, to a degree, be reconciled with the others. The major conflict and inconsistency would appear to lie with the question whether all nodes in the hierarchy of central places are growth poles. Issues are raised regarding appropriate criteria through which poles may be distinguished from other nodes in the hierarchy. Hermansen, for example, has suggested that a distinction can be made between geographic poles which are merely a clustering of economic activity and geographic poles which are expressions of economic polarizations.[35] There is perhaps a more fundamental issue here and this is the possible lack of empirical correspondence between polarization as conceived in the economic dimension by Perroux and as conceived in the realm of service activity by Christaller. The possible lack of correspondence between the polarizations in these two types of spaces would seem to be fundamental and to raise important issues regarding the organization of society in supra urban space.

Social and Political Activity and Supra Urban Space

The relatively brief treatment given to these final considerations is not because they are considered to be comparatively unimportant, but reflects the relative lack of attention that has been paid to them. In the light of this neglect no more than an outline - of emerging trends is noted, together with an indication of potentially desirable directions of development.

Although sociology has from its origins had a greater concern for the spatial dimension than has economics, the development of this concern and its formal incorporation into the central body of sociology has not proceeded very far; the development of urban sociology which might have aided this, has, in fact, been fraught with difficulties.[36] A concern for social activity in supra urban space might have alternatively developed out of the initial thrust made by economics in its concern for economic performance in supra urban space. However, this thrust has been so recent and the recognition of the significance of social considerations in economic development equally so,[37] that it is only within the last few years that an explicit concern for the social dimension in regional economic development has gained ground. Ziolkowski, for example, records the social disruption that accompanies economic development where insufficient concern is paid to social issues, in addition to their potentially constraining effects on the total process of economic development.[38] Similarly reports of Regional Economic Councils and Boards in Great Britain have stressed the importance of social and cultural amenities and facilities in their identification of factors limiting regional economic performance. Klaasen's recent work is an attempt to examine the need and provision for social amenities in a more formal and systematic way but still from a perspective of maximizing an area's attraction to industry rather than from strictly social perspectives.[39]

It is possible, however, that Pahl's fresh and creative work might begin to provide the basis for the development of a body of knowledge which is directly and explicitly concerned with the relationship between social activity and social performance on the one hand and spatial structure on the other.[40] Pahl contends that an individual's location in the spatial structure fundamentally influences his life chances; and this is so because it places constraints on his access to scarce social resources in the form of social amenities and facilities. In so far as social opportunities of this nature are not distributed randomly but rather in some regular pattern, then the way is open for some individuals to experience deprivation in terms of their access to these facilities and for others to enjoy a much more easily expressed choice of opportunities. Thus within the urban area two individuals within the same socio economic class who occupy different locations can be expected to experience differential access to city centre and job opportunities and thus to life chances. At the supra urban scale and within the context of central place hierarchy the same two individuals, one at the bottom of the hierarchy the other in the city of the first rank, may experience very considerable differences of social opportunity. Thus the contention is that an individual's life chances and opportunities for self realization vary not only with location in the social structure, but also with location in the spatial structure. If this is accepted then it follows that spatial policy may contribute to the achievement of social equity, and more fundamentally that the achievement of social equity ultimately requires policy and action addressed to the spatial structure.

The critical issue in Pahl's thesis is clearly the degree to which the social facilities and amenities which he identifies are crucial to the achievement of social fulfilment. This will in turn reflect the structure of society. To the extent that certain norms and values are held universally and that these facilities are the passports to their achievement then the thesis would seem very significant; to the extent that society is strongly pluralistic with a variety of quite different life styles, then these facilities may be less crucial to self fulfilment and the thesis loses its power. However, despite local and regional differences in life style, most individuals hold to certain universal societal values and some of these may only be achieved through the channels identified by Pahl; it would accordingly seem to be a potentially significant thesis.

If Pahl is right, then one might expect in the context of a hierarchy of settlements that the socially disadvantaged occupy the peripheral smaller settlements in a concentric circle form of model. Inquiries which might begin to test this model or even attempts to elaborate alternative models of the social ecology of regions have, however, hardly begun. Apart from drawing attention to the need for a greater understanding of the way in which social groups are distributed in supra urban space, Pahl opens up certain other potentially important and fruitful lines of advance. One line of inquiry which immediately follows on concerns what Ziolkowski has termed 'spatial democratization'; that is, how to achieve equality of access to critical social services and facilities.[42] This could be taken to imply a concern for uniform city size and this in turn to a concern for optimum city size.

This is a topic which has attracted a considerable degree of interest in the past and useful summaries of this body of thought have been made by Duncan,[43] Shindman[44] and Allen.[45] There are, too, indications of a recent revival of interest in this issue in the USA as part of the growing concern to evolve a national urbanization policy.[46] In much of the work on optimum city size, however, initial enthusiasm wanes into despair and this would seem to be inevitable in so far as it is motivated by a concern to establish the optimum. A good deal of the work too has been economic in orientation, and what would seem to be required is work which is more explicitly social and which is concerned to develop understanding of the social consequences of different settlement sizes. Unlimited by a concern to establish the social optium, this more open approach could ultimately provide the basis for a more meaningful discussion of it; at the least it could provide a rudimentary form of input into regional planning decisions which may otherwise be dominated by more limited physical and economic considerations.

The concept of a universal optimum and thus uniform city size jars with the reality of a hierarchy of settlements of quite different sizes and it jars too with the appeal of such a central place arrangement in so far as this can deliver high order services and facilities. For these reasons the issue of an optimum system of settlement sizes has occasionally been raised. Although this raises awesome problems there are again certain elementary but useful lines along which inquiry might proceed. In particular, it would seem very desirable to develop understanding of the way in which people move within supra urban space, the difficulties of access that are experienced and especially the degree to which these are real or inspired by particular perceptions of regional space.

Armed with this type of understanding it might be possible to begin to appreciate the implications of a particular increment of population or social equipment in one settlement, not solely in terms of its social consequences for that settlement, but for the population of the other settlements of the region. Linked with this and following on from Pahl, it would be desirable to develop understanding of the way in which managers and controllers of regional institutions perceive regional space and from this of the way in which the needs of particular client groups are inadequately served due to a mismatch in the perceptions of supplier and client. Finally there is the intriguing but more complex issue concerning the degree to which improved personal mobility may change perceptions, break down the rigid hierarchical forms of social disposition implied by central place theory, and open up new opportunities in terms of providing facilities for different combinations of settlements of different sizes.

Although the concern to study the effect of spatial structure on the social system at the supra urban scale is a very recent one, it has at least gained some recognition as a field of study pertinent to regional planning. No such recognition has been gained for the study of the effect of spatial structure on the performance of the political system. This is a neglected field of study. In the succeeding discussion an attempt is made to identify some of the major issues which this field of study should seek to confront.

Pahl's work can provide a fruitful lead in to the discussion. As has been noted, Pahl contends that access to social resources varies with location in the spatial structure. The question arises whether or not access to political resources varies with location in the spatial structure.

It has already been noted that the tendency for the spatial structure to crystallize into settlements of different sizes is a well established empirical fact. *A priori* it would seem very difficult if not impossible to ensure equal representation in government for the populations of such very different settlements; to design a formal system of representation which ensured that a citizen in village town or city had exactly similar representation would require extraordinarily complex arrangements, and even if achievable, it would be destroyed as population movement affected the relative size of settlements. It must be recognized that political influence embraces a variety of other informal channels of power outside those formally created by the state, such as membership of special interest groups; and the degree to which ability to exercise this type of influence varies with location, and the degree to which these informal channels develop in compensation for the lack of formal representation offered by particular locations are interesting questions but they are not pursued further here.

Given then that there are grounds for suggesting that representation in the formal organs of government may vary with spatial location, then attention to methods of ensuring greater equality of access to these would seem to be warranted. Ultimately one can recognize again here the question of an optimum and uniform city size in terms of ensuring equal opportunities for participation in the local system of government and equality of influence in representation at higher levels of government. Unfortunately, although considerable attention has been given to reforming the system of local government in Great Britain, none of this appears to have considered these vital political issues. It is notable that more aggressive political ideologies such as communism have gone further in identifying the scale and character of settlement forms suited to their revolutionary objectives.[47] Although no doubt a great deal has been written on the scale of settlement suited to western democratic ideologies, less seems to have been done to codify this and to move aggressively towards its implementation.

Although the degree to which concentration in the form of a capital is a prerequisite to the development of a nation state is problematical, it is worth noting in passing that political geographers have debated the concept of the core area and the influence of this on the evolution of nations.[48] The core area is defined as the area in which or about which a state originates. It is characteristically described in terms of a super abundance of resources, and the example of the Paris basin is commonly cited, and Pounds and Bell in an attempt to test this thesis established that some 15 out of 25 European states have grown via accretion from a core area.[49] The role of concentration in the evolution of the modern state is thus as yet unclear. However, it is possible to surmise more readily about the impact of the capital on the ongoing political performances of states.

Given the unique distinction implied by designating one settlement to be the capital, then as intimated above, serious doubts arise regarding the degree to which there can be equality of political resources between different points in the spatial structure. This is so, not because the population of the capital enjoy greater formal representation, but because they enjoy a greater visible presence before the nation's government. Friedmann has advocated a strategy of deliberate urbanization for poor countries in order to aggravate this incipient political pressure to realize economic and political change.[50]

The corollary of the national government's awareness of the problems of the capital is the very real possibility of ignorance of more distant issues. This potential decay of awareness with distance has been caught by Kohr in his formulation of the law of peripheral neglect, which states that 'the concern of the capital for its surrounding political space decreases with the square of the distance from it.'[51] Ultimately Kohr's formulation dramatizes what would appear to be a basic inconsistency in the way the modern nation is spatially organized. This inconsistency arises because decisions are made at a single point, the capital, but applied to a set of contiguous points, the area or territory of the state. This may be resolved as Kohr suggests by neglect; it may also be resolved in principle by limiting the number of contiguous points, the small nation argument; by making the capital mobile between all the points—the pre modern state solution; or by devolving some of the capital's power—the contemporary regional government solution.

Unless the problem is resolved in terms other than neglect, then it is possible that the spatial inconsistency between capital and territory may threaten the integration and survival of the political unit. A much clearer understanding of the incidence and causes of the neglect expressed in Kohr's law is thus clearly called for. To the degree that it is confirmed and inherent in the structure of the modern nation state, then there may be a case for entertaining the idea that political representation in the organs of central government should increase with distance from the capital; some form of equality of political resources between all the points within the nation might thereby be achieved.

The underlying idea of giving certain portions of the national space 'unequal' representation has been touched upon by Ullman in the context of economic development. Ullman has noted that in the USA equal state representation in senate gave in effect unequal power to the less developed western and southern states, and this he suggests stimulated their rapid economic development and thus the rapid development of the national space as a whole.[52] It would appear that there is a strong case for examining the role of manipulating political space, conceived in terms of the representation accorded to different parts of the nation, in order to realize both economic as well as political goals.

Hirschman has been alone in regional planning theory in giving this concept of the manipulation of political space any degree of considered attention.[53] In particular Hirschman has noted that the creation of new autonomous political units may radically affect the flows of backwash and trickle down which characterize the working of economic space. Where a peripheral region is given independent sovereign status, the flow of backwash may be cut down because of the ability to deploy economic instruments reserved for national governments and because of the frictional effect of political boundaries on economic movement.[54] Simultaneously, however, the peripheral region in gaining independent status, may very likely lose the favourable trickle down effects from its formerly associated core. The solution to the problem is, Hirschman suggests, to create sub national political units which can be treated in some ways as regions and are thus permeable to trickle down effects and in other ways as nations and thus impermeable to backwash effects.

Unfortunately this creative contribution of Hirschman's appears to have remained undeveloped and has not been brought to fruition. Hirschman appears to be looking for some single new form of sub national political unit which will express the desired balance of permeability and impermeability and this may be the central difficulty in giving practical expression to the idea. It is possible that the solution is to be found not in the creation of any one unit, since no one unit may be expected to have all of the desired qualities, but in the development and toleration of a complex multitude of institutions, some of which give the region a degree of autonomy and others which tie it into the nation. Rather than fostering the creation of institutions with similar boundaries in the interests of co-ordination and rational action, a movement currently apparent in institutional reform in Great Britain and elsewhere, what may be necessary as a step towards Hirschman's solution is the acceptance of ambiguity—a lack of areal correspondence in the design of supra urban institutions.

Conclusion

Although clearly fragmented and undeveloped, it is suggested that the above discussion warrants the conclusion that it is possible to speak of an emergent regional planning theory; of a relatively unified set of concepts and propositions regarding the way in which society works in supra urban space.

The most insistent theme that emerges from this discussion is that of polarization; that is, the postulated tendency for economic, social and political systems to concentrate or polarize spatially in some significant sense. In keeping with this both Friedmann[55] and Hermansen,[56] in their attempts to produce a synthesis of regional planning theory, have emphasized the central idea of society evolving through a process of successive differentiations. The challenge now is rigorously to test both this central idea and the associated supporting ideas that have been advanced. Much greater understanding is needed of the process of polarization, its causes and implications and the degree to which it is being affected by long run secular changes within society. This applies to each of the dimensions that have been distinguished, the economic, the social and the political, but it is perhaps particularly the latter two where more work is imperative. More understanding is needed too of the interrelationship between the polarizations in these different dimensions, of the degree to which and why they correspond or fail to correspond in empirical reality. This is important because it may be that it is the failure of these different systems to express themselves in some reasonably coincident way that provides much of the pressure for regional planning action.

Over and above greater penetration into and articulation of the major facets that have been discussed, it is also necessary to recognize that the whole field of regional planning theory may need to be expanded outside the realm delineated here. The ultimate challenge for regional planning is not to test and fill out some given body of regional planning thought, but to remain responsive to society's needs and to contribute to the development and extension of knowledge in however a rudimentary a form which will allow courses of action to be recommended for the fulfilment of those needs.

References

1   Hightower, H., 'Planning Theory in Contemporary Planning Education', *AIP*, September, 1969.

2   See, for example, Lichfield, N., 'The Scope of the Regional Plan', *Regional Studies*, May, 1967. Robertson, D.J., 'The Relationship between Economic and Physical Planning', Town and Country Planning Summer School 1965.

3   Thorburn, A., 'The Process of Sub Regional Planning', in *Procedures of the Nottingham Symposium on Sub Regional Planning*, (Regional Studies Association, 1969).

4   Ullman, E.L., Regional Development and the Geography of Concentration. Papers and Proceedings of the Regional Science Association, Volume IV, 1958.

5   Lampard, E., 'The History of Cities in the Economically Advanced Areas', *Economic Development and Cultural Change*, Vol. 3, No. 2, 1955.

6   Pred, A.,*The Spatial Dynamics of US Urban Industrial Growth 1800–1914*, (MIT Press, 1966).

7   Friedmann, J., 'An Information Model of Urbanisation', *Urban Affairs Quarterly*, Vol. IV, No. 2, 1968.

8   Perroux, F., 'Note sur la Notion de la Pole de Croissance', *Economic Applique*, Vol. 8, 1955; translated from the French in Livingstone, I. (ed), *Economic Policy for Development* (Penguin, 1971).

9   Perroux, F., op. cit.

10 Lasuen, J.R., 'On Growth Poles', *Urban Studies*, Vol. 6, No. 2, 1969.

11 Hansen, N.M., 'Development Pole Theory in a Regional Context', *Kyklos*, Volume XX, 1967. The article has also been reprinted in Richardson, H.W., *Regional Economics, A Reader* (Macmillan, 1970).

12 Hansen, N.M., op. cit. page 721. See too, Penouil, M., 'An Appraisal of Regional Development Policy in the Aquitaine Region', in Robinson, E.A.G. (ed), *Backward Areas in Advanced Countries* (Macmillan, 1969).

13 McCrone, G., *Regional Policy in Britain* (Allen & Unwin, 1969) page 87.

14 Hansen, N.M., op. cit. page 718.

15 Lasuen, op. cit.

16 Friedmann, J., *Regional Development Policy* (MIT Press, 1966). Friedmann refers in particular to the work of Prebisch who uses a centre periphery model to explain the plight of the underdeveloped *vis-a-vis* the developed world.

17 Friedmann, J., (1966) op. cit., page 10.

18 Myrdal, G., *Economic Theory and Underdeveloped Regions* (Methuen, 1957).

19 Hirschman, A., *The Strategy of Economic Development* (Yale University Press, 1958).

20 Hilhorst, J., 'Regional Development Theory', in *Multi-disciplinary Aspects of Regional Development* (OECD, 1968).

21 Williamson, J.G., 'Regional Equality and the Process of National Development, a Description of the Patterns', *Economic Development and Cultural Change*, Vol. 13, 1965, reprinted in Needleman, L. (ed), *Regional Analysis* (Penguin, 1968).

22 Friedmann, J., *Regional Development Policy* (MIT Press, 1966).

23 Friedmann, J., 'A General Theory of Polarized Development', mimeo, The Ford Foundation Urban and Regional Advisory Programme in Chile, Santiago, 1967.

24 Friedmann, J., 1966, op. cit. p. 35.

25 Shachar, A.S., 'Israel's Development Towns', *AIP*, November, 1971.

26 Friedmann, J., 1966, op. cit. p. 31.

27 Berry, B.J.L. and Neils, E., 'Location Size and Shape of Cities as Influenced by Environmental Factors: the Urban Environment Writ Large', in Perloff,

H.S. (ed) *The Quality of the Urban Environment* (Johns Hopkins Press, 1969).

28 Moseley, M.J., 'The Impact of Growth Centres in Rural Regions, An Analysis of Spatial Patterns in Brittany, *Regional Studies*, March, 1973.

29 Hagerstrand, T., 'Aspects of the Spatial Structure of Social Communication and the Diffusion of Innovation', Regional Science Association Papers, Vol. XVI, 1965.

30 Thompson, W.R., 'Internal and External Factors in the Development of Urban Economies', in Perloff, H. and Wingo, L., *Issues in Urban Economics* (Johns Hopkins Press, 1968).

31 Hagerstrand, op. cit.

32 Berry, B.J.L. and Neils, E., op. cit. 1969.

33 Misra, R.P., 'Growth Pole Hypotheses Re-examined', in Kuklinski, A., (ed), *A Review of the Concepts and Theories of Growth Poles and Growth Centres* (United Nations Research Institute for Social Development, 1970).

34 Berry, B.J.L., 'Some Relations of Urbanisation and Basic Patterns of Economic Development', in Pitts, F. (ed) *Urban Systems and Economic Development* (University of Oregon, 1962).

35 Hermansen, T., 'Development Poles and Development Centres', in Kuklinski, A., op. cit.

36 See, for example, the discussion in Pahl, R.E., 'Trends in Social Geography', in Pahl, R.E., *Whose City?* (Longman, 1970).

37 See, for example, Drewnowski, J., *Social and Economic Factors in Development*, (United Nations Research Institute for Social Development, 1966).

38 Ziolkowski, J., 'Sociological Problems of Regional Development,' *Proceedings of the First Scandinavian – Polish Regional Science Seminar*, (P.W.N. Warsaw, 1967).

39 Klaasen, L., *Social Amenities in Area Economic Growth* (OECD, 1968).

40 Pahl, R.E., *Whose City?* (Longman, 1970) and Pahl, R.E. *Patterns of Urban Life* (Longman, 1970).

41 One of the few attempts to generate and test such models is Ray, D.M., 'The Spatial Structure of Economic and Cultural Differences: A Factorial Ecology of Canada,' Regional Science Association Papers, Vol. 23, 1969.

42 Ziolkowski, J., 1967, op. cit.

43 Duncan, O.P., 'Optimum Size of Cities', in Hatt, P.K. and Reiss, A.J., *Cities and Society* (Free Press, 1957).

44 Shindman, B., 'An Optimum Size for Cities,' in Mayer, H.M. and Kohn, C.E., *Readings in Urban Geography* (University of Chicago Press, 1959).

45 Allen, K., 'Growth Centres and Growth Centre Policy, in Allen, K. and Hermansen, T., *Regional Policy in EFTA*, University of Glasgow Occasional Paper No. 10 (Oliver and Boyd, 1968).

46 See, for example, the special issue of *Urban Studies*, February, 1972.

47 See, for example, the discussions in Kaspersen, R.E. and Minghi, J.V., *The Structure of Political Geography* (University of London Press, 1970).

48 See, for further elaboration, Kaspersen, R.E. and Minghi, J.V., op. cit.

49 Pounds, N. and Bell, S., 'Core Areas and the Development of the European State System', in Kaspersen and Minghi op. cit.

50 Friedmann, J., 'The Strategy of Deliberate Urbanisation', *AIP*, November, 1968.

51 Kohr, L., *Is Wales Viable?* (Christopher Davies, 1971).

52 Ullman, E., 1958, op. cit.

53 Hirschman, A., 1958, op. cit.

54 Thus Belassa and others have pointed to the increased polarization effect that can be expected with the development of units such as the Common Market, see Belassa, B., 'Regional Problems in a Common Market', Chapter 5 of *The Theory of Economic Integration* (Allen and Unwin, 1962).

55 Friedmann, J., 1967, op. cit.

56 Hermansen, 'Development Poles and Development Centres', in Kuklinski, A., 1970, op. cit.

4 National Regional Policy and Regional Planning

Regional policy has evolved in Great Britain since the 1930s as an *ad hoc* response by national government to distributional issues of a mainly economic character. Since then the meaning of regional policy has been specifically related to those measures adopted by government at national level regarding the distribution of, mainly, economic resources for part or all of the national space. Thus regional policy is an element of national planning and a means through which the spatial dimension has been introduced into national government decision making. But to a large extent regional policy has been an 'extra'; the spatial element attached to national policy making which is traditionally non spatial. The main characteristics of regional policy have been, therefore, conceived in interregional, national economic and functionally distinct terms.

However, the purpose of this chapter is not to examine the nature and role of central government's regional policy *per se*,[1] but rather to consider both regional policy and regional planning as forms of planning action, to seek to overcome the confusion[2] that has arisen over these two terms, and to enhance understanding of the relationships between them. In particular, this chapter attempts an assessment of the complementarity or substitutability of these two forms of planning action, and sets out to identify their relative strengths and weaknesses.

The need for a fundamental appraisal of regional policy and regional planning as forms of planning action has become even more urgent in the context of recent developments in this sphere, most notably the operation of the new local government authorities and the recommendations of the Kilbrandon Commission on the Constitution together with the establishment of the EEC Regional Development Fund and the movement towards a common regional policy among member countries. The former will have important implications for the operation of regional planning as a form of planning action in the institutional framework, and the latter might be expected to lead to central governments paying greater attention to regional policies.

Linkages between Regional Policy and Regional Planning

An understanding of regional policy is necessary to regional planning for a number of reasons. The regional planner has to know and understand the basic nature (i.e. its structural character) of regional policy because, first, this form of action may logically induce regional planning; secondly, regional policy constrains regional planning; and thirdly, regional policy and regional planning are partial substitutes and partial alternatives.

First, while a regional policy may help national governments to achieve national objectives (e.g. fuller employment), or a particular town to cope with an urgent problem (e.g. the reduction of unemployment in a Special Development Area), it may induce regional planning in a functional sense. This is so because if resources are to be allocated and articulated (e.g. achieve maximum economic growth) then it is necessary to discriminate within regions as well as between them. For example, knowledge may be required of where resources are needed (problem areas) and of how resources can be developed (e.g. growth points), and this can only be done with regional planning. Regional policy also induces regional planning in a political and organizational sense with a view to gaining those resources allocated by regional policy. Regional planning undertaken by the Standing Conferences of local authorities in the regions of Britain, together with action taken by the regional developmental agencies (e.g. North East Development Council) has been closely linked to the operation of regional policies. In a situation where central government allocates resources between regions it may be expected that regional planning agencies will make claims upon those resources.

Secondly, the operation of a regional policy may constrain and influence the operation of regional planning. A good example to illustrate this situation may be drawn from the growth point philosophy of regional policy. In relation to South Wales, regional policy is focused on centralizing investments in a small number of growth points (Bridgend, Port Talbot and Swansea) located in the coastal belt. If a regional planning authority in South Wales had a policy of pursuing a more even distribution of development, then this objective would be constrained and conflict with the operation of regional policy. In fact, the major planning authority in South Wales, Glamorgan CC has also adopted, implicitly at least, a growth point policy.[3] It is difficult to assess to what extent this policy has been influenced by a similar approach being adopted by central government in its national regional policy; in the case of Glamorgan CC, its growth point strategy had been based on the philosophy of the mid 1960s when population growth forecasts were at a level three times those of current estimates. In practice, regional policy has attempted to do both things at once, i.e. follow a growth point policy on the one hand, while pursuing a Development Area policy on the other. This is a complex issue, and one which is taken up later.

A fundamental reason why regional policy constrains regional planning is because central government must demarcate a territory over which specific measures of the policy apply, and this demarcation may be divisive and disruptive of any horizontal regional action. It would therefore appear to follow that it is necessary to know not just about specific regional policy measures themselves, but also about the nature of regional policy in terms of its fundamental characteristics.

Thirdly, it is important to clarify the role of regional policy in so far as it might be seen as a substitute for regional planning and vice versa. This latter point requires further explanation. In the process of distributing resources within a given part of national space, either regional policy or regional planning may be considered as being appropriate forms of planning action. Considered from this point of view the essential difference between regional policy and regional planning focuses upon a number of key points, identifed here but developed further later in this chapter. First, as already noted, in distributing resources. between areas in a region, central government, through its regional policy, must designate areas with specific boundaries (for example, Special Development Areas, Development Areas and Grey Areas all within a single region) thereby imposing in a mechanical way, distinct subdivisions within a region. Regional planning on the other hand is able to distribute resources within a region without resort to this procedure. Secondly, regional policy, being a national regional policy, standardized in its operation, is often insensitive to local needs because of the need to implement a national system. Regional planning, however, is able to be sensitive to local needs. Thirdly, a national regional policy in designating subdivisions, standard in operation, and having taken considerable time to operate, is not capable of adopting rapid changes which may be required. Regional planning, being free of these constraints, may be able to react more swiftly to any changed situation. Regional policy may be an effective means by which resources are distributed between regions but not within a region; regional planning therefore has a particularly important role to play in distributing resources within a region and may therefore be preferred to national regional policy.

Rationale and Aims of Regional Policy

The current objectives of regional policy in Great Britain, *vis-a-vis* the operation of sub national planning, have never been stated comprehensively by national governments, although considerable attention has focused on the areas, measures and administrative machinery which should be used. While the aims of regional policy have certainly been largely economic ones, there have been recent developments in the articulation of social objectives.

The Labour government of 1964-70 published a number of volumes relating to national and regional planning, with references to regional policy,[4] but a list of the objectives was never fully stated, except in general economic terms, emphasizing the need for economic growth and a reduction in regional differentials in rates of unemployment. The Conservative government also failed to publish a list of the aims of regional policy in any comprehensive way. Once again, the references which are available[5] have been related to either White Papers or debates in the House of Commons.

The goals of regional policy have changed substantially since the operation of the policy began in the 1930s. The objectives of regional policy have moved from those essentially concerned with social welfare towards those concerned with the problems of the Development Areas, of growth, and of equality in the distribution of economic resources.

Official statements on regional policy have tended to confuse economic objectives with political and social aims; the objective of utilizing unused resources to achieve faster growth may not necessarily be compatible with equity objectives such as creating similar job opportunities in different areas. Regional problems raise fundamental points of principle and ideology in attitudes to public expenditure, control of industry and to the whole complex field of planning. It might be expected that governments will vary in the degree and extent of commitment in operating a national regional policy, placing differing degrees of emphasis on both the objectives and measures used. While there is little disagreement that the existence of areas with low incomes, persistently high unemployment, high outward migration, and slow growth of output within a national space is a matter of national concern, there is less agreement on the extent to which central government should become involved in operating a regional policy to solve 'the regional problem'.[6]

A list of objectives which has been largely adopted by British central government in recent years has included:

1 To utilize unused resources, mainly manpower, and consequently to increase potential economic growth, both in the depressed regions themselves and also for the country as a whole.
2 To reduce inflationary pressures and achieve stable economic growth.
3 To overcome the deficiencies and social consequences of the free market mechanism for decision making on the location of industry.
4 To increase the standard of living and secure a substantial narrowing of the regional differentials in rates of unemployment between less prosperous regions and the rest of Britain.

In addition those objectives might be added which have, as yet, not been precisely formulated; these have particular relevance to social aims, whereas the more established objectives listed above, are mainly economic in nature (although, of course, there are many key social issues involved with inflation and unemployment).

    5 To provide similar social and economic opportunities to those living in the less prosperous regions as those living in the more prosperous regions.

    6 To provide an attractive environment in which the advantages of economic growth can be equitably enjoyed by all regions.

    7 To avoid high social costs of congestion and economic agglomeration.

The major question at stake here is the suitability of regional policy as a form of action, given its characteristic and basic nature, to achieve these objectives. A number of arguments can be put forward which suggest that some of the most used justifications for regional policy may contain serious weaknesses.

The argument that a more even distribution of economic activity will enable the government to manage the economy with lower unemployment without inflation is not convincing. Britain has for a number of years experienced regional unemployment and record national inflation rates. A labour shortage in London may not justify the transfer of activities to a region of high unemployment; workers possessing particular skills may be as scarce in the North East as in the South East. The Confederation of British Industry has also emphasized[7] that throughout the world the highest economic growth rates have been consistently attained in congested areas such as Greater Tokyo and the seaboards of the United States. This argument does, however, neglect the social consequences of congestion and long term versus short terms costs and benefits.

In many cases regional policy is regarded as a means of redistributing income from rich to poor areas, being justified on social equity grounds. With the exception of Northern Ireland, regional variations in income in Britain are relatively small, certainly when compared with other countries such as France, Italy, West Germany and USA.[8] This situation is illustrated in Table 4.1, with reference to regional per capita income and gross domestic product. A more detailed analysis of interregional variations in economic and social performance in EEC countries is given in Appendix 1. There is no guarantee that the recipients of transfers of incomes will be the lower paid or poorer families; indeed, probably the contrary. Poverty is experienced by families living in inner city areas in prosperous regions; the Community Development Projects sponsored by the Home Office in Newham (London), Coventry and Birmingham, have confirmed social and economic deprivation in the generally prosperous South East and Midlands. Regional policy is not necessarily a suitable means of pursuing income redistribution objectives; in this case, national fiscal policies may be the most appropriate instrument. On the other hand, if regional policy is seen as having a relevant role to play in this field, then changes will be required in the measures used.

Table 4.1. *Regional Differentials in Per Capita Gross Domestic Product and Income Great Britain and EEC Countries*

Index Numbers:
National Average = 100

	Gross Domestic Product per capita (1962)			Income per capita (1968)		
	Highest region	Lowest region	Difference (index points)	Highest region	Lowest region	Difference (index points)
Italy	148.1 (Valle d'Aosta)	56.4 (Calabria)	91.7	148.0 (Lombardia)	59.0 (South)	89.0
France	131.5 (Paris)	78.4 (West)	53.1	147.0 (Paris)	84.0 (South West)	63.0
West Germany	161.7 (Hamburg)	77.0 (Rheinland-Pfalz)	84.7	180.0 (Hamburg)	85.0 (Rheinland-Pfalz)	95.0
Belgium	128.7 (Brabant)	68.1 (Limburg)	60.6	126.0 (Brussels)	93.0 (Flamande)	33.0
Netherlands	123.0 (Zuid-Holland)	81.0 (Friesland)	42.0	114.0 (West)	87.0 (North)	27.0
Great Britain	111.0 (South East)	86.0 (Scotland)	24.0	109.0 (South East)	94.0 (Scotland)	15.0

Sources: (a) A Regional Policy for the Community: Commission of the European Communities.

(b) *National Institute Economic Review*, No. 40, 1967.

(c) *Abstract of Regional Statistics*, No. 6, (HMSO, 1970).

(d) *Regional Statistics*: Statistical Office of the European Commission, 1971, Luxembourg.

The objectives of regional policy must be identified with specificity, and any conflicts recognized; and more thought must be given as to whether or not regional policy is the most appropriate form of action for attaining the objectives stated.

The relatively sophisticated meshing of social and economic objectives has been comparatively recent in origin. However, the recognition that regional policy must engage itself with social problems as well as economic ones is an important development in the potential of regional policy. In a debate in the Commons on Tuesday June 12th 1973 on the Northern region, the Opposition moved a motion demanding 'urgent action from the Government in activating a positive regional policy which will create new jobs, sustain economic growth, expand the social services, and improve the environment, thus closing the gap between the more prosperous areas and the Northern Region'.[9] The motion expressed concern not only of the lack of job opportunities in the Northern region but persistent social inequalities and low household incomes.

This increasing awareness of the need for national regional policy to embrace both social and economic policy has been illustrated not only in debates on UK regional policy but also over the emerging EEC common regional policy. In a Commons debate on June 26th 1973, Mr. Grimond emphasized that while an important aim of regional policies was to close the gap in regional variations of income per head, (quoting Hamburg at one end of the scale with an average of 4,700 dollars, and Calabria in Southern Italy on the other, at 756 dollars per head) this was 'only one of the aims that should be in the forefront of regional policy. One feature that these figures do not take into account is the differences of life in these places'.[10] Similarly, at the European Parliament in Strasbourg, during a debate on the Community's regional policy, in October 1973, emphasis was placed on the fact that regional policy could not, and must not, be seen simply and exclusively as an economic exercise. Regional policy is not only about jobs, but about infrastructure, education, culture, and the whole quality of life.[11]

The effectiveness of regional policy to achieve its objectives through a variety of means is examined in the following section for a number of reasons; first, an examination of the effectiveness of regional policy contributes to an understanding of the policy as a form of planning action. Secondly, an assessment of regional policy identifies its main strengths and weaknesses. Thirdly, such an assessment enhances understanding of the relationship between regional policy and regional planning as forms of public planning action.

The Effectiveness of Regional Policy as a Form of Action

The Report of the Royal Commission on the Distribution of the Industrial Population (the Barlow Report) in January 1940 was the first major study of regional policy in Britain. In recent years there has been a growing awareness[12] in many countries that a regional policy has become indispensable for supporting a general policy of economic and social progress. Although regional policy is comparatively recent in origin, and having gained in substance only since the mid 1960s, it has become an accepted and integral element of national government's policy making. Despite its significance, the case for regional policy must be questioned and its form and scope continuously reassessed. Evaluations of regional policy have been made almost wholly in economic and political terms; this is probably due to the fact that regional policy as a form of government action needs to compete with other possible resource uses.

Perhaps it is not surprising that regional policy has been evaluated in economic and political terms when the objectives of the policy have also been set within this context. However, as social issues have become an integral part of regional policy any evaluation must include this dimension. In addition to the extent that social policy has been neglected within regional policy making, then this aspect must also be assessed.

In general, two aspects of regional policies may be distinguished for analytical purposes; first, those objectives and measures which relate to regions with special problems, and secondly, those which relate generally to all regions of a country. This follows from an important change in regional policy with the extension of concern from merely solving specific, urgent problems in some regions, notably the peripheral ones, to embrace also the needs and aspirations of people throughout the national space. During the past 40 years national regional policy has been concerned mainly with 'make work' programmes in Development Areas. Regional development, however, is more than a matter of creating jobs, although even this achievement has never been anything like fully realized. If regional policy for the regions succeeds only in providing work, but the regions fall short of other parts of the world as congenial places in which to live, or to run a business, then in the long run they will fail as communities. While regional policy has been related almost exclusively to the needs of Development Areas, its meaning for the prosperous regions has been seen in a negative rather than positive way, through a system of controls. Regional policy operated by national government in Britain has been criticized as being only a Development Area policy.[13]

An evaluation of the effectiveness of regional policy is not an easy task. While any public policy should be based on a full analysis of the problems it tackles, a clear set of objectives, identified means and estimated costs involved, regional policies in the past must be criticized on all these points. Indeed, the situation has been reported by the 1971/72 Expenditure Committee as follows — 'We were struck by the paucity of . . . information which indeed seems to have decreased rather than increased in recent years, despite the emphasis placed by the Treasury on quantification of evidence before decisions were taken . . . There must be few areas of Government expenditure in which so much is spent but so little known about the success of policy'.[14]

An evaluation of the effectiveness of regional policy in achieving its objectives, and the extent to which it meets specific societal needs (which might be a different matter because the objectives of regional policy have not been established in any systematic and comprehensive manner), really falls into two parts; first, the effectiveness of regional policy in distributing resources between regions; and secondly, its effectiveness in distributing resources between areas within a region. In both cases, this effectiveness of policy must be measured in terms of objectives being realized. Clearly, regional planning does not have the capability to do the former, but it does have the potential for the latter. Unfortunately, there is little information available to evaluate these two dimensions of regional policy; it is not known with any specificity what the allocation of resources in financial terms has been between regions through regional policy. However, since 1967, the cost of regional policy has been approximately £300 million per year, which over the period 1967-74 amounted to over £2000 million; for such a huge expenditure, the lack of measurement and of knowledge of effects is a matter of some concern. Following on from this point, so long as subsidies have to be given to regions by central government, in the way of investment incentives etc., it might be better for central government to control the total sum rather than the detailed distribution, which might be left to regional planning agencies within the region. However, any development of regional policy in this direction will require a much improved accounting system which can measure the distribution of resources in financial terms between regions. As far as measuring the effectiveness of resources used at regional level is concerned, a regional distribution system might be expected to maintain an accounting procedure more efficiently than is possible with a national one.

A priori it seems unlikely that a single regional policy, or even a single group of assisted area policies, will meet the needs and aspirations of people living in different regions and parts of regions. A priori it seems unlikely that a central authority is able to formulate sufficiently sensitive policies to meet regional needs; rather than a single policy, it might be expected that many policies will be required and decided by the regions themselves.

As regional policy is concerned with distributing resources between regions, and may be an effective form of action for this purpose, an evaluation must be made of this aspect of the policy. In this respect, a number of studies illustrate the extent to which regional policy has realized its objectives. In the process of discussing these the potential of regional policy as a distributor of resources between regions is assessed.

Reducing Regional Differentials

The basis of present regional policy consists of a combination of both negative controls and financial inducements, together with measures to encourage the improvement of the environment and infrastructure of the Development Areas where this will assist industrial development. Three main categories of attractive measures may be used by governments to implement the traditional 'developmental' and 'dispersal' aspects of regional policy.

Firstly, those relating to the development of infrastructure. In Britain, central government takes account of the needs of different regions in preparing its programmes of public expenditure in infrastructure. Investment in infrastructure is an important contributory factor to economic growth in areas where growth has been lacking. The size of the public sector in total gross fixed capital formation, at approximately 45 per cent, is large enough to have a significant impact on total regional investment. Particularly important in regional policy are housing, communications, construction of advance factories and provision of their basic services. Britain has pioneered the use of the technique of industrial estates provided by a central authority on a large scale. The separate English, Scottish and Welsh industrial estates corporations are financed by and are responsible to the Department of Trade and Industry and act as their agents in estate development. The use of industrial estates has been a particularly appropriate method as an inducement to industry to locate in a specific place, and has been used in this respect especially in coal mining districts where there has been a substantial decline in employment. The Department of Trade and Industry factories are sold or rented at current market value, and as this is often less than the cost of building the factory in the Development Areas some element of government subsidy is involved.

The measures announced by the government in October 1970 relating to public expenditure included savings in the operation of the nationalized industries. Any cuts in public expenditure might be expected to have an impact in regions where the industrial structure is dominated by having industry within the public sector. In the Welsh economy, for example, South Wales is largely dependent on the vitality and growth of the coal and steel industries. The use of public sector industry as a positive instrument of regional policy is examined further later in considering appropriate measures to use within regional policies, from both central government's and region's viewpoint.

In some cases, national programmes have been adapted to serve particular regional needs, as for example, the approval by central government in May 1971 for the construction of the Humberside bridge. The White Paper on regional policy published in March 1972[15] illustrated central government's intention of accelerating the strategic road and port development programmes.

Secondly are those measures relating to manpower mobility, education and vocational training. Many countries have implemented training and mobility policies as an integral element of their regional policies.[16] In Britain a number of measures have been taken in recent years to improve the working of the labour market. The Employment Exchange service has been modernized and the government has commenced a major programme to expand the training facilities which will be available to individuals through the new Training Opportunities Scheme. Government spending on the TOPS is to be doubled from £50 million 1973-74 to £100 million in 1976-77, which will raise the number of trained people from 38,000 to 70-75,000 a year. An extensive coverage of the facilities available under the government's manpower training and mobility programmes is available in a series of leaflets from the Department of Employment.

The role of government employment and training facilities has become an important element of regional policy and may be expected to assume even greater significance in the future as the mechanisms of the labour market are improved.

The third and major category of measures contained within regional policy consists of inducements offered by central government to industry to move to or expand in the assisted areas. The new measures introduced by the government in 1972 focus on, first, countrywide and improved tax allowances for investment in plant, machinery and buildings, and secondly, regional development grants in the form of cash payments. These are available towards capital expenditure on both new plant and machinery and buildings in Development Areas and Special Development Areas, and towards capital expenditure on buildings only in Intermediate Areas and, temporarily, in Derelict Land Clearance Areas. The new cash grants are available to industries already located in the qualifying areas concerned as well as to incoming industries. The system of regional development grants are available at the rates shown in Table 4.2.

Table 4.2   Rates of Regional Development Grants

	Plant and machinery	Buildings
Special Development Areas	22 per cent	22 per cent
Development Areas	20 per cent	20 per cent
Intermediate Areas	—	20 per cent
Derelict Land Clearance Areas (for two years only)	—	20 per cent

Source: White Paper: Industrial and Regional Development, Cmnd. 4942, March 1972, Appendix B.

Britain is not alone in facing problems of congestion in particular parts of the country and especially in the metropolitan areas. Many countries, faced with similar problems, have taken positive countervailing action by giving investment incentives in uncongested areas, creating new towns, investing in infrastructure etc. However, Britain and France are the only countries in Western Europe to adopt restrictive measures. The government uses a system of industrial development certificates (IDCs) as an essential element in its regional policies. Negative controls are also used in Britain to control office development in the metropolis. A White Paper published by the government in 1963 showed that of 40,000 jobs created in London each year, only 8,000 were in manufacturing industry. The exclusion of office development from regional policy was clearly a serious omission as it was the main source of employment growth. In 1965 the system of Office Development Permits (ODPs) was introduced through the Control of Office and Industrial Development Act.

The most comprehensive statement of measures contained within central government's regional policy relates to that made by the Chancellor of the Exchequer on March 21st 1972 in the Budget, which was more fully described in the White Paper subsequently issued.[17] The Department of Trade and Industry also issues, periodically, booklets which set out the incentives available to industry in the assisted areas.[18] A summary of the incentives contained within regional policies is given in Table 4.3, together with the appropriate legislation, from the 1930s to the present time.

While it is extremely difficult to assess the effectiveness of regional policy, the evidence that does exist suggests that regional disparities between the assisted areas and the more prosperous regions have narrowed. The 'regional problem' in Britain has, hitherto, centred upon the relationship between regional growth differentials and regional differentials in industrial composition. This relationship has been analysed in terms of the standardization technique of shift and share analysis. An application of this technique in a modified form, to the regions of the United Kingdom[19] has demonstrated that regional policy in the 1960s did appear to have had at least some effect in securing a more favourable industrial mix in the less prosperous regions.

Table 4.3   Financial Incentives to Industry in Assisted Areas.

Legislation	Financial incentives	Development controls
Special Areas Acts 1934, 36, 37	Loans to firms moving to SAs Contributions to rent, rates and tax. Exemption from national defence contributions	None

Legislation	Financial incentives	Development controls
Distribution of Industry Act 1945	Loans for sites, buildings. Treasury loans and grants on 'lender of last resort' basis, for approved projects	None
Town and Country Planning Act 1947		IDCs required for over 5,000 sq.ft. and favoured Development Areas
Distribution of Industry Act 1958	Extended treasury loans and grants	None
Local Employment Act 1960	Loans and grants without 'lender of last resort' restrictions; building grants	IDCs to favour Development Districts
Local Employment and Finance Acts 1963	25 per cent building grant. 10 per cent plant and machinery grant. Accelerated depreciation	None
Industrial Development Act 1966	40 per cent investment grants replace all investment tax allowances	IDC limit lowered and ODPs started
Further action by Labour government 1967	REP introduced for Development Areas and SDAs. 35 per cent building grants in SDAs. Investment grants raised to 45 per cent 1967/68 only	None
Local Employment Act 1970	25 per cent building grant. Training grants for new jobs	IDC exemption limit raised from 5,000 to 10,000 sq.ft. nationally, except in South East and Midlands. Exemption limit for ODPs raised

Legislation	Financial incentives	Development controls
Action by new Conservative government 1970-71	Investment grants replaced by 'free depreciation'. Larger building grants. 30 per cent operational grants in SDAs	None
Industry Act 1972	Return to investment grants of 22 per cent in SDAs and 20 per cent DAs free depreciation to remain	IDC exemption limit raised further.
Action by Conservative government 1973	New grants to help decentralization of office jobs. Training grants scheme phased out in favour of training opportunities scheme	None

A more comprehensive evaluation of the effect of British regional economic policy has been undertaken by Moore and Rhodes.[20] Once again, the evaluation involved a quantitative assessment of how much activity has been diverted to Development Areas as a direct result of that policy. The overall conclusion of the study was that regional policies operated between 1963 and 1970 (1963 marked the introduction of regionally differentiated investment incentives in British Development Areas) diverted 220,000 jobs to the assisted areas, as well as helping national output and the balance of payments. The study concluded that spending on regional policies did not strain national resources, and that the regional employment premium had a beneficial effect in terms of jobs and export competitiveness.

One of the major objectives of national regional policy has been to reduce the high rates of unemployment in the Development Areas. While it may appear logical to look for the effects of regional policy by examining the unemployment figures in Development Areas and other parts of Britain, there are several reasons why unemployment figures may give a misleading picture of the impact of regional policy. Firstly, those industries reducing manpower nationally are concentrated in the Development Areas, and may release relatively more labour in a period of active regional policy. Secondly, while regional policy may increase the demand for labour in Development Areas, it may also stimulate an increase in the labour supply, for example in the form of lower net migration losses and increased labour participation rates. For these reasons, Moore and Rhodes in their evaluation of regional policy chose employment growth and investment as indicators of effectiveness rather than traditionally used unemployment figures.

In relation to the creation of jobs in the Development Areas, a study published by the Board of Trade in 1968[21] illustrated to some extent the effectiveness of regional policies in the United Kingdom since the war, although the study terminated in 1965, just before regional policies were further intensified. The study divided the United Kingdom into 50 areas for recording the movement of firms. Every new manufacturing establishment was investigated to find out whether its origins were in the region where it was located or to another region or even country. The study demonstrated that by the end of 1966 nearly 1 in 10 employees in manufacturing industry was working in a factory opened since the war by a firm whose base was in another area. The Development Areas illustrated the gains from regional policies, with nearly 30 per cent of all employment in manufacturing industry in Wales being attributed to moves into the region during the 21 years.

Another important finding of the study was that the movement of industry in the United Kingdom has not taken place at a constant rate. From 1945 to 1951 there was a high volume of movement with approximately 53,000 new jobs created per year by firms new to the areas, of which 37,000 were in the Development Areas. However, between 1952 and 1959, when distribution of industry policy was pursued less vigorously, only 34,000 new jobs of this kind were created each year. With greater government activity in operating regional policies in the period 1960-65, the number of new jobs created by the movement of industry increased to 46,000 in the Development Areas. With the intensification of regional policy since 1966, the impact of this policy upon the movement of industry might be expected to have increased, and the recent studies seemed to have confirmed this situation.

Progress in reducing regional disparities in economic and social performance might be expected to be greatest in those countries where expenditure on regional policies is relatively high, or where these policies have been in operation for long periods of time. Table 4.4 illustrates the level of expenditure on regional policies by certain member countries of OECD together with expenditure per capita.

Owing to difficulties in international comparisons of expenditure on regional policies (some nations exclude spending on infrastructure), these figures should be taken as orders of magnitude rather than specific values. Indeed, as the total amount of expenditure spent on regional policy in Britain 1967-70 approached something in the order of £280 − £300 million, the OECD figures appear rather

Table 4.4.   Expenditure on Regional Policies in Certain OECD Countries, 1969

Country	Millions US dollars	Population in millions	Expenditure per capita $'s
France	90 − 108	50.0	1.8 − 2.2
Germany	75 − 125	60.2	1.2 − 2.1
Sweden	45	7.9	5.7
Norway	35	3.8	9.2
Belgium	200	9.6	20.8
Netherlands	20	12.7	1.6
Italy	750	53.8	13.9
United Kingdom	552	55.4	9.9

Source: Adapted from Table 2, Chapter V, OECD Report, Paris 1970 op. cit.

on the low side. The current sums of money being spent on regional policy are relatively large when it is realized that over the whole period of the Distribution of Industry Acts 1945-60, only £12 million was spent by the Treasury through loans and grants, and Board of Trade Expenditure on constructing factories and industrial estates reached £78 million; a total of £90 million or an average of just £6 million per year. To a large extent this spending was regarded as an investment as the government received rent from the factories it let. Measured by the yardstick of expenditure, regional policies have become more effective.

While much of the preceding discussion has centred upon the needs of the assisted areas, an important development in recent years has been the increasing concern of the prosperous regions to maintain their relative position. As national regional policy has allocated extra resources to the assisted areas in recent years, the prosperous regions have emphasized the importance of growth in their economies for other regions and the nation as a whole. On the topic of migration and mobility, some mention should be made of the extent to which the South East of England is the seed-bed for growth in the less prosperous areas. It is important to recognize that national regional policy operates within this context of continuous pressures by both assisted and non assisted areas. This pressure must, itself, place a constraint on the operation of regional policy.

The results of the Board of Trade study[22] into the movement of firms illustrated that movements originating in the South East gave rise to 200,000 jobs in other regions over the period 1945-65; and that movements originating from the West Midlands gave rise to 93,000 jobs in other regions. The generation of growth in the prosperous regions has important implications for growth in the less prosperious regions, and after an intensive effort to encourage the movement of industry and offices from the South East to the Development Areas, attempts have been made to reverse present policy, especially in relation to office location policy. The GLC in a policy statement to the Greater London Development Plan

Inquiry in May 1971 sought to allow 29 million extra square feet of office space and 14.5 million square feet of industrial development in the GLC area 1971-76 on the grounds that London is the key to prosperity in the South East, and that some action is required to counteract the falling demand for labour in the London area.[23]

The South East Regional Economic Planning Council in their 1967 report 'A Strategy for the South East' destroyed one of the long held myths of regional planning, namely the 'drift to the south' which occupied the minds of so many people in the 1960s. The 1966 Census of Population gathered data on migration for the first time on a regional basis in any comprehensive way. The report of the SEEPC illustrated that in 1965-66 the South East region recorded a total net loss through migration of 1000 people; in the 1960s the region had consistently registered a net migration loss with other regions but gained overall due to overseas immigration. The figures contained in the SEEPC report are illustrated in Table 4.5.

Table 4.5   Extract from SEEPC Report

Time period	Net migration balance with other regions of England and Wales	Net migration balance with other countries
1961 – 62	−40,000	+141,000
1962 – 63	−14,000	+ 42,000
1963 – 64	−17,000	+ 49,000
1964 – 65	−36,000	+ 42,000
1965 – 66	−29,000	+ 28,000

Source: 1967 Report of SEEPC, *A Strategy for the South East* (HMSO, 1967)

This assessment of the effectiveness of regional policy must be seen in relation to the potential of new measures which might be developed. It must be recognized that central government has considerable potential for influencing and determining the distribution of resources between regions, although in many ways this potential has been under-used. The use of public sector expenditure as an instrument of regional policy has not been fully developed in Britain, although it has considerable potential. The size and growth of public expenditure is considerable. Approximately half of all spending in the economy is done by the public sector; public expenditure as a proportion of GNP has increased from 41 per cent in 1956 to the current figure of 50 per cent. Public expenditure comprises the current and capital expenditures of central government and local authorities, together with the capital expenditure of the nationalized industries and other public corporations, and their debt interest. Table 4.6 illustrates the allocation of this expenditure by sector.

Table 4.6   Public Expenditure by Sector: (£ millions) 1971-72

(a)	Central government	£15,172 M
(b)	Local authorities	7,096 M
(c)	Public corporations	2,202 M
		£24,470 M

Source: Adapted from Treasury Economic Progress Report. No. 31, September 1972.

Clearly the nationalized industries (i.e. public corporations) are an important sector of the national economy, contributing 10 per cent of GNP, employing 2 million people and providing many of our basic needs for energy, transport, steel and communications. Their performance has a vital influence on the health of the economy as a whole. In some communities the dependence on the nationalized industries is substantial. The public sector also exerts a strong influence on the private sector to the extent that the public sector purchases a substantial part of its output of goods and services from the private sector. It follows that a major contribution towards increasing economic and social opportunities in the development areas might be made by injecting a regional bias in the allocation of public sector contracts through the form of a quota system whereby a specific proportion of the total must be bought from particular regions, rather than the system at present of competitive tendering. An injection of regional allocation into the programmes of public expenditure, especially the nationalized industries, may conflict with national policy. For example, in the mid 1960s governments sought to make the nationalized industries more commercially minded.[24] However, in the 1970s there has been, to some extent, a reversal of previous policy; in the case of Rolls Royce and Upper Clyde Shipbuilders, the government realized the extent to which economic and industrial policy must be seen within a social and political context.

Regionalizing the public sector has been an instrument used within regional policy in Italy, where, as early as 1957, the Italian government passed a law which instructed the nationalized industries to promote industrial activities in the south by allocating at least 40 per cent of their total investment, and at least 60 per cent of their new investment, in the Mezzogiorno.

Another opportunity for central government to influence the distribution of resources between regions arises because national governments have a number of tools with which to manage their economies which are not available to planning agencies at the regional level. In particular, central government may establish regional variations within the national structure of taxation. This could be applied in relation to Corporations Tax, or a system of regional differentials with Value Added Tax. Within the general structure of taxation might also be considered social security benefits. The Welsh Council in its document 'Wales: Employment and the Economy'[25] suggested that one way to stimulate demand in Wales was for central government to increase social security benefits throughout the United Kingdom; in fact, central government has now accepted the need to revise all benefits annually in future. The Welsh Council also drew the government's attention to the need to maintain the relative position of recipients on social security benefits in the face of relative increases in food prices which were likely to be a consequence of EEC entry. This point assumes significance in Wales, which is particularly dependent on social security benefits (£62.0 per head on average in Wales compared with £51.9 in the UK as a whole in 1967/68); this situation is also likely to apply in other assisted areas.

Finally, the importance of the New Towns programme in determining the location of industry and public investment requires that it be considered as an integral element of national regional policy. The accommodation of urban growth is likely to be a major challenge for most regional planning authorities, and the role of central government in providing extra resources for this purpose assumes some significance. The contribution of the New Towns programme to a regional policy may be seen in both an inter- and intraregional context. Within an intraregional context the role of the new towns has been to accommodate population growth and problems of urban renewal. It is generally agreed that new towns have been largely successful in fulfilling this role and will continue to do so. In relation to the interregional context there has been less agreement on the use of the New Towns programme as a positive instrument of regional policy on a national scale. The New Towns, however, can be conceived as counter magnets to London and the major conurbations, both in terms of economic and social opportunities. A study of New Towns designated 1947-55 outside the London ring supports this hypothesis.[26] As the New Towns programme requires a substantial element of public finance and control, there is an opportunity for central government to exert some influence on the location, size and form of urban growth in the future, and hence, the distribution of resources.

Some Weaknesses of Regional Policy

While regional policy may have been successful in reducing regional disparities in economic performance in recent years, this form of action contains a number of weaknesses which reduce its effectiveness in meeting societal needs within regions. This section focuses upon three important aspects of regional policy which illustrate the extent to which regional policy as presently conceived has been unable to meet successfully a range of regional needs. In part, the weaknesses of regional policy can be attributed to the very nature of the policy itself, and partly, also, because regional policy has not engaged itself with a fuller range of societal problems. Firstly, attention is given to the fact that in distributing resources between areas within a region, central government must designate areas with specific boundaries, a mechanical process which may be avoided through regional planning. Secondly, a national regional policy by its very nature, being standard in operation and having taken considerable time to operate, e.g. by Act of Parliament, is not capable of adopting changes rapidly although these may be required. Thirdly, the effectiveness of regional policy in meeting societal needs is examined where its impact is perhaps most marked, namely on individuals and families in the regions. In this context, local needs are examined in both economic and social terms; regional policy is assessed for its ability to cope with urgent social problems, not only in the assisted areas, which remains the primary focus of the policy, but also in the non assisted regions, with particular reference to the inner cities, whose problems must be engaged by some form of planning action. Some evidence is drawn upon from the national programme of the Community Development Projects, sponsored by the Home Office through the Urban Aid Programme, which has, among other things, examined the relevance of regional policy in meeting societal needs in the regions.

THE DESIGNATION OF AREAS IN REGIONAL POLICY

The operation of regional policy in Britain has involved the designation of assisted areas with specific boundaries which has imposed distinct subdivisions within a region. The development areas contain Special Development Areas, Development Areas, and Grey Areas, all within a single region, and each of these categories has become firmly cemented as blocks, fiercely competitive in maintaining or enhancing their designated positions, and introducing inflexibility into the distribution of resources within a region.

An important characteristic of regional policy in Britain in recent years has been the expansion of the long established concept of using measures to assist the Development Areas to embrace also the prosperous regions. Hitherto, an unsystematic basis had been used whereby the boundaries of regions were drawn to focus upon a specific problem; one example is that of unemployment, whereby areas with relatively low rates of unemployment have been denied special assistance to encourage the creation of jobs. A more systematic basis has begun to emerge by which the national space has been regionalized to cater for needs in a much wider context than hitherto. One of the criticisms of the choice of areas in Britain justifying special treatment has been that the policy has not been sufficiently selective. In France, for example, both the variety of aids given and the areas involved are marked characteristics of the system of incentives given to encourage growth in depressed regions. Until 1967 financial aid in Britain was based on a twofold classification; the Development Areas versus the rest of the country. However, with the establishment of Special Development Areas in 1967, and the publication of the Hunt Report on Intermediate Areas in

April 1969,[27] the basis for areas receiving special treatment was widened from the twofold classification. In a note of dissent in the report of the Hunt Committee, A. J. Brown recommended that the incentive system should be based on four classes of area (excluding Special Development Areas) or zones. Firstly, development areas with similar levels of incentives as at present; secondly, intermediate areas with something less; thirdly neutral areas, being prosperous but uncongested with no incentives, and finally, the congested areas where a congestion tax might be levied to reflect social costs to the community from industrial location. The system advocated by Professor Brown is similar to that operated in France based on five zones. In Britain the government has added the new town and town expansion programme as a fifth level in the structure, receiving less priority than the three special problem areas, but more than the rest of the country.

A variety of criteria may be used for the designation of areas qualifying for special government attention; the criteria used in the past have focused mainly on economic phenomena, such as unemployment, income, migration, activity rates etc. However, the criteria used in selecting areas within a government's regional policy may not be confined to those used in the past. There is no unique set of criteria that can be recommended for use in all countries and in all circumstances. In Britain between 1945 and 1958 regional policy was concerned with providing employment and reducing unemployment in fairly large areas. Table 4.7 illustrates the nature of the areas designated in regional policies operated from the 1930s, and the use of large assisted areas for 20 years up to the end of the 1950s. By 1958, however, it had become evident that parts of the scheduled Development Areas were no longer places where there was high unemployment or any special danger of it. On the other hand, a number of places had become prominent, most of them small, and many of them coastal towns, in which there was a relatively high rate of unemployment. Accordingly, the Development of Industry (Industrial Finance) Act 1958 extended the power of the Treasury to give assistance by way of grant or loan to firms both inside and outside the Development Areas, providing the Board of Trade was satisfied that the assistance would contribute to lower unemployment in a locality.

The 1960 Local Employment Act attempted to consolidate and clarify the situation, replacing the broad development areas by narrower development districts which were selected administratively by the Board of Trade, on the sole criteria of actual or prospective high unemployment. The 1960 Act did not stipulate any specific rates of unemployment which were regarded as high for the purpose of listing a development district. The Board of Trade adopted initially an annual average rate of 4½ per cent as the *prima facie* measure of high unemployment for the purposes of the Act. This rate was selected as appropriate at a time when the national average was 2 per cent.

Table 4.7   Areas Designated by Regional Policies 1934-73

Areas designated	Date
North East England, West Cumberland, South Wales, Clydeside	1934
South Lancashire (1946) Merseyside (1948) part of Scottish Highlands (1949) and North East Lancashire (1950) added to SAs	1946-50
Concentrated on areas, in or out of DAs where unemployment more than 4½ per cent	1958
DAs replaced by narrow Development Districts areas with more than 4½ per cent unemployment	1960
Return to DAs; most of Scotland, Wales, Merseyside, Cornwall, N. Devon and Northern England	1966
Special DAs added — focused on coalfields; Northumberland, Durham, Cumberland, Scotland and Wales	1967
Intermediate Areas created; assisted areas extended to Yorkshire/Humberside and Lancashire	1970
SDAs extended in Development Areas	1970-71
No changes in The Industry Act 1972	1972

During the 1960s the need began to emerge for further evolutions of policy, from action designed merely to relieve the immediate unemployment problems of particular localities towards the broader concept of promoting the economic development of regions as a whole. The concept of the 'broad area' became an important element of regional policy; rather than attempting to encourage investment to specific locations, attention focused on larger areas within which choices might be made. Fresh legislation was required to meet these new objectives, and under the Industrial Development Act 1966 the development districts were replaced by wider continuous Development Areas. In selecting the Development Areas the Board of Trade considered not only unemployment, but employment growth, population growth, migration, and the objectives of regional policy. In November 1967, certain parts of the Development Areas suffering, or likely to suffer, particularly high and persistent unemployment, often as a result of colliery closures, were designated Special Development Areas. In February 1971 the coverage of the SDAs was increased, as too were the Development Areas and Intermediate Areas. In a period of relatively high unemployment, at both national and regional level, central government extended aid to specific blackspots. The extension of areas justifying special treatment has raised another important issue within regional policy in addition to the broad area versus specific location concept. In the case of Special Development Areas, (and also of Intermediate and Development Areas to some extent) for example, the number of designated areas has increased substantially in recent years, thereby reducing the effectiveness of such status. While all SDAs receive similar benefits the problems and needs of communities within them may be subject to significant variation, not reflected by regional policy in Britain.

The government re-examined the boundaries of assisted areas in March 1972[28] and concluded that there should be no significant changes in the extent of the existing Development Areas or Special Development Areas. However, the government did announce extensions to Intermediate Area status and the Derelict Land Clearance Areas. Figure 4.1 illustrates the nature and extent of those areas which receive assistance through the government's regional policy.

By the 1970s the selection of areas justifying special treatment had developed on a more sophisticated basis, both in the range of areas used within regional policy, and in the criteria adopted in designating the areas. While these refinements to designated areas have been made in an attempt to recognize a variety of needs, which undoubtedly exist, the fixing of specific boundaries for different types of assisted areas (or areas of negative control in other regions) has become an integral feature of regional policy; regional policy, not surprisingly, has often seemed to be more concerned with defining areas and drawing boundaries than the solution of urgent problems.

THE INFLEXIBILITY OF REGIONAL POLICY

The inflexibility of regional policy to meet local needs stems from a number of aspects of the policy. Whereas the previous section identified the inflexibility of regional policy in relation to the designation of areas, this section focuses attention on the inflexibility of the instruments of the policy in meeting the needs of different regions. First, regional policy is a national regional policy which must be standardized in its operation. An example of this dimension of the policy has been seen in relation to the areas used; all areas with a similar designation receive standard treatment irrespective of the nature and scope of the problems they experience. In the case of the Special Development Areas for example, the measures contained within regional policy are quite specific and standard in their application; however, while some SDAs may benefit from investment incentives offered to industrialists, perhaps because they have a supply of industrial sites available, other SDAs may not be in this position but require subsidies for public transport to gain access to job opportunities in growth points. The need for standardization in operating a national policy must impose constraints upon meeting local needs.

Secondly, a national regional policy must, necessarily, take considerable time to operate, and will not be capable of adopting changes rapidly although these may be required. The present administration of regional policy rests upon a

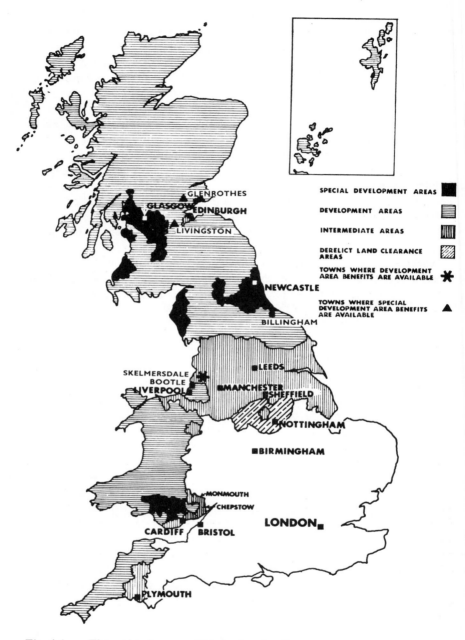

Fig. 4.1   The assisted areas within regional policy.
           Source: White Paper, Cmnd. 4942, op. cit. Appendix C, March 1972.

considerable input of resources, including the March 1972 White Paper and the August 1972 Industry Act. In addition, the form of regional assistance has been administered by the new Industrial Development Executive, whose structure is illustrated in Figure 4.2. Regional policy has become firmly established as one of the main national policies of a central government, and has, not surprisingly, become institutionalized within the structure of government.

An example of the inflexibility of regional policy, both in terms of its standardization and its inability to change quickly, can be drawn from the decisions made in recent years over the use of investment grants or investment tax allowances as a form of investment incentive to industrialists. The present system of investment allowances and regional development grants have been generally welcomed as being more substantial than previous incentives. Taking the case of a £5,000 investment (£4,000 plant and machinery, £1,000 buildings) Table 4.8 shows the values cf the grants and tax allowances received, both absolutely and as a percentage of the initial investment. The table illustrates the substantial improvement in the position of the Development Areas and Special Development Areas. Taking present values over a 10 year period the absolute improvement in the advantage of the Development Area investment over the national area investment has become £954, compared with £686 under the cash grant scheme operated by the Labour government 1966-70, and only £447 under the system of investment allowances operated by the Conservative government from October 1970 until the new measures were introducèd in March 1972.

Table 4.8   Comparison of Present Values of Grants and Allowances for the First Ten Years

	Pre-October 1970		Post-October 1970		New system	
	£	%	£	%	£	%
National	1830	36.6	1448	28.9	1660	33.2
Special Development Areas	2516	50.3	1895	37.9	2710	54.2
Development Areas	2516	50.3	1895	37.9	2614	52.3
Intermediate Areas	2007	40.1	1651	33.0	1851	37.0

Source: Review of 1972 Budget Measures, Welsh Council, 1972.

In addition to the improvement for Development Areas, it is important to note that the new system is scheduled to be maintained at least until January 1978. Certainty and stability of practice are necessary elements of any investment incentive scheme, and these requirements of a policy need to be safeguarded. However, this aspect of the policy need not preclude changes in the form of policies.

The decision of central government to adopt either a system of investment

HEADQUARTERS ORGANIZATION

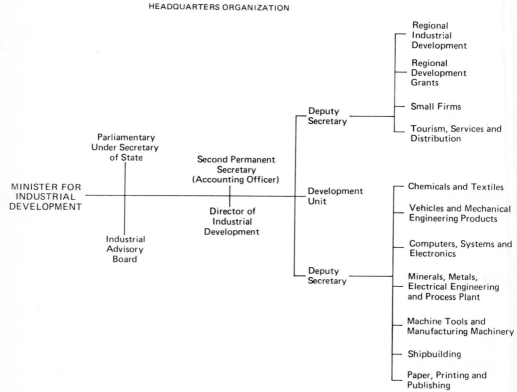

Fig. 4.2   Administrative structure of the Industrial Development Executive.
Source: White Paper, *Industrial and Regional Development,* March
1972, Appendix D.

grants or allowances is of some importance for the generation of jobs and income in the less prosperous regions. In the past, national regional policy has been standard in its practice; until recently, the two forms of investment incentives were considered separately and as mutually exclusive. It was not until 1972 that a mix of the two kinds of measure was chosen. However, the present system is applied nationally, without variation, whereas some areas may benefit from one kind of policy and another area from a different policy. The system of investment grants established in 1966 had three advantages over the previous system of tax allowances; it covered replacement machinery, it assisted new projects which did not make profits in the earlier years, and thirdly, payments to firms were made within six months instead of about eighteen months under the former system. The system of cash grants, while not related to profits were restricted to manufacturing industry, although this need not have been the case. Indeed, in 1973 certain grants were made available to service industry moving to the assisted areas. In the White Paper[29] which gave effect to the system of investment allowances in 1970 the government stated that in their view the old system of investment grants had involved a high public expenditure without achieving its objectives (investment grants were paid to the value of £430 million[30] in Great Britain in the financial year 1968-69). In addition the government outlined three specific disadvantages of the investment grants scheme. First, that investment grants benefit firms whether or not they are making profits and can therefore result in uneconomic investment leading to a waste of resources. Secondly, that the previous system discriminated unjustifiably against the service industries which made an important contribution to economic growth and the balance of payments. Thirdly, the government believed that the investment grants scheme had imposed a considerable administrative burden and cost on industry, and also on government itself requiring a staff of 1000 at an annual cost of £2 million (although this represented only 0.4 per cent of the total cost of the scheme which does not seem excessive). One of the advantages of the investment allowance scheme which began in 1970 was its availability to service industry as well as manufacturing industry.

However, it soon became apparent that the system of investment allowances was less likely to benefit the Development Areas than the old system of investment grants. Firstly, the growth of the Development Areas depends to a large extent on small firms investing in buildings, plant and machinery who expect to receive little profit in the early years of an investment project. These firms will receive little tax relief because they have little profit to be taxed. This weakness of the new system for depressed areas has been emphasized in the OECD report published in 1970 on regional policies in fifteen industrialized countries.[31] The governments of other countries in Western Europe favour incentives based on investment grants, and with a view to British entry to the

EEC this might have been borne in mind by the government in re-introducing a system of regional investment grants alongside investment allowances.

The Trade Union Congress in its 1971 Economic Review was one of many agencies which criticized the then system based exclusively on investment allowances. It estimated that the £100 million differential that had existed between the less and more prosperous areas under the investment grant scheme 1966-70 had been replaced by a differential of only £75 million.

The second major criticism made of the system of wholly investment allowances was that many Development Areas depend upon foreign capital, especially Central Scotland with American firms, and German/Japanese firms in Northern Ireland. American firms have also become important contributors to economic growth in Wales, with 20 American owned firms being established in 1966-72 employing 6,000 people. If foreign firms are taxed according to legislation of their own country, a system of investment allowance may provide no incentive to invest for these firms, whereas under a system of investment grants they are eligible.

The Welsh Council has explored in its report[32] 'Wales: Employment and the Economy' the case for instituting a system of lower Corporation Tax for firms located in the Development Areas. While the government did not accept this proposal the 1972 Finance Bill included a clause for the introduction of a lower rate of Corporation Tax on profits up to £15,000 liable to Corporation Tax, and for marginal relief to be applied to the balance over £15,000 and up to £25,000. These provisions were scheduled for the whole of the United Kingdom with the reform of Corporation Tax in April 1973. Measures of this sort are likely to be of particular advantage to rural areas where the majority of firms tend to be small, and also in tourism where the proportion of small firms is higher than in other sectors. Both these points are important to many Development Areas. The measures will also help firms in the first few years of their operation, when profits are liable to be low; this is of advantage to many assisted areas since they must hope to attract new firms and the success of such firms is of vital importance to them.

It seems undoubtedly the case, that, but for the standardization of national regional policy, many innovations in the forms of regional measures used could have been introduced where they were considered to be appropriate. One of the most disappointing features of national regional policy has been its seeming inability to be innovative. One of the advantages of regional planning as a form of action, given the necessary financial context, is that policies can be designed to suit particular needs without encountering many of the inflexibilities of regional policy.

THE FAILURE OF REGIONAL POLICY TO MEET SOCIETAL NEEDS

The focus of attention in regional policy has been on the assisted areas in which the SDAs have been designated as exhibiting some of the most severe economic and social problems facing individuals and families. Regional policy specifically purports to be directed at these very people; however, there is some evidence to suggest that regional policy has failed in this respect, and that a national regional policy may not be an appropriate means of providing solutions to these problems. In addition, there is further evidence to suggest that regional policy has failed to embrace a range of societal needs which must be met in the non assisted areas.

A Working Group on Regional Policy of the Community Development

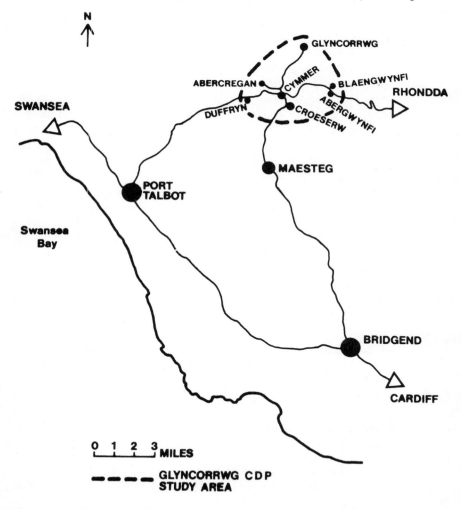

Fig. 4.3   Glyncorrwg CDP study area.

Projects (CDPs) involved in the national CDP programme has illustrated a number of ways in which regional policy has failed to meet social and economic needs of people to whom it purports to be directed, and in other cases, where regional policy has not even sought to become positively involved.

The number of areas covered by the CDP programme in Britain has now reached the planned total of 12, with 10 being located in the inner cities, both in assisted and non assisted areas, and two, Glamorgan and Cleator Moor, focused on older industrial areas. The Home Office has described[33] the CDP programme as a modest attempt at action/research into the better understanding and more comprehensive tackling of social needs, especially in local communities within older urban areas, through closer co-ordination of central and local official and unofficial effort. While the concept of community development of this kind is not new, it is the first time that central and local government have made a joint venture into this field themselves.

The Glamorgan CDP has undertaken a considerable amount of work on examining the operation of regional policy and the extent to which it has provided solutions to urgent economic and social problems.[34] The Glamorgan CDP is focused upon a group of former mining communities in the Upper Afan Valley, situated within Glyncorrwg UD (now part of the new Afan district), some 10-14 miles north of Port Talbot; the location of the study area is illustrated in Figure 4.3. In essence, Glyncorrwg, a Special Development Area, is faced in a dramatic way with all those dimensions which have come to be known as 'the regional problem'. Apparently sensitive regional policies are ineffective because they rest on invalid assumptions about the convenience of travel, the multiplier effect of special investments, and the availability of trained labour that can take advantage of theoretically available investment. No firm future is foreseen because there is no local plan that gives substance and expression to these policies, and no backcloth against which men and women and investors can decide whether or not to invest themselves, and their children, or their money, in the future of such communities. It might be expected that this situation is replicated elsewhere in South Wales and in communities in other parts of Britain.

All these factors are themselves root causes of the familiar problems which take quantifiable forms:

1 High unemployment — 10 per cent in 1973 compared to 3 per cent nationally.
2 High dependency on social security benefits. With a population of 8,600, and 2,500 households, there are 2,750 beneficiaries of social security benefit with a weekly value of £23,000.
3 Declining population: 1961 9,400: 1971 8,600.
4 Severe outward migration: between 1951 and 1961 a net loss of 400 people; between 1961 and 1971 a net loss of 1,500 people.

5 Poor housing stock.
6 Poor transport facilities.
7 Poor economic prospects; the local economic base had 3,000 jobs in 1961; by 1971 this figure had fallen dramatically to 600, with the closure of the last three collieries 1966-70, and a major redundancy by the main firm in the valley.

This does not mean that the community is without its strengths — the close knit life and family ties of traditional South Wales coal mining valleys still linger, and environmentally the valley has few equals in South Wales. Nevertheless, urgent and drastic remedial action is required if the downward spiral of community life is to be halted, let alone reversed.

The Upper Afan Valley was designated an SDA in November 1967 in the first round of such designated areas. However, even as an SDA, the area has had to compete not only with a whole range of different areas receiving different benefits, but also with other SDAs, not only on the doorstep in South Wales, but also in other regions of Britain. Since 1967 there have been 20 SDAs designated in Wales, and this was further increased to 28 in February 1971. It seems certain that the attractiveness of the Afan Valley for the location of industry has been devalued by the increase in the number of SDAs, particularly in South Wales. Regional policy has not been sufficiently selective and flexible in matching its system of benefits to the needs of particular communities.

The Upper Afan Valley, like many other communities in South Wales, and elsewhere, is marginal to the growth points which regional policies have promoted.[35] At present this SDA has not benefited to any significant extent from regional policy in creating local jobs, nor from growth point policy due to poor accessibility of people in the communities concerned in jobgetting and jobholding. It is difficult to assess the objectives of central government's regional policy at a particular point in time. In *Wales: The Way Ahead* published by the Welsh Office in 1967, the government stated[36] that 'one element in an integrated plan must be the establishment of new employment in the valleys themselves, in so far as this is practical, so as to reduce emigration or travel to work, to encourage the fuller use of female labour and to help provide jobs for men with disabilities incurred in the mining industry'. As far as the Afan Valley is concerned, this part of the government's regional policy has not been implemented. From what has been observed, it is extremely doubtful if regional policy, as presently conceived, will be able to achieve these objectives.

Regional policy relies very largely for its success on the financial inducements to industrialists to create jobs in the assisted areas. While these benefits are of some importance for improving the economic base of the assisted areas, non financial items may be equally important yet outside the scope of regional policy. In South Wales, for example, the solution of economic and social problems requires planning on a regional scale, establishing an agency which is able to assess the needs of individual communities, establish priorities, and take effective action, backed by an appropriate financial framework. To some extent, the reorganization of local government into larger units in South Wales can be expected to enable the kind of action required to be implemented, and the recommendations of the Kilbrandon Report on the Constitution do provide the opportunity for additional support.[37]

Finally, an illustration of the extent to which regional policy is constrained by its standardization and inflexibility, and its national objectives set against needs which are local (which require regional action), may be drawn from work undertaken by the CDP in Canning Town in East London. Alongside the Coventry and Birmingham CDPs, the Canning Town Project has identified and measured the extent of social and economic problems in their part of the Metropolis. An examination of Canning Town's industrial structure reveals its dependency on the docks, road haulage, container services, storage and wholesale distribution, followed by heavy refining industries such as sugar, flour and animal foodstuffs, together with chemicals, ship repair and cable manufacture. London's traditional 'seed-bed' industries in light electrical and instrument engineering are poorly represented. In summary, both the total structure and manufacturing alone are atypical of the South East and closer to the dockland of Liverpool or Hull. In 1966 there were 50,000 jobs in and around Canning Town, with 85 per cent in manual jobs. Since 1966 the area has lost 14,000 manual jobs and gained 2,500—3,000 new manual jobs; a net decline of some 25-30 per cent. Redundancies have resulted in unemployment twice the national average, re-employment in service jobs at far lower wages, and increased travelling in terms of both cost and time.

The social and economic problems faced in communities like Canning Town, within regions designated as 'prosperous', lie outside the scope of regional policy; none of the benefits of that policy are available to these areas. Attempts made by the Canning Town CDP, and others, to gain assisted area status for the community have not, hitherto, been successful; this is not surprising given the nature, structure and pressures upon regional policy. While the inner cities of prosperous regions may have social and economic needs as great as the SDAs in the assisted areas, regional policy seems unable to help. The kind of changes required would raise fundamental issues within the national policy; the assisted areas would certainly emphasize the need to withhold inducements from the South East and Midlands and maintain controls over development to retain their advantage in this field. In addition, changes to the existing policy require substantial pressure which individual communities may not possess, and the administrative and legislative machinery is slow to adopt change.

A Working Group on regional policy comprising a number of the CDPs has attempted to make regional policy more sensitive to local economic and social problems by suggesting a number of experimental schemes, in keeping with the spirit of the CDP programme, with which regional policy might engage. However, central government has refused to take on experimental schemes, such as the provision of subsidies for travel to work for people living in the Upper Afan Valley in Glamorgan, as these fall outside the scope of regional policy (i.e. the 1972 Act subsidizes capital rather than labour, with the exception of the REP) and also, because if local CDP schemes were accepted this might lead to a demand for replication elsewhere. This demonstrates the essence of the weakness of regional policy; it cannot respond to specific situations because it is a national policy and because of its emphasis upon standardization of application. However, experimentation is necessary for innovations to be introduced into policy making, and once again, regional planning offers a form of action which can have this capability.

Regional policy is not sufficiently sensitive or flexible enough to cope with economic and social problems for two main reasons; first, it gives inadequate recognition of social problems, and their linkage to economic ones. While the social dimension of regional policy could be expanded to fill the gaps that at present exist, this development of the policy has been extremely slow to effect. Secondly, and more important for the role of regional planning, national regional policy has an administrative and legislative base which seems unable to be sufficiently sensitive to specific economic and social problems, or to keep pace with changes which are required in policies for their solution. This insensitivity of regional policy really stems not from any sinister or deliberate approach of central government, but rather its sheer inability to be informed adequately about what is happening and required in a wide range of very different regions within the country. The experience of regional policy to date points towards the need for greater decentralization of government from the national level.

On the basis of past experience, the ability of regional policy to provide solutions to individual and family problems has been seen to have many limitations. In so far as the solution of a wide range of problems requires regional action, given the potential of regional planning, then this form of action seems to offer the most hopeful means of success. The task for regional planning is clearly not an easy one. Regional policy and regional planning, as forms of planning action in principle, have different capabilities and can be expected to make individual and corporate contributions to meeting various societal needs. In practice though their contributions and capabilities, and thus the degree to which they substitute and complement one another, will depend on the relative strengths of national and regional decision making. This raises the whole question of the strength and capacity of institutions for regional planning action; this question is taken up in the following chapter.

Regional Policy, Regional Planning and the EEC

With Britain's entry to the EEC there are important implications for central government's regional policy, and consequently for regional planning. There are a number of crucial issues which together form the essence of the regional dimension of British entry to the EEC; first, the ways in which membership of the EEC will affect the nature or magnitude of British regional problems; secondly, the extent to which existing instruments of regional policy are likely to be compromised by accession to the Treaty of Rome; and thirdly, the nature of Community regional policy to which Britain is likely to be committed in the long run as a consequence of membership of the Community.[38]

At present there is no common EEC regional policy, although the reduction of regional differentials is one of the fundamental objectives of the Treaty of Rome. However, in its Report of May 1973 on the regional problems in the Community, the Commission of the European Communities emphasized that members had agreed to co-ordinate their regional policies and establish a Regional Development Fund before December 31st 1973[39]; unfortunately, progress has been slower than was anticipated. The purpose of the Report was not only to examine the main regional problems in the enlarged Community, but also to present the ideas of the Commission for a Community regional policy.

The implementation of a common Community regional policy might be expected to place further constraints upon the flexibility of individual member's policies; not only will Britain's regional policy have to be standarized in a national context but in an international one as well. While member states of the EEC are free to use their own national funds for their own regional policies, Article 93 instructs the Commission constantly to examine all systems of aid existing in member states. The EEC Commission has already taken action against member states because of regional aid policy. In 1971 the Commission took action against the Belgian regional aid programme contained in the industrial expansion law, against Germany for the aid which it gave to industry in the Ruhr, and against aid given by Italy to the extreme north west which borders Austria and Yugoslavia. In the case of Italy, for example, the subsidy given to industry was held to distort competition within the EEC and thereby banned under Article 92 of the Rome Treaty.

The European Commission, in formulating and implementing a Community regional policy has examined the choice of areas used for national regional policies. The coverage of assisted areas in Britain is not out of line with that of the members of the Community. For example, whereas 27 per cent of the population of the UK live in assisted areas, in France, Italy and Belgium, the figures are 40 per cent, 38 per cent, and 35 per cent respectively. It seems, therefore, that fears that the assisted areas in Britain are too widely drawn to satisfy the Community appear to be unfounded. It should be noted, however, that whereas the assisted areas in Britain, in terms of population at least, are predominantly urban industrial areas, the assisted areas in the Community states are predominantly agricultural. This, together with historical and social differences, makes comparisons between regional policies of Britain and the Six difficult in any meaningful way. In October 1973 the European Commission defined the 'central' and 'peripheral' areas which will be eligible for aid from the Common Market regional development fund, which, it is hoped, will have resources of some £1,200 million in the first three years. Basically, two general criteria must be satisfied by all regions from which projects are put up to Brussels for aid. They must be included in a national system of regional aids, and they must have a gross domestic product per head below the Community average. In Britain, it seems likely that all the assisted areas will be eligible for benefit from the Fund, certainly the Development Areas and SDAs.

The importance of regional disparities in the Common Market are recognized in relation to both the application of the common agricultural policy (Article 39(2)), and the free movement of labour (Article 49(d)) which seeks to equate labour supply with demand to avoid unemployment in the various regions. In addition, Article 80 provides for account to be taken of the requirements of an appropriate regional policy in application of the Common Transport Policy. Articles 123 and 128 provide for the setting up of the European Social Fund which provides assistance for retraining and resettling workers. It also grants aid to workers whose employment is reduced or totally suspended (important changes have been approved recently which will lead to increased funds being made available for this purpose). The other major reference to regional policy is contained in Articles 129 and 130 which established the European Investment Bank, one of whose major tasks is to finance projects designed to promote expansion in the less developed regions.

Regional planning authorities might expect to supplement their resources by drawing upon the various funds of the EEC. In Wales, for example, industries which provide work for redundant steelworkers, following the British Steel Corporation's plans to reduce 18,000 steel jobs by 1980 in the Shotton, Ebbw Vale and Cardiff areas, are eligible to apply for loans from the £20 million European Coal and Steel Community Fund. The ECSC Fund was also used to compensate the dependants of the miners killed in disasters at Markham Colliery in Derbyshire, and Lofthouse Colliery, Yorkshire, in 1973. The EEC possesses a number of other agencies for dealing with regional problems within the Community, including the European Social Fund, and the European Agricultural Guidance and Guarantee Funds (FEOGA). The European Social Fund promotes labour mobility between occupations and regions by reimbursing 50 per cent of the expenses incurred by member states on the retraining and resettlement of workers. The United Kingdom has been allocated £31 million from the European Social Fund, which will be handled by the Department of

Employment, although the areas which are to receive assistance from the social fund are yet to be decided. The FEOGA provides assistance to projects of structural improvement, and favours low income, agricultural areas in the south of Italy, France and Germany. The European Investment Bank might be expected to play an important role in solving regional problems; the Bank has already found that in most cases the industrialist is influenced more by infrastructure and environmental considerations than the value of cash handouts. The European institutions may play an important role in the development of national regional policies of member governments.

The future of regional policy in an integrated Europe might be expected to increase its focus upon the market price philosophy inherent in the whole Common Market concept. The implications of this are likely to determine the nature of regional policy in the future. Any policy instruments which directly affect the cost structure of particular enterprises or industries will clearly conflict with the *modus operandi* of the market system. It might be expected, therefore, that entry to the EEC will maintain, or even enhance, the economic content and emphasis in national regional policies.

The concern for regional planning, given the context of a strong national regional policy, and an emerging Community regional policy, stems from the lack of institutions to articulate regional action, and the increasing dominance of national and international institutions over decision making which attempts to meet local and regional needs. If regional institutions were more of a force as a countervailing power to those at national and international level, then the solution of urgent economic, social and environmental problems in the regions might be realized more readily. Given the context of an EEC regional policy, it seems extremely likely that the relationship of national regional policy to regional planning as forms of planning action will become a major focus of attention in the years ahead.

References

1   See, for example, McCrone, G., *Regional Policy in Britain* (Allen and Unwin, 1969), and *Regional Policy for Ever?* by Hallett, G. Randall, P. and West, E. G., Institute of Economic Affairs, Readings 11, 1973.

2   This confusion can be seen in many cases, for example in IEA Readings 11, 1973 op cit, page 13, where the two terms regional policy and regional planning are used very loosely.

3   The Glamorgan Planning Study, 1965, Glamorgan CC.

4   See, for example, (a) *The National Plan*, Chapter 8. Cmnd. 2764. September (HMSO, 1965) (b) *The Task Ahead: An Economic Assessment to 1972*, Chapter 9.

5   See, a range of White Papers and debates in the House of Commons. White Papers: *Investment Incentives*, Cmnd. 4516, October 1970, and *Industrial and Regional Development*, Cmnd. 4942, March 1972. For reports of debates in Hansard, see, for example, (a) Friday 19th February 1971, and Monday June 11th 1973 debates on the Northern Region; (b) Friday 5th March 1971, debate on the Investment Grants Bill, and (c) Friday 12th March 1971 and Monday June 11th 1973 on regional policy.

6   For a concise discussion of the two main schools of thought on the approach to be adopted by central governments, i.e. the 'national demand approach' which asserts that in the long run the free market mechanism creates an optimal spatial distribution of economic activity; and the alternative hypothesis, the 'theory of planned adjustment', which assumes that regional problems persist precisely because competitive forces don't create an optimal spatial distribution of economic activity, see Cameron, G. C. *The Regional Problem in the USA, Some Reflections on a Viable Federal Strategy*, Regional Studies Association, Vol. 2, No. 2, 1968.

7   Confederation of British Industry, *Reshaping Regional Policy: An Analysis of Present Policy and Proposals for the Future*, 1972.

8   For an assessment of regional differentials in Britain *vis-a-vis* other countries, see Brown, A. J. 'Regional Economics, with Special Reference to the UK', *Economic Journal*, December 1969, and Kaldor, N. 'The Case for Regional Policies', *Scottish Journal of Political Economy*, November 1970.

9   Motion moved by Mr. Urwin, MP, Hansard for 25th June 1973, op. cit.

10 Part of speech made by Mr. Grimond in the Commons debate on EEC regional policy, 26th June 1973.

11 See proceedings of debate on EEC regional policy at the European Parliament in Strasbourg, on 18th October 1973 especially the speech by Mr. R. Johnston, MP for Inverness.

12 This awareness is illustrated in the report of the Organization for Economic Co-operation and Development 'Regional Policies in Fifteen Industrialised OECD Countries', Paris, 1970.

13 See, for example, 1972 Report of the CBI, op. cit.

14 1971/72 Expenditure Committee (Trade and Industry Sub-Committee) Vol. 1. pp 56/57; extract from paper 'British Regional Policy. A Critique' Allen, K., presented to Seminar on Regional Development, held at Peterlee New Town, October 18-19th 1973.

15 op. cit.

16 See, Government Financial Aids to Geographical Mobility in OECD Countries, Paris 1967. In particular, the Swedish government has recognized the need to regard regional and employment policies as a single entity and not as separate alternatives. See, Swedish Labour Market Policy 1972/73. National Labour Market Board. Sweden.

17 op. cit.

18 *Incentives for Industry in the Areas for Expansion,* (DTI, 1973).

19 Stillwell, F. J. B., 'Regional Growth and Structural Adaptation', *Urban Studies,* June 1969.

20 Moore, B. and Rhodes, J. 'Evaluating the Effects of British Regional Economic Policy', *Economic Journal,* March 1973. See especially, Appendix A — 'Measuring the Major Elements of Government Regional Economic Policy'.

21 *The Movement of Manufacturing Industry in the United Kingdom,* Board of Trade (HMSO, 1968).

22 op. cit.

23 The GLC has estimated that half a million jobs will be lost in London 1966-76. Also on this topic, see 'Industrial Development Certificates and Control of Growth of Employment in SE England', Holmans, A. E., *Urban Studies,* November 1964.

24 (a) White Paper, *The Economic and Financial Objectives of the Nationalised Industries,* Cmnd. 1337, 1961.
(b) White Paper, *A Review of the 1961 Paper,* Cmnd. 3437, 1967.

25 *Wales: Employment and the Economy,* 1972, Welsh Council. Welsh Office.

26 Thomas, R., 'Aycliffe to Cumbernauld: A Case Study of Seven New Towns in their Regions', PEP Broadsheet 516, 1969.

27 *Report of the Hunt Committee on Intermediate Areas,* Cmnd. 3998, April 1969.

28 op. cit.

29 White Paper, *Investment Incentives,* Cmnd. 4516, October 1970. (HMSO, 1970).

30 *Abstract of Regional Statistics,* 1970.

31 op. cit.

32 Welsh Council, 1972 op. cit.

33 'CDP: A General Outline', Background Paper, Home Office, 1971.

34 See Working Papers of the Glamorgan/Home Office CDP, especially 'Jobholding and Jobgetting' June 1972, and the 1972 and 1973 Reports to the Management Committee.

35 *Marginal Regions: Essays on Social Planning*, Ed. Broady, M., (Bedford Square Press, 1973).

36 *Wales: The Way Ahead*, Welsh Office (HMSO, July 1967).

37 Kilbrandon Report, *Royal Commission on the Constitution 1969-73*, Volume 1, Report, Cmnd. 5460 (HMSO, 1973).

38 These issues have been considered in greater depth by Nevin, E. in *Europe and the Regions, Three Banks Review*. June 1972, Also see, 'Regional Policies in Britain — and in Europe', a survey by the North East Development Council 1971.

39 Report on the Regional Problems in the Enlarged Community. Commission of the European Communities, Brussels, 3rd May 1973.

5   Regional Planning Institutions

Introduction

Regional policy is a form of decision making undertaken at the national level in which action is applied to the whole or some part of the national space. Regional planning is quite different and involves decision making at the regional level in which action is applied to the whole or some part of a regional space. It follows that regional forms of public institution are required in order to generate these actions and to sustain a decision making process, and in this chapter the different types of public governmental and administrative institution which have been developed and proposed for regions are discussed. The main focus is on first identifying these alternative institutional models and secondly on a critical assessment of their respective strengths and weaknesses.

The rationale for this appraisal of regional planning institutions is self evident. If regional planning actions are to be developed and promoted then it is necessary to inquire into the different forms of institution capable of these actions. If regional planning actions are to be improved in effectiveness then it is necessary to inquire into and to be sensitive to the weaknesses, constraints and potential capabilities of these different forms of institution.

There is an additional but more specific reason for undertaking this institutional appraisal. This derives from the popular view that regional planning institutions are invariably weak institutions. Kuklinski, for example, has argued: 'If we would try to find a common feature in the agencies responsible for regional planning in various countries, then behind the impressive display of differences in political and social backgrounds, in managerial solutions and in technical perfections, we would find one basic common feature, the regional planning agency, as a rule, has only an advisory capacity in the process of investment decisions.'[1]

The weakness implied in this statement is echoed in the writings of many commentators. If this view is valid then it follows that here is an additional reason for regional planners, perhaps even more than other planners, to be knowledgeable about and sensitive to institutional issues. Through this knowledge and sensitivity some of the weaknesses may be tempered and longer run improvement achieved.

Following on from a discussion of the main institutional alternatives, consideration is given to the character of the institutional environment at the regional level. In particular the number and nature of private and quasi governmental institutions which organize themselves on a regional scale are discussed. These warrant consideration because it may be contended that they influence the working and performance of the core public institution and the quality of its regional planning actions. For a similar reason attention is also paid to the distant but powerful institutions of government at the local, national and supra national levels.

Throughout the discussion is orientated to Great Britain and developed within the context of the governmental system and political culture of this country. However, attention is also paid to institutional developments in Europe, the USA and the Third World, particularly to those developments which might have a potentially wider application.

Alternative Institutional Models

Five regional institutional formulas can be readily identified in the British context and these are:

1 Administrative decentralization by central government.
2 Administrative devolution from central government.
3 *Ad hoc* regional institution created by central government.
4 Regional or provincial government.
5 Inter agency institution created by local governments.

It is possible to identify variations of each of these main models and combinations between them have also been conceived. Some of these main variations and combinations are identified in the succeeding discussion on each of the five main models.

ADMINISTRATIVE DECENTRALIZATION

Comment has already been made to the effect that, although the regional idea in Great Britain was first put forward as a solution to local government problems, it was taken up and implemented by central government as a solution to central government problems.[2] Administrative decentralization to regional offices by central government departments increasingly gained favour, during the 1940s, as a means of reducing administrative overloading at the centre and of gaining better information about local conditions and the effects of policies on those conditions. The need to reduce this overloading and gain this information were in turn a product of the increasing role of government in societal affairs. Currently these regional arms of central government departments comprise the most important institutional structure for generating regional planning action in Great Britain.

The initial movement towards decentralization began in the early decades of the century and it was spurred on by crises in the form of World War I, the General Strike and then World War II.[3] During the latter period a regional government structure was devised for implementation in the event of the breakdown of central government. This institution took the form of 12 appointed Regional Commissioners who in the light of this eventuality would have taken the place of central government in the regions and who would thus have controlled the regional or Divisional Officers of central government departments.

The Commissioners were viewed critically both because they posed a potential threat to local government and because of their lack of political accountability.[4] For these reasons they were eliminated following the end of the war. Even though it is not given very much consideration in the British context, the appointment of a Commission or commissioner is one possible means for securing regional planning action.[5]

The regionalization of central government departments which was stimulated by war conditions in general and by the Regional Commissioner contingency arrangement continued to develop in the immediate post-war years. In 1946 the regionalization efforts of individual departments were further regularized and standardized through the Treasury's creation of Standard Regions to which they were expected to conform.

At the same time interdepartmental organization continued to be strengthened in the form of interdepartmental committees of senior officials; these included Regional Physical Planning Committees, Regional Building Committees and Regional Distribution of Industry Panels. The Regional Boards for Industry were rather different in that they not only offered the basis for more coherence between the work of individual ministries, but they also provided a means of contact between government departments and industry in the regions, and they were formed of representatives of both.

The Boards were, in fact, one of the very few points of contact between the life of the region and the emerging regional machinery. It is particularly noteworthy that local authorities had no formal link with the regional committees. Indeed there was substantial antipathy by local government to the regional machinery. This antipathy derived from the fact that regional administrators had little autonomy and consequently referred critical issues from

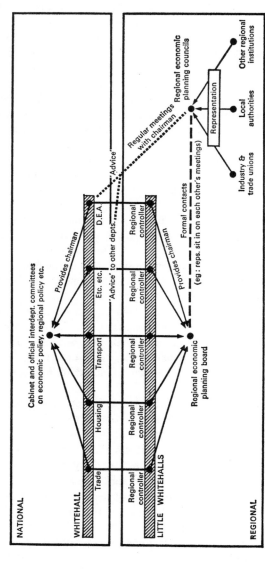

The Structure of Regional Planning Machinery (in England only)

Fig. 5.1   The structure of regional planning machinery (England only).
Source: Mackintosh, J.P. *The Devolution of Power* (Pelican, 1968).

local government up to central government level. The regional offices were consequently viewed as a new frustrating level of officialdom interposed between them and the centre of decision making.[6]

In consequence when the regional offices of central government were closed down by the Conservative Government in the 1950s, there was no outcry from local government authorities. More surprisingly, when the regional offices were re-created in a new and strengthened form by the Labour Government in the 1960s, no serious attempt was made to gain the confidence of local authorities and to ensure them a proper place in the revived institution.

The current regional machinery of central government remains basically that created by the Labour Government in 1964 (Figures 5.1 and 5.2). This involved the establishment of 11 economic planning regions, each with an Economic

Fig. 5.2   Economic planning regions.
Offices of Economic Planning Councils and Boards.
Economic Council set up by Northern Ireland government.
Source: Mackintosh, J.P. *The Devolution of Power* (Pelican, 1968).

Planning Council made up of nominated individuals and Economic Planning Boards made up of the regional representatives of the main government departments, and chaired by the regional representative of the simultaneously created Department of Economic Affairs.[7]

The Council consists of part time members, appointed as individuals and not representatives. Approximately one third are chosen from industry, one third from local government and one third from prominent regional institutions, for example, universities. The Councils were initially charged with three tasks. First to aid in the formulation of a regional plan, secondly to advise on steps necessary for its implementation, and finally to advise on the regional implications of national economic policy. The Councils have no executive power. The Boards consist of interdepartmental committees of 15 to 20 civil servants, and their tasks were initially to aid in the formulation of regional plans and to co-ordinate the work of the departments concerned with the implementation of these plans.

A considerable number of criticisms have been made of this machinery, and many of these illustrate the limitations and difficulties of a regional planning institution formed through administrative decentralization.

The Boards are the least innovative part of the new institutional arrangement for they are little more than a more elaborate expression of the interdepartment committees that developed after World War II. Although similar in structure to these committees, they were nevertheless charged with a radically new task, namely to prepare regional plans, and this is the crux of their limitation for they are required to produce a new horizontal synthesis (a regional plan) within an unchanged vertical decision making structure. The regional directors or controllers of each central government department were not given any new powers of discretion and the Board itself has no more powers than that possessed by its individual members. Each official accordingly acts strictly in keeping with central directive. Thus as Cross has emphasized the regional controllers are regional in the sense of being informed about regional views and circumstances but not in the sense of possessing a discretion which is readily susceptible to regional pressures.[8]

The underlying issue here is the impossibility of significant discretion at the regional level within the context of administrative and not political decentralization. The Minister in Whitehall alone remains accountable for the decisions taken in regional offices, and thus the authority of a regional controller must remain strictly limited. The product of this arrangement is not only that civil servants are centrally orientated and directed in decision making, but ultimately centre orientated in terms of careers and motivations. Thus it is frequently asserted that regional civil servants are mainly concerned to please their masters in Whitehall so that they may return from exile in the provinces. Under these circumstances they may not even develop a regional perspective let alone a regional commitment. Nevertheless, experience of sitting on the Boards may have helped to begin to introduce a greater regional orientation and outlook amongst their members. In terms of actual effect, however, Self has suggested that they have achieved little more than co-ordinate and adjust matters of detail.[9]

Although more of an innovation than the Boards the essence of the idea expressed in the Councils had been discussed over a considerable period of time. A number of commentators, for example, had argued that the Regional Boards for Industry should have been expanded to include local authority representation in the post-war years. Despite this the Councils revealed a number of basic flaws when they were created, suggesting that they were intended as no more than a temporary measure and a stage in the process of regional devolution.[10]

The Councils, particularly in their early period, inadequately related to local government institutions. The local—regional hiatus noted earlier rather than being eliminated was revived by the new machinery. Local planning authorities thus felt threatened by it and joined together to form Standing Conferences to withstand the threat. This was a poor start for the Councils who could only hope to advise these authorities and whose active co-operation was necessary for plan implementation. The fault at least in part appears to have been due to the assumption by the designers of the new system that local authorities would simply co-operate automatically, and fit into any plan produced by the new machinery and endorsed by central government.[11] Their significance in terms of their weight of composition on the Council was also possibly underrated. George Brown, the DEA's minister was particularly concerned that the Councils should not represent local authorities but have a character of their own. Also, Painter, in his study of the West Midlands Economic Planning Council, suggests that membership of this body in terms of domination by members of the Confederation of British Industries and Trades Union Councils simply reflected the established web of central government relations at central government level.[12]

These points would again seem to be indicative of a basic problem associated with administrative decentralization, namely the difficulty of institutional initiatives which derive from central government and from a central government perspective, adequately and sensitively articulating with local agencies.[13]

In addition to the weak relationship to the powerful local government machine, the Councils also suffer because their members sit as individuals not as delegates and are unable to commit interests, local authority or otherwise, to any course of action. The Councils have also found it difficult to effect any regional alignment of interests due to their non elective base and their role as regional advisory bodies to central government concerned to achieve central government goals.

As well as being weakly related down into the life of the region the Councils are weakly related into the actual government machine. Their advisory status means that their actions and pressures can be readily ignored and there is ample evidence that their views have been overridden and little evidence that they have elicited significant decisions from central government.

In addition to these weaknesses the Councils not only have no-staff or finance of their own but they are all part timers, usually combining a number of other public offices with that of membership of the Council. The 26 members of the South West Economic Planning Council, for example, held 56 positions in public and private voluntary bodies at the time they were surveyed by Smith.[14] This most probably further denies the Council leverage over affairs within the region and at central government level and encourages a dependence on civil service briefing. For all these reasons the Councils are best characterized as weak appendages to the Boards.

Despite these shortcomings, the Councils have undoubtedly stimulated regional discussion of regional issues and they have fostered a stock of regional knowledge, and had a marginal effect on some policy changes by central government. Many of the difficulties of relationship with local planning authorities have been overcome and albeit inadvertently the latter have been brought closer together in the form of regional conferences. In at least one instance of creative institution building by the new regional machinery the formula of the Councils has been repeated at the sub regional level and in this sense they have provided a useful precedent.[15]

Many of the weaknesses of the Boards and Councils briefly noted here would appear to be generally acknowledged, but as yet these are either tolerated or being modified through relatively *ad hoc* tinkering and changes of emphasis. In January 1972 it was announced by the Conservative government that regional strategies were to be produced and that the responsibility for these strategies was to be tripartite, involving the Economic Planning Councils, local planning authorities and central government. At the same time it was determined that the regional director of the Department of the Environment should handle an increased range of decisions formerly dealt with by Whitehall.

Also as part of the newly created Industrial Development Executive within the Department of Trade and Industry, Regional Industrial Directors have been established with 'an important degree of devolved authority' in order to stimulate industrial expansion in the regions. The directors are to be advised by Regional Industrial Development Boards.[16,17]

The archetypal regional planner no doubt considers that administrative decentralization is a far from satisfactory arrangement and that an institution altogether more autonomous and powerful is to be preferred. But at least as far as Great Britain is concerned, this is the institution which has been able to develop and become established. Over and above this pragmatic point, it is perhaps too an arrangement which has not yet been fully exploited. It could develop further through the inclusion of departments not at present in the regions, through Board members committing more time and effort to regional and Board affairs, and thus through the development of a greater regional outlook amongst civil servants. This in turn would help to ensure that central government was more widely and more deeply penetrated by regional information which could increasingly come to be used more sensitively to inform decision on regional issues, and to initiate central government policy changes. In order to achieve these improvements the Boards need to be fired with new directives, directives which have been lacking since the demise of the DEA and its national planning exercise.

A further component in a strategy for improving the performance of administrative decentralization in Great Britain is further study of foreign and especially European experience. Brief reference to the French approach to the

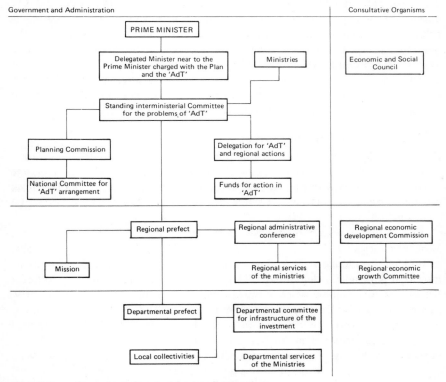

Fig. 5.3   French regional planning institutions.
Source: Viot, P. 'The Process of Interregional Plan Formation in France', Chapter 11 in *Issues in Regional Planning,* Dunham, D.D. and Hilhorst J.G.M. (eds.) (Mouton, 1971).

problems of administrative decentralization may serve to illustrate and underline this general point.[18] Under the regional reform of 1964 the French government created a series of wide ranging innovations. These included the creation of advisory councils, Commissions de Developpement Economique Regionale (CODER) on which indeed the British Councils are modelled. More interestingly however, the CODER's advise a powerful regional prefect appointed by the Prime Minister. The regional prefect is also the prefect of the Department in which the capital of the region is situated and thus penetrates into the life of the region. He has also a considerable degree of discretion in welding together vertically compartmentalized ministries, he has the duty to 'animate and supervise' the activity of the department prefects, the directors of public institutions and mixed corporations (Figure 5.3).

The underlying lesson here may be that it is only an individual, and a powerful individual who can hope to handle and manipulate the subtle and complex patterns of pressures that are inherent in the administrative decentralization formula. Such an appointment as previously noted tends to be ruled out by commentators as inappropriate to Britain but at this stage in the development of regional planning institutions the onus is to open out and explore the alternatives rather than prematurely to foreclose them. It is encouraging in this respect that identification of these alternatives will become increasingly possible as European countries come to recognize their common problems and to pool and systematize their experiences.[19]

ADMINISTRATIVE DEVOLUTION

Given that one of the fundamental limitations of administrative decentralization arises from the vertical accountability of civil servants to their minister, then one is led to consider how this pattern of political accountability at the national level can be changed in order to overcome this limitation and to realize horizontal co-ordination.

Two solutions suggest themselves. In the first place it is possible to appoint a Minister of Regional Planning at the central level. Such a Minister would be able in principle to induce at central government level a degree of regional thinking into each government department. This formula has in fact been tried in Great Britain: as for example when Edward Heath was created Minister of Industry, Trade and Regional Development. Proposals for this type of solution continue to be made. However, it is clearly a formula which is more a vehicle for regional policy making rather than for regional planning. One Ministry can hardly be expected to impose horizontal co-ordination at the regional level between different departments without confusing the pattern of responsibility of the civil servants at this level: to make all regional officials responsible to one Minister is a possible solution but this would be an overwhelming burden for one Minister to sustain. The way out of this impasse is to limit the range of functions involved. Thus Luttrell has suggested that such a Ministry would be essentially involved with land-use, local government and location of industry policy. Such an approach severely circumscribes the scope for regional planning action.[20]

The second solution therefore presents itself, that of creating a Minister within each region. This is at once a more amenable administrative arrangement, and also a more sensitive political arrangement allowing individual Ministers to be responsible for a graspable range of functions, to be close to and familiar with their charge and to be accessible to regional pressures and to be able to fight for these at national government level. This formula is to be found in both Wales and Scotland and again proposals have been made to expand it to all the regions of Great Britain.

However, those assessments that have been made of the Scottish and Welsh Offices have not been altogether favourable. Both Mackintosh and Rowlands point out that national government policies and practises are little changed by this formula and that few specifically regional adaptations are made to these. The fundamental reason is that the regional minister has one focus of political responsibility, namely the Cabinet and Parliament, and any regional shifts and biases are, therefore, heavily constrained by the political consideration of the implications of these on the remainder of the nation. Thus Mackintosh has suggested that 'The great pride of the civil service is not that it has developed special methods of a different emphasis in Scotland but rather that no gap can be found between Edinburgh and London methods so that no politically awkward questions can be raised.'[22]

Both Mackintosh and Rowlands also stress that administrative devolution has not assuaged the need for more local control and decision making by the nationalists and others within these regions.

Rowlands identifies a number of possible modifications to the machinery. These include the development of opportunities for more democratic pressure to be applied from the region, including, for example, the creation of a more powerful Welsh Grand Committee, the region's grouping of Members of Parliament; and the establishment of a Select Committee for Welsh Affairs. Although perhaps welcome in themselves they do not resolve the fundamental issue.

· This issue is that, under administrative devolution, Ministers are responsible to the electorate through a nationally elected assembly. It is an issue, which Mackintosh and others go on to argue, that can only be resolved through making the Minister(s) responsible to the regional electorate through a regionally elected assembly. This provincial government model is considered at a later stage.

THE *AD HOC* REGIONAL INSTITUTION
The creation by central government of a new special institution in order to embrace and tackle some regional problem is a potentially far more effective

institutional formula than devolution or decentralization. Through an autonomous or semi autonomous institution, extra resources can be channelled and directed towards problems occurring in supra urban space. The *ad hoc* innovative institution is at once powerful, transforming and dramatic.

The *ad hoc* regional institution is found in a large number of countries. In the USA, for example, there is the Tennessee Valley Authority, in Brazil the Sudene, in Italy the Cassa per il Mezzogiorno, in Venezuela the Corporacion Venezolana de Guyana, in Britain the Highlands and Islands Development Board and in Germany the SVR. These institutions all represent attempts to deal with deeply ingrained and spatially extensive problems. The Cassa, for example, was established in order to channel resources to the whole of the impoverished southern half of Italy, and the Sudene to tackle the drought ridden North East of Brazil, an area of over 25 million people. The Highlands and Islands Development Board has the task of achieving economic renovation in an area totalling one sixth of the land area of the United Kingdom.

In addition to their extensive territorial scope these institutions are also usually given very significant and wide ranging executive powers, relative freedom and autonomy in the initiation and operation of these powers, and a substantial budget to help give expression to them. Thus the Highlands and Islands Development Act 1964 gave the Board power to acquire land compulsorily, to carry out projects itself, to run its own industrial and commercial undertakings and to support and stimulate economic activity through the provision of financial inducements. It receives an annual grant in aid from central government currently in excess of £3.5 millions. The Cassa per il Mezzogiorno was brought into being in 1950 to administer a large expansion of extraordinary public works and to do this outside the confines of traditional slow working bureaucracy. It was voted a sum of 1,000 billion lire for a period of 10 years but this sum has constantly been increased and so too has its realm of intervention.[23]

The innovative regional institution frequently experiences problems regarding its relationship to the population within its area. This is so because the agency is essentially designed by central government and the usual difficulty of adequately taking into account local conditions and feelings may here be added to by the fact that the innovative institution is frequently the product of political manoeuvering behind closed doors. The regional population thus may have little say in its design as well as in its running. This issue is highlighted in one of the few sociological studies made of these institutions, namely Selznick's 'TVA and the Grass Roots'.[4] Selznick hypothesizes that the TVA's grass roots doctrine must be seen, in part at least, as the result of the subsequent need to come to terms with powerful local interests. Moreover he shows how in implementing this doctrine through various forms of co-optation, the choices of the authority became seriously curtailed by the co-opted groups and its ability to act as a front line conservation agency blunted.

The Corporacion Venezolana de Guyana (CVG) has quite consciously sought to resist regional political pressures. This is so because of its fundamental concern to retain a politically neutral style, orientated to national goals in order to free itself of a turbulent political environment and maintain its existence. In this case, therefore, a political strategem has added to the difficulties of articulating with the local situation.[25] And not surprisingly Rodwin has commented that the CVG has produced intensified feelings of political inadequacy and anxiety amongst regional groups and individuals.[26]

The American political culture is evident in the way *ad hoc* regional commissions have been formed in this country: the emphasis is very much on local initiative and local attitudes in determining the incidence and particular territorial scope of these institutions.[27,28] Strong emphasis is given too to the role of local groups in the development process. The Appalachian Regional Commission is in the process of creating local development organizations made up of groups of counties to prepare their own plans for development. However, Wildner has admitted that the fundamental issue of how to engage with the local population so that ultimately it is them who decide the future course of the regions development has remained untouched.[29]

The Cassa per il Mezzogiorno has also developed an attempt to articulate local groups and interests and to bring them into the development process.[26] This revolves around the creation of local consortia made up of local authorities and local chambers of commerce and trade, who are responsible for formulating industrial development plans which may then be supported by the Cassa. The latter has, however, had to increasingly take over this local role where local groups have lacked the necessary initiative and skill.

Even where the high powered central government agency does overcome the problem of relating to the local population, difficulties may well arise regarding its relationships with central government ministries. *Ad hoc* institutions usually supplement rather than replace other central government functions and activities, and this together with their autonomy often poses severe relational problems. Thus the Cassa frequently engaged in expenditure for which it was not intended because some ministries saw it incorrectly as a substitute for their work: at the same time where the Cassa did establish working relationships it became constrained by the procedures of the ministry concerned, thus failing to exploit its flexibility. These problems gave rise to various reforms in 1965. It is intended that the creation of a Minister for Southern Development and consequent interministerial changes will overcome these interagency problems.[30]

Similar problems have been experienced by the CVG which has found it hard to get funds for projects which are the responsibility of other government agencies and the weight of its strategy lies towards those areas requiring limited co-ordination with other ministries for both administrative reasons and the political reasons noted earlier.

One less commonly identified problem may be mentioned tentatively. This concerns the apparent inclination of at least some of these institutions to adopt preconceptions and perspectives of the nature of the problem they confront and for these to become ingrained into its operation. These preconceptions shape its very design and even where that design is relatively open and flexible they may influence its work style. Thus the TVA may have become an essentially hydrological agency not solely due to external political constraints but to internal administrative and technical assumptions about the problems of the valley and its role in changing these.

Mackay[31] has criticized the Highlands and Islands Development Board for its emphasis on economic as opposed to social and cultural factors in development. Certainly the Board's invidious labelling of the latter as non economic and the relatively small proportion of the budget allocated to these give some tentative grounds for the criticism.[32] Valid or not in this context, the fundamental point is that like all institutions the *ad hoc* innovative institution operates on the basis of certain assumptions but that in order to establish the institution these are repeatedly and heavily emphasized: it may accordingly be difficult to throw them off later especially given the administrative and sometimes too the political autonomy of these institutions which preserves the assumptions from challenge. In keeping with this MacMurray has suggested that the New York State Development Corporation and these *ad hoc* institutions in general may never get further than tackling visible and pressing symptoms rather than root causes.[33]

There is an additional way in which root issues may not be tackled by these institutions despite their apparently radical nature. The point here is that they can act as a substitute for and thus serve to delay more fundamental reform within government institutions. In other words the fundamental problem may lie in the poor structure and performance of the main established institutions and the new institution may serve simply to cover up this fundamental weakness.

Despite these problems the power of the *ad hoc* institution ensures that it is a formula to which regional planners are favourably disposed. The problems identified here are, therefore, more likely to be viewed as challenges rather than as constituting a fundamental case against this type of institution. Although a strict evaluation of their achievement is not possible the available evidence does provide support for this view. Thus the Highlands and Islands Board over the seven years to December 1972 invested £10.2m in the region and private enterprise £16.9m. Some 8,000 jobs have been created and interestingly and probably in strong comparison with the centralist Regional Economic Councils and Boards, 80 per cent of approved financial assistance has gone to indigeneous enterprise. For the first time in 100 years the decline in the population of the Highlands has been arrested.[34] McCrone[35] has claimed that it has indeed had a greater impact on the Highlands and Islands than any other institution. Evidence from other experiences generally tends to portray a good record of their achievement.[36]

In Britain this form of institution has generated considerable professional and academic interest. One suggestion particularly in tune with it is Self's proposal that New Town Development Corporations should be adopted on a regional scale.[37] It is also an institutional formula which has become an idea in good currency in political circles whenever solutions for problem regions are debated.

The fundamental significance of the *ad hoc* institution would appear to lie in the fact that problems may develop in national space in a way which fails to fit the institutional structure of a society, and in such cases a new institution may be required in order properly to confront these problems. In terms of the tentative theory advanced earlier, it would appear that the innovative institution is needed because, on occasion, social and economic space may fail to match political space. This, of course, may be the case however strong and coherent a system of regional government and administration exists in a given situation. A point visually dramatized by the incidence of the regional commissions in the USA (Figure 5.4).

Despite this, it is an institutional device which suffers from severe disadvantages particularly in terms of its potentially undemocratic eruption into society, its often tentative relationship with the people it is designed to serve, and with other government agencies. For these reasons it has been suggested by Pastore[38] that there is a need to develop clear criteria for determining where it is an appropriate institutional solution. Pastore, for example, has suggested that it should be resorted to only where there is a marked discrepancy between an area's actual and potential level of development, where its sphere of operation can be clearly separated from those of established agencies, and where an area's development strategy as such clearly calls for unconventional methods. Others have emphasized that it is only likely to be implemented anyway when it touches deeply felt national sentiments.[39]

It would seem highly desirable that greater study should be made of these institutions both on an individual and comparative basis in order that their strengths and weaknesses may be assessed, their role and contribution more clearly explicated and their capability improved.[40]

PROVINCIAL GOVERNMENT

Provincial government is a term used here to embrace a wide range of institutions all of which are characterized by regionally elected assemblies which exercise control over executive functions or both legislative and executive functions. It is distinguished from the federal model which involves the transfer of sovereignty from the national parliament as for example in the USA, West Germany and India.[41] The provincial formula thus involves the devolution of

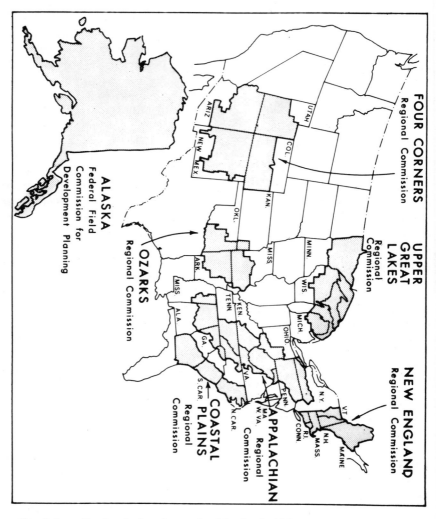

Fig. 5.4   Regional planning authorities in the USA.
Source: 'The Beginnings of a New Era. Regional Planning in the
USA', *JTPI*, May 1971.

power by central government but the degree of this power and the checks exercised over it preserve the essential unity of the state.

A number of fundamental social and political arguments are advanced in favour of some form of provincial government. In the first place regional elected government is a means of bringing power and control over decision making closer to people. It serves the democratic ideal of participation for its spreads out the opportunities for that participation. Secondly it also divides up power, protecting the individual from its over concentration. In Maas's terms, it adds an areal division of power to the traditional division between legislature, executive and judiciary.[42] It may be argued also that in order to serve the welfare of the population certain services need to be provided on a larger than urban scale, and that these in turn need to be controlled by the regional population. It was this particular argument which informed much of the early movement for regionalism in Great Britain. Local government units, it was argued, were too small in area and in terms of population thresholds to support efficient service provision, the continued creation since then of *ad hoc* boards and agencies at the regional scale has served to underline this argument.

Some of the points that are advanced against provincial government[43] include the argument that Britain enjoys a rich institutional structure which already articulates the individual into central government decision making[44] and that provincial government is no more than a diversion. It is argued too that it spells diversity whereas the population, particularly given high mobility rates, demands uniformity of standards between one region and another. Further, because of this and because of the lack of regional identity, it is pointed out there has been no popular demand for provincial government apart from the special cases of Wales and Scotland.[45] Other commentators have stressed the difficulties of predicting the far-reaching consequences of such a scheme;[46] its threat to national development planning;[47] and to national unity allowing the wealthy regions to forge ahead of the less fortunate regions;[48] the reluctance of the centre and centre politicians in particular to accept such a scheme; the difficulties of designing a scheme in terms of a clear understandable division of functions; and in terms of ensuring financial independence and financial accountability.

Despite these drawbacks there are examples of provincial government in the United Kingdom and a sequence of authoritative proposals continue to be made for such an institution.

Within the United Kingdom there have been until recently two institutions which fall within the provincial government category: these are the Greater London Council (GLC) created in 1963 and the Stormont parliament of Northern Ireland created in 1921 and terminated in 1972.

The directly elected Greater London Council exercises executive control over strategic physical planning including major roadbuilding and overspill schemes, housing development drainage and a number of other services. Within its area 32 borough councils exercise typical borough council functions including housing, personal social services and sewage; and land-use allocation functions.

Mackintosh has provided a recent and valuable assessment of the GLC.[49] He identifies a number of weaknesses. These include the inadequate division of functions between the GLC and the boroughs leading to confusion, constraints on the strategic planning work of the Council both in terms of traffic and land-use development, and the manner in which the typical precise over detailed controls on local government have been foisted on to the GLC. Early protagonists for provincial government in Great Britain such as Cole[50] saw the need for regional government very much in terms of an enlarged local government both in terms of scale and functions and in terms of internal methods of working, and it is interesting that Mackintosh is especially critical of the GLC from this point of view. More fundamentally, his criticisms point to the need for a rethink of the basic form which a regional institution should take and underline the difficulties of implementation of such an institution, many of the problems of the GLC stemming from the reluctance to give it too strong powers.[51]

The Stormont model is a much more complex institution and much more difficult to evaluate. Until 1972 Northern Ireland enjoyed a substantial degree of devolution with its own parliament and cabinet wielding extensive powers. These powers have amongst other things allowed a substantial amount of innovation to occur in the institutional structure of the region, including for example a distinctive education system, a highly successful Industrial Development organization within the Ministry of Commerce and a range of institutions to tackle distinctive health and housing problems. All of these are regarded by Oliver as successful aspects of public administration that might never have come into being without the encouragement of a regional parliament.[52]

Many of the fundamental assumptions of the 1920 Government of Ireland Act have been seriously challenged by subsequent experience and this particularly applies to the way in which powers and finance were divided under the Act.

Two assumptions in particular both of them fundamental to many federal solutions proved in Mackintosh's view to be too simplistic.[53] In the first place it was assumed that functions could be divided neatly into external and domestic functions; this has been made increasingly difficult given growth in the size and complexity of government and the exactitude of the division has not been conducive to sensitive adaptive changes with time. In the second place it was assumed that financially Northern Ireland should live off its own. This has resulted in the need to track down very complex financial flows in detail and in practice has led to the view that finance from central government is a subsidy or topping up thus permitting very detailed Treasury control.

The complexity that has grown up consequently has led in the view of Lawrence to the situation whereby 'nobody, it seems, outside a narrow circle of Ministers and civil servants can forecast whether departures from British practice are likely to be feasible in any particular case.'[54] It would seem from the Northern Ireland experience that cutting into the fabric of the unitary state requires a broader based set of assumptions than those that seemed applicable in the interwar period. Certainly some of the more recent and authoritative proposals for provincial government in the United Kingdom have learned from the Stormont experiment and adopt different sets of assumptions. Some of these provincial government proposals are considered below.

As part of its proposals for the reform of local government in England, a Royal Commission under Lord Redcliffe-Maud advocated the creation of a comprehensive system of Provincial Councils[55] (Figure 5.5). The main function of these councils was to be the creation of a broad economic land-use and investment framework for the planning and development policies of operational authorities. It was recommended that this provincial strategy should be binding on the main authorities within the province and that the council membership would be indirectly elected by authorities. It was also recommended that the council would take over the functions of the existing regional Sports, Arts and Economic Planning Councils. The Royal Commission recognized in the light of substantial devolution of central government powers, then under consideration by the Commission on the Constitution that the provincial councils could become directly elected. As they stood, however, the provincial councils were relatively weak bodies, their main strength being that they could substantially add to the weight of advice flowing from the regions to central government.

A much more substantial form of provincial government has been elaborated by Mackintosh (Figure 5.6). This proposal involves the creation of nine elected Regional Councils in England plus Elected Assemblies in Scotland and Wales with powers over all forms of intermediate government including, for example, highways, housing, agriculture, forestry, countryside amenities, police, fire, water supplies, river pollution, education and hospitals. The need to learn from the experience of Ireland is stressed and accordingly no attempt is made to allocate functions in their entirety 'it is unsuitable in modern times to try and allocate functions in their entirety, because there is a real popular pressure for uniformity of standards in some fields and the extent of this demand may alter rapidly'[56] and thus Mackintosh's approach is for central legislation to lay down major policy lines and then to leave the rest to the regional councils and assemblies. 'For instance in education the most appropriate method would be for the UK Parliament to pass an Act declaring that all state education must be fully compulsory to a certain age and that certain minimum standards of pay and qualifications for teachers must be maintained. Thereafter, the regional councils

THE NINE STANDARD TREASURY REGIONS

Fig. 5.5   Provincial council proposals of the Redcliffe-Maud Commission.
Source: *Local Government Reform, Report on Local Government in England,* Cmnd. 4039 (HMSO, 1969).

PROPOSED ELEVEN REGIONS

Fig. 5.6   Regional government proposals of J.P. Mackintosh..
Source: Mackintosh, J.P., *The Devolution of Power,* (Pelican, 1968).

would be empowered to organize and run all aspects of education, making, where necessary, subordinate legislation for their own region.'[57] Under this system the precise limits of responsibilities and powers between central government and regional government would not be fixed thus allowing continuing alterations to be made without incurring the confusion that has arisen in the Northern Ireland context.

The councils and assemblies would be directly elected and would be organized on a parliamentary model with a Prime Minister and Ministers responsible for departments: each council would recruit its own staff.

In terms of finance the regional governments might exercise a surcharge on personal income tax giving them their own source of revenue, but it would not be intended to raise much money in this or any other way within the region; most of the finance would come from central government on the basis of annual negotiations. The Treasury control implied by this scheme would be kept to a minimum and the regions would be free to switch resources between different items of expenditure once national minimum standards had been achieved.

Hanson and Walles[58] have queried the need for such an elaborate proposal for regional government and Hanson[59] in particular has underlined the almost complete absence of financial responsibility of the proposed authorities and the radical departure in the tradition of government which this implies. More extended discussion of Mackintosh's proposal has had to wait upon the report of the Commission on the Constitution.

The Commission on the Constitution

In 1969, in the context of a rising tide of Welsh and Scottish nationalism, a Royal Commission on the Constitution was established 'to examine the present functions of the central legislature and government in relation to the several counties, nations and regions of the United Kingdom' and to consider 'whether any changes are desirable in those functions or otherwise in present constitutional and economic relationships.' The majority report under the chairmanship of Lord Kilbrandon and a dissenting report produced by Lord Crowther-Hunt and Professor A.T. Peacock were published in 1973.[60]

The majority of the Commissioners under Kilbrandon quite consciously sought to circumscribe the very wide ranging terms of reference and they concentrated their detailed examination and recommendations on the issue of devolution, that is on the case for transferring the responsibility for government functions from the centre to new institutions in the regions. Lord Crowther-Hunt and Professor Peacock adopted a different interpretation of the terms of reference, and they offer a different diagnosis and prescription. Their dissenting report is considered following a discussion of the majority Kilbrandon report.

Kilbrandon concludes from the evidence that, although there is not serious dissatisfaction with the system of government in Great Britain, the population has less attachment to it than in the past and there is substantial and persistent discontent. This discontent is seen to arise from the feeling that there is too much centralization of government in London and that government as a whole is becoming insensitive, remote, or more generally less democratic. The Commissioners reporting under Kilbrandon go on to argue that, although it is not a complete solution to all the complaints and discontent identified, devolution would do much to reduce overcentralization and to strengthen democracy and would be a welcome response to national feeling in Scotland and Wales (Figure 5.7).

The majority report accordingly proposes the establishment of a directly elected assembly for Scotland and Wales. However, the Commissioners disagree on the nature and extent of the powers that should be conferred on these assemblies. A majority of the signatories to the Kilbrandon report favour a scheme involving legislative devolution. This would give them responsibility for legislating on specifically defined subject matters, although Parliament would retain ultimate authority in all of these. The matters suggested as suitable for transfer include the following:

Local government
Town and country planning
New towns
Housing
Building control
Water supply and sewerage
Ancient monuments and historic buildings
Roads (including the construction, use and licensing of vehicles)
Road passenger transport
Harbours
Other environmental services (e.g. prevention of pollution, coast protection and flood prevention)
Education (probably excluding universities)
Youth and community services
Sport and recreation
Arts and culture (including the Welsh and Gaelic languages)
Social work services (including, for Scotland, probation and after care)
Health
Miscellaneous regulatory functions (including matters such as betting, gaming and lotteries, obscene publications, shop hours and liquor licensing)
Agriculture, fisheries and food (with certain exceptions)

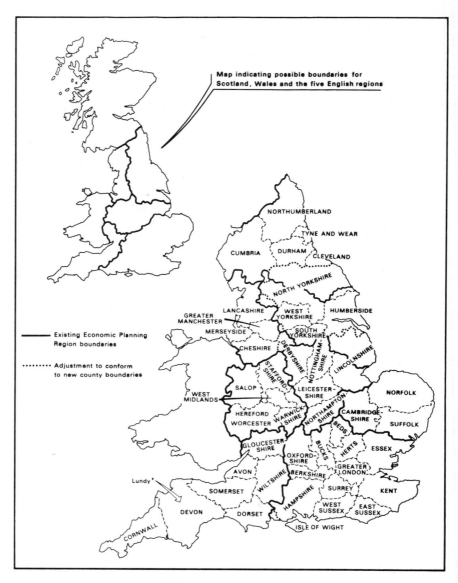

Fig. 5.7   Proposals of the Kilbrandon Commission.
Main map: Boundaries of the eight English regions proposed in the main report. Heavy lines indicate the existing economic planning region boundaries, and broken lines indicate adjustments to conform to the new county boundaries.
Inset map: Possible boundaries for the five English regions suggested in the memorandum of dissent.
Source: *Royal Commission on the Constitution 1969-1973,* Vol 1, Report, Cmnd. 5460 (HMSO, 1973).

Forestry
Crown estates
Tourism

Following a detailed examination of alternative financial arrangements for the assemblies, the Commissioners recommend the creation of an independent exchequer board which would mediate between Parliament and the assemblies in allocating them their financial resources. In determining this allocation the Commissioners underline the principle that the regions would be allocated sufficient monies to finance United Kingdom standards in all transferred services. although the assemblies would not be obliged to adopt those standards. The assemblies would be a single-chamber body of about 100 directly elected members.

This scheme is objected to by a number of Commissioners on several grounds, including the view that membership of the Common Market will increasingly limit the scope for such legislative freedom, and that legislative devolution is unsuitable for England and that it is accordingly unfair to grant these powers to Scotland and Wales and not to the English regions which would indeed still be legislated for by Scottish and Welsh MPs in Parliament.

Two Commissioners argue accordingly for a uniform scheme of executive devolution throughout Great Britain which would secure for regional assemblies executive responsibility for policies laid down by Parliament but also the ability to fill out the details of these policies; funds would be negotiated directly with central government. This scheme is seen to offer the disadvantages that the division of power between policymaking at the centre and execution in the regions is not clear cut thus possibly producing blurred responsibilities and difficulties in safeguarding the assemblies' legitimate field of interest. The latter might also be compounded by their limited financial freedom.

The majority of Commissioners propose a scheme for England which would create eight non executive co-ordinating and advisory councils. These would consist of approximately 60 members, four-fifths members of, and elected by, local authorities, and one-fifth nominated by central government. The councils would have the function of viewing the needs of the region as a whole and of expressing these needs to all levels and agencies of government. They would make representation to central government and advise on government spending and also play a co-ordinating role *vis-a-vis* local government.

The Kilbrandon Commissioners have identified a wide spectrum of alternatives, and within this spectrum make a number of alternative recommendations, only the major of which have been noted here (for a summary of all the alternatives see Table 5.1). They clearly hope that public response to their analysis and to these alternatives will crystallize into a firm decision on devolution for the regions.

However the Commissioners do not appear to have been sufficiently fundamental and rigorous in their approach to the encouragement of such a decision. The report is inspired not by a fundamentalist concern to redesign government to meet the needs of society, but by a concern to cure well articulated discontents. Just as the orientation is remedial, so too does the analysis tend towards the superficial. Problems are categorized into groups rather than analysed in terms of underlying causes; accepted at face value rather than interpreted in terms of changes within society at large. Problems are seen as threats to the existing system that need to be accommodated rather than as the eruption of new concerns and new values which may augur fundamental changes in the governmental system. The inbuilt commitment to consider only certain

Table 5.1   Commission on the Constitution: Alternative Schemes

	Scotland	Wales	England
Recommended	Legislative devolution to a directly elected assembly. Executive devolution to a directly elected assembly. Advisory and some legislative functions devolved to a directly elected assembly.	Legislative devolution to a directly elected assembly. Executive devolution to a directly elected assembly. Deliberative and advisory functions devolved to a directly elected assembly.	Co-ordinating and advisory councils partly indirectly elected by local authorities and partly nominated by central government. Executive devolution to a directly elected assembly. Regional committees of local authorites. Indirectly elected representatives of local authorities.
Rejected		Separatism. Federalism.	

types of proposals, namely those involving devolution, served to weaken the approach, simultaneously preventing a more fundamental analysis and producing a set of solutions which on their own admission do not solve all the problems. In summary, the concern for well articulated discontents and for devolution appears to have produced an unbalanced set of recommendations from the Commissioners, the majority of whom recommend radical legislative devolution for Scotland and Wales, but very weak muted changes for the English regions.

The dissenting memorandum of Lord Crowther-Hunt and Professor Peacock embodies an entirely different approach. The terms of reference are interpreted by them as a remit to examine and to make appropriate recommendations for changes in the entire government system of the United Kingdom. Their approach too is fundamentalist, they are concerned with ensuring that this system meets the needs and aspirations of the people, not simply with curing a number of discontents. Further, their analysis is more rigorous, problems are interpreted in terms of underlying trends in the structure and organization of government, trends which are seen to add up to an erosion of the extent to which people govern themselves. Their response is directed to this issue in a wide ranging set of proposals embracing changes in the organization of Parliament, political parties and the House of Lords as well as fundamental changes in the intermediate level of government.

Within the latter context the two Commissioners recommend a scheme for elected regional assemblies in Scotland, Wales and for five regions of England. Each assembly would have substantial but not legislative powers. They would be in control of all regional outposts of central government, take over the functions of the non commercial, non industrial *ad hoc* bodies currently operating on a regional basis; be given supervisory responsibilities over the commercial and industrial *ad hoc* bodies and be responsible for devising policies for the general welfare and good government of their regions.

The Commissioners reject the idea of an independent exchequer board as undemocratic and propose that the regions should have independent revenue raising powers. Taxes could include a supplementary income tax, a retail sales tax and taxes on vehicles and fuel consumption. Further income would be derived from the United Kingdom government. The latter would control the total amount but not the pattern of expenditure by the assemblies.

The scheme is seen to have the following advantages. It would reduce the burden of ministers, departments and MPs at the centre, enabling them to play a more positive role in policymaking at that level and in the European institutions of government. It would enable the people of each region to devise their own policies and to adapt policies of the United Kingdom government to their own needs. It would enable these peoples to bring under democratic control the bureaucratic decision making which takes place in the regional outposts of central government and *ad hoc* regional authorities.

Although this is a scheme which is attractive and demands serious consideration, and although the context within which it is elaborated is more fundamental and comprehensive than the majority report, the report needs questioning. Although it starts off by evoking needs and aspirations, the report moves farther away from this perspective as it proceeds, and increasingly evolves received democratic ideals. This is not to say that these ideals are rejected here, but that they are never reinterpreted in a wider context of current needs and aspirations. As with the majority report, preserving the legitimacy of the existing system of government and the consent of the governed to it is paramount. This conservatism unfortunately affects the whole quality of the analysis and eventually it is given trends, for example towards larger scale units, rather than the problems and ideals of people which inform it. Thus, much of the logic for devolution is seen to derive from a concern to allow the centre to shed burdens so that it can engage in higher and assumedly more important European circles of decision making. A concern brought out frequently in comment to the effect that local government would have limited contact with central government.

As in the majority report too, the unquestioned commitment ot economic growth is used as an argument for unity and in this, in its conservatism, its concern for legitimacy of existing institutions, its centralist orientation it is open to question to what extent it has captured the needs and aspirations of the people and the spirit of the age.

Both reports, then, have their limitations. In the face of an overwhelmingly large task the majority report circumscribes it and produces a set of unbalanced proposals. The dissenting report falls back on received ideals, the perspectives of the centre, irreversible trends and thus a set of proposals in which it is difficult to feel confident that the requirements of society are adequately reflected. Indeed, the size and complexity of the task make it unlikely that any one report could produce the ideal solution and it may be that this can be forged only through reaction by people expressing their various views in an ongoing interative debate. In this respect the reports have certainly marshalled a very great deal of knowledge and information for the public to bite on. However, response to both reports has as yet been very muted and the obtuseness of some reactions[61] and negative responses of others[62] is not encouraging.

It is therefore difficult to envisage the immediate implementation of any of the recommendations of the Royal Commission on the Constitution. However, the Commission has brought a provincial government model within the United Kingdom closer within sight by indicating its significance to key issues, and by ordering information about the alternative organizational and financial forms that it could take.

It would seem a reasonable assumption that the provincial government model is viewed as an ideal by some regional planners offering as it does a very powerful base for action, a base comparable in strength to that enjoyed by local and national planning and thus one capable of reversing the basic structural weakness of regional planning which Kuklinski and others have identified. Whether or not this is a practicable ideal must however be seriously questioned in the light of the foregoing discussion, and this may apply not simply to the United Kingdom but also to other countries of a comparable political structure.[63] It is also to be questioned whether or not the provincial formula is a desirable ideal as far as regional planning is concerned.

The provincial solution cannot in itself be expected to be the complete answer, however well it is devised. This is because problems will evolve and form in ways which do not neatly fit into the formula, and this, of course, is where the *ad hoc* institution can be expected to play its role. Clearly in so far as a concern for and attachment to the provincial arrangement detracts from the need to map changing problems and to devise proposals for their solution, perhaps through new institutions, then its esteem amongst planners may be questioned.

It is feasible that the favour in which the provincial formula is held may be based upon a misconception of regional planning. The point here is that the thesis that regional planning institutions are weak is probably informed by a comparison with the established monolithic institutions at local and national levels and by the underlying assumption that regional planning needs to be like local and national planning and, therefore, needs similar institutions. This, however, may be seriously questioned and a more open perspective to the nature of regional planning and the forms of institution appropriate to it would seem to be a potentially more fruitful way of proceeding.

INTER LOCAL AUTHORITY INSTITUTIONS

A fifth type of institution capable of generating regional planning action consists of the arrangement whereby a group of local government agencies combine together into some form of association. In Great Britain this type of institution is generally both little developed and invariably weak. It is, however, usually an institution that has developed from below, from local rather than national initiative. It is too an institution that could perhaps be developed, and whose potential could be better exploited than has been the case in the past.

Probably the most common form that this type of institution takes is that of the industrial development association. This typically consists of a group of local authorities together with other established interest groups, formed in order to attract industry into their area. Fogarty[64] identified a considerable number of these institutions in Great Britain in the early post-war years: but no comprehensive survey or appraisal of them appears to have been made since then.[62] In the USA Gilmore also identified a significant incidence of this form of institution in the late 1950s.[66] More recently it has been established that just over one third of all of the local authorities in South Wales belong to some form of inter local authority industrial association.[67]

A number of these organizations such as the North of England Development Council and the Development Corporation for Wales were initiated not by the local authorities but by private enterprise and this may in part explain the almost ingrained concern within them for the same policies of attraction of industry over periods of a decade and more.[68] The limited policy analysis that this implies may also reflect the often weak financial status of these organizations and this in turn the generally weak commitment which local authorities are prepared to make to this type of grouping.

It is not surprising, therefore, that only one tenth of local authorities in South Wales have found their membership to be significant in explaining their success in attracting industry.[69]

Although weak in articulation and limited to promotional activity, these industrial associations are a potential institutional resource which could conceivably be further developed. Given encouragement, industrial attraction could provide an entree into the co-ordination of industrial development, physical development and other programmes. Smith indicates that the North East Development Council has in the past made progress towards the co-ordination of physical development plans of constituent local authority members.[70] And the Scottish Council has produced wide ranging and imaginative reports on the future of the region which indicate its potential role as a forum for discussing alternative regional futures.

A second form of inter local authority institution that can be distinguished in Great Britain is the Standing Conference arrangement. Standing Conferences of Local Authorities developed rapidly in Great Britain during the early 1960s as a reaction to the creation of the Regional Economic Planning Councils which were seen as a potential threat by the authorities to their traditional planning role.

These Conferences function in a consultative and advisory capacity only and have no power to bind or commit any of their members. The Standing Conference on Regional Planning in South Wales and Monmouthshire is typical of the provincial Conferences. It consists of all county councils and county borough councils in South Wales, and has four objectives:

1 To keep under review the principal planning issues affecting the area of the constituent authorities, and to assemble, assess and disseminate the planning information for the area.

2 To make recommendations to the constituent authorities with a view to establishing a joint policy with regard to matters of mutual concern.

3 To co-ordinate the action subsequently taken and in particular to consult, liaise and co-operate with the Welsh Economic Planning Council and Board on the principal planning issues affecting the area of the constituent authorities.

4 For the foregoing purposes to consult the Welsh Office, other appropriate Government Departments and other authorities and bodies concerned.

The Conference only meets twice yearly and so far has confined its work to questions regarding data collection and co-ordination and planning techniques. In the West Midlands, Painter has underlined the existence of strong centrifugal forces that can be expected to emerge and fail to be contained when more controversial and vital questions are raised than the merely technical.[71] Nevertheless they do provide authorities with a wider perspective for their operation and thus the possibility of developing similar and harmonious responses to situations.[72] They have provided an alternative and informed view of their region's future, particularly so in the case of the oldest and perhaps strongest Standing Conference on London and the South East.[73] They have become a firmer part of the regional planning machinery and are now expected to play a role in the preparation of the current round of regional strategy plans.

The crucial issue for this type of institution is clearly the problem of achieving sustained and genuine co-operation between traditionally autonomous and frequently jealous and insular authorities. Little consideration appears to have been given to this issue and to how bridges can be built between them. Perhaps one of the reasons for this is that government in the political core, which has the knowledge and capability to devote to this issue, has little reason for doing so, and traditionally either implicity or explicity is content to pursue a policy of divide and rule. Thus the administration of regional policy in Great Britain unlike in the USA has not encouraged inter authority co-operation and perhaps inadvertently encouraged insularity. Thus there is some evidence to suggest that in South Wales those authorities who look to national government for assistance to achieve industrial development do not tend to engage in horizontal or regional groupings.[74]

What would appear to be necessary is further investigation into why some industrial development associations are stronger than others, into where and under what conditions harmonious and committed actions develop between local authorities, and to consider which institutional devices break down insularity and promote integration and so on. The experiences of inter local authority groupings in Europe such as the Ruhr Planning Authority (SVR) or the Milan Intermunicipal authority would need to be drawn into such an analysis.[75]

Although it is possible to identify a number of potential lines of development for inter local authority institutions, including for example, their transformation into regional forums,[76] or into components of regional industrial development machinery,[77] it does seem that by far the most desirable step forward involves the creation of knowledge of means of inter authority bridge building, knowledge which can then be used by the authorities to further the role which they themselves determine upon. It is encouraging in this respect that current local government reform in England and Wales[78] through creating divided planning responsibilities is forcing a concern for means of achieving adequate collaboration between local authorities.[79]

The Main Models — A Summary

There are a number of points which need emphasis in the form of a summary at this stage. In the first place the discussion has been ordered in terms of very broad alternative models; numerous variations within each of these are conceivable in principle and current in practice. Further the list is not conclusive; other models can be broken out and the source of some of these such as a prefect system or a regional groupings of MPs have been touched upon in passing. Also it needs to be emphasized that the alternatives are not mutually exclusive, numerous permutations are again conceivable in principle and current in practice. To underline this point it may be noted that Bray has advocated the development of a regional council made up of two chambers. An upper made up of a region's Members of Parliament, acting also as a Select Committee in the House of Commons and a lower house directly elected on local authority constituencies, both exercising a range of major functions.[80]

It may indeed be the case that given the difficulties of realizing substantial institutional innovation at the regional level, in the form of provincial government, that one fruitful way forward for regional institutional building will be through developing different forms of combinations. Combinations both in terms of the integration of aspects of different models into a single new model and in terms of the development of different institutions in the same time—space. This seems likely to be one of the most practicable ways forward in the British context.

It does seem then that there is no shortage of alternative means for institutionalizing regional decision making, but what does seem lacking in many of the proposals and critiques reviewed above is a consideration for the basic objectives of the exercise. Few studies have been concerned to elaborate basic principles, to derive criteria for design and to develop a systematic set of proposals. Institutions are criticized for lacking power, for being unresponsive but rarely are these underlying concerns made explicit, debated and ordered. More academic professional and popular discussion on the ends rather than just alternative institutional means would seem to be required if regional institution building is to progress. Obviously what is wanted is the development of an institutional system capable of articulating and responding to societal needs, but unless the debate returns to or derives from such a perspective it is likely to become bogged down in hollow discussions about structures.

The Institutional Environment of Regional Planning

The number and variety of institutions that organize themselves on a regional basis and which thus constitute a part of the immediate environment of the regional planning institution are of considerable significance. They can be expected to influence the work style and performance of the regional planning institution. Further than that, institutions within this environment may be embraced by the planning institution to become an integral part of the regional planning structure. An *ad hoc* board, whether for water or manpower, hitherto independent and part of the environment, may become associated with the main base of regional planning; for example, a set of decentralized central government offices, and thus form part of the regional public planning system. For these reasons the character of the institutional environment in Britain is briefly noted here.

In the first place it is notable that within Britain a considerable number of powerful public corporations possess a regionalized administrative structure. The BBCs regional structure was developed in the 1930s as a result of the desire to give listeners a choice of programmes,[81] the Post Office in early 1973 introduced new regional boards for its postal and telecommunications businesses in order 'to push down the decision making nearer to where the customer is served'.[82] The Central Electricity Board has 12 area electricity boards, although the British Gas Corporation has recently dissolved its previously strong regional structure. The British Waterways Board, the British Railways Board, the National Coal Board and the British Steel Corporation all have a regional administrative structure. In the context of the latter organization Fisk and Jones have underlined the significance of this in encouraging the two way flow of information and assistance between the regional planning authority and the steel industry and the consequent matching between company and regional strategy to their mutual benefit.[83]

A number of public services are also organized on a regional basis. It has recently been decided that responsibility for water and sewerage in Great Britain is to become the responsibility of ten regional Water Development Authorities[84] with full executive powers, although it has been argued that too little power has been given to the national level of decision making in this case.[85]

Police services are organized on a regional basis and other minor public service institutions have also adopted a regionalized structure, including for example the Regional Sports Councils and Regional Arts Councils.

It has also been determined as part of the restructuring of the health service to create 14 new regional health authorities.[86] The National Health Services Act which came into being in April 1974 will make it possible to tackle the health needs of the nation on a regional basis. But more than that, like the new water authorities, it is particularly noticeable how these regional innovations are being accompanied by changes at the local and national level and by the way the whole operation is informed by a planning orientation. They are being structured *de novo* in a way which will encourage them to search for needs, alternative ways of meeting them and to evaluate their effectiveness[87] (Figure 5.8).

In the private sector many of the large industrial companies, particularly in the services sector, including for example, the commercial banks, and insurance companies, have regional structures and so too does the Confederation of British Industry. The Trades Union Congress has recently announced plans to set up

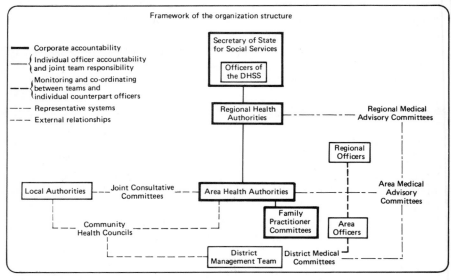

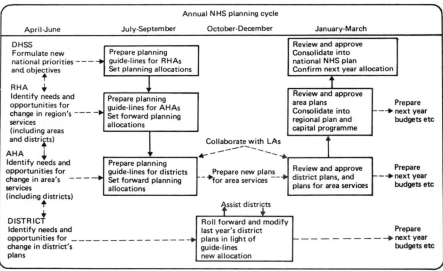

Fig 5.8   Organization and planning structure of the reorganized NHS.
Source: *Management Arrangements for the Reorganized Health Service.*

eight regional councils in England and one for Wales in order that 'the various planning and administrative bodies at regional and local level should be made fully aware at all times of the view of the trade union movement'.[88]

This roll call of regional institutions will no doubt enjoy extension and suffer erosion; the strength of the regional level within each institution may also be expected to ebb and flow. Nevertheless, one major characteristic stands out at this stage, and this is that the overall weakness of the institutional environment is certainly not as rich as the environment of local and national planning. Further it is not apparent what underlying factors cause some institutions to adopt a regional basis and others not. This would appear to be an issue requiring much closer investigation. It would appear to be particularly desirable to establish first, which types of institution can most readily have a regional level induced into them particularly where regional planning requires to widen the base of its actions; secondly, what conditions foster the development of a regional level; and thirdly, what conditions induce variation between institutions in the amount of power allocated to this level. These and related questions need to be answered if the regional planner is to understand and harness the potential of the institutional environment and to widen the scope of regional planning actions.

However, there is another, more fundamental, issue which makes the development of this type of regional institutional knowledge imperative. This issue derives from the marked absence in the above institutional inventory of the various forms of voluntary and special interest groups in which the individual citizen plays a formative role. The community action groups, clubs and societies which proliferate in the urban environment are by and large absent in the regional environment. At one level of consideration this forces a concern for how the citizen is to participate in the regional planning process and thus for the need for institutions which can achieve this. This drives home the point that creating institutions with decision making power, the underlying concern in the early part of this chapter, is not enough; institutions may also need to be developed to ensure that these actions do reflect regional aspirations. Regional institutional knowledge may thus be needed not simply so that the regional planner can expand his power base but also so that individual feelings and attitudes can gain expression in the regional planning process through appropriate institutions.[89] At another and more fundamental level of consideration, knowledge about how to build regional institutions is needed so that groups where they themselves see it as desirable to develop regionally, can do so; not because this is helpful to the regional planner in obtaining his portion of participation but because these groups for one reason or another may see it as advantageous to develop regionally. Knowledge needs to be developed and disseminated not simply about how government can develop regional institutions but how the entire spectrum of societal institutions can do so.

In penetrating into these questions and in clarifying the relative constraints which operate on groups in developing a regional orientation, it is possible that light will be thrown on the ultimate and most abstract institutional question, namely why in some regions or for some groups a sense of regional identity and belonging develops. In other words why the region becomes institutionalized in a cultural sense.

One of the advantages of the regional scale for a wide variety of services and functions is that it offers economies of scale in terms of the size of the population to be served. This particular advantage has hardly revealed itself as yet in encouraging the development of a whole new type of planning institution. Nevertheless it is to be expected and to be hoped that in the future a wide variety of institutions might develop concerned, for example, to foster independent knowledge and information within regions, or to act as future institutes or to provide specialist planning services to local community groups in their local planning work. Such institutes would not only be critical for the regional public planning institution but also for the whole spectrum of other institutions contained within the region.

The Supra National Environment: The EEC

Britain's membership of the European Common Market transforms the institutional environment of British regional planning at the national and supra national levels. The nature and implications of this transformation are still unclear but it is important to speculate on this question.

A progress report on the negotiations between the UK and the EEC, which began in June 1970, was published by the government in a White Paper in July 1971.[90] The government stated[91] that no problems arose over Britain's participation in the institutions of the Communities. It had been agreed from the start that the UK should have a position in these institutions equal to that enjoyed by France, Germany and Italy.

The body which takes all the major decisions about Community policy is the Council of Ministers. Of the 61 votes allocated in the Council, France, Germany Italy and the UK have 10 votes each. The European Commission is the authority responsible for executing the decisions of the Council of Ministers, for putting forward proposals which take into account the interests of the Community as a whole, and for safeguarding these interests. The members of the Commission are nominated by member governments and are staffed by a Community 'civil service'.

The European Parliament's present role is largely consultative, though it has certain powers of control over the Commission. In the European Parliament the number of members total 208, of which 36 are nominated by each of the national Parliaments of France, Germany, Italy and the UK. The Economic and Social Committee also has a consultative role, it consists of representatives from employers, trade unions, professions, agriculture and is similar to an international version of the UK Regional Economic Planning Council or the French CODER.

While Britain should not have to change the way in which it governs itself[92] or its methods of making and enforcing its own laws, in certain fields it will have to accept some Community decisions about what goes into these laws. The EEC rules mainly concern issues such as customs duties; agriculture; movement of labour, services and capital; monopolies and restrictive practices; state aid for industry; and the regulation of the coal, steel and nuclear energy industries.

Nevertheless the institutional arrangements and agreements noted above would seem to suggest that the EEC will not place constraints on the development of regional planning institutions within the United Kingdom. Nevertheless, disagreements among the Kilbrandon Commissioners underline the fact that there is room for considerable differences of opinion on this point.

At the same time membership of the enlarged community seems unlikely *a priori* to reduce the need for such regional institutions. Indeed it may well increase this need partly because of the possibility of increased economic polarization on the European scale.

Conclusion

Since regional planning involves decision making and action which allocates values and resources at the regional level, the main concern of the chapter has been to discuss those alternative institutional arrangements capable of providing a sufficiently powerful base for such decisions and actions. A wide variety of institutions are conceivable and a considerable number actually exist. However, the likelihood of any of these matching the executive power and scope of government at the local and national level seems very slim. Regions are new and vague and feelings for their importance and potential significance are not strong. In these circumstances each and every type of institution that has been identified may have a role to play either singly or more especially in combination. This type of open ended inductive strategy for regional institutional development is perhaps the most appropriate, and this is more likely to be fostered where conceptions of regional planning as a phenomenon similar to local and national planning and therefore, requiring similar institutions are abandoned.

Although governmental power remains a significant dimension in the debate on regional planning institutions an exclusive concern for this alone is a narrow perspective. Institutions for participation need to be developed, knowledge disseminated which will allow institutions other than government to act regionally, and opportunities grasped for building entirely new forms of institutions capable of providing planning services. This broader based strategy may in the long run provide the environmental setting for a firmer regional government institution to develop. Whether or not this proves to be so, it does seem that institutional change at the regional level is likely to take an evolutionary rather than a revolutionary sequence.[93] This does not, however, mean that it will be a process devoid of innovation, and it may well be that one of the characteristics of this innovation will be the development of a particular planning style adapted to the particular institutional context and institutional environment of regional planning.

References

1   Kuklinski, A.R., 'Regional Development, Regional Policies and Regional Planning, Problems and Issues', *Regional Studies*, October 1970.

2   See Chapter 2, and Smith, B.C., *Regionalism in England*, Vol. 2. 'Its nature and purpose' (Action Society Trust, 1964).

3   For a fuller account of this movement see Smith, B.C., *Regionalism in England*, Vol. 1, 'Regional Institutions' (Action Society Trust, 1964).

4   See, for example 'Regionaliter', *The Regional Commissioners, Political Quarterly*, Vol. 12, No. 2, 1941. Reprinted, in part, in Thornhill, W., *The Case for Regional Reform* (Nelson, 1972).

5   See the proposal for an appointed commission for regional planning in Ireland and the hostile reaction to this reported in Viney, M. (ed), *Seven Seminars, An Appraisal of Regional Planning in Ireland* (An Foras Forbatha Dublin, 1969).

6   These attitudes are clearly expressed in the memorandum submitted by the various local government associations to the select Committee on Estimates: 'Regional organisation of Central Government departments: 1953/54' reproduced in Thornhill, W. op. cit. For a further indication of these attitudes see The West Midland Group, Local Government and Central Control (Routledge, 1956).

7   The machinery is described in greater detail in Turnbull, P., 'Regional Economic Councils and Boards', *JTPI*, February 1967, and by Chester, T.E. and Gough, J.R., 'Regionalism in the Balance: Whitehall and Townhall at the Crossroads', *District Bank Review*, March 1966 and critically assessed in Mackintosh, J., *The Devolution of Power* (Penguin, 1968).

8   Cross, J.A., 'The Regional Decentralisation of British Government Departments', *Public Administration*, Winter 1970.

9   Self, P., 'Regional Administrative Machinery and Planning', *Proceedings of the Conference, Regional Planning before and after Crowther* (Regional Studies Association, 1970).

10   This view is confirmed in the autobiography of George Brown, part creator of the DEA and the regional machinery and its head during its initial years: see George Brown, *In My Way* (Gollancz, 1971).

11   This assumption is, for example, expressed in Rodgers, W., 'Regional Planning', *JTPI*, June 1966. Rodgers as Under-secretary of State in the DEA was. one of the designers of the new machinery.

12   Painter, C., *The Repercussions of Administrative Innovation, Public Administration*, Winter 1972.

13   For further evidence on the weakness of this link see Williams, G., *Economic Planning Machinery in Wales 1965–1968* (Regional Studies Association, 1971).

14   Smith, B.C., *Advising Ministers. A Case Study of the South West Economic Planning Council* (Routledge & Kegan Paul, 1969).

15   McGuiness, J., 'Regional Economic Development', *JTPI*, March 1968.

16   *Industrial and Regional Development*, Cmnd. 4942 (HMSO, 1972).

17   These recent additions to regional machinery are summarized by Thorburn, A., 'Towards an Effective Regional Framework', *Built Environment*, April 1972.

18   For accounts of the regional institutional pattern in France see, for example, James, P.M.B., 'The Organisation of Regional Economic Planning in France', *Public Adminstration*, Winter 1967, Gremion, P., 'Regional Institutions in the French local political and administrative system, in Kalk, E. (ed), *Regional Planning and Regional Government in Europe*. (International Union of Local Authorities, The Hague, 1971).

19   See for example, 'Function of Local and Regional Authorities in the Preparation of Regional Plans' (Council of Europe, 1972); and Kalk, E., op. cit.

20   Luttrell, W.F., 'Industrial Location and Employment Policy', Report of the Town and Country Planning Summer School Exeter, 1964.

21   Rowlands, E., 'The Politics of Regional Administration: the Establishment of the Welsh Office, Conference on Regional Development Cardiff (Regional Studies Association, 1971).

22   Mackintosh, op. cit., p. 132.

23   The Cassa is discussed in Watson, M.M., *Regional Development Policy and Administration in Italy* (Longman, 1970).

24   Selznick, P., *TVA and the Grass Roots* (Harper, 1966). The TVA is also examined in Lilienthal, D., *TVA* (Penguin, 1944) and in Huxley, J., *TVA* (The Architectural Press, 1945).

25   Dinkelspiel, J., 'Administrative Style', in Rodwin, L., *Planning Urban Growth and Regional Development* (MIT, 1969).

26   Rodwin, L., *Nations and Cities*, Chapter III, 'National Planning of an Urban Growth Region. The Experience of Venezuela' (Houghton Miffin, 1970).

27   See Edwards, J.A., 'The Beginning of a New Era. Regional Planning in the USA during the 1960s', *JTPI*, May 1971.

28   See Levin, M., *Community and Regional Planning*, Chapter 12, 'The Big Regions', (Praeger, 1969).

29   Wildner, R., 'Appalachia After 5 Years', A progress report on Appalachia's Experiment in Regional Development. Fourth Annual Meeting of the Appalachian Education Laboratory Charleston 1970.

30   Watson, M.M., op. cit.

31   Mackay, G.A., 'Scotland' in *Marginal Regions, Essays on Social Planning*, Broady, M. (ed) (Bedford Square Press, 1973).

32   For an elaboration of the Board's attitude on this issue see Grieve, R., 'Scotland: Highland Experience of Regional Government', *Town and Country Planning*, March 1973.

33   MacMurray, T., 'Innovation for Urban Problems', *JTPI*, September/October 1971.

34   See Grieve, R., op. cit. and 'Developing the Highlands and Islands — 4', A Board News Briefing, June 28th 1973.

35   McCrone, G., *Regional Policy in Britain* (Allen & Unwin, 1969), p. 235.

36   See, for example, Friedmann, J., 'The Implementation of Regional Development Policies: Lessons of Experience, *International Social Development Review*, No. 4, 1972. Kleinpenning, J., 'Objectives and Results of the Development Policy in North East Brazil', *Tijdschift voor Economishe en Sòciale Geographie*, September/October 1971.

37   Self, P., 'Regional Planning in Britain', *Urban Studies*, May 1964.

38   Pastore, J.M.D., 'Regional Development in Argentina, Administrative and Organisational Problems' in *Multi-disciplinary aspects of Regional Development* (OECD, 1969).

39 See in particular Grieve and Dinkelspiel, op. cit.

40 *Ad hoc* institutions are discussed further in the context of innovative planning in Chapter 6.

41 Federation in general and the case for a federal scheme in Great Britain is discussed in Banks, J.C., *Federal Britain? The Case for Regionalism* (Harrap, 1971).

42 Maas, M., 'Division of Powers', in Maas (ed), *Area and Power*, (Free Press, 1959).

43 For a lively discussion of the case for and against, see *Local Government Reform* (Regional Studies Association, 1969).

44 See, for example, Donnison, D., 'Planning and Government', in *The Future of Planning*, Cowan, P. (ed) (Heinemann, 1973).

45 See, for example, Clarke, R., *New Trends in Government* (HMSO, 1971).

46 See, for example, Thornhill, W., op. cit.

47 See, for example, Hanson, A.H. and Walles, M., *Governing Britain*, Chapter 10, 'Regionalism and Decentralisation' (Fontana, 1971).

48 See, for example, the fears of Southern Italy, discussed in Fried, R.C., 'Administrative Pluralism and Italian Regional Planning', *Public Administration*, Winter 1968.

49 Mackintosh, op. cit.

50 Cole, G.D.H., *The Future of Local Government* (Cassell, 1921), reprinted in part in Thornhill, op. cit.

51 For further references on the GLC see, for example, Donnison, D. and Eversley, D., *London Urban Patterns and Policies* (Heinemann, 1973). Although it appears that the GLC has received more research attention than any other regional institution in the UK little of this has been translated into practicable and imaginative reform. The prospects for other regional institutions which cannot expect the same degree of academic and professional attention would accordingly appear poor.

52 Oliver, J.A., Synopsis of talk on Northern Ireland as a practical case of Regional Administration (Regional Studies Association, 1973).

53 Mackintosh, op. cit.

54 Lawrence, R.J., *The Government of Northern Ireland 1921–1964*, (Clarendon Press, 1965) reprinted in part in Thornhill, W., op. cit.

55 *Royal Commission on Local Government in England 1966–69*, Cmnd. 4040 (HMSO, 1969).

56 Mackintosh, op. cit. pp. 196–197.

57 Mackintosh, op. cit. pp. 197.

58 Hanson and Walles, op. cit.

59 Hanson, A.H., 'The Region Why', *New Society*, November 28th 1968.

60 *Royal Commission on the Constitution 1969–1973.* Vol. 1, Cmnd. 5460 and Vol. 2, Cmnd. 5460–1 (HMSO, 1973).

61 See, for example, *The Guardian*, leader November 1st 1973.

62 See, for example, *The Times*, leader November 1st 1973.

63 See, for example, Woodcock, G., 'Regional Government: The Italian Example', *Public Administration*, Winter 1967.

64 Fogarty, M.P., *Plan your own Industries, A Study of Local and Regional Development Organisation* (Blackwell, 1948).

65 For some useful general comments, see Smith, B.C., *Regionalism in England*, Vol. 1, 'Regional Institutions: A Guide', Action Society Trust, 1964.

66 Gilmore, D.R., 'Developing the "Little" Economies', Supplementary Paper, No. 10, Committee for Economic Development, New York 1960.

67 Morgan, R.H. and Hockaday, M., 'The Role of the Local Authority in Regional Development', *Research Papers*, Vol. 1, No. 1, UWIST, Cardiff 1973.

68 For an analysis of the North of England Development Council on this point see Rowntree Research Unit, University of Durham, 'Aspects of Contradiction, in Regional Policy: the Case of North East England', Paper presented to the IX World Congress of International Political Science Association Montreal August 1973.

69 Morgan and Hockaday, op. cit.

70 Smith, op. cit.

71 Painter, op. cit.

72 See, for a statement of this role, Macmillan, A., 'The Role of the Local Authority Standing Conference, in *Proceedings of the Nottingham Symposium on Sub Regional Planning* (Regional Studies Association, London 1969.

73 See, by way of example, 'Population Employment and Transport in the London Region', November 25th 1964. (LRP 340) and The Conference Area in the Long Term, 20th July and 23rd November, 1966 (LRP 680).

74 Morgan and Hockaday, op. cit.

75 See, for example, Wiesling, L., 'The Ruhr Planning Authority (SVR)', and Mazzocchi, G., 'The Intermunicipal Planning Authority in the Milano Metropolitan Area', in Kalk, E. (ed) op. cit.

76 See, for example, Smith, op. cit.

77 See, for example, Fogarty, op. cit.

78 *Local Government in England*, Cmnd. 4585 (HMSO, 1971).

79 See, for example, the studies commissioned by central government to aid the new local authorities and especially *The Sunderland Study*, Vol. 1 and Vol. 2 (HMSO, 1973). These issues are critical to the regional planning process and are discussed further in the following chapter.

80 Bray, op. cit.

81 See, 'Broadcasting and Regionalism', in Thornhill, W., op. cit.

82 Announcement by Chairman of the Post Office, *The Guardian*, December 2, 1971.

83 Fisk, T.A. and Jones, T.K., 'Regional Planning from the View Point of a Major Employer', Conference on Regional Development Cardiff (Regional Studies Association, London, 1971).

84 See Chapter 2 for a further discussion of these changes.

85 See, for example, the comments by Rees, J. on the paper 'The Management of Water in England and Wales: the Case for Reform', *Town and Country Planning*, September 1972.

86 *The Re-organisation of the National Health Service*, Cmnd. 5055 (HMSO, 1972).

87 Grey Paper, *Management Arrangements for the Reorganised National Health Service* (HMSO, 1972).

88 Announcement by the General Secretary, TUC, *The Times*, September 5th, 1973.

89 See, for example, Morsink, H., 'Regional Plan Formulation and Popular Participation with Special Reference to Latin America, in Dunham and Hilhorst, op. cit.

90 White Paper, *The U.K. and the European Commission*, Cmnd. 4715, July 1971.

91 See paras. 69–76, op. cit.

92 For a more detailed account see the White Paper of the Labour government, 'Legal and Constitutional Implications of UK Membership of the European Commission.' May 1967. Cmnd. 3301.

93 A similar conclusion is arrived at by Pajic, R., 'From Regional Planning to Regional Government, the Case for Yugoslavia', in Kalk, E. (ed) op. cit.

6 The Regional Planning Process

Introduction

Consideration focuses in this chapter on the process of planning at the supra urban scale. The main approaches to the way in which this process might be conducted and the main methods for ordering it are identified and critically assessed. An attempt is also made to consider what a theory of this process should concern itself with, what it should attempt to explain and predict. In other words an attempt is made to outline the major dimensions and concerns of regional planning procedural theory as opposed to the substantive theory of Chapter 3.

It has already been emphasized that regional planning is most appropriately viewed as a particular type of public planning, one of many that may be invoked by society to serve its needs. Implanted and developed at a certain level or at certain points within society the basic nature of the regional planning process, it is contended, is similar to other types of public planning with differences deriving from the fact that it is implanted at a particular scale and within a particular type of environmental setting.

The approach of the chapter, therefore, is firstly and basically to consider the emerging methods and theory of public planning in general. Then secondly regional planning methodology and theory are discussed within this context and consideration is given to how and in what ways its particular characteristics modify and produce variations from the general.

It should be emphasized that public planning itself is not a well defined or highly structured corpus of thought and knowledge. Indeed, its study, development and evaluation have only just begun. In locating regional planning within this context one is therefore locating it within an emerging rather than a developed field of thinking and knowledge. It is a field to which regional planning can expect to contribute perhaps as much as it gains, for as regional planners seek to develop this new field so they will be forced to elaborate and systematize its basic nature and this will, it is contended, inevitably mean spurring on an understanding of public planning.

These points serve to underline the essentially initial and undeveloped perspectives of public planning that are offered here. They also underline the difficulty but also the potentially wider significance of developing the method and theory of regional planning.

Outline of the Chapter

Planning has already been defined as a means by which society induces change in itself. This process is essentially a scientific one in which action is undertaken in the form of a hypothesis which is tested; in other words the action is evaluated in the process of its implementation.

Action is, of course, a means to certain ends, and ends and means interact with one another in what is most fruitfully regarded as a learning process; as a consequence of evaluating the action, means and ends may be changed due to the learning gained. Evaluation may also be seen as the essence of the activity which sets off a means-ends chain; in other words a situation is evaluated. Are there problems? Can the situation be improved? This outline suggests then that the planning process is one in which situations are evaluated, ends are set and action undertaken. The whole sequence forming a learning process. Public planning may be regarded as one particular type of decision making going on within society which produces these acts; it is a particular type of social decision making, or, as Friedmann terms it, a particular type of societal act.[1]

Haltingly, but with increasing pace, in recent years attempts have been made to elaborate different methodologies through which the sequence noted above can be ordered and structured. These methodologies form the substance of the first and major section of the chapter. In each case they are discussed in general terms, but an attempt is made wherever possible to discuss their applicability to regional planning and how they might need to be modified by it.

The majority of public planning methodologies are still far from properly elaborated, but at least their development can now be said to be underway. This is not the case as far as public planning theory is concerned. There is as yet no planning theory and not even a generally agreed view on what it should seek to embrace and explain. Recently, however, one significant line of thought has emerged. This views planning theory in terms of a concern for the causal relationships between the social system, or the societal environment of planning (the independent variable) and the nature of planning activity carried out within and appropriate to that environment (the dependent variable). This planning activity may most fruitfully be conceived in terms of alternative planning methodologies. Planning theory according to this line of thought would, therefore, predict the methodology appropriate to a given social situation. These developments in planning thought are discussed in the second section of the chapter. In this section particular attention is paid to the societal environment of regional planning and the way in which this may influence the incidence of alternative methodologies: in this way an attempt is made to explore the nature of regional planning procedural theory.

THE RATIONAL PARADIGM IN PLANNING

Although planning is a universal human activity, self conscious attempts to understand its nature and systematically to improve and develop it have been undertaken only recently and within the context of a few of society's institutions. Government and private industry have been the sources of the two main drives to develop the field, and their attempts have largely been restricted in time to the post-war world. Within this limited compass the benefit of mutual interaction and exchange has moreover been lacking. Physical and economic planning have developed separately within government circles, and in turn government and industry have developed their planning methods independently. However, there is increasing interaction between all of these and this is of considerable significance for the future development of public planning. This future will no doubt involve changes in the paradigms of planning—its dominant thoughtways. Currently the rational paradigm is already subject to considerable criticism; nevertheless it remains at this stage predominant and for this reason it is given extended consideration here.

The rational model of decision making is the fundamental base for the majority of currently practised planning methodologies. Even those methods not based on the model gain clarity and meaning in terms of their opposition to it. Many of the latter methods too can only operate where they complement rather than replace rational planning methodologies. The pervasiveness of the model thus gives it paradigmatic significance.

Bicanic[2] has suggested that the three elements of man, aims and instruments were fundamental to the elaboration of the rational model by Weber and Parsons. In other words man, who is goal seeking, is faced with the problem of choice of means or instruments in order to realize his goals or aims, and a rational decision was seen to be forthcoming when this choice was made in certain ways. Two particular authorities are important for their elaboration of the model within the context of government planning. In the realm of economic planning, Tinbergen, and in the realm of physical planning, Banfield played seminal soles. Both elaborated the criteria by which a decision on means could be judged to be rational. Banfield, for example, identified three steps which he considered to be necessary in realizing a rationally calculated decision.

1 The decision maker considers all of the alternatives (courses of action) open to him, i.e. he considers what courses of action are possible within the conditions of the situation and in the light of the ends he seeks to attain.

2 He identifies and evaluates all of the consequences which would follow from the adoption of each alternative, i.e. he predicts how the total situation would be changed by each course of action he might adopt.

3 He selects that alternative the probable consequences of which would be preferable in terms of his most valued ends.[3]

Rational choice of instrument, then, follows from a consideration of all available instruments and the implications of each of these for the values of the decision maker. A number of characteristics of the planning process would seem to follow on from this model. In the first place planning is a technical exercise involving the elaboration of means and the prediction of their consequences, it thus provides the technical base for the political decision maker. Secondly, planning is characterized by its comprehensiveness. The planner is required to consider all of the alternatives and all of the consequences of each of these. Even where the expressed aims are relatively few he is required to consider the implications of each alternative on the other values of the decision maker. In Banfield's terms ends may be of a contextual as well as an active nature; that is, in addition to the explicit aims of a planning exercise there are a host of other ends in the background which ought not to be violated in trying to achieve the active elements.

A third implication for planning is that it is essentially an allocative mechanism—a means through which resources are allocated in the most efficient manner within a comprehensive framework. It might be added that it is allocative in a value sense as well, for decisions by government entail discrimination—they emphasize some values to the relative neglect or sacrifice of others.

The model was elaborated further within the physical planning world. The most formal and systematic statement undertaken in elaboration of the model is discussed first, before turning to the criticisms that have been made of the model. The model, it has been suggested, led clearly to a technocratic interpretation of the planner's role; it emphasizes the problem of choice of means or instruments. This was not accepted by physical planners especially it would seem by those informed by the utopian and social reform traditions of physical planning. This issue received its most systematic consideration in Davidoff and Reiner's *A Choice Theory of Planning*.[4] According to their formulation, choice permeates and constitutes the central act of the planning process; but it was suggested that choice is not confined to means but embraces the issue of ends as well. The planner, they argued, is involved in widening the range of goals or ends to be considered and in explicating values not given much consideration in a situation. The utopian tradition within physical planning was one technique through which this could be achieved.

Davidoff and Reiner thus extended Banfield's rational model and firmly anchored planning in the stage where aims are elaborated and determined. They further extended the model in another direction by emphasizing that the planning process did not halt when means had been identified but rather continued into a third phase of implementation or effectuation. This was seen as essential if the planner was to engage in redirection and change of the plan. Through becoming involved in the process of effectuation the planner may achieve feedback and goals or means may be modified accordingly.

Davidoff and Reiner thus envisaged three fundamental phases in the planning process, value formulation, means indentification, and effectuation. The rational model was extended by this formulation firstly in the direction of ends and secondly in the direction of greater concern for implementation. It appears that the first of these extensions took place partly under the influence of a long standing tradition of utopianism, the second under the influence of more recent developments in administration and cybernetics. This formulation has culminated in the current orthodox view of the planning process as one involving first, the establishment of goals, secondly, development of alternatives, thirdly, testing and evaluation, fourthly, choice, fifthly, implementation, and, finally, evaluation and monitoring of the progress of the plan.

Criticisms of the Rational Model

Despite the pervasiveness of the rational model in planning thought, it has been subject to very considerable criticism. These criticisms have come from many quarters but particularly from those who urge a rejection of the model in favour of a strategy of disjointed incrementalism. A more orthodox reaction to the criticisms views the model as an ideal but a relevant and meaningful one for planning practice.

A number of criticisms revolve around the issue of ends. It is argued by Lindblom and others that the variation in values held by individuals prevents agreement on ends from being realized.[5] It is not, therefore, possible to establish goals and thus follow the sequence of the model. The obvious means of combating this problem also proves of no avail. Aggregating individually varying value preferences into a single scale of values which reflects these has been mathematically demonstrated to be not possible.[6] The implications of this are very significant, for it means that those goals which do become the generators of planning proposals are goals agreed upon within the political system. It is here that the issue is resolved and it is resolved in accordance with the realities of political power. It follows that goal statements will be preferred which reflect this distribution, and that planning proposals developed to realize these goals will be to the advantage of some but inevitably, too, to the disadvantage of others. Planning is thus inevitably a political activity.

Even within this political context, however, the model is still open to criticism, and this derives from the problem of the relative weighting of values or ends. Lindblom argues that it is not possible for the individual to indicate exactly his relative preferences for different values. Individuals can only be expected to do this, he suggests, where they are confronted with different policies which express different combinations of values. This makes the problem of agreement on ends apparently more difficult, but in fact makes it easier in so far as the problem becomes one of obtaining agreement on policies incorporating different combinations of values, and this may be more possible than striving for agreement in higher order terms. The model, it is therefore argued, is incorrect in suggesting that ends are first agreed and then means sought to realize these ends. Ends and means interact and are interdependent in a manner quite unlike that suggested in the rational model. This is so too because investigation and knowledge of means can readily lead to changes in already articulated ends.

These points although important do not, it might be argued, alter or destroy the model's fundamental features. However, consideration of the issues surrounding choice of means exposes further problems and these taken in conjunction with those outlined above seriously challenge its validity. In the first place it is argued that the model mistakenly assumes that adequate knowledge is available for the identification of alternative means. But our knowledge is imperfect and this viewed realistically, within the time constraints of a given situation, must mean that not all of the alternatives can be investigated.

One of the most significant ways in which new knowledge is acquired is, of course, through the evaluation of existing means; learning from these and then designing new means as a result of this learning process. Yet this may not be possible where attempts are made to follow the rational model since the rational model may require a range of different policies, devoted to the achievement of ends, but where this is the case evaluation may prove impossible because of the difficulty of ascribing a particular result to a particular policy input. This is one of the arguments Popper has put forward in opposition to what he terms holistic social engineering. [7]

Lack of knowledge also clearly inhibits another requirement of the rational model. This is the prediction of all the consequences of a course of action. This again is strictly speaking not possible, for the consequences of an act may go on reverberating into infinity. It was the impossibility of predicting the consequences of holistic planning operations that led Popper to argue that this form of planning must degenerate into unplanned planning; hasty attempts to overcome the unpredicted consequences of large scale planning action. Popper here seems to have misinterpreted the nature of the planning process; his argument implies a rapid and thus uncontrollable *volte-face,* whereas a comprehensive range of policies may be employed but gradually so as to gain feedback from their consequences, minimizing, if not obviating, unplanned planning. Thus, although prediction in the form called for in the rational model is not possible, this does not mean that attempts to order a range of instruments should not be attempted because of the Popper argument of unplanned planning. It does, nevertheless, underline the need for great care in the deployment of these.

Even where the range of means and the details of predictions of these are incomplete, it is possible that the amount of information involved may well be too great for the decision maker capably to scan and absorb and thus realize a choice. Even with the aid of computers the vast amount of information involved and the need to scan this simultaneously may possibly pose severe constraints on the operation of the model.

A final problem is more open to manipulation than those which revolve around man's finite intellectual abilities and limited knowledge. Although not inherent in the model, it is, nevertheless, worth noting at this stage. This is the problem of the institutional structure of governments within which planning is undertaken. This structure is characterized by the division of the tasks faced by an organization of government into separate predefined parts; duties are allocated to different positions, agencies are allocated to a variety of territories. Yet the rational model clearly requires that these separate divisions are overcome in order that a comprehensive and coherent range of instruments can be developed to realize aims. Where this cannot be done then clearly the hope of realizing a rationally calculated set of actions diminishes. Thus Wheaton, in attempting a brief evaluation of the success of metropolitan planning through a comparison of the conditions in planned and non planned metropolitan areas, concluded that the planned metropolitan areas had gained very little from planning and this was so because 'the major failures of comprehensive planning stem from its definition of comprehensiveness in a world that lacks any comprehensive political power or institutions. With political institutions utterly lacking in power, much less a broad range of powers, it is scarcely credible that comprehensive plans could be implemented.'[8] Given the structure of regional planning institutions outlined earlier, doubt must be cast by these comments on the appropriateness of the rational model for regional planning.[8]

The Strategy of Muddling Through

A great deal of the criticism launched against the rational model derives from a group of analysts of policy-making who advocate its rejection in favour of a strategy of disjointed incrementalism or muddling through. Lindblom, the main advocate of this form of approach, totally rejects the more common form of adaptation to the rational model's weaknesses, which is fo use it as an ideal to work toward. This, he suggests, is not a realistic or a useful approach. It is preferable he argues to observe how decision making is actually carried on in practice and then to systematize and develop this. The strategy that is deployed in practice is he suggests a strategy of muddling through. Lindblom has developed and codified this stategy in a number of writings[9] and only an outline is presented here.

By definition the aims with which muddling through is concerned are not the realization of some value but the solution of immediate, pressing problems; the process of muddling through is a process of continuous reaction to a succession of problems. This, it is argued, immediately confers the advantage that social agreement is more likely to be forthcoming than is the case where targets are ideal values. Lindblom reaffirms Popper's view that it is easier to obtain agreement on some evil than on some ideal goal.

Muddling through attacks these evils or problems incrementally, that is, through considering alternative policies which differ marginally from current policies. This immediately restricts the number of alternatives considered and thus makes the problem of choice very much more manageable. Choice may be aided too because prediction of the consequences of these marginal changes may be more feasible and it may also be easier for decision makers to evaluate a range of policies where they involve only marginal change in the existing allocation of values. It may also be easier to develop knowledge regarding the problem under consideration than in the case where a mass assault involving a battery of radically new measures is applied.[11]

Just as the strategy ignores a vast range of possible instruments, so too does it ignore predicting all the consequences of alternative decisions. The obvious danger of this is overcome, it is argued, by the serial nature of the process. In other words thorough prediction is not attempted because any unforeseen, unpredicted consequences can be tackled by later decisions in the serial chain of decisions. Lindblom anticipates criticism that the method may be conservative and thus fail to solve problems by pointing to the strategy's ongoing continuous attack on problems through this chain of decisions.

A further major characteristic of the strategy is that analysis and policy making are seen as fragmented, undertaken by different agencies inside and outside government in a disjointed manner. Lindblom thus rejects the view of authority or government associated with the rational model where values are centrally aggregated and allocated. In reality government is only one of many decision making agencies. This fragmentation ensures that freshness and distinctiveness of outlook between different agencies are maintained, and the different facets of a problem are exposed; that the unforeseen value consequences of a particular choice are highlighted through the agencies concerned with their articulation. Further, through each of these fragmented bodies engaging in mutual adjustment and adaptation to one another, it is possible to realize co-ordination other than in a centrally imposed manner and thus to move to a more rational overall solution.

A major feature of disjointed incrementalism is that quite unlike the rational ideal there is no comprehensive overview, no attempt to articulate and order all values, to consider all of the alternatives and their consequences. The major strength of the strategy immediately follows and this is its manageability. Thus, this, it is claimed, is the strategy which policy makers actually do follow. Moreover, the way to improve policy making is to improve what is done in practice rather than struggling to realize some logical but unattainable ideal. The empirical base of the strategy points to an equally fundamental contrast to the rational model with it logical base. This empiricist development will be taken up further at a later point.

Reactions to and Criticisms of the Strategy of Muddling Through

The reaction of planning theorists to Lindblom's work, at least in the United States where it had been formulated, was one of some concern and discomfort. Some interpreted his work, and that of Popper too, as a blow to the very idea of planning; others saw it pointing to a very limited role for planning, where all it could hope to achieve was marginal improvement in a given situation. Webber, in an important article depicts the clouded state of planning theory in the USA in the 1960s as a consequence of Lindblom's work, and it is worth noting in passing that Webber's own reaction is to support a probabilistic programming strategy until the problems might be resolved.[12] By this Webber had in mind an updated version of Myerson's central intelligence function.[13] He suggested that planners might attempt to increase the probability of rational decisions in a situation simply through the provision of information. Although a potentially powerful instrument capable of benefiting groups and individuals in the community, its weakness as a tool of intervention is the uncertainty surrounding who will use the information and how they will use it; it is an undirected form of intervention, the results of which are problematical.

Since the time of Webber's article, serious criticisms of the strategy of muddling through have begun to emerge and these are briefly discussed here.[14] In the first place the strategy is limited in terms of its ability to confront certain types of situations and problems. Where the consequences of past policies in tackling a problem have been unsatisfactory, then incrementally changing these may be of little benefit. There is the additional point here that incrementalism, in so far as it incorporates Popper's concern to undertake only those actions, the results of which can be measured, may mean that complex problems demanding a battery of different actions remain unsolved. In addition to this where entirely new problems confront the decision maker, then again past policies may be no guide simply because there are not past policies. The concern marginally to adjust current policies may mean too that new possibilities, the consequence of some technical breakthrough, are not exploited; the strategy may then be over-limiting and lead in the long run to overcautiousness and inertia. Thus in an earlier work written with Dahl. Lindblom acknowledged that 'unaided by the imaginative impact of utopias incrementalism might easily degenerate into petty change, fear of the future, placid tolerance of existing distress and an irrational unwillingness to take calculating risks'.[15]

The strategy may also be limited in terms of the nature of the societal environment within which it can be practised. The strategy depends upon a highly articulated structure of different interests and values in order that a relatively frictionless process of mutual adjustment and adaptation can be made; where that structure becomes excessively fragmented, then this sophisticated balancing process may not be possible.[16] On the other hand the strategy may be unworkable and unacceptable in a situation where political culture and political structure veer towards centrality and intervention. Disjointed incrementalism may in other words by particularly suited to the United States where a liberal political theory[17] and highly fragmented pluralistic structure of government[18] may be its ideal environment. More generally it may be limited in operation to 'the stable, well established deeply rooted democracies of the world'.[19] It is not surprising, therefore, that Leys, for example, is sceptical of its validity in the less developed countries.[20]

A final point is that the model may be incomplete. It seems difficult to accept that where the strategy is practised there are no long term aims impinging on the decision maker. In fact Lindblom has acknowledged that the role of long term goals in the process is uncertain. Although it is claimed that this is the strategy policy makers pursue, this seems to underline the point that there is insufficient empirical grounding to the formulation.[21]

Although there has been a natural tendency to criticize and list the weaknesses of the strategy because of the negligible role it holds out for planning and planners, it is important that some of its potentially important advantages should not be ignored. Its concern for manageability and thus non comprehensiveness, its concern to be empirically grounded, its openness and fluidity and thus readiness to perceive new problems are all significant.[22] It is too in sympathy with the increasing groundswell of feeling in many democracies that decision making needs to be more decentralized and more sensitive to the values of different groups. It is to be hoped that, following the initial concern to criticize disjointed incrementalism and to dismiss it as equivalent to *laissez faire*,[23] it may be acknowledged as a method of planning and one whose advantages need to be more positively explored. As far as regional planning is concerned, then there may indeed be a certain affinity with and sympathy for disjointed incrementalism. This is so because regional planning itself may well represent and express a greater dispersal of power, lack a monolithic base, and operate in an environment with both strong local and central agencies. Rondinelli[24] in his analysis of regional planning and development in the USA certainly portrays a policy making structure in accordance with Lindblom's work. Rondinelli develops from this a proposal for adjunctive planning which would attempt to articulate and oil the wheels of the disjointed policy making process. To the extent that this is successful then changes other than of incremental nature might be forthcoming, but they might be changes more firmly grounded in the values of different groups than are changes associated with the highly centralized form of decision making implied by the rational model.

Rondinelli's suggestions however ultimately imply a return to more co-ordinated and centralized decision making; a proposal more in keeping with Lindblom's thesis might involve the building of independent centres of knowledge at the regional level or encouraging the development of institutions for articulating unrepresented interests: the fact that this might allow overall changes of only an incremental nature may not in itself be disadvantageous in certain situations. These few points do perhaps serve to underline the fact that Lindblom is a fruitful source for thinking about the regional planning process and that his formulation is one which deserves serious attention.

Comprehensive Planning : The Strategy of Maximizing Bounded Rationality

An alternative to the response of rejecting the rational model is to acknowledge that the model has weaknesses but nevertheless to use it as an ideal to work towards. This is probably the approach taken by the majority of planners and planning methodologies. It is an approach that accepts that rationality is bounded, that not all of the alternatives or all of their consequences can be considered, and that the basic task of planning is 'to maximize bounded rationality.'

Within this context a number of different methods can be identified. Comprehensive policies planning is an imprecisely formulated method. Basically, it works within the rational ideal through seeking integration or co-ordination between policies developed for different dimensions of reality. The most commonly used perspectives to date recognize a tripartite division into social, economic and physical policies planning. Local authority policy planning or corporate planning is a more precisely formulated method, it perceives the planning process in terms of synthesizing the policies of separate government departments. Also within the context of 'maximizing bounded rationality' but confined to the spatial dimension, is a fashionable and precisely formulated methodology for spatial policy planning which applies systems thinking to the planning process. Each of these three methodologies is reviewed below.

Social Economic and Physical Policies Planning

The most ambitious attempts to live up to the requirement of the rational model in the sphere of public planning have revolved around concepts such as societal planning which is concerned to manipulate all of the available public planning instruments in order to realize societal goals.[26] These instruments and their attendant professional skills are conceived at their broadest as being social, physical and economic, although it is implicitly recognized that as new instruments are developed so might this list be added to. The ideal which is aimed for by societal planners is integrated policies plans which would bring together physical social and economic instruments in as rational a manner as possible.[27,28] The outline working framework for the Lerma-Santiago regional plan illustrates the comprehensive policies planning approach (Figure 6.1) and at the same time draws attention to the central problem of how articulation between alternative means is to be achieved. Most protagonists accept that this can only be done inductively that is through building up a total package of policies from different policy areas. Foley's work is interesting in this context because he advocates a different approach.[29]

Foley has developed a very appealing model which views the pattern of physical development as the outcome of human activity patterns which are in turn generated by values. In keeping with this it is argued that the way to construct comprehensive statements is, therefore, first of all to elaborate social and economic policies and then to derive from these physical policies. The substantive regional planning theory developed in Chapter 3 points to a different relationship. The theory developed there suggests that spatial structure may exercise a very powerful effect on societal performance—that spatial structure does not passively reflect social phenomena but actually helps to shape them. If this is the case then clearly what is logically required is for spatial considerations to be conceptually integrated with social and economic policy making. To this extent, Foley's approach to policies integration is misguided.

One particularly notable example of regional planning which is in keeping with this argument is the Yorkshire and Humberside regional strategy.   Here an attempt is made to relate decisions regarding economic allocations and decisions about spatial allocation. Sub regional (the spatial element) economies (the economic element) form the crux of the analysis and policy making process. Alternatives are presented and decisions may be made not about alternative economic policies and alternative spatial policies but about alternative combinations of economic- spatial allocation; for example decisions about the encouragement of an existing industry in certain towns because the spatial conditions are acceptable to this expansion as opposed to decisions about economic expansion which are divorced from, and possibly in conflict with, policies for physical development. It is not difficult to conceive of this method

GENERAL AIM: RAISE THE POPULATION'S STANDARD OF LIVING

Economic planning	Infrastructure planning	Social planning
Plan	**Aims**	
Raise the population's per capita income. Reduce income disparities between different social groups, economic activities and sub regions	Create favourable conditions for economic and social progress.	Raise the population's standards of education, culture and health. Break down social rigidities, and create human conditions favourable to rapid change without serious friction
	Specific aims	
Increase employment and productivity of the labour force in various sub regions, social groups and economic activities. Rationalize the use of the factors of production.	Establish adequate infrastructure for agricultural and industrial development and social progress. Balanced growth of urban centres and rural population.	Generalize opportunities for apprenticeship in conventional and vocational training schools. Arouse an attitude favourable to progress in the various ethic groups, and secure the population's active participation in the achievement of its material and cultural progress.
Programmes		
	Sectoral instruments	
Industrial development. Agricultural development. Rational exploitation of forest resources. Stimulation of craft activities.	Communications. Irrigation. Electrification. Building schools, hospitals, clinics, recreation centres, etc. Rural and urban housing.	Attack on illiteracy. Rural social welfare. Extension of general and technical education. Public health measures.
Projects		
	Specific instruments	
Planning by branches of industry. Intensive growing of certain crops. Consolidation of farms. Exploitation of certain forest products.	Siting on roads, dams, hydro-electric plants, schools, hospitals etc. Urbanization of population centres.	Establishing centres for the literacy campaign, social welfare and the promotion of general education and training.

Fig. 6.1   Overall planning levels of the Lerma-Santiago region.
Source: Berrueto, E.M. 'Regional Planning in Mexico' in *Multidisciplinary Aspects of Regional Development* (OECD, 1969).

being developed to include social and other dimensions of public policy making. Alternative regional strategies could be developed, each derived from the inductive build up of sub regional analyses and alternatives which in themselves incorporate a reiteration between economic, social and physical considerations (Figure 6.2).

In principle regional planning is potentially capable of allocating greater social and economic resources than local planning. At the same time, it can have a closer and more sensitive regard for spatial structure than national planning which can only deal with space in a gross and crude way through dividing the nation into regional blocks. All of this implies that regional planning faces the challenge and the opportunity of forging its own particular style of comprehensive policies planning. It is possible in the light of the Yorkshire and Humberside example that this style will be characterized as much by the inductive integration of sub regional policies as by the integration of social economic and physical policies for the region as a whole, and more especially by a complex reiteration by the sub regional and regional planes.

Corporate Planning

Corporate planning is an important, though recently developed, planning method. The main development so far has taken place in the local authority context where it is sometimes termed local authority policies planning. Corporate planning in general and its particular expression in the local authority context warrants consideration, not only because it is a possible model for the regional planning process, but because it might be adopted at the level of local and national government, in which case it will constitute an important feature in the environment of regional planning.

The essence of corporate planning in general, and local authority policy planning in particular, is that the attempt to grapple with the complexity of comprehensive policies planning is undertaken with the government institution itself as the frame of reference for the development of policies. Policies are generated not for the social or economic system but for the department of education or the department of public health, and the policies *in toto* are policies for the affairs of government as a whole and not for the societal system as a whole. This makes the development of comprehensive plans less complex because the comprehensive scope involved is more limited and more precisely defined.

Local authority policy planning has developed recently due to doubts about the ability of the decision making structure at local government level to solve increasingly complex problems. In particular the criticisms of the Maud Report on the Management of Local Government have provided the immediate cause for and context of attempts to develop this method of planning.[32] The report argues for the need to draw together the complex fragmented array of government departments through the creation of a centralized management function. A logical corollary is seen to be the diffusion of planning into all government departments and at the same time its elevation to a key role within the central management of the authority's affairs conceived as a whole.

One of the first attempts to give expression to the idea of a policies plan for the total range of governmental activity was undertaken by Fagin in 1959.[33] It is worth noting in passing that Fagin's formulation was particularly careful to emphasize the close intertwining of government and private affairs, hence 'governmental planning must take into account not only the things government does directly, but also the much larger range of things affecting and affected by governmental activity.' It is argued that more recent British elaborations of the model have been less outward looking in perspective and narrower, more bureaucratic in scope.[34]

The central problem for corporate planning as for societal planning is how to articulate and synthesize separate policies. The issue is dramatized in Fagin's formulation regarding the content of the policies plan. This would contain, he suggests, 'physical plans co-ordinating spatial relationships, schedules co-ordinating time relationships, budgets co-ordinating financial relationships, and narrative texts and tables describing and co-ordinating proposed activity programmes. Maps schedules and texts would also set forth the physical economic and social facts, assumptions and goals underlying the government policies.'

In recent elaborations of the approach, central emphasis is placed on the use of a new method of decision making the planning programming budgeting system as a means of confronting the central problem. PPBS is defined as 'the process by which ends and means are combined to achieve a coherent and comprehensive programme of action for any organisation conceived as a whole.'[35] It attempts to achieve this aim through combining a number of both established and new techniques integrating these into a coherent method of decision making, which embraces all government affairs and which moves in a sequence which reduces goals to actual budgeting decisions. In outline PPBS requires all departments explicitly to state their goals; to state these in such a general way that they do not automatically involve policies by the department concerned. It then requires alternatives to be developed in cost effectiveness terms, thus obliging a greater concern for the evaluation of a department's policies in order to support its proposals. Given the completion of these initial stages a programme structure may be established indicating both the goals and the varying alternatives open to the authority to meet each of these. Analysis of these terms of cost effectiveness and other technologies of choice potentially allows the optimum combination of alternatives to be chosen. In principle it would be possible at this stage to make this choice regardless of departmental structure. Since alternatives are submitted in budgetary terms, with resource requirements structured on an annual basis, it is intended that actual expenditure decisions become related to what it is government is basically trying to achieve rather than to the maintenance of existing functions and departments. PPBS has proved extremely attractive to governments at both the national and at the local level. In the USA its use throughout all Federal departments was ordered by President Johnson in 1965 and its establishment at state and local level has also been encouraged. In Great Britain experimentation with the technique is more recent, but it is currently being employed both in Whitehall and amongst a range of local authorities.[36]

Although both corporate planning and PPBS are too new to allow any firm judgement on their acceptability, some assessment of their possible weaknesses and limitations is necessary in considering them as possible models for the regional planning process. In the first place, as it has already been implied, it would appear that corporate planning is narrow and circumscribed in terms of its subject matter. This subject matter is defined as the affairs of the authority rather than in more embracing community or societal terms. This raises doubts regarding the perceptiveness of corporate planning to new issues and problems arising beyond the duties and affairs of the authority as these are defined at any one moment in time. This problem is recognized by the advocates of the method. Stewart, for example, has emphasized that it has a 'special responsibility' for identifying the need for innovation, for discovering problems that are not being met by the existing structure of government duties and responsibilities.[37] This attempt to overcome the problem of perception of need through the development of an extra precautionary device tacked on to the core of the process is disconcerting.[38] More recently Stewart[39] and Stewart and Eddison[40] have argued the need for community planning. Explicitly acknowledging that local authority policies planning is narrow in scope, community planning is viewed by them as an attempt to meet the needs and problems of the community as a whole. However, unfortunately a narrow view of government planning prevails in these recent modifications because government is seen to be incapable of community planning, and only capable of government or corporate planning. Community planning is seen to require some other agency. This would seem to suggest that corporate planning is ultimately informed by the inappropriate traditions of public administration and private enterprise. In physical and social planning, government has always been viewed very differently. Public planning has not planned the affairs of the whole community but it has intervened in a way which attempts to conceive the community as a whole, to recognize the consequences of intervention on the whole and to recognize the role of other agencies in inducing change in the whole. These traditions of public planning which view it as an outward looking means of intervention into society are tapped in Fagin's formulation but not in Stewart and Eddision's.

Another issue derives immediately from this first limitation of corporate planning. The point here is that its circumscribed view of the focus of planning *vis-a-vis* the community might engender the community to take a limited view of the role of planning and the aims it may entertain: There are two points that might be noted in this context. In the first place Stewart and Eddison emphasize in their work that it is social needs which are the focus of planning action. This, it might be suggested fosters an apolitical view of planning in so far as needs unlike wants or aspirations are non controversial, a concern for their satisfaction being basically beyond dispute. In the second place and following on from this, planning is accordingly viewed by them as the provision of certain obligatory services in order to satisfy needs.[41] This formulation again in its stress on obligatory provision places government planning beyond the realm of political debate, and again reflects on administrative orientation of thought. The implication of these two points is then that corporate planning may not encourage the community and the groups within it to see planning as a means for their self realization. It would in turn affect the whole tempo and quality of political life. In a recent review of British corporate planning experience, Stewart has acknowledged that the objectives which are set by the process are often hollow and non controversial. Stewart also notes in this review how the whole question of policy formulation and development can be readily reduced to a set of administrative and thus rigid procedures.[42]

It is a tenable thesis that the employment of PPBS might reinforce the limitations of corporate planning identified above. It might reinforce rather than break down its lack of perception and sensitivity to community issues and political debate, and its administrative orientation. In the first place PPBS forces a concern for quantification and for the expression of alternatives in cost effectiveness terms. This could possibly lead the analyst to underplay consideration of policies not amenable to such analysis however socially desirable they might be. Secondly, PPBS and its underlying impetus to achieve economy and efficiency might force a concern for judging policies too much in terms of coherence one to another—a bureaucratic criterion. This too might make the entertainment of new innovative policies more difficult in terms of the complex array of policies into which they would be required to fit. Thirdly, as Dror has pointed out, the concern to translate all policies immediately into financial terms may inhibit the elaboration of inventive and expensive looking innovations.[43] Fourthly, given the mammoth dimensions of the operation entailed in PPBS, it is possible that attention might focus on existing known policy alternatives, on reshuffling these rather than generating new ones.[44] Any such tendency might encourage an emphasis on narrow analytical skills and training which would in turn reduce the incidence of reactive new policies. A final issue relates to the centralization of decision making which PPBS, following the rational model, logically requires.[45] It would appear that decisions currently within the political arena might be pre-empted by bureaucrats sifting out the lower level but nevertheless meaningful alternatives of different departments, thus presenting policy makers with strategic alternatives for the authority as a whole. Whilst this might, as Stewart suggests, promote a politics of issues and enliven political life,[46] it also fails to open up the decision making process to public view and influence at a time when the community is beginning to demand this of its planning system. Overall there remains the technical complexity of the operation and this together with some of the points noted above has produced some pessimistic evaluations of PPBS.[47]

In conclusion, obviously the tentative arguments outlined above do not constitute a basis for rejecting corporate planning and PPBS as possible models for the regional planning process; they do, however, provide a basis for enjoining caution in their implementation.

Over and above the desirability of corporate planning as a model for regional planning, there is a final question regarding the feasibility of its employment at this level. The issue here is an institutional one. Policy planning and PPBS would clearly require considerable power at the regional level over the allocation of resources and in the determination of policies for departments. Such power, it has been seen, is not as yet normally held at the regional level. Further than that, it might be pointed out that they are both very demanding in their resource requirements, and may best be implemented where there is an established rich institutional environment which can provide counter weight to their internal orientation and where there are adequate stocks of expertise. Something at once simpler and more robust may be required in developing a regional planning process. Leys and Morris have held out PPBS as an ideal for the less developed countries[48] of the world, but for these reasons its implementation here, as at the regional scale, may not be feasible. Further, given the current structure of manpower and institutional resources at the regional scale in the developed countries and in the less developed countries generally, then their value as ideal models must also be placed in doubt. Some form of inter corporate rather than corporate planning appears to be eminently more suitable at the regional scale. This is a suggestion which is developed further below.

A Systems Method for Spatial Policy Planning

Consideration focuses next on a recently formulated method of spatial policy planning. The formulation considered is that developed by Mcloughlin in *Urban and Regional Planning — A Systems Approach.*[49] Although confined to the spatial dimension it is a method which does within this context attempt to realize the strategy of maximizing bounded rationality. The methodology is of interest for two reasons. In the first place it may be adopted as a means of regional planning where this is seen to involve entirely or in part spatial policy making. In the second place, although Mcloughlin's is only one particular formulation, it may be illustrative of the methodology of systems planning in general, whether in the spatial economic or social realms. This does not mean that all forms of systems planning will bear all the characteristic strengths and weaknesses of his formulation, but nevertheless certain similarities are to be expected.[50]

Unlike local authority policy planning which is being forged out of the weaknesses revealed in institutional performance and consequent institutional reform, Mcloughlin's systems approach is more the product of academic research and is concerned to translate the concepts of new fields of knowledge such as operations research, cybernetics and systems engineering into terms that provide an entirely fresh way of viewing the nature of urban and regional planning; to the extent that the formulation draws on practice, then it is largely American practice, especially in the realm of land-use—transportation studies.

The major characteristics of the formulation that have been derived from these origins are briefly as follows. At the urban level the town is conceived as a system, made up of activities which are going on at a particular location plus activities which relate these localized activities. This activity system is accommodated in a physical framework, the localized activities in adapted spaces, the flow activities in channels. Although the framework is seen to be important in the method, it is not the core of the system; the core of the system is the localized and flow activities. The nature of the system at the regional scale is rarely explicitly defined, but it may be assumed at this scale that the town as a whole is viewed as an activity node with flow activities conceived in terms of intra urban movement between the nodes. The system at both levels is conceived as an ecological system and thus is tied into and is part of wider system of relationships which embrace the whole of the planet's ecology. Man, like plants, is located within a physical environmental context which is affected by and in turn affects the organism.

The nature of planning in the systems approach is most appropriately viewed in terms of the way in which change occurs in the activity system. This is seen to be the product of competitive decisions which arise out of the decision maker's dissatisfaction with the physical environment and which attempts to change his relationship with it. Any such change is seen to alter the state of the system and thus other decision makers may be impelled to act; a chain reaction of change may thus develop. In this way the system is driven and impelled forward, it experiences systemic change. This systemic change is by definition change throughout the system and it affects all of the individuals and decision makers within it.

Planning is seen to be necessary to guide systemic change in order to protect the welfare of these individuals and decision makers. Thus planning is defined as the guidance and control of systemic change in the public interest; guidance because the system is seen to be too complex and driven by too powerful pressures to be handled in any other way.

The nature of plans again follows on closely from this formulation. In the light of explicitly stated goals, plans are generated by simulating the real world system in a mathematical model, experiment on the latter providing a means of exploring a range of possible plans for the real world system. These simulations take the form of trajectories or sequences of states through which the system might pass; whereas the plan is the trajectory through which the system will be required to pass. A plan is thus a chart of the course to be followed and the planner a steersman or helmsman who acts to ensure that the system follows the chosen course. This involves the systems planner in system guidance and control and the general principle through which this is seen to work is termed error controlled regulation. Quite simply, this means that control is activated where the actual course of the system as revealed through continuous monitoring differs from the intended course as depicted in the plan, greater than previously determined allowable limits. The planner is seen to have two types of regulator in instigating control; he may recommend appropriate action in the public sector of the system, or he may, more indirectly, control development proposed by the private sector. With these two regulators the planner may either put the system back on course or, where this is not possible, recommend basic policy changes.

The approach is undoubtedly extremely attractive and persuasive at first sight; it is a remarkably coherent and systematic codification; it clearly defines its field of application and its rationale, and deploys a rich range of techniques. Nevertheless, it is a very new approach, and, although case studies are now rapidly increasing, relatively untried. Within this context it is possible to identify a number of potential limitations of the approach.

It might be argued in the first place that the use of an ecological model is constraining. Gans has argued that it is a model most applicable where one is dealing with an organism with limited choice. It is thus more useful in dealing with the poor than with the rich segments of the human population, with plants rather than man, because with increasing power and choice the impact of the physical environment and other species within it becomes increasingly insignificant. Mcloughlin accepts this argument but counter argues that since man is only relatively more powerful than a flower, the ecological model remains valid. The limited view of human nature and its capabilities implied by this counter argument gives some cause for concern. Although it would be clearly misguided to ignore man's ecological relationships, there is a clear danger that, by placing these at the centre of concern, physical constraints and the physical repercussions of man's actions will inevitably be overestimated. They are best viewed against man's social problems and aspirations and it is surely these that are the only valid bases for any planning exercise.

The formulation that change in the system is the product of atomistic competitive pressures would appear at least in part to derive from the ecological model; just as plants compete for air and water, so too does man. Although competition is indeed a central social process and its importance cannot be denied, its exclusiveness is questionable. Man, unlike a flower, is born into a culture and shares as such certain core values and bonds of sympathy which can and do provide the basis for co-operative action. The acts of government may on occasion express such a co-operative process. To hold that such acts are competitive would appear to be a reflection of American liberal political theory and one is reminded in this context of the American origin of the approach.

However, the fundamental informing idea of the systems approach is not ecology but that of the town or region as a system. As such it is argued that a change in one element or part will set off a chain reaction throughout all of the other parts. The systems planner may accordingly be very sensitive to change, perhaps even hypersensitive, and one notes here the conceptualization of change in the approach as a 'disturbance'. It may indeed be the case that this hypersensitivity is justified, but this can only be determined given a much more rigorous examination of the system; rather than assuming that everything is related to everything else, it is necessary to find out what is related to what and in what ways. Unless this sort of examination is forthcoming, there is the possibility of the system being planned in such a way as to make it more system-like than in fact it is, through, for example, the planner concentrating on giving emphasis to interactions and through viewing the parts too exclusively in terms of the whole and not as entities in themselves. As with many of the criticisms raised here, this last point could have a very considerable conservative implication.

It follows from a number of the points outlined above that the systems approach tends to see the basic source of change as arising from outside the system of interest. This is, for example, implied in the view of change as a competitive, chain reaction process; the parts respond to changes in the environment. This formulation of behaviour as a reactive response to external changes is not made explicit, although Mcloughlin's statement that 'an exogenous influence will tend to have more widespread and general effect than a change arising within the system'[51] gives further foundations to the point, and thus further cause for concern that the approach articulates a passive view of human nature; man is seen to react and adjust to change rather than inducing it.

It has already been noted that the central concept—systemic change—gives purpose and definition to the planning process, and that this systemic change is the product of man's attempt to overcome dissatisfaction with the physical environment. Thus an industrialist may adapt or develop his space *in situ* or seek a new location for his activity because of dissatisfaction with his existing adapted space. The problem is thus seen to reside in the physical environment and as such is of interest to and the concern of the physical planner. Clearly it is not dissatisfaction which drives the system forward, but rather values, and dissatisfactions are simply a derivative of these. Although this may be acknowledged in the approach, there is cause for concern that the focus on dissatisfaction, on the frustration of values at the interface with the physical, might in turn lead to a lack of concern for more fundamental social and cultural processes, and this in turn to a lack of articulation with social and economic planning Certainly the approach is more concerned to carve out a niche for the physical planner than to develop some form of comprehensive policies planning. The fundamental concept of systemic change is essentially based on man affecting man in some physical way and the consequent need to intervene to control these physical changes. Man is not seen as a socio cultural entity, nor is he seen as a social instrument by which he may realize himself.

Given that the purpose of planning is to influence and intervene in the process of systemic change, there would appear to be strong limitations on the extent of the intervention that it entertains. In the first place plans are generated in the form of simulations of the real world system which start with the present system and shows how it might evolve. In other words, only those alternatives that evolve in a logical programmed way from the present are considered; the future is limited by being an extension of the present. In the second place planning attempts no more than to guide and control the process of systemic change. This is seen to be the most it can expect to achieve because 'brute force' is simply incapable of confronting a system so complex and driven by such powerful competitive pressures. Given a different view of the system, one where man is capable of acting co-operatively, because he is a socio cultural entity, then the concept of brute force becomes inappropriate and radical change may be induced within the system.

These points in turn give grounds for some concern regarding the extent to which the approach is purposive in its orientation. In this context it is worth noting that Catanese and Steiss have stressed that systems analysis has traditionally been concerned with the solution of immediate present problems and not with the long term. They accordingly argue the need to combine systems thinking with traditional planning into a systematic planning approach.[52]

The final consideration in this outline of possible limitations of Mcloughlin's systems approach brings together a number of previous points by developing a general perspective on the approach. It is argued that the approach misinterprets the nature of the urban and regional system and is in its current stage of development both mechanistic and static. This argument is derived from the work of Deutsch.[53]

Deutsch has distinguished a number of different types of feedback within systems. First order feedback consists of a feedback of information regarding action taken to achieve a given goal. Simple mechanistic systems are only capable of this form of feedback and thus are able to control their actions only within a highly circumscribed area; they may change their actions in order better to realize a given goal but not the goal itself. Third order feedback, however, consists of a feedback of information from the memory device of a system, from its accumulated experience, and it is equivalent to consciousness. As a result of this consciousness, a system may not only switch actions but change goals. These goals are not predetermined but arise out of inner reflection, that is out of third order feedback. This basically involves a process of evaluation of experience to date and of learning in response to this. Thus a system capable of employing third order feedback is also capable of engaging in a process of self development and self realization. Such systems are typically complex human systems. Basically it is argued here that the systems approach is based on first order feedback. The principle of error controlled regulation is in essence first order feedback, that is the monitoring of a system providing feedback in order to realize the predetermined goals. Mcloughlin's formulation does not, of course, assume the continued viability of the same goal with which the system has to operate as in simple mechanistic systems, but it does appear that new goals are brought in rather mechanistically when the system goes off course. The operation of learning through evaluation of changes in the system does not appear as an integral part of the approach.

Clearly the systems that urban and regional planners are concerned with are complex human systems capable of third order feedback. Within such systems planning may be seen more appropriately as a means through which a system may provide information about itself enhancing its consciousness; as a means through which it may determine its own future through providing feedback regarding the effects and success of its actions.[54,55]

It is to be expected that systems thinking will exercise its attraction as much at the regional level as it has at the urban and sub regional level: indeed the need for a perspective which can integrate and synthesize the complexity of regional change, including the performance of different towns and the way they interact upon one another, is likely to make systems approaches especially appealing for the regional planning process.

As yet, however, there are very few examples where a systems approach has been explicitly adopted as a regional planning method. One example is the East Anglia regional strategy. This is still in preparation, but Townroe's description of the work involved tends to confirm the argument developed above.[56] It is assumed in this strategy for example that external pressures will initiate most of the changes and that apart from these that there are no dominant problems in the region. This would seem to fit very neatly with the underlying conservative idiom of the systems method. It may well be that here is an entirely appropriate juxtaposition between a particular type of regional setting and a particular type of planning method.

STRATEGIES FOR MODIFYING RATIONALITY

So far consideration has been given to those planning methodologies which either reject the rational model, or which accept it, attempting in the process to maximize bounded rationality. Recently, another approach to the rational model has begun to be formalized. This is characterized by a concern to modify the basic requirements of the rational model in the light of the complexities of real life planning practice. Although still very new this would appear to be a significant development. Two particular contributions to this emergent strategy are discussed briefly.

The first contribution derives from the work of Boyce and his studies of metropolitan planning in the USA.[57] Boyce has examined the performance of a number of agencies preparing metropolitan land-use transportation plans against the requirements stipulated by the rational model. He found, not surprisingly, an inability to live up to the latter. However, the main thrust of Boyce's work is to explain this disparity not so much in terms of the inadequacy of the planners concerned, but in terms of the insensitivity of the rational model to practical real life complexities. These complexities included, for example, the reluctance of politicians to predetermine ends without first acquiring a knowledge of means, and the inability due to time and cost contraints to consider more than a very few alternatives.

In addition to these complexities which constrained the usefulness of the exercises, Boyce also found that many fundamental problems remained unaddressed in these planning studies. This was so because the planners concerned were trained in the comprehensive rational tradition and thus produced comprehensive metropolitan area plans. But many of the problems, although metropolitan in significance, existed at a less than metropolitan scale consequently they were not considered adequately.

Boyce's recommendations for a revised planning process accordingly stress in the first place the need to focus on the identification of problems for solution. Not only would this ensure a concerted focused attack on fundamental problems; Boyce also implies that it would provide a sharper more focused basis for the generation of alternatives and for decisions on these. In the second place, a relaxation in the requirements of the rational model is recommended. In effect Boyce argues that decisions regarding the conduct of the planning operation should not be externally determined by the rational model, but internally by the planner himself, in the light of the complexities of the situation on which he practises. Thus he suggests that the planner should explicitly determine the purpose of the planning operation, the number and range of alternatives to be considered, in the light of considerations of the kind of decisions that need to be made.

This explicit rejection of the rules of the rational model is also echoed in the work of Etzioni.[58] Etzioni starts from the thesis that the rational ideal is unmanageable and incrementalism too conservative, and he has attempted to produce a new synthesis which is characterized by being more manageable and also more active than both. The resulting formulation, termed mixed scanning, is in summary a combination of fundamental or contextuating decisions and bit or item decisions plus rules for relating these two types of decisions. Thus fundamental decisions are made after a brief overview of the main alternatives that come to hand; bit decisions are made incrementally within the context set by the fundamental decisions which they in turn test. The decision maker is then required to follow certain rules which ensure an interplay between these levels. Thus after a few bit decisions the decision maker is required to undertake a semi-encompassing review; when a series of bit decisions appear to be running into difficulties, then it is necessary to undertake a fully encompassing review and to be prepared to make fundamental decisions.

Although these formulations are too new to be properly evaluated, they do represent a potentially significant shift in planning thought; both spell the end of the rational paradigm.

Whether or not these evolving strategies for planning prove particularly applicable and appropriate to the regional planning process cannot be clearly assessed as yet, although some speculations can be made. Thus, in so far as regional planning is conceived as part of a comprehensive national economic exercise, then clearly this will require a comprehensive regional planning approach rather than the issue orientated approach identified by Boyce. Thus, although the regional Economic Planning Councils have acknowledged their limitations of resources they have still persisted in producing comprehensive and thus, too, superficial regional planning strategies.[59] The current emphasis in regional planning in Great Britain is on the need for regional physical strategies which can provide a strategic context for the preparation of statutory development plans by new local government authorities: regional planning is seen to be critical because of the way in which these authorities, especially the metropolitan councils, have been territorially circumscribed. This need for a strategic context is likely to encourage a detailed comprehensive approach rather than an issue orientated approach or an approach which concentrates on a non detailed scanning of broad alternatives.

It is possible too that issue orientated approaches require reasonably mature established institutions, for issue orientation implies concentration of effort on some matters to the neglect of others; this may pose difficulties for weak and young regional planning institutions. Thus, where specific issues have been tackled by some regional Economic Planning Councils, they have been abstracted and generalized from any specific geographical or group context.[60]

NORMATIVE PLANNING

All the methods considered above are distinguished by the common characteristic that they require the planner to play a neutral, apolitical role. In all of them the planner is an adviser to a politician whose word and decision are accepted as final. One term that might, therefore, be used to describe all of these approaches is functional The planner is a means, he plays a functional role in society. In contrast to functional it is possible to identify normative planning. In this tradition the planner becomes politically engaged, and this is so because of his personal commitment to certain ideas, values or groups in society. Two types of normative planning have been formulated to date—these are advocacy planning and innovative planning.

Advocacy Planning

The essence of advocacy planning is that the planner here represents the interests of a particular social group in the planning process and his allegiance and responsibility is solely to this group.[61] The advocate planner might represent well established and powerful interest groups, but he is more interested in and concerned to represent those groups who are poor, marginal or disadvantaged in some way.

It follows, where advocacy planning is an established mode, that a plurality of plans are generated with plans for each advocate as well as the government planner. It further follows that such a situation is characterized by political contention and conflict with the advocate fully engaged in this process in order to represent the interests of his client. It would appear that a basic argument underpinning advocacy is that a pluralistic social situation demands a relatively fragmented and pluralistic planning structure to articulate the variety of interests and values in such a situation.

The practice of advocacy planning would clearly appear to hold out a number of advantages and benefits. It can ensure involvement for the disadvantaged, expose a richer range of plans to the whole community, expose the government planner to expert criticism, mutally educate the client group on the one side and the government and community on the other. However, there are problems regarding feasibility, and in particular of providing the advocate with the support with which to practice. At the same time the advocate may be very limited in terms of what he can hope to achieve. Radical solutions in particular may require nationally applied pressure and action, and engagement in this may mean loss of contact with the client group.[62] At the same time the concern to avoid organization and manipulation of the interests of the weak, may mean that the latter must identify and organize themselves first, so only the most capable can, therefore, be helped.

Advocacy planning has until now operated at a neighbourhood or urban area scale, and interesting questions are posed regarding its feasibility at a supra urban scale. The advocate here is clearly placed in greater difficulties regarding the problem of maintaining contact with a group whilst representing their interest in regional decision making. Whether advocacy planning can be practised at the regional level whilst retaining its essential characteristics, therefore, remains to be seen. It is, however, more likely to develop given a significant politically accessible form of government decision making at the regional level and the development of institutional knowledge which will enable groups to organize themselves in order to gain access to it. One particular innovation which regional planning might make to advocacy planning is the development of advocacy institutes—independent sources of information and advice which possibly can be supported by regions because of their very size.

Innovative Planning

Innovative planning is a potentially much more powerful form of planning than advocacy, and one with a stronger affinity with planning at the regional level. First formulated by Friedmann in 1966[63] it has attracted rather less attention than advocacy planning and relatively few attempts have been made to develop and formalize the idea of planning as innovation since that date.[64] It would appear, however, that this is not a reflection of its insignificance in practice.

Friedmann distinguished between two types of planning—allocative and innovative. Allocative planning is concerned to achieve the optimal allocation of resources between all of the competing needs or uses within a system. An allocative plan is a balanced comprehensive plan and thus almost all of the approaches considered under the term functional, and especially those adopting the strategy of maximizing bounded rationality, can be considered as allocative. Friedmann is concerned not to criticize allocative planning but to deny its exclusiveness and its status as the current orthodoxy in planning. It is argued that there is another form of planning—innovative—which is just as prevalent as allocative but not so visible and therefore less consciously formulated and practised. More than that, innovative planning may be even more prevalent than allocative planning where conditions of crisis are experienced.

Innovative planning attempts to mobilize and channel resources to some single new or neglected use, achieving in the process the legitimization of new social objectives or a major realignment of existing objectives. It seeks to do this by creating a new institutional arrangement. The chief characteristic of the operational style of this new institution is that it fuses plan making and plan implementing; the essential output is therefore not plans or intentions for other agencies to act on, but action—action which changes the nature of reality. The innovative planner is concerned to mobilize and harness the largest possible share of resources through this institution for a single particular use, even though this may have severe implications for other uses and the achievement of other values elsewhere. The innovative planner thus acts rather as a public entrepreneur. As such he portrays different behavioural characteristics to the allocative planner and these include a fairly immediate and intense commitment to one particular solution, an engagement in the political process in order to mobilize support for the solution, a concern to justify rather than to predict consequences and an attachment to experimental approaches in its testing and development.

Probably the best example of regional innovative planning in Great Britain is the Highlands and Islands Development Board. Grieve's descriptions of the planning method employed by this institution accord closely with Friedmann's formulation. Thus following a rapidly prepared and brief strategy pointing out the broad direction of change[65] the Board 'moved as quickly as possible into performing a multitude of fruitful actions';[66] planning and action were initiated in parallel with a central concern to attack the long history of neglect and to convince the population that changes were going to occur. The Board's first activity map (Figure 6.2) conveys this central concern to initiate actions in broad conformity with rather than rigorously deduced from a strategy.

Friedmann does not view innovative planning as a substitute for allocative planning; even in times of severe crisis, he suggests, it is extremely unlikely that innovative would completely replace allocative planning. Allocative planning remains necessary in order to ensure that the interests of the societal system as a whole are safeguarded. The allocative planner thus acts as a guardian of the system and upholds its traditional values; he, therefore, necessarily acts as a check on, and comes into conflict with, the innovative planner. Where the latter is successful in implanting new projects into the societal system, then these various innovations may be regarded as nodes of intense change within it and are typically unco-ordinated and competitive. The role of the allocative planner in this context will usually consist of attempts to bring these independent thrusts together, to co-ordinate them and bring them within an allocative purview; a situation which one can well envisage arising should the Scottish experiment be repeated in a few other areas of the country. It follows that the essence of the relationship between innovative and allocative planning is that innovative planning changes the parameters within which allocative planning works, achieving in the process a major as opposed to a minor re-allocation of resources. resources.

Despite the attractions of innovative planning in terms of its ability to come to grips with serious problems and conditions of crisis, it does suffer from a number of disadvantages. Society may experience disbenefits in the form of, first, a waste of resources during the period when the separate innovations remain outside an allocative purview; secondly greater complexity of the government machine and thus inability to understand and manipulate it; and thirdly delayed reform of the basic government machine itself. A further criticism of innovative planning is that it induces a harsh process of change, causing hardship and suffering in those areas and sectors which are the responsibility of the allocative planner. This cut throat approach, it may be

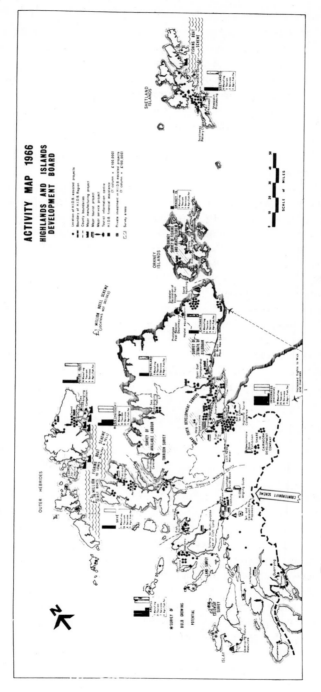

Fig. 6.2   Activity map 1966 – Highlands and Islands Development Board.

Source: Annual Report, Highlands and Islands Development Board 1966.

argued, is inevitably a part of the process of rapid social change and the resetting of value priorities, but nevertheless in so far as innovative planning formalizes and condones this type of insensitivity, then it is unacceptable.

A final weakness of innovative planning which immediately follows on is that it may readily become, even if it is not inherently, an undemocratic form of planning. The innovative planner in his intense commitment to one idea, his biased mustering of data in support of it, his engagement in behind the scenes persuasion, may lose contact with and sensitivity to the initial problem and impose some unwanted project on to a society which has insufficient check and control over the process of innovation.

It has already been suggested that regional planning and innovative planning have a strong affinity with one another. The reason for this would appear to be that problems arise which fail to correspond with the existing institutional structure of society which then requires some new institutional form to tackle it. Thus Wingo[68] has suggested that regional problems occur at the interface between different institutions. At the same time because such problems are greater in scope than existing local authority areas, their solution may be imperative. National government is obliged to act, changing its pattern of resource allocation, because of the weight and significance of such large areas.

Innovative planning would appear to be a valuable tool with which society may tackle a changing constellation of problems. And there is thus a clear need to tackle the problems posed by this method of planning. Nevertheless it may be necessary to accept that some of its weaknesses are the inevitable price that has to be paid for the solution of the critical problems which it confronts.

SOCIETAL ACTION

A final and brief consideration of the different types of societal action distinguished by Friedmann[69] provides a useful perspective on the different methods of applying scientific knowledge and intelligence to societal action—societal action being any deliberate action taken with regard to society or a major sub system within it. All of the methods considered may be classified as system maintaining in intention; that is they are concerned to maintain or improve an existing system of societal relationships. They may in turn be classified as either adaptive or developmental. Adaptive methods generate actions which are concerned to maintain the equilibrium of a societal system in the face of changing conditions; whereas developmental methods generate actions which propel a society towards new forms of realization. In an earlier paper[70] Friedmann suggested that the incidence of each depends partially on the autonomy of the system under consideration, so that developmental planning is more possible at a regional than at an urban scale where limited autonomy may mean that adaptive response to external change is all that is possible. However, given the characteristic lack of autonomy amongst regional institutions, it might be argued that regional planning is more likely to evidence adaptive rather than development actions.

System transforming actions are generated by methods which strongly contrast with all those that have been considered so far. These are actions taken by disaffected groups who challenge the existing power structure and attempt radically to transform society substituting new rules and institutions by which society governs itself. This is achieved through revolutionary action and that form of planning concerned with the ends and means of revolutionary action Friedmann terms counterplanning—counterplanning because it is directed against the dominant system of institutionalized power. Friedmann thus draws in and identifies as part of evolving planning thought radical critiques of the existing order and proposals for its overthrow including manuals on guerilla warfare. By definition, planning at the regional level cannot generate system transforming actions, for action here cannot hope radically to transform either the region or society at large.

PLANNING THEORY

This second and briefer part of the chapter discusses firstly the nature of planning theory in general and then secondly the nature of regional planning in theory in particular. Planning theory is still in the initial stage of its evolution but nevertheless encouraging signs of its development have begun to appear recently, and these warrant identification and discussion.

Broadly and simply it is suggested that planning theory is concerned with four major variables: planning methods, the societal environment, the planning system, and the planner; and that more specifically it is concerned with explaining the relationship between these variables and with making predictions about any one of them in the light of this knowledge about their interrelationships.

It has been suggested by a number of commentators[71] that a theory of planning might hinge on the relationship between the first two of these variables. Etzioni for example, suggests that it is pointless discussing which is the ideal planning method in the abstract since the ideal can only be determined in the light of the situation within which planning is being practised.[72] Accordingly this line of thought suggests that planning theory should build up knowledge about how planning methods vary with environmental circumstances. It would then predict the planning method appropriate to a situation given the characteristics of that situation. Burby's model (Figure 6.3) is one particular expression of this line of thinking and one which has indeed been used to generate some interesting empirical data supportive of the underlying idea.[73]

A priori it seems unlikely that the relationship is one which is as straightforward and simple as these emerging ideas suggest. It may well be for

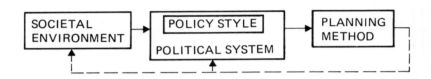

Fig. 6.3   Planning theory – a model.
Source: adapted from Burby, R., *Politics and Planning* (University of North Carolina Press, 1968).

example that the planning methods discussed above are not mutually exclusive and that a given societal environment determines a range of planning methods rather than a particular method. Implied in this is the view that the environment may determine the range within which planning methods may be practised effectively and that beyond this range other methods become ineffective or impossible to practise. One way of meeting this point is to argue that planning theory is concerned not with explaining how the societal environment produces a particular planning method, but with how it produces planning behaviour where planning behaviour is conceived in terms of the methods or the mix of methods used and the effectiveness of these.[74]

Further issues, however, still remain. Planning changes the societal environment within which it operates. It may do this not only in the way intended by plans but also unintentionally; latent effects may be produced which transform the environment as Friedmann and others have emphasized.[75] It would seem important to recognize this feedback effect from planning to the environment, and to recognize in the process that planning behaviour is rather more than a passive reflection of the environment. Further, it would seem to be desirable to incorporate into planning theory a concern to predict the latent consequences of planning methods on the societal environment.

A more fundamental consideration underlines these points. It is readily conceivable that, although the environment may imply a method or a range of planning methods, policy makers may require some other form of planning to be practised and are prepared to transform those aspects of the environment which are critical in permitting the practice of preferred methods. Thus although some form of incrementalism may be implied by a given environmental situation, policy makers may prefer some more active and radical form of planning and may consider inducing changes that would allow the latter to operate. Planning behaviour is thus not necessarily derived from or an output of a given societal environment; it may be conceived not solely as the dependent but also the independent variable. This in turn suggests that it is necessary for planning theory to incorporate a concern for the environmental prerequisites of different types of planning method; in other words that planning theory needs to incorporate knowledge of the environmental features that need to be brought into being in order to allow a particular method to be practised—it would predict failure or ineffectiveness where these were not so produced.

Speculating further on the nature of planning theory it would seem desirable to separate out two further categories from the societal environment both of which may exercise an influence over planning method, or more broadly, planning behaviour. Both too may be readily open to influence in seeking to effect a particular change in planning behaviour.

The first and most important of these is the nature of the government institution responsible for public planning. It is apparent from the foregoing discussion that the nature of the institution at the regional level is critical in determining regional planning behaviour. What is necessary now is more adequate conceptualization of the planning institution or planning system[76] and then to develop understanding of what dimensions are a critical influence on planning method, and how they influence planning method. At the same time it would also be desirable to know more about the relationship between the planning system and the societal environment; about where and under what conditions it exercises a strong independent effect on method because of its autonomy from the societal environment. This line of thinking would bring into planning theory the whole question of institutional design; it would provide that basis for institutional reform which the previous chapter has shown to be completely lacking as yet; ultimately then it would envisage institutions being changed in order to deliver the type of planning method and thus type of planning actions which policy makers determine. This line of thinking would also logically but more tenuously bring into planning theory knowledge about how different institutions capable of different types of planning behaviour could be implanted into different environmental settings; with this knowledge policy makers would not only know what institutional changes might be necessary to deliver a particular type of planning behaviour but also whether these institutional changes could be introduced into a given environmental setting.[77]

Alongside the planning system but possibly of lesser significance on planning behaviour is the planner.[78] It is conceivable that the planner may exercise an independent influence on planning behaviour and that in turn the latter may be manipulated through influencing the former. Again this points to a number of specific challenges for planning theory. In the first place it is necessary to consider what differences there are if any between the amount and type of influence planners exercise and how this varies with different attributes, including, for example, social origin, education, professional orientation.[79] Further there is the consideration of how these influences are mediated by the institutional context of the planner's work: the need to establish which type of institutions institutionalize and thus neutralize the planner, and which type of planners succumb more readily than others to this influence.[80] Ultimately, although again how practicable or desirable this is, is open to debate, this line of thinking points to the development of knowledge about planning the planner.

Regional Planning Theory

Given that societal environment, planning system, planner and planning method provide the critical ingredients of public planning theory, the question arises whether or not this theory applies across the board embracing regional planning, or whether there is a need for a distinctive body of regional planning theory. Basically it is contended that, although regional planning must develop within the context of public planning and derive a great deal in terms of methodology and technique from this broader field, some of the dimensions of planning in the regional context vary in significant and fundamental ways and this provides a basis for and the need for a distinctive body of regional planning procedural theory. This theory would seek to explain why some public methods are adopted by and prove effective within the regional context, how each method would have to be modified for it to be practised regionally and how the regional context would have to change in order to accommodate each public planning method.

The subsequent discussion attempts to identify the distinctive characteristics of the environment and the planning system at the regional level and attempts to draw out the implications of these in terms of their influence on planning method.

As far as the regional societal environment is concerned, three fundamental and fairly distinctive characteristics immediately present themselves for consideration. In the first place regional planning is by definition sub national. That is it is subject to control by a superior decision making body in its environment. The power of the regional authority, however great, cannot rival this, nor can it match it, therefore, in terms of its ability to intervene within the region. 'Regions are open economies in a relatively closed system',[81] and as such 'they have limited ability for closing in on themselves and closing others out'.[82] It has already been noted that this may incline the regional planning process to an adaptive rather than a developmental mode of planning, and also from system transforming actions.

In the second place, and also by definition, regional planning is supra urban, that is it deals with a lower tier form of government which is near universally well established and well entrenched, which exercises important functions and which is often seen to be an important bulwark of democracy. Regional planning may thus usually have to seek to work with and through these urban institutions and this may in turn impose an important environmental constraint on planning methods adopted at the regional level. It may, for example, incline the regional planning process to the development of actions emerging out of consensus and bargaining rather than towards the imposition of a comprehensive plan. Although conventionally seen as an allocative mechanism between local and national levels in traditional rational comprehensive terms, the need for regional planning to articulate with powerful local and national institutions may in practice require a form of planning in sympathy with strategies, which explicitly modify the demand of the rational model. Indeed it may be the case that the impossibility of persisting with the rational ideal becomes more readily exposed and more obvious at the regional than at other levels with their apparently less complicated input- output relationships with the environment.

A further structural characteristic of the regional planning environment is questionably not such an inherent or universal feature. This is the fact that the immediate institutional environment is a relatively barren one; relatively few institutions as yet structure themselves on a regional basis. This amounts to a possible paucity of channels through which the regional planning system can communicate with the region and similarly through which it may receive inputs from it. This could mean a certain lack of sensitivity to the slowly developing and diffuse problems of a region and a consequent focus on the large clearly identifiable project or problem. At the same time it could result in a relatively slow feedback on the consequences of action which would incline regional planning towards a static blueprint rather than a dynamic process form of planning.

To a certain extent these three environmental features are a product of the nature of the regional planning system in the sense that it is partly because government institutions at the regional level are weak that national and local government appear as such powerful environmental features and that relatively few institutions organize themselves regionally. However, even with a very powerful regional government institution, the first two of these three environmental features would probably remain.

Nevertheless, the critical point is that the regional government system is generally speaking without the executive power of local and national government and it is this institutional factor regarding the power of the regional planning system which seems likely to be critical in shaping the regional planning process and in compelling the need for a distinctive body of regional procedural theory.

In this context interesting evidence is emerging which suggests that regional planning might recompense its lack of executive power through building up networks and bridges between different national and especially local and regional institutions. This is certainly in keeping with suggestions made previously but more pointedly it is a conclusion derived from recent studies of the English regional planning process undertaken by Friend, Yewlett and Power.[83] They contend that regional planning is likely to be effective only if it can develop connectivity between the executive actions of many agencies, that its lack of power will force this but also provide the freedom to play this outwardly connective role. They also suggest that in fact the regional planner has already begun to perform a new role of 'regional reticulist' in order to secure this bridge building across agency boundaries.

These findings and suggestions are very much in keeping with those of Rondinelli[84] on the basis of his study of regional planning in the United States. Rondinelli argues for the need for regional planning to concern itself with promoting co-ordination along lines of interest and concern shared by agencies, and accordingly to identify agencies most likely to be susceptible to joint action and policy making integration.

This again echoes the French experience recounted by Rouvre.[85] Rouvre comments on his experience in devising a strategic plan for the Region Nord as follows: 'A strategy for the North cannot be implemented by merely programming the State's investments; it involves too many other local or private interests. Even the government administrations do not feel strongly committed to a regional structure plan. So inside the region the OREAM (Organization d'Etudes d'Alles Metropolitaine) studies try to detect what agreements could be achieved and what links may be tied between local authorities to implement the different aspects of this strategy.

The crux idea is that of complementary relationships. Each local government has its own interests and objectives: but even if there are objective divergencies or rivalries between neighbouring local authorities they may unite for the purpose of achieving some sort of development or investments which are to be mutually profitable.'

Of course, it could be argued that the need for some form of inter corporate planning and for reticulist skills is necessary at all levels of planning but it may nevertheless be needed in proportionately greater quantities at the regional level, simply because the concentration of 'in-house' executive power is less. Further, at the regional level the skill may be one which can penetrate across agency boundaries at an intermediate level in their power structures, for example, building links between the regional levels of the National Health Service and the National Coal Board rather than between the central, highest decision making level of these authorities.

It, therefore, seems possible to suggest that the regional context does possess a number of near universal characteristics which are sufficiently fundamental to evoke peculiar patterns of response in terms of planning method; this in turn suggests that there is a case for a regional planning theory to order and understand these relationships and to predict those changes in methodological style or environmental context necessary to secure a chosen form of regional planning.

Two final considerations remain; these concern the nature of the regional planner and the nature of the subject matter of planning, the region itself.

The regional planner may exercise an influence over regional planning behaviour and it may be that the lack of any clear tradition or expectation of the nature of regional planning will allow that influence to be marked at least in the initial phase of its history. To the extent that the influence is marked and to the extent that regional planners tend to be characterized by a particular social origin, education, professional orientation or ideology, then a further source for the distinctiveness of regional planning has been identified. The regional planner would need to be embraced in explaining regional planning behaviour and in making predictions regarding the adoption of particular forms of planning method.

A final component of regional planning theory is the subject matter of the region itself. In so far as this has distinctive structural characteristics that impinge upon the incidence of methodology, then again an important source of a distinctive body of theory has been identified. At this stage a few features may be tentatively identified. The territorial scope and thus information handling demands of the region would seem in the first place to force a concern of abstraction, for techniques of synthesis and thus for planning methods which can handle such techniques. Harris[86] has also suggested that a region (and thus regional planning) is to be distinguished from a metropolis (and thus metropolitan planning) by its greater availability of space, that it can be concerned with the location of activities within space, whereas metropolitan planning must be concerned with the allocation of competing activities to space.

Thus whereas the generation of alternative metropolitan plans might be heavily constrained,[87] regional space is at the least more likely to make it easier to indulge in alternative spatial strategy generation which might in turn induce an encouragement for certain types of planning method.

Clearly this is no more than a tentative treatment of some of the major dimensions of regional planning theory. What is required is a concern for the way in which all of the complex of elements interact to produce regional planning behaviour. It is to be hoped that headway can be made in explaining this behaviour and that in the process society will be provided with the means of predicting this behaviour and thus intervening to effect it in the interests of its own self articulation.

References

1 Friedmann, J., 'Notes on Societal Action', *JAIP* September 1969.

2 Bicanic, R., *Problems of Planning – East and West* (Mouton, 1967).

3 Banfield, E. and Myerson, M., *Politics Planning and the Public Interest* (Free Press, 1955) p. 312.

4 Davidoff, P. and Reiner, T.A., 'A Choice Theory of Planning,' *JAIP*, May 1962. Also reproduced in Faludi, A., *A Reader in Planning Theory* (Pergamon Press, 1973).

5 See Reference 9.

6 These issues are discussed in Seeley, J., 'Central Planning', in Morris, R. (ed), *Centrally Planned Change'* (National Association of Social Workers, 1964).

7 Popper, K., *The Poverty of Historicism* (Routledge and Kegan Paul, 1961).

8 Wheaton, W. 'Metropolitan Allocation Planning', in Hufschmidt, M., *Regional Planning* (Praeger, 1969), p.28. Portions of this paper are reproduced in *JAIP,* March 1967.

9 Lindblom, C.E., 'The Science of Muddling Through' in Ansoff, H.I., *Business Strategy* (Penguin, 1969). Also reproduced in Faludi A., 1973, op. cit. Hirschman, A. and Lindblom, C.E., Economic Development Research and Development and Policy Making. Some Converging Views', in Emery, F.E., *Systems Thinking* (Penguin, 1969). Lindblom, C.E., 'Policy Analysis', *American Economic Review,* Vol. 48, 1958. Braybrooke, D, and Lindblom, C.E., *A Strategy of Decision* (The Free Press, 1963).

10 Popper, op. cit. p. 92

11 Popper, op. cit, p. 67

12 Webber, M. 'The roles of Intelligence Systems in Urban Systems Planning,' *JAIP,* Vol. 31, No. 4, 1965. Also reprinted in Eldridge (ed) *Taming Megalopolis,* Vol. 11 (Praeger, 1967).

13 Myerson, M. 'Building the Middle Range Bridge,' *JAIP*, September 1956.

14 A number of the criticisms are drawn from Dror, Y., *Public Policy Making Re-examined* Leonard Hill, 1968).

15 Dahl, R.A. and Lindblom, C.E. *Politics Economics and Welfare* (Harper and Row, 1953).

16 Hirschman and Lindblom, op. cit. p. 370.

17   Fainstein, S.S. and Fainstein, N.I., 'City Planning and Political Values,' *Urban Affairs Quarterly,* Vol. 6, No. 3, 1971.

18   Broady, M., 'From Planning Techniques to a Theory of Planning,' *SCUPAD Bulletin* 4, 1967.

19   Lindblom, 1958, op. cit, p.301.

20   Leys, C., 'The Analysis of Planning,' in Leys, C. (ed) *Politics and Change in Developing Countries* (Cambridge UP, 1969), p. 252.

21   Braybrooke and Lindblom, op. cit. p. 110.

22   Hirschman and Lindblom, op. cit. p. 364.

23   Faludi, A, 'Problems with Problem Solving', *JTPI,* November 1971. Faludi attempts a more systematic refutation in Faludi, A., op. cit. 1973; many of his substantive points have already been noted, others are mainly methodological rather than substantive criticisms.

24   Rondinelli, D., 'Policy Analysis and Planning Administration. Toward Adjunctive Planning for Regional Development,' Department of City and Regional Planning, Cornell University 1969.

25   Seeley, J., 'What is Planning?', *JAIP,* May 1962.

26   The term is described and used in Gans, H.J., Memorandum on Social Planning in Gans, H.J., *People and Plans* (Basic Books, 1968).

27   Webber, M. 'The Prospects for Policies Planning' in Duhl, L. (ed), *The Urban Condition* (Basic Books, 1965).

28   Hansen, W. 'Metropolitan Planning and the New Comprehensiveness,' *JAIP,* September 1968.

29   Foley, D., 'An Approach to Metropolitan Spatial Structure' in Webber, M. (ed) *Explorations into Urban Structure* (Pensylvania UP, 1967). See too Chapin, F.S. *Urban Land Use Planning* (Illinois UP, 1965).

30   Yorkshire and Humberside Economic Planning Council. *Yorkshire and Humberside Regional Strategy,* (HMSO, 1970).

31   One of the least studied ingredients of this complex is the nature of regional social planning. One example is Lomas, G.M., *Social Planning at a Metroplitan Scale* (Regional Studies Association, 1971).

32   *Management of Local Government* (HMSO, 1967). The recommendations of this report have now been followed up by the Report of the Bains Committee. *The New Local Authorities Management and Structure* (HMSO, 1972).

33 Fagin, H., 'Organising and Carrying out Planning Activities within Urban Government,' *JAIP,* August, 1959.

34 Particularly significant here has been the work of the Institute of Local Government Studies University of Birmingham, see Stewart, J., *Management in Local Government* (Charles Knight, 1971), and Eddision, T., *Local Government Management and Corporate Planning* (Leonard Hill Books, 1973).

35 For an elaboration of PPBS see Millward, R.B., 'PPBS — Problems of Implementation,' *JAIP,* March 1968, and Leyden, F. and Miller, E., *PPBA Systems Approach to Management* (Markham Publishing Co., 1970).

36 PPBS is clearly a set of techniques brought together in an overall method of decision making. It is thus considered further in Chapter 8 where techniques of choice are examined.

37 Stewart, J.D., 'The Case for Local Authority Policy Planning,' Town and Country Planning Summer School Proceedings, 1969.

38 This problem is further acknowledged in Stewart, J., 'Developments in Corporate Planning in British Local Government,' *Local Government Studies,* No. 5, 1973.

39 Stewart, J.D., 'The Management of Local Government', 1971, op. cit.

40 Stewart, J.D. and Eddison, T., 'Structure Planning and Corporate Planning', *JTPI,* September/October, 1971.

41 Eddision, T., 'The Wider Role of the Development Plan,' *JTPI,* December 1968.

42 Stewart J. 1973, op. cit.

43 Dror, Y., 'Policy Analysis A New Professional Role in Government Service,' *Public Administration Review,* Vol. 27, No. 3, 1967.

44 Stuart, D.G., 'Rational Urban Planning,' *Urban Affairs Quarterly,* December 1969.

45 See Millward, op. cit.

46 Stewart, J.D., 'Management in Local Government,' op. cit.

47 See in particular Cassett. J., *The Management of Government* (Pelican, 1972).

48 Leys, C. and Morris, P., 'Planning and Development' in Seers, D. and Joy, L. (eds), *Development in a Divided World,* (Pelican, 1970).

49 Mcloughlin, J.B., *Urban and Regional Planning. A Systems Approach* (Faber and Faber, 1969).

50 For an alternative formulation see Chadwick, G., *A Systems View of Planning* (Pergamon, 1971).

51 Mcloughlin, J.B., 'Notes on the Nature of Physical Change', *JTPI*, December 1965.

52 Catanese, A.J. and Steiss, A.W., 'Systematic Planning', *JTPI*, April 1968.

53 See Churchman, R., *Introduction to Operations Research*, Chapter 4 (Wiley, 1967), and for a more extended treatment Deutsch, K., *The Nerves of Government* (The Free Press, 1966).

54 This has been described as a process of evolutionary experimentation in Dunn, E.S., *Economic and Social Development. A Process of Social Learning* (Johns Hopkins, 1971).

55 For a further source of criticism of the systems approach see Dimitriou, B. (ed), 'The Systems View of Planning', Oxford Working Papers No. 9, Oxford Polytechnic, Oxford, 1972.

56 Townroe, P., 'And Then in the East: a New Regional Strategy for East Anglia', *Town and Country Planning*, April 1973.

57 Boyce, D.E., Day, N.D. and McDonald, C., 'Metropolitan Plan Making', Regional Science Research Institute 1970. For a precis of this work see Boyce, D.E., 'The Metropolitan Plan Making Process', in Wilson, A. (ed), *Urban and Regional Planning*, (Pion, 1971).

58 Etzioni, A., *The Active Society*, (Collier Macmillan, 1968). See too, Etzioni, A., 'Mixed Scanning. A Third Approach to Decision Making', in Faludi, A. (ed), op. cit. 1973.

59 See for example, Northern Economic Planning Council, *Outline Strategy for the North*, 1969.

60 See, for example, North West Economic Planning Council, *The Social Planning of Urban Renewal*, 1972, *Social Planning in New Communities*, 1971.

61 See, for example, Davidoff, P., 'Advocacy and Pluralism in Planning,' *JAIP*, November, 1965. Peattie, L., Reflections on Advocacy Planning,' *JAIP*, March 1968.

62 See Davidoff, P. and Gold, 'Suburban Action,' *JAIP*, January 1970.

63 Friedmann, J., 'Planning as Innovation,' *JAIP*, July 1966.

64　However, see, MacMurray, T., 'Innovation for Urban Problems,' *JTPI* September/October, 1971.

65　See, *First Report, Highlands and Islands Development Board*, 1967.

66　Grieve, R. 'Infrastructure in the Planning Process – the Local Level,' Town and Country Planning Summer School, 1972.

67　The relationship between allocative and innovative planning is discussed in Friedmann, J., 'A Conceptual Model for the Analysis of Planning Behaviour', *Administrative Science Quarterly*, Vol. 12, No. 2, 1967.

68　Wingo, L., 'Regional Planning in a Federal System,' *JAIP*, May 1964.

69　Friedmann, J., 'Notes on Societal Action,' *JAIP*, September 1969.

70　Friedmann, J., 'Regional Development in Post Industrial Society,' *JAIP*, May 1964.

71　See in particular, Friedmann, J., 'The Institutional Context,' in Gross B. (ed), *Action Under Planning* (McGraw Hill, 1967), Bolan, R., 'Emerging Views of Planning,' *JAIP*, July 1967. Faludi, A., 'The Planning Environment and the Meaning of Planning,' *Regional Studies*, May 1970.

72　Etzioni, A., op. cit. 1968.

73　Burby, R., *Politics and Planning* (University of North Carolina Press, 1968).

74　See Faludi, A., 'Towards a Three Dimensional Model of Planning Behaviour, *Environment and Planning*, Vol. 3, 1971.

75　Friedmann, J., *Venezuela*, Chapter 3 (Syracuse UP, 1965). Selznick, *T.V.A. and the Grass Roots* (Harper, 1966).

76　See Friedmann, J., *Notes on Societal Action*, op. cit. and Faludi, A., *Towards a Three Dimensional Model of Planning Behaviour*, op. cit. for interesting initial conceptualizations.

77　For an interesting example of planning coming to terms with the societal environment see Buck R.C. and Rath, R.A., 'Planning as Institutional Innovation in the Smaller City,' *JAIP*, January 1970.

78　For an interesting discussion which identifies the significance of understanding the planner himself, see Reade, E., 'Some Notes Towards a Sociology of Planning, *JTPI*, May 1968.

79　For some interesting and comparatively British data on some of these dimensions see Marcus, S., *Planners Who Are You?* For a discussion on interplay between these dimensions in effecting behaviour see Heraud, B., *Sociology and Social Work* (Pergamon, 1970).

80 Broady provides an interesting insight into the way in which the more immediate structure of interpersonal relationships may affect planner's behaviour, including attitudes to innovation, see Broady, M. 'Social Theory and the Total Environment,' in Broady, *Planning for People* (National Council of Social Service, 1968).

81 Friedmann, J., *Regional Development Policy* (MIT, 1966).

82 Perloff, H., 'Key Features of Regional Planning', *JAIP,* May 1968.

83 Friend, J.K. and Yewlett, C., Interagency Decision Processes, Practise and Prospect, Power, J.M. 'Planning Magic and Technique,' *Institute of Operational Research,* 1971. Friend, J.K., Power, J.M. and Yewlett, C. *Public Planning, the Intercorporate Dimension,* forthcoming.

84 Rondinelli op. cit.

85 Rouvre de, J.B., 'Implementation of Metropolitan and Regional Plans,' Town and Country Planning Summer School; Town Planning Institute, 1972.

86 Harris, B., reply to Friedmann, *Regional Planning as a Field of Study,* op. cit.

87 See for example, Powell, G., 'The elements of the Regional Plan – The Lessons of the South East,' Conference on Regional Planning before and after Crowther, (Regional Studies Association, London 1970).

7 Analytical Techniques for Regional Planning

Introduction

THE ROLE OF TECHNIQUES IN REGIONAL PLANNING

Broadly speaking, regional planning techniques may be placed in one of two categories; firstly, those analytical techniques which enhance our understanding of how a regional system functions, i.e. related to the substantive theory of Chapter 3; and secondly, those techniques which assist the planner in the use of methods of planning, i.e. related to the procedural theory of Chapter 5. Techniques, unlike methodologies, are capable of very precise formulation, but more than that they are contained within methodologies. The same technique may of course be employed by different methodologies but the issue of the applicability of different techniques to each planning method is one requiring much closer elaboration and one prompted by the succeeding chapters.

The techniques which enable the planner to analyse the functioning of a region, and which are discussed in this chapter, include forecasting techniques, model building, focused particularly on input-output analysis, economic base analysis, regional multiplier analysis, industrial location analysis, spatial interaction and gravity models, social accounting, social area analysis, and monitoring. This choice of analytical techniques stems mainly from the development of regional planning which has been dominated by economic planning, but also reflects the current realization for a need to develop equivalent techniques in the social field. However, it must be pointed out at this stage that techniques are social or economic in terms of the end to which they are addressed, and a narrow categorization of these as economic or social must be avoided. For example, gravity models, social accounting and social area analysis, all have a capability to analyse opportunity for both social and economic interaction. While input-output analysis and regional multiplier analysis are traditionally described as 'economic' techniques, their usage in achieving and maintaining full employment and maximum levels of income has important implications for the development of both economic and social opportunities.

As most analytical techniques require the use of data, the discussion of individual analytical techniques is preceded by an examination of data needs and availability at the regional scale. The techniques which assist the planner in the planning process itself are considered in Chapter 8, and include checklist of criteria; comparative cost and investment appraisal; threshold analysis; cost benefit analysis; goals achievement matrix; and planning, programme and budgeting systems.

To some extent techniques may be used for both analytical and procedural purposes; for example, indicators of regional development and performance may be used both for monitoring in an analytical way or in the process of plan evaluation. The technique of forecasting may also be used for two purposes, either as an essential ingredient of a modelling technique or to help simulate alternative futures in plan making itself.

Both Chapters 7 and 8 are intended to provide an introduction to the role of the techniques in regional planning. An assessment is made of their usefulness, together with a critical analysis of the state of individual techniques, their main strengths and weaknesses, and their potential use. In particular, emphasis is given to why, how and when individual techniques may be used. These aspects of technique application are as important as knowledge of the techniques themselves. The task of handling techniques in a meaningful way is an immense one; the application of a technique which may seem appropriate in a certain situation, or with a certain methodology, will require constant reappraisal for an assessment of its usefulness. At the same time the question of the relationships between techniques is one demanding constant consideration. Although no doubt some techniques may complement and reinforce one another, attempts which have been made recently to produce a grand synthesis between all of them may be far from desirable.[1] While valuable knowledge and understanding of regional planning techniques may be gained from reading the literature, there is no substitute for actual application to appreciate the use and abuse of individual techniques.

The development and advancement of techniques in planning gathered momentum in the 1960s as a more scientific approach was made to the activity of planning. This movement toward a more scientific approach to planning has necessarily focused upon greater weighting being given to objectivity and quantification. However, this increased awareness of the need for a more scientific approach in seeking solutions to the problems and issues of society has not been solely concerned with placing numerical values on previously unmeasured variables, but also with arranging thoughts in a more orderly and logical manner.

A bibliography has been included in Appendix 2 which may be used for further reading in relation to the individual techniques. The bibliography provides a summary list of the main pieces of published work, both books and articles, on the respective techniques.

Information Needs

This section on information needs is a prerequisite for the following section on the availability of information. One of the main technical difficulties which has faced planners in recent years has been to manage the available stock and flow of statistics. Many regional planning studies undertaken in the 1960s illustrated the adoption of a 'marshalling' approach whereby the maximum amount of data was gathered but little or no account taken of the real questions which needed answering and for which data might be required. This section is not intended to be a guide to the information needs of regional planning *per se* but rather in so far as the application of techniques depends to a large extent on the availability of data. The availability of data itself cannot be assessed in any meaningful way without considering what kind of information is required.

Any attempt to influence the course of events in a regional system presupposes a knowledge of the economic and social relationships which control the variables it is desired to influence. However, for decision making, it is not sufficient to know just how a regional system works; it is essential to have accurate and recent information on the state of the system at the time of applying a policy. The information needs of regional planning are required to give both a quantitative and qualitative measure of the stocks and flows of social and economic variables which underlie the planning process. The extent to which existing data are adequate must be examined within this context.

The list of questions which may be posed for which solutions, and therefore information, may be required is endless. But a list of questions has been included here to illustrate the point that a simple question may require a complex technique for its solution, and that techniques have a very real practical use. To what extent, and for what reasons, is the level of personal income higher or lower than in other regions? Does the region contain a high proportion of growth industries? Does the region receive a net gain or loss of population through migration with other regions? Is this of any practical significance? To what extent is the labour force fully employed? What impact would be made by the growth or decline of industry X on the region's economy? What are the major deficiencies in the region's housing stock? To what extent does the existing provision of social services meet the needs of individuals and families in the region? To what extent does the supply of recreational facilities meet the demand for them? What changes in central government's regional policy would be beneficial to the region's rate of economic growth? What are the likely effects of locating a major investment project (e.g. airport, steel works, roadbridge, new town, or channel tunnel) inside or outside the region? What impact has been made on the region by entry to the EEC? Clearly, the nature and scope of the questions to which answers must be found will depend on the circumstances peculiar to the region. The need for information must stem from the nature and scope of the issue being considered; information must not be used simply because of its availability.

The Availability of Information

There are two main aspects of the availability of statistics; firstly, the collection of new information, and secondly, the use of data which are already available.

The effectiveness of regional planning depends to a large extent on the quality of information available, yet there have been many criticisms in recent years of the existing supply of statistics. These criticisms include the irregularity of the flow of data, slowness in their availability, absence of links between old and new series of data (e.g. (a) old and new standard regions; (b) 1958 and 1968 SIC), difficulties in aggregating statistics for areas required, and the need to tap unused sources of information (such as the Inland Revenue, or market research surveys).

Until 1964 only a small amount of national statistics had been provided with a regional breakdown. With the establishment of the new Planning Regions, the need for regional information became urgent, and in 1965 the first issue of the annual *Abstract of Regional Statistics* was published. In the last few years, and particularly since the work of the Hunt Committee on Intermediate Areas which reported in March 1969 having encountered huge problems of data availability in assessing the performance of regions, the need has been felt for a finer breakdown of statistics.

Two important developments in the improvement of data availability and their usage have been the use of computerized cartography and the collection of data on a grid square basis. With a view to improving the availability of data the East Anglia Regional Economic Planning Council commissioned in 1968 a piece of research undertaken by the Experimental Cartography Unit at the Royal College of Art into the feasibility of mapping regional planning data by computer. The work included the compilation of a comprehensive register of data available, and the results of this experiment have been published.[2] Computerized cartography enables census, survey and other data to be presented in the form of maps printed directly by the computer. Closely linked to the operation of automatic cartography is the availability of information on the basis of grid squares. One of the major problems in data availability for regional planning in Britain has been the variety of areas for which statistics have been collected and analysed. The OPCS for example, has published data from the

Census of Population for areas as small as Enumeration Districts, which vary in size. However, before the use of automatic processing of data it had been impracticable to produce sophisticated tabulations for areas as small as EDs. The 1961 Census was the first to be processed on an electronic computer, and it then became possible to produce standard tabulations for wards, civil parish and ED irrespective of whether the demand was stated beforehand or not.

The 1971 Census of Population has been operated on the basis of one kilometre squares to provide uniformity, yet also flexibility, in the availability of data. This system provides building bricks which may be used to provide information at the regional level, in a way not possible by disaggregation of national data.

The advantages for analytical purposes of a wide range of information on a national grid square basis are fairly clear; firstly, it provides statistics for divisions of a country which are uniform in size; secondly, squares on the National Grid are easy to identify on the map; and thirdly, there is greater comparability over time as the squares on the National Grid will not change in definition from one Census to another. Unfortunately, due to the technical difficulties involved, the production of the magnetic tape containing the 1971 census statistics for squares on the National Grid will be available only three or four years after the Census was taken. Another difficulty may arise over confidentiality, for while some squares will be densely populated, others may be sparse. The OPCS may have to suppress the data for squares with only one household. The challenge facing planners will be substantial; for each of some fifteen million grid squares a large amount of statistics will become available from the 1971 Census of Population alone, and it remains to be seen whether such a mass of information can be absorbed efficiently and in a meaningful way. Within this context, automatic cartography offers some new opportunities in data handling and extension of the information base.

In assessing the adequacy of information, based largely on statistics, a number of criteria may be used, including those of relevance, availability, reliability and timeliness. While the key criterion must be that of relevance, the other criteria are also important. It is necessary to have some definition of what is meant by the term 'available'. There is in fact a range of availability, from the figures published in statistical volumes to the detailed tabulations of the Census returns which may only be obtained by payment to the OPCS. A summary list of published sources containing regional data on a regular time series is contained in Appendix 3.

Description and Forecasting

FORECASTING TECHNIQUES

As mentioned at the beginning of this chapter, it is important to note that forecasting may be both an analytical and procedural technique. On the one hand a forecasting capability is an integral element of most modelling techniques; on the other hand, forecasting is an essential stage in the process of plan making, and must therefore also be considered in an examination of procedural techniques. As an analytical technique, forecasting is a fairly specific, self-contained operation, whereas as a procedural technique, forecasting may be used within a much wider context.

There are various types of forecast ranging from the subjective hunch or 'guesstimate' to the objective approach of sophisticated forecasting through model building as illustrated within economic policy by econometrics. Between these two extremes forecasts can be made on the basis of extrapolating trends, either by adopting a manual approach, or by more complicated mathematical methods of statistical analysis. Sophisticated forecasting depends largely on developing and improving models of a system which enable the workings of that system, whether a city or region, to be simulated in such a way that the consequences of given policies can be predicted. The accuracy of the prediction depends on the extent to which the model can produce the complexities of the actual system. To a large extent the reliability of prediction depends on the quality of the information used as an input to the model, and as has already been indicated, the present information base is still limited. Although forecasting may involve a high level of sophistication, it is important to remember that one of its objectives is to influence action, and that forecasting is not to be seen merely as an isolated tool of the technocrat. In addition, the efficacy of forecasts is dependent upon the goals that are sought. Within the forecasting field some important developments have been made in recent years, and especially with regard to technological forecasting. As Gordon Willis has illustrated in his book,[3] technological forecasting emphasizes the role of normative forecasting, where the problem of finding out what will be needed in the future is more than just a problem of adding up the figures for what is lacking today; it involves the exciting and demanding task of conceiving what it is that might be wanted if only it were invented or could be imagined. In his conclusion to the book Willis emphasizes an important point in relation to forecasting techniques: 'morphological analysis, relevance trees, the Delphi method of time scaling, scenario writing and the rest are all valuable techniques in the hands of wise men but dangerous in the hands of the ignorant or foolish. All techniques are the same'.[4]

Forecasting techniques may be applied to project either a system as a whole or individual sub systems; for both the methodology and techniques are similar. While a common forecasting approach may be applied to many situations, for example, population growth, manpower, shopping, leisure and recreation, office space, education and housing, two particular ones have been selected for analysis to illustrate the value of forecasting; these are population growth and manpower, which are both key variables in a regional system.

POPULATION FORECASTING

Forecasts of population growth and decline are the focal point about which a great deal of planning revolves. Forecasts of population growth play an important role in the formulation of policies on housing, education, welfare, transport and communications, water supply, sewerage, location of industry, and all the other interrelated elements which constitute the complex discipline of planning. However, despite its central importance in planning, planners have been able to claim only limited success in population forecasting. Forecasts can be made only on the basis of a certain set of assumptions and these are based on the best information available to the planner at the time of making a forecast. Over a period of time these assumptions become less valid as birth or death rates change or as migration flows into and out of an area alter in response to conditions outside the control of the planner. Thus there has been a tendency in recent years to produce a range of forecasts based upon different assumptions about natural increase and migration.

It is important to recognize that there are two elements in population growth, natural increase and net migration; natural increase is defined as the excess of birth over death, and net migration represents the balance between the number of people moving into an area and the number of people moving out. The major difficulties in forecasting population growth have focused on the migration element rather than that of natural increase. Although there are not large differences in rates of growth of natural increase between regions of Britain, there are significant interregional variations in migration rates. The most reliable sources of information on migration are the population Censuses; that for 1961 was the first to cover migration on a 10 per cent sample basis, and similarly for 1966 and 1971.

Various methods of population forecasting can be used in regional planning. These include the following; first, graphical techniques where population is plotted as a dependent variable and time as the independent variable. This method assumes that relationships which have existed in the past will continue to exist in the future and no account is taken of the composition of change. The main advantage of this method is its simplicity. Secondly, ratio and apportionment methods where changes are a function of those experienced in wider areas; thirdly, migration and natural increase methods where natural change and migration change are computed separately; fourthly, simple extrapolation where past trends of a sufficiently long time period (say 15 years) are projected into the future by use of regression and correlation analysis, and, fifthly, the cohort survival method, which is the standard method of population forecasting in current use.[5] The cohort survival technique traces what happens to each five year age group of the population over a period of time. As a cohort progresses it becomes subject to different mortality, fertility and marriage risks at different periods of time. These risks are applied to each cohort so that at the end of the period, the cohort which survives will be substantially different from the cohort which sets out at the beginning of the period. While the cohort survival method of population forecasting may be managed manually, computer programs are available or may be written to produce the forecasts.

There have been many examples[6] of planning studies using the cohort survival method for population forecasting. However, in recent years the reliability and accuracy of population forecasts has been challenged. The South East Joint Planning Team in preparing their regional planning strategy for the South East of England in 1970 decided to use 'design figures' rather than rely on mechanical population projections.[7] The South East Joint Planning Team stressed that these design figures did not represent either target populations for the region or firm forecasts which were likely to remain unchallenged. They indicated, on the basis of the best information available at the time, the general level of population that plans should be designed to accommodate. In view of the difficulties involved in making accurate forecasts over a long period, plans must be flexible enough to cope with unforeseen changes.

However, it must be stressed that the design figures used by the South East Joint Planning Team were used in conjunction with the current population projections for the South East region. While design forecasting may be sufficient for strategy planning, this might not be the case in formulating policies for individual programmes; for example, education, housing, or social services, where, for purposes of allocating scarce resources, more precise population forecasts are required. The 'design' and 'mechanical' forecasts need not be seen as mutually exclusive, but rather as complementary tools to assist the planner in the difficult task of planning.

MANPOWER FORECASTING

The rate of growth of any regional economy will depend on two elements; first, the rate of growth of the level of employment; and secondly, the rate of growth of output per man. As the level of income depends on the rate of economic growth, regional planners must be able to anticipate changes in the level of output and employment. An essential element of regional planning is therefore to forecast the future demand and supply of labour. A number of regional planning studies in Britain have used manpower forecasting techniques to identify and assess the potential surplus or deficit between the supply and demand for labour. For example, the Northern Regional Economic Planning Council in its report 'Challenge of the Changing North' published in 1966 forecast 27,000 more workers than jobs by 1971 and recommended further restrictions on industrial development certificates in the South East and Midlands, and greater inducements to development areas for the location of industry.

Forecasting the supply and demand for labour may be seen as comprising two essential steps; firstly, the demand for labour forecasts may be prepared, and then, secondly, these may be matched with the supply of labour forecasts.

Demand for Labour

Of the two elements of manpower forecasting the demand for labour is the most difficult. The South East Joint Planning Team, in preparing the strategic plan for the South East of England, tried various methods of forecasting the demand for labour but they resulted in a wide range of employment figures (from 9.3. million to nearly 10.75 million jobs in 1981). In forecasting the demand for labour there are two basic approaches which complemented each other; these are the 'inquiry' methods and the 'statistical' methods.

The 'inquiry' methods assume that future manpower requirements are already known to, or can best be estimated by, the employers themselves. The planner is essentially an agency for collecting the replies by employers to questions about their future expectations. In the short run, this method has proved to be a satisfactory one, but less reliable in the long run as few employers forecast more than three to five years ahead. The project team working on the Nottinghamshire and Derbyshire sub regional planning study found that in estimating future demand for their products or for labour, firms did not look normally more than two years ahead, with very few experimenting with five year forecasts.[8] Another major difficulty arises over problems of disclosure; even if employers do forecast their demand for labour, they are often unwilling to release this information to planners. The planner has, hitherto, failed to establish a professional rapport with the private industrial sector.[9] However, the forecaster who does not make direct inquiries of employers is probably neglecting his most reliable source of information.

A good example of the methodology of forecasting demand for labour may be found in the 1965 National Plan.[10] The keystone of The National Plan was a 25 per cent increase in Gross Domestic Product 1964-70. The government sought industry's views on the implications of a 25 per cent increase in national output for their own growth prospects up to 1970 by means of an Industrial Inquiry (Appendix C of the National Plan). Industry as a whole projected a demand for labour in 1970 above the supply likely to be available. The demands for extra manpower were 800,000 over the planned period. This compared with an expected increase in the labour force of about 400,000; an extra 200,000 were to be found by increasing activity rates and reducing the rate of unemployment, especially in the Development Areas. However, even if regional policy had been successful in achieving this aim (which it wasn't) there would have been a manpower gap of 200,000 not large in relation to a total labour force of 25 million in 1965, but still a serious problem.

The second main category of methods for forecasting the demand for labour include the statistical ones, in which the future evolution of manpower demand is deduced by the forecaster from recorded past and present trends. If medium term forecasts of employment by industrial sector are required, the first step is the tabulation of employment series covering broad industrial groups (i.e. Standard Industrial Classification orders in the UK) over a period of years. The simplest method is to extrapolate these series as they stand by fitting appropriate regression curves to them.[11] Compared with the inquiry methods, statistical methods have the advantage of producing figures by a single consistent method. Their main disadvantage is that they cannot directly take into account information of a qualitative nature, available at the plant or industrial level.

While statistical methods can be applied to forecast the demand for labour, the conditions under which an economy has grown in the past may not necessarily be sufficient to guarantee its growth in the future. So vast is the complexity of factors which influence the pattern of economic activity that any attempt to produce a forecast, however tentative, of the future industrial structure of a regional system must be subject to a wide range of qualifications and in many circumstances put its value into doubt. As a region becomes smaller in size, so the importance of local conditions becomes greater and prediction more difficult.

The method of approach most suitable for planning at regional level appears to be joint usage of the inquiry and statistical methods. With a limited number of firms each can be visited individually to make an assessment of market conditions, trading prospects, labour recruitment intents, and other aspects affecting the economic environment of industry in an area. As the inquiry method suffers from the disadvantage of being short term and based on personal opinion, this can be complemented by a statistical method. Many variations of regression analysis may·be used, ranging from a straightforward extrapolation to a method which gives greater weighting to the most recent years. This mechanical process may be supplemented by a number of studies on individual industries which are central to the economic performance of a region. The end result of a demand for labour forecast may, therefore, combine three lines of approach; first, the inquiry method, secondly the statistical method, and thirdly, the special industry studies. An example of a final employment projection, which used these approaches, is illustrated in Table 7.1. For example, if only the statistical method had been used, and extrapolated the employment trend 1961-66 for agriculture, forestry and fishing (order 1), then a situation would have arisen whereby no people would be employed at the end of the time period. Both the inquiry and special study approaches found that this would not be the case and the statistical method was amended.

Supply of Labour
People are the largest economic resource of any economy, earning between 65 per cent and 75 per cent of the national or regional income. Labour is, of course,

Table 7.1.   Projected Employment Growth Esk Valley 1961–86

		1961	1966	1971	1976	1981	1986
Primary industry							
I	Agriculture, forestry fishing	1,522	1,644	1,345	1,195	1,095	960
II	Mining and quarrying	11,561	9,168	6,200	6,200	6,200	6,200
Manufacturing industry							
III	Food, drink and tobacco	612	405	455	455	455	455
IV	Chemicals	53	33	30	30	30	30
V	Metal manufacture	63	109	180	200	200	200
VI	Engineering and electrical goods	683	2,122	3,650	4,000	4,500	4,900
VII	Shipbuilding and marine engineering	100	85	95	95	100	100
VIII	Vehicles	55	120	130	160	195	225
IX	Metal goods n.e.s.	1,216	1,119	1,190	1,190	1,200	1,200
X	Textiles	1,101	1,384	1,480	1,500	1,500	1,500
XI.	Leather and leather goods	4	4	5	5	5	5
XII	Clothing and footwear	25	95	125	165	215	255
XIII	Bricks, pottery etc.	339	383	435	455	480	495
XIV	Timber, furniture etc.	322	97	105	105	105	105
XV	Paper, printing, publishing	2,587	2,680	2,530	2,675	2,900	3,025
XVI	Other manufacturing industries	23	145	220	295	365	440
XVII	Construction	2,395	3,898	3,250	3,250	3,250	3,250
Service industry							
XVIII	Gas, electricity, water	424	570	710	710	710	710
XIX	Transport and communication	1,165	1,152	1,100	1,100	1,100	1,100
XX	Distributive trades	2,939	2,931	2,980	2,950	2,925	2,900
XXI	Insurance, banking, finance	325	364	335	335	335	335
XXII	Professional and scientific services	1,737	2,656	3,390	4,200	5,100	6,025
XXIII	Miscellaneous services	1,706	2,239	2,740	3,220	3,685	4,160
XXIV	Public administration	1,519	996	735	735	735	735
	Total	33,144	34,569	33,415	35,225	37,385	39,310

Source: Table 6.25, page 84, Esk Valley Study, op. cit.

only one factor of production; capital is the other major contributor to economic growth. There is, however, general agreement that labour is a scarce resource and should be used carefully. This point has been made quite forcibly in a number of references on the labour market.[12]

The problem of labour supply forecasting is to identify and assess the component elements of the availability of labour. In general terms the future work force may be forecast by applying projected activity rates to the population over 15 years of age predicted by the population projection. The limitations of this process lie in the reliability of the population projections and on the accuracy of the activity rates used. However, a number of different dimensions of labour supply need to be identified and measured to enable activity rates to be projected with any degree of accuracy. In forecasting labour supply the following elements need to be measured.

The unemployed   It has long been held that where the rate of unemployment is high ample supplies of labour are available or can be made available through training, and that where the rate of unemployment is low, then labour shortages are intense and few workers can be found by firms seeking labour. A low rate of unemployment may represent a large number of unemployed, but these persons may not constitute a labour reserve. A low rate of unemployment might mean that any potential labour is being used, and if a rate is low this is the 'hard core' of unemployables. On the other hand, in many cases where the rate of unemployment is high, the number of persons involved is quite small. In estimating the labour potential of the unemployed, two pieces of work are essential, the first being quantitative, and the second qualitative in nature. By applying a standard statistical technique known as Time Series analysis, the long term trend of unemployment may be measured. The results of a Time Series analysis of unemployment data for Great Britain, Scotland and Edinburgh, are illustrated in Table 7.2.

Table 7.2   Percentage Change in the Long Term Trend of Unemployment January 1952 − December 1966.

Edinburgh	− 20.9
Scotland	+ 34.3
Gt. Britain	+ 30.7

Source: Esk Valley Study, op. cit.

The time series analysis of unemployment data shows a rising trend of approximately equal force for Great Britain and Scotland, but an opposite situation for Edinburgh, where the underlying trend of unemployment was falling over the time period selected.

The significance of the unemployed as a potential pool of labour for industry, and an earner of an income themselves, depends upon to what extent the unemployed can be regarded as capable of work. The relevant information in this field is not only the numbers of unemployed people but includes their characteristics of age, mobility, desire for full or part time work, training received, capacity to benefit from training, job sought, and duration of unemployment.

The Department of Employment undertook a study of the characteristics of the unemployed, nationally, in October 1964; the national survey was based on questionnaires completed at all local offices in Britain. The survey placed the unemployed into three main categories; those who should get work without difficulty, those who will find difficulty because of the lack of local opportunity, and those who will find difficulty in getting work on personal grounds. The findings of the 1964 survey illustrated that the distribution of unemployment in these three categories were 20 per cent, 20 per cent, and 60 per cent respectively. The Department of Employment has not undertaken any comprehensive survey work since 1964, one of the main reasons being given that the results reflected to a large extent the subjective judgements of the local employment exchange managers when completing the questionnaires. The qualitative attributes of the unemployed remains an aspect of labour supply which has been inadequately researched in this country.

Labour activity rates   The unemployed can really be regarded as part of the labour force but temporarily out of employment. However, large numbers of people of working age do not participate at all in the labour force. An activity rate is defined as the proportion of the population of working age who work. Estimates of labour supply can be made by calculating activity rates and matching them with the figures of the population fo working age.

Example
given (a)   Population 15 years and over = 150,000
     (b)   activity rate = 75 per cent
then (a)   labour supply = 112,500
     (b)   inactive persons = 37,500

Differences in activity rates between areas are not necessarily attributable to economic differences, and therefore indicative of potential labour reserves. This may be the case, but differences may also be due to demographic, social and educational factors. As an article in the January 1971 issue of the *Department of Employment Gazette* has emphasized, many spatial differences in male activity rates can be explained by variations in population structure. In addition, male activity rates, nationally, are falling, mainly due to early retirement and the provision of occupational pension schemes.

Table 7.3   Activity Rates 1961: 1966: 1971

	Male				Female		
	1961	*1966*	*1971*		*1961*	*1966*	*1971*
Great Britain	86.3	84.0	77.0		37.3	42.1	40.7
Wales	85.0	81.1	72.5		28.1	33.4	33.6
Scotland	87.1	83.9	73.9		35.7	41.2	40.5

Source: 1961, 1966 and 1971 Censuses of Population

However, in the case of female activity rates, it can be expected that spatial differences can be explained by variations in industrial structure; this is certainly true of regional variations in Britain, although the position for individual localities might vary.

As variations in female activity rates are likely to indicate potential labour reserves, and female activity rates are increasing, the extent to which regional variations are explained by reference to economic factors may be analysed by means of a standardization technique. For example, the effect of variations in the age composition of the population on activity rates can be measured by standardizing the ratio of retired to total population in each age category for all regions. The expected number of retired for each region can be estimated given its age composition. This information is central to the calculation of retired inactivity rates (standardized for age composition) which may be compared to actual inactivity rates. The standardization technique is used to explain regional variations in activity rates. In an analysis of male activity rates undertaken in the planning regions of Scotland using 1966 Census data, the standardization technique for age composition explained a considerable amount of the variation in regional activity rates.[13]

Female activity rates have, nationally, increased considerably in recent years, and the fact that the activity rate has reached nearly 50 per cent might suggest that further increases may not be so easily obtained. To test the hypothesis that the labour reserve among potential female labour is exhausted, in the absence of the necessary data, requires sample survey work. It is necessary to have some measure of the propensity to work of inactive females, i.e. those women at present without a job.[14]

In preparing forecasts of labour supply, the activity rates are crucial; however, a number of other elements of labour supply must also be considered, and these are discussed briefly below.

Migration and travel to work   An addition to the supply of labour in a region may be made if the region receives a net migration gain of working population.

The potential gain will depend upon both the size of the net flow and the socio-economic characteristics of the immigrants. Communities in certain regions may find activity rates rejuvenated due to receiving a disproportionately large number of young people in relation to the present age structure. One example of this movement has been the case of the old established coal mining communities in Midlothian Scotland which have in recent years received a relatively large increase in young people buying thier own houses and working in Edinburgh. Table 7.4 quantifies the activity rates of people moving into communities in Midlothian between 1961 and 1966.

Table 7.4   Activity Rates of Immigrants to Midlothian 1961-66

Area	Activity Rates	
	Male	Female
Bonnyrigg/Lasswade SB	100.0	44.1
Dalkeith SB	90.0	59.4
Musselburgh SB	100.0	49.2
Loanhead SB	100.0	42.0
Penicuik SB	100.0	39.7
Newbattle DC	95.6	50.9
Musselburgh SB	92.6	35.0
Gala Water SB	94.0	48.6
Penicuik SB	89.2	35.7
Lasswade SB	86.2	34.3

Source: 1966 Census of Population, Unpublished tables.

On the other hand, regions may experience persistent net losses of population through migration, as in South Wales where the labour supply has been depleted by out migration of economically active persons. Table 7.5 illustrates the net losses in population through migration experienced by valley communities in South Wales during the period 1961-71. One of the most serious aspects of loss of population is the depletion of community resources through migration of the economically active. The implications of such relatively large scale population shifts on employment, economic resources, social support networks and social relationships on these communities are enormous.

Benefits may also accrue to individual areas within a region through travel to work patterns and the situation of a town as a labour catchment area. The Census of Population provides information on travel to work and the extent of local labour catchment areas. In addition, the demand for labour in a dominant adjacent urban centre outside a region may have an important bearing on the availability of labour within the region. Two examples of the pull of large urban centres may be taken from the situation in Edinburgh and Cardiff in relation to their city region. The complex relationships which may exist between a

Table 7.5   Changes in Home Population 1961–71: Valley Communities in South Wales

Area	Home Population 1961	Population Changes 1961–71				Home Population 1971
		Total	Natural Change	Armed Forces	Net Civilian Migration	
Glyncorrwg UD	9,360	− 750	+ 820	—	− 1,570	8,610
Maesteg UD	21,510	− 590	+ 880	—	− 1,470	20,920
Ogmore & Garw UD	21,010	− 1,490	+ 750	—	− 2,240	19,520
Aberdare UD	39,170	− 1,390	+ 140	—	− 1,530	37,780
Mountain Ash UD	29,530	− 1,730	+ 860	—	− 2,585	27,800
Pontypridd UD	35,430	− 900	+ 1,040	minus 10	− 1,930	34,530
Rhondda MB	100,240	− 11,250	+ 340	—	− 11,590	88,990
Gelligaer UD	34,640	− 930	+ 1,980	—	− 2,910	33,710
Bedwelly UD	27,300	− 2,020	+ 1,400	—	− 3,420	25,280
Blaenavon UD	8,410	− 1,260	− 110	—	− 1,150	7,150
Brynmawr UD	6,470	− 480	+ 40	—	− 520	5,990
Ebbw Vale UD	28,610	− 2,580	+ 1,120	—	− 3,700	26,030
Nantyglo & Blaina UD	11,010	− 340	+ 550	—	− 885	10,670
Pontypool UD	39,570	− 2,750	+ 700	—	− 3,420	36,850
Rhymney UD	8,870	− 860	+ 170	—	− 1,035	8,010
Tredegar UD	19,790	− 1,920	+ 650	—	− 2,570	17,870

Source: Welsh Office, June 1972

dominant urban centre and its periphery may necessitate demand for labour studies of the industrial structure in the centre;

Labour from industries with declining employment opportunities In Britain, coal and agriculture industries have released a constant supply of labour which has been utilized by the newer growing industries. The 1965 National Plan forecast a loss of 142,000 jobs in agriculture, and 179,000 jobs in the coal industry in 1964-70. Special attention must be given to industries in an area which faces declining employment opportunities as a potential source of labour.

Young persons Finally, an important contribution to the supply of labour is made by young persons leaving school and entering the labour force for the first time.

Forecasting Labour Supply
All the labour market studies provide information to forecast activity rates, which can be matched with population projections to give labour supply forecasts. A central issue arises over the assumptions used in preparing the activity rate projections. The assumptions will cover many aspects of human behaviour, including raising the minimum school leaving age after 1973/74, the increase in numbers of young people going on to full time education, the demand for part time jobs by married women, together with some statement on the overall demand for labour. The actual supply of labour which is forthcoming will depend upon the level of the demand for labour at any particular time. As activity rates are affected by the demand for labour it must be emphasized that the supply of labour cannot be calculated independently from the demand for labour; both aspects of manpower forecasting need to be meshed together.

In conclusion to this section on forecasting it should be mentioned that at the present time planners do not have any knowledge of the probable ranges of error implicit in the use of techniques. Furthermore, it cannot be said, at the present time, whether complicated and expensive techniques give better forecasts than naive ones. However, the process of monitoring will give planners the opportunity to check the accuracy of their forecasts, which is something that has not been done before on any systematic basis.

The activity of forecasting is an integral element of model building; the analysis of manpower forecasting considered on the preceding pages may be placed within the framework of an overall model of the labour market. It is to the task of model building that the following section focuses its attention.

Model Building

The purpose of this section is to provide an introduction to the task and scope of model building; it illustrates some of the methodological and technical problems involved in their application, and makes some comments on their potential use. Wilson[15] identifies their role as being twofold; firstly, model building is at the root of all scientific activity, and regional modelling is an attempt to achieve a scientific understanding of cities and regions; and secondly, model building may be used in providing solutions to a variety of urban and regional problems.

The concept of scale is central to both the theory and operation of model building.[16] While theories and models may be applicable at various aggregate levels, the level of spatial aggregation of concern in this section is the regional level. This will, necessarily, in many cases, include references to national urban and intra urban levels as human behaviour may be represented as a flow as well as a stock. In other words, any regional model may embrace a number of spatial levels; for example, regional multiplier analysis will be concerned not only with regional income and expenditure flows but also those at the national and international level. Again, a model to examine regional growth in terms of population movements will be concerned with flows between towns and cities as well as between regions.

As Wilson has indicated[17] a brief definition of a model is a 'formal representation of a theory or a hypothesis'. A model is used by the planner to provide both understanding and an explanation of phenomena in systems of concern to him. In addition it might be expected that a useful model will provide a forecasting capability. Formal representation of theories has for some time been considered as models. While current interest in modelling may be considered as a sign that the urban social sciences have reached a particular level of development, this is a natural accompaniment and development of scientific inquiry. As models are representative of theories, model building cannot be isolated as an activity away from the theoretical base. A number of basic steps are contained within the method of model building;[18] these steps include the following:

1 Identifying the purpose of using the model, and the questions to which the model builders are attempting to provide solutions.

2 Identifying the components of the system which will form the variables of the model.

3 Identifying the time scale involved in providing an explanation of, or forecasting behaviour. The time scale involved will determine the use of static techniques or the construction of a dynamic model in which time is handled explicitly.

4 While a model is a representation of a theory there may be a range of model building techniques available from which one might be selected to represent a theory.

5 Assessing whether or not a model is a good or bad one, the model will have to be calibrated and tested.

Although it is possible to construct a list of planning problems to which model building might provide solutions, or make a contribution to providing solutions, the approach used in this section is to consider the range of models available to the planner and outline the uses to which each model might be put. Faced with a particular problem or issue, this range of models may be used as a check list against which the selection of the most appropriate model can be made.

As outlined at the beginning of this chapter, this section is concerned with those techniques which enable planners to increase their knowledge and understanding of how a regional system functions at different points in time, rather than those techniques which may be used to assist choice in plan selection. This latter aspect of regional planning techniques is considered in Chapter 8. Even within the broad category of model building techniques, attention is focused on the role of those techniques which might be expected to be used both regularly and frequently within the regional planning process.

INDUSTRIAL LOCATION ANALYSIS

Industrial growth is the key to economic development in the UK. While economic growth at a national level is a central issue, the problem also arises as to how this can be achieved, at a regional or sub regional level. In the Development Areas, for example, to realize the objectives of the future in terms of lower net migration, lower unemployment, higher activity rates, better employment opportunities, and higher incomes, higher rates of growth may be the most appropriate policy. Below regional level there are no figures of output available on which to base forecasts or projections and thus all analysis below regional level must be based on statistics of employment. Even at regional level, the availability of data on output for a recent time period is poor. While a forecast may be made which shows no increase in employment, this need not necessarily be interpreted as meaning that no increase in output is expected, for output could increase as a result of an increase in output per head, i.e. productivity. Industrial location analysis may be used to answer important questions related to a region's industrial structure; these questions include the following; is the industrial structure specialized or diversified? If the industrial structure is highly specialized, is this a weakness or a strength? What are the reasons for a region achieving a certain rate of economic growth?

A useful first task in an analysis of the industrial structure of a regional economy, is to compare its growth against the growth of the national economy; or if a sub region is taken, then a comparison with the region of which it is a part. In Scotland, for example, total employment in 1967 was barely above the level of 1959, whereas the corresponding figure for Great Britain was an increase of nearly 10 per cent. Between 1959 and 1964 employment in Scotland actually grew faster than in the rest of Great Britain, but since then employment has declined sharply.

When analysing growth in employment, it is important to bear in mind two aspects of the choice of time scale. First, the time scale should be consistent with any changes in the Standard Industrial Classification which might have occurred (e.g. major changes for 1958 and 1968 SICs); and secondly, the time period adopted should conform to a complete trade cycle, that is representing two points of equality in the level of economic activity as this will have a significant effect on job creation. In other words, as with all comparisons, it is important to compare like with like; for example, 1961-1966 was one trade cycle period with the rate of unemployment nationally at 1.5 per cent in both 1961 and 1966. Fortunately, 1961 and 1966 were also years in which a Census of Population was undertaken.

Disparities in rates of growth of employment are obvious indicators of differences in the employment structure of different areas. In regional analysis a number of more sophisticated techniques have been developed for the purpose of analysing the structures of regional economies to assess the strength and performance of a system in economic terms. While a number of analytical techniques have been developed in the literature in relation to industrial location analysis, emphasis is placed here on those which might be used most frequently.[19]

The first of the techniques of regional analysis on industrial structure is the *location quotient,* which has been developed to demonstrate the region's share of employment in particular industries. The location quotient has sometimes been used as a self sufficiency ratio. In computing the location quotient the base used depends upon the problem and region under study. In terms of employment a necessary first step is to divide industry into four major sub divisions; primary, manufacturing, construction and service industry. The location quotient can then be calculated in two ways.

1 Numerator: the region's percentage share of total employment in industry.
  Denominator: the region's percentage share of total national employment in primary/manufacturing/construction/service industry.

Dividing the numerator by the denominator gives the location quotient. Where the value of the quotient is less than 1, the region has less than a 'fair share of a particular industry'; where the quotient is greater than 1, the region has more than a proportionate share.

2 Numerator: the percentage of the region's total primary/manufacturing/construction/service employment accounted for by industry.
  Denominator: the percentage of national total primary/manufacturing/construction/service employment accounted for by industry.

Dividing the numerator by the denominator gives the location quotient. This method yields the same results as the first method and the same interpretation can be put on the values of the quotient.

Example of Location Quotient for Welsh Economy 1970
e.g. Mining and Quarrying (Order II of 1968 SIC)

1 Numerator: number employed in coal industry in Wales as a percentage of total employed in coal industry in UK = 13 per cent.
2 Denominator: number employed in primary industry in Wales as a percentage of total employed in primary industry in UK = 8.9 per cent.

location quotient: $\dfrac{13.0}{8.9} = 1.5$

The corresponding location quotient for metal manufacture in Wales for 1970 is:

$$\frac{16.1}{4.1} = 3.9$$

The location quotient illustrates a region's dominance in a particular industry. The location quotient, together with the other industrial location/structure techniques, has been used in relatively few planning studies.[20] While the location quotient does have a limited use on its own, it is a useful technique when used in conjunction with related techniques on industrial location and structure. It may also have a useful role to play in economic base analysis in distinguishing between local and export markets. If a given region is highly specialized relative to the nation in the production of a particular commodity, the product is presumed to be an export item. The distinction between local and export economic activities is important in economic base analysis because regional growth is seen to be dependent on the demand for goods external to the region.

From the table of location quotients a number of further indices or coefficients can be calculated to demonstrate the degree of concentration of specialization of industry which has taken place within a region. Perhaps the most useful is the *coefficient of specialization*. This coefficient measures the extent to which the distribution of employment by industry groups in a region deviates from the national distribution (or sub region from a regional distribution).

The method of calculation of the coefficient of specialization is as follows:

1 Numerator: ratio of employment in industry X in the region to employment in primary/manufacturing/construction/service industry in the region.

2 Denominator: ratio of employment in industry X nationally to employment in primary/manufacturing/construction/service industry in the nation.

To calculate a coefficient of specialization the numerator is subtracted from the denominator, without regard for sign, yielding values between 0 and 1. If the region had a mix of industry identical to that of the nation (or sub region to region), the coefficient would be 0. Alternatively, if all the employment in a region is concentrated in a single industry, the value of the coefficient of specialization would approach 1.

Taking the examples of the mining and quarrying industry in Wales shown above, the coefficient of specialization is:

Example of Coefficient of Specialization

Mining and Quarrying Wales 1970

(a)   Numerator: 0.82
(b)   Denominator: 0.07

Subtract (a) from (b)   = 0.07 − 0.82
                                      $\doteqdot$ 0.75

This coefficient illustrates the extent to which the Welsh economy in comparison to the UK economy is specialized on the mining and quarrying industry.

The extent of specialization within a region can be shown diagrammatically be means of specialization curves. The industries within a region are arranged along the horizontal axis at equal distances, and on the vertical axis is plotted the cumulating percentage of total employment within each major subdivision accounted for by each individual industry.[21]

Having calculated coefficients of specialization, which assess the extent to which an economy is specialized in its industrial structure, the next task is possibly to assess whether or not the degree of specialization is something which need be a cause for concern. For example, is a situation in an industrial region specialized in, say, the coal and steel industry, any cause for concern? A technique which can be adopted to answer this type of question is the *shift ratio*. In other words, while the coefficient of specialization provides information on the degree of specialization in an industrial structure, the shift ratio is a tool which assesses whether or not the degree of specialization is harmful or beneficial to the region.

This technique applies to the employment structure of a region the changes which have taken place over a period of time in the employment structure of the national economy. The employment estimates for the region thus obtained are compared with the actual growth which has taken place in the region, i.e.

national growth rates are applied to a region's industrial structure. If the actual growth has been greater than the estimated growth, then the regional economy may be said to have performed better than the national economy of which it is a part. The shift ratio is obviously an important technique in assessing the strengths and weaknesses of a regional economy.

Two examples of the application of the shift ratio technique are illustrated below; one example, that of Cymmer, a Special Development Area in South Wales, shows that if the local economy had grown as fast as the economy of Great Britain as a whole, then more employment would have resulted; the other example, that of the Esk Valley in Midlothian (a Development Area), Scotland, shows that actual growth in recent years in the regional economy has been greater than that for Scotland as a whole, and that, if the Esk Valley had grown at the same rate as the Scottish economy, fewer jobs would have resulted.

Example 1   Esk Valley: Midlothian Scotland[22]

The Esk Valley is a sub region of the Edinburgh City region consisting of a number of towns with populations of 10-20,000 with an industrial structure equally dependent on coal mining, paper, engineering and textiles. The 1961-66 percentage changes in employment in Scotland, by SIC Order, were applied to the Esk Valley 1961 employment structure. This produced an estimated employment structure for 1966 which was then compared with the actual structure of 1966.

Industry group	Estimated employment	Actual employment	Differences
Primary	9,382	10,812	+ 1,430
Manufacturing	7,222	8,782	+ 1,560
Construction	2,730	3,898	+ 1,168
Service	10,460	11,018	+ 558
Total	29,794	34,510	+ 4,716

If industry in the Esk Valley had grown at the Scottish rate between 1961 and 1966 there would have been 29,794 people in employment in 1966, a fall of 3,350 on the total employed in 1961. However, the actual number of people employed in the Esk Valley in 1966 was 34,510 resulting in a positive surplus of 4,716 in employment over the number who would have been employed had the Esk Valley performed at the Scottish rate. The industrial location analysis undertaken in the Esk Valley Study illustrated that despite its specialization in primary and manufacturing industry the Esk Valley had grown at a much faster rate than the Scottish economy as a whole.

Example 2.   Cymmer: A Special Development Area in South Wales[23]

The Cymmer employment exchange, scheduled as a Special Development Area in 1967, comprises several communities, with a total population below 10,000, located in the Afan Valley in West Glamorgan; originally heavily dependent on the coal industry, the domestic economic base has been eroded away and, increasingly, access is sought to jobs in the Port Talbot sub region.

The shift ratio technique has been applied to Cymmer over the period 1959-69. The changes which took place in employment in Britain between 1959 and 1969 were applied to the 1959 employment structure of Cymmer, which produced an estimated employment structure for 1969. This was compared with the actual structure of 1969.

Industry group	Cymmer actual employment 1959	Employment growth Gt. Britain 1959-69 (per cent)	Cymmer estimated employment 1969	Cymmer actual employment 1969
Primary	2,856	− 43.4	1616	1,086
Manufacturing	3	+ 5.0	3	311
Construction	31	+ 4.6	32	83
Services	382	+ 11.5	426	464
Total	3,272	+ 4.8	3397	1,944

The results of the analysis shows that if Cymmer's overall industrial structure had grown at the national rate between 1959 and 1969 there would have been 3,397 people in employment in 1969. However, the actual number of people at work in 1969 was 1944, resulting in a loss of 1,453 jobs; i.e. a fall of 40 per cent who would have been employed had the local economy of Cymmer performed at the national rate.

The shift ratio technique is particularly suitable for analysis of industrial structure at regional level. However, for small regions, as in the case of the Cymmer employment exchange area, it must be recognized that a detailed application of the technique may be subject to small changes leading to substantial effects, especially where employment growth may be strongly influenced by the fortunes of perhaps a single firm. For small areas it is desirable to supplement these mechanical methods with analysis of non statistical data. Unless the mechanical techniques are related to sound local knowledge the results may not be very meaningful. As with all techniques it is necessary to relate the sophistication of the method to the subject under study.

In using the shift ratio technique, one further qualification should be made. It is possible that the faster (or slower) rate of employment growth in a region could be attributed to it having a faster (or slower) rate of population growth. For example. between 1961 and 1966, the population of Scotland rose by only 2.5 per cent, whereas the population of the Esk Valley rose by 4.8 per cent. This possibility can be examined by means of *relative growth charts*.[24] These are calculated by relating the employment growth in a region over a specific time period to the population growth over the same period. The same calculations are carried out for the national economy (or that of the region if this is being compared to growth in a sub region). The ratios are plotted in charts and indicate per capita growth in employment.

The scope of industrial location analysis may be extended by the use of a more sophisticated standardization technique known as *shift and share* analysis which may also be used to analyse the relationship between regional growth differentials and regional differentials in industrial composition. The application of this technique, in a modified form, to the Planning Regions of the UK by Stillwell[25] has demonstrated that regional policy in the 1960s had at least some effect in securing a more favourable industrial structure in the less prosperous regions.

ECONOMIC BASE ANALYSIS

Economic base analysis is based on the hypothesis that the existence and growth of a region depends on the goods and services it produces locally and sells, or exports, beyond its borders. The economic base theory is applicable to the analysis of cities or regions, and while economic base analysis may be used to estimate regional multipliers, many urban and regional economic base studies have been used in a descriptive function to improve understanding of how a community earns its living.

Regional economic base analysis distinguishes two types of actitivy within the regional economy; first, 'basic' activities which export goods and services; and secondly, 'service' activities which are consumed locally. The economic base of a region consists of those activities which provide the basic employment and income on which the rest of the economy depends. As Tiebout has emphasized,[26] an economic base study identifes the basic sources of employment and income and provides an understanding of the source and level of all employment and income in a region. Therefore the economic base study is able to develop information which will help a community solve local problems.

While the measurement of the economic base was developed in the 1940s by Daly and Hoyt,[27] economic base analysis has been linked with regional multiplier theory in the form of the regional 'export base' theory which states that the growth of a region depends upon the growth of its export industries. This theory suggests that it is expansion in demand external to the region which is crucial in determining growth within the region. The regional export base theory was developed by North and Tiebout in the 1950s.[28]

Economic base analysis has been related to the idea of a 'basic service' ratio, which is calculated in one of two ways:

1 The proportion between total employment in a region's basic or export activities and total employment in its service or local activities.

2 The proportion between the increase in employment in basic activities and the increase in employment in service activities.

From either of these basic service ratios a regional multiplier can be easily calculated.

Formula

The multiplier =

$$\frac{\text{total (or increase) employment in both basic and service activities}}{\text{total (or increase in) basic employment}}$$

The economic base study has not been undertaken on any large scale in Britain; it was, however, a technique used in the South East Lancashire and North East Cheshire (SELNEC) transportation study.[29] The study undertaken by Tiebout[30] in the USA serves as a useful reference work on the theoretical base and empirical mechanics which form the core of an economic base study.

A number of criticisms have been made of economic base analysis.[31] Firstly, as Isard[32] has emphasized, there are serious difficulties involved in measuring the economic base. Economic base studies have used employment as the unit of measurement mainly because data on employment are more readily available than data related to other possible units of measurement, such as income or net output. However, data on jobs do not take account of different wage levels in different industries; for example, the same increases in employment in two industries paying significantly different wages (such as the coal and steel industries in South Wales) will lead to different secondary (i.e. multiplier) effects.

Secondly, there are problems involved in distinguishing between basic and service activities. Many industries are mixed in the sense that they cannot easily be wholly allocated to either basic or service activities. One solution to this problem has been the application of location quotients to determine the basic service division. For example, ratios greater than unity may be taken to indicate an export or basic industry, and the amount by which the ratio exceeds unity may be an indication of the extent to which employment is basic.

Thirdly, there are substantial methodological problems involved in economic base theory which question its validity. The theory overemphasizes the role of exports suggesting that a large weighting of basic industry will necessarily result in growth, and as Blumenfeld has argued, underestimates the significance of imports.[33] The existence of imports as a leakage from the circular flow of income questions the usefulness of distinguishing between basic and service activities.

Fourthly, the economic base analysis has been used as a planning technique to predict the growth of cities and regions. Some preliminary research by Pfouts[34] in the 1950s illustrated that little relationship existed between basic activity (measured by location quotients) and growth (measured by population growth) but rather found a closer relationship between service activity and growth. It might be expected that the ratio of basic to total activity will tend to fall as cities become larger, which will seriously weaken the base concept as an explanation of long term growth.

In the SELNEC study in Britain the economic base analysis was used as a predictive technique to assess the quantity of non basic employment versus basic employment which is to be expected in an urban or regional system of a given size. The size of the non basic element of employment may be taken as directly related to population size, i.e. it can be expected that the larger the region the more it is self sufficient in local services.

While economic base analysis may be used as a technique to predict what type of employment/industrial structure is required in relation to certain population sizes, it must be recognized that the technique is constrained by a number of technical difficulties, and is too simple in its present form to analyse regional growth. However, the main advantage of the economic base concept is its simplicity, and it does provide a useful technique for purposes of both preliminary analysis and prediction.[35] While the economic base method may not be very accurate in making forecasts in the context of other forecasting techniques, this is not necessarily critical. The real value of an economic base study is its ability to pinpoint the problem areas of a region; it may, for example, reveal what sectors are in trouble and how they are related to other elements in the economy.

REGIONAL MULTIPLIER ANALYSIS

If money is injected into an economic system the income of that system will increase not only by the value of that injection but by some multiple of it. The income multiplier has been used for many years as an important tool of national economic analysis and forecasting and has been one of the first national economic models to be applied at regional level.

The regional multiplier is an important concept because it enables an assessment to be made of the consequences of changes in expenditure for regional income and employment.

Formula

$$\text{The multiplier} = \frac{\text{change in income}}{\text{change in expenditure}}$$

and the size of the multiplier depends on the size of the marginal propensity to consume.[36]

The size of the multiplier depends on the proportion of income allocated to consumption. The marginal propensity to consume identifies the proportion of any increase in income which is consumed, and the marginal propensity to save, the proportion in any increase of income which is saved. The size of the multiplier depends upon the size of the MPC. The higher the MPC, the higher is the multiplier as consumption represents an injection into the circular flow of income and savings as a withdrawal from this system.

For example, if the government spent £10 million on road building in region A, this initial injection raises incomes to the building industry and economy by £10 million. Assuming 20 per cent of this increase in income is saved, i.e. the MPS = 0.2, and 80 per cent, i.e. £8 million, is spent on services, the service industry has an increase in income of £8 million. The income of the region has, therefore, increased by £18 million. With a constant MPS of 0.2, and therefore an MPC of 0.8, (MPC plus MPS must equal 1. i.e. income) the people in the service industry spend 80 per cent of the income they receive and save 20 per cent, i.e. £6.4 million spent (80 per cent of £8 million) and £1.6 million saved; the income so far generated is £10 million plus £8 million plus £6.4 million etc. With an MPS of 0.2, the multiplier will be 5, i.e. the reciprocal of the MPS. Therefore, £10 million of investment in a region with an MPC of 0.8 and MPS of 0.2 will create £50 million of income.

The use of multiplier analysis is also important in that it stresses the linkage between regions, and especially the point that money injected into one region frequently leaks out into other regions. Recent research into variations between regional multipliers in the UK has illustrated that these variations are fairly narrow, and that multipliers for the development areas as a whole probably fit within the range 1.14 and 1.28.[37]

When income is earned there are numerous leakages which reduce local consumption, and therefore the multiplier.[38] Firstly, there are the income leakages; these include savings, national insurance contributions, and direct taxation. Therefore a relatively large amount of income (these three items account for approximately 25 per cent of personal income) is never spent; it is taken out of spending, either to the national exchequer, or into personal savings. Leakages to other regions may not only occur in consumption but also in savings; savings placed with building societies and insurance companies in the peripheral regions may, for example, be invested to accommodate urban growth in the South East of England.

While the income leakages are relatively easy to calculate, the expenditure leakages are more difficult to measure. There are three main items to take out of expenditure made in a region to find expenditure on goods and services produced in a region itself. Firstly, an estimate must be made of expenditure undertaken on services. If it is assumed, for example, that most expenditure on services is attributed to the region itself, then some estimate is required of the proportion of personal expenditure made on goods from which there may be leakages. Secondly, in the UK indirect taxes take approximately 12 per cent of personal expenditure. The third main item consists of import leakages caused by importing goods from abroad; this may comprise both other regions within national space as well as other countries. Therefore, some estimate has to be made of the extent of self sufficiency within a region. In the absence of the necessary data, i.e. trade flows between regions, one method suggested by Allen[39] is to use the ratio of employees in consumer goods industry in the region as a proportion of employees in the UK consumer goods industry to the population of the region as a proportion of the UK population. In the case of Wales, the ratio of self sufficiency works out at 2.8 : 4.8 or approximately 60 per cent.

Some research work undertaken by the authors on the Welsh economy illustrates that of total personal income of £900 million in 1966/67, total leakages amounted to £498 million. Therefore, for every £100 injected into the Welsh economy only £44 is likely to remain. The regional multiplier is, of course, inversely related to leakages; the Welsh expenditure will be significantly reduced by the relatively high leakages from the circular flow of income. The essence of the multiplier lies in the size of the possible leakages, all of which reduce the MPC. Without any leakages the MPC would be unity and the multiplier infinity. A lot of work remains to be done on regional multipliers.[40] As the availability of data improves, especially knowledge of regional trade and of the destination of the regional import flows to sectors within the region, less reliance need be placed on the use of national ratios for regions, and regional ratios for local economies in estimating multipliers.

A low regional multiplier means that solving regional problems, of high unemployment and low incomes, will necessarily be a slow process; as one author has remarked, it is like trying to fill a bath with the plug out.[41] Modern economies are characterized by high levels of interregional trade and high levels of taxation, all of which make for high leakages and therefore low multipliers.

Regional multiplier theory may help to solve some important problems involved with regional planning. Firstly, regional multipliers are important in determining whether or not regional policy should be undertaken on a selective basis; and secondly, when a regional policy is agreed regional multipliers may help in choosing regions most likely to benefit from particular kinds of policy. The regional multiplier provides a measuring rod for determining the effects of regional policies.

Disparities in Gross Regional Products may be modified by the application of fiscal policy and monetary policy contained within a regional policy. The extent to which regional policy is able to reduce disparities in employment and economic growth depends to a large extent on the degree to which higher expenditure in poorer regions gives rise to either higher local production which will raise Gross Regional Products, or higher imports from other regions and abroad which will be a leakage from the circular flow of income.

Multiplier analysis may also provide a basis for favouring certain types of industrial development. Central governments, for example, could operate a selective investment allowance scheme whereby higher rates of allowance would be given to industries which yield high multipliers, i.e. those which increase regional production rather than stimulate demand outside the region.

Important changes in taxation have taken place in the 1970s, especially that of Value Added Tax. Regional differentials in taxation may help to reduce regional disparities by making an impact on a person's marginal propensity to consume and therefore the size of the multiplier. At present taxation, other than the local rateable value tax, is operated by central government. However, there are a number of ways in which taxation may be regionalized.[42]

Any rise in a region's disposable income resulting from an injection of money will depend upon the importance of certain leakages. These leakages will not only vary with a region's industrial structure, but also with a region's size. It can be expected that regional size will make a significant impact on regional multipliers because larger regions are likely to be more self sufficient than smaller ones, thereby leading to smaller leakages.

Regional multiplier analysis may not only be an instrument of regional policy at national level, but also a powerful instrument for regional planning agencies in seeking to increase their allocation of central government resources. Agencies in less prosperous areas, with relatively high MPC's, may be able to justify claims on the nation's resources in so far as a given piece of autonomous investment expenditure by central government would lead to a relatively large increase in regional income compared with that investment in a more prosperous region. On the other hand, numerous difficulties face the least prosperous areas. The Special Development Areas in the UK for example, suffer many disadvantages; firstly, the necessary data on income, investment, consumption, and saving, are virtually non-existent at local level to calculate regional multipliers; and secondly, the Special Development Areas, being small in size with a weak economic base, have relatively high leakages which reduce the power of the multiplier and therefore a claim on extra resources. However, regional multiplier analysis does contribute to the knowledge and understanding of how a regional system operates, and in the case of the Special Development Areas, with their relatively high expenditure leakages, the size of the problem involved can be both identified and measured, and a basis provided on which to operate a regional policy.

INPUT-OUTPUT ANALYSIS
Input-output analysis was pioneered by Wassily Leontief in his standard work.[43]

Many of the principles developed by Leontief still apply today. It is another of those models which have been found useful at the national level and which have therefore been extended to the regional, and in some instances, even sub regional level, on the basis that regions are similar in many ways to nations. The problems of using national models at regional level in relation to input-output analysis have been examined by Edwards and Gordon.[44] The two major problems of using the nation-region model are, the lack of adequate data and the validity of applying national models to smaller and more open systems. This latter difficulty has already been encountered in the application of regional multiplier analysis. Hitherto, regional input-output tables in Britain have been based on national data as little regional data are collected on interindustrial relationships. This necessarily entails the use of more assumptions in preparing regional input-output tables than national ones.[45]

The input-output table is a system of accounts prepared for an economy which examines the linkages between different sectors of an economy as they combine to produce the regional product (i.e. gross regional product, or gross national product of a national economy). An input-output analysis for South Wales, for example, would provide an assessment of the impact for each sector of the economy of changes in particular sectors. For example, such an input-output analysis could measure the impact of a decline in the coal industry sector or growth in the steel industry sector on other sectors in the region. Input-output analysis can provide a tool for predicting the likely impact of growth and decline in particular sectors on the rest of the economy. The usefulness of the input-output table lies in changes occurring in individual sectors on the rest of an economy. For this, however, assumptions or estimates must be made of the technical relationships which exist between outputs of the different sectors and the inputs absorbed by them.

The first official input-output table was published in the Blue Book for 1952; it consisted of only eight industry groups, whereas that for 1963 consisted of 28 industrial groups. Although during recent years a number of regional and interregional input-output tables have been constructed, and substantial progress has been made in improving the methodological aspects of the input-output technique, it still remains a very expensive tool of analysis. This is probably the major reason for its relatively slow development and application by planning authorities in Britain.

The high cost of preparing an input-output table is due to the enormous amount of statistical data which is required. To construct an input-output table; information is required from the Census of Production on both sales and purchases for the industrial groups. The collection and processsing of information for a transaction table consumes a great deal of time and money. Although Hewings[46] has surveyed input-output models in the UK with a view to using non survey techniques to prepare a set of regional tables for the West Midlands on the lines of recent research in the USA, he eventually came to the conclusion that it is doubtful whether present methods will obviate local surveys completely.

National Input-Output Analysis

Input-output analysis is based on preparing input-output tables. The Central Statistical Office prepares input-output tables and publishes these in the National Income and Expenditure Book. The most recent and comprehensive input-output table is that for 1968, published in the Blue Book of 1971. Most regional and local input-output tables are based on these national tables. This table illustrates two important points; first, it shows the interindustrial relationships within the national economy; and secondly, the national table illustrates the difference between 'intermediate' buyers and 'final' buyers, who use goods and services as finished goods. The electricity supply industry, for example, uses coal as an intermediate buyer, whereas households use coal as final buyers. The intermediate buyers use a product in the process of production, while final buyers purchase a product for its own use.

In addition to difficulties regarding the availability of data, the input-output tables take a considerable time to prepare; the tables for 1954 were not completed until 1961, and those for 1963, not until 1968. The latest detailed Census of Production relates to 1968. To help overcome timing problems the Central Statistical Office prepares updated tables projected forward from an existing base year. The Central Statistical Office has recognized that, in addition to the need for central government, industry, research workers in universities and research institutions are showing greater interest in input-output studies. The Central Statistical Office therefore undertook a special table of more than 70 industries based on the 1963 Census of Production, which was published in 1970.[47]

Input-Output Tables used in Analysis

The input-output table shows for each sector what it must buy from other sectors in order to produce its own product; it also shows for each sector the destination of the finished product. Input-output analysis is based on three types of table; first, the descriptive table which illustrates sectoral linkages; secondly an analytical table showing input coefficients which defines the technology of the sectors of the economy; and thirdly, an analytical table which shows the completed pattern of linkages when changes occur in particular sectors.[48]

The input-output table describes the intersectoral flows of goods in an economy. A simple example of the descriptive input-output tables is given in Table 7.1

Table 7.1 illustrates an input-output table for a region with only two production

Table 7.1   The Descriptive Input-Output Table

Region X

Sales by	Purchases by		£ millions Final buyers	Total output
	A	B		
A	—	10	40	50
B	30	—	40	70
Domestic income	10	50	—	60
Imports	10	10	10	30
	50	70	90	210

sectors A and B. Sector A buys £30 million of product from B. £10 million of domestic income (i.e. the services of factors of production; land/labour/capital); and £10 million of imports (either from other regions or abroad); the value of total purchases by Sector A must equal the value of total output of Sector A (£50 million).

This description need not only apply to the time when the data were assembled because an assumption can be made that the basic production characteristics of industry are likely to remain the same even if some of the circumstances change. In fact, one of the basic assumptions in the Leontief input-output model is that 'output in each industry is proportional to each input' i.e. if 400 units of a given product are produced with 100 units of input A and 50 units of input B, it is assumed that an expansion of output to 800 units would create a demand for 200 units of input A and 100 of input B. Therefore, output is assumed to be proportional to each input; or in other words, factors are combined in fixed proportions. As output is proportional to input, sectoral dependants can be shown without reference to output levels, but rather to technical coefficients; i.e. purchases by each sector from other sectors can be shown as a percentage of total input in each sector. This is illustrated in Table 7.2.

Table 7.2   Direct Requirements per £100 of Sectoral Output £

Sales by	Purchases by		Final buyers
	A	B	
A	—	15	44
B	60	—	44
Domestic income	20	70	—
Imports	20	15	12
	100	100	100

Table 7.2 illustrates that whatever the actual level of output of, e.g. sector A, 60 per cent of that output will be purchased from Sector B, and 20 per cent will be imported. Table 7.2 shows only the direct requirements of sector A; however, if sector A increases its purchases by X amount from other sectors, then these sectors must increase their own output by this amount and therefore their own input requirements, which adds indirect effects. The total impact of any changes in the production patterns of any one sector upon other sectors can be calculated.

The input-output analysis adopted for a single region can be extended to provide an interregional/interindustry input-output matrix whereby the impact of changes in one sector of a region upon sectors in another region can be assessed. Such complex analysis requires calculations to be made by using computer facilities. The potential of interregional/interindustry input-output matrices are considerable and the development of this particular technique for regional planning is still in its formative stages in Britain.

A number of problems face the user of input-output analysis, problems which are both conceptual and technical; while the technical problems of data availability are gradually being overcome, many problems of methodology may be expected to remain. Amongst these might be included the choice of regions, the choice of a set of industries or sectors, the validity of constant input coefficients, use of the input-output approach for prediction, and regional variations in the behaviour of final buyers.

Applications of Input-Output Analysis

A number of input-ouptut studies have illustrated the usefulness of the technique in regional planning. One of the first applications of the technique at regional level in Britain was that used by Nevin for the Welsh economy.[49] The Welsh input-output table was based on the format of the UK tables. The input-output model was used for predictive purposes, taking the national growth estimates of the 1965 National Plan for 1964-70 to anticipate likely developments for the Welsh economy. The expected situation in 1970 as predicted by use of the model in fact came extremely close to the actual situation.

The first major attempt to prepare an input-output table for a single town in Britain was undertaken by Blake and McDowall for St. Andrews in Scotland.[50] The model was prepared to help solve a longstanding dispute about the relative importance to the town of St. Andrews of its two staple industries, namely tourism and the university. The main conclusion of the St. Andrews study was that the university was nearly three times more beneficial to the town in £s of household income generated per £100 expenditure than tourism. It is surprising that the technique has not been extended to similar circumstances in other towns.

Another interesting use of an input-output model was that made in the USA in the Philadelphia Regional Impact Study. The project used input-output methodology for description, and as a model for projection and impact analysis. The Bucks County Inter-regional Input-Output Study was made as part of the Philadelphia Regional Impact Study, Bucks County being one of the eight counties in the region.[51] The input-output model was concerned with the economic structure of Bucks county and its economic relationships to the Philadelphia Region.

While the Bucks County input-output model was used to examine linkages of neighbouring areas, the California/Washington model was prepared with different objectives.[52] The technique was used to examine linkages between two States in the USA situated far apart from each other. One of the main objectives was to assess the influence which California's growth has had in Washington's gross regional product. As California has a gross regional product eight times the size of that of Washington, California is far less influenced by fluctuations in the final demand for Washington output.

While most of the regional planning techniques have been developed in the USA and Western Europe, it is perhaps important to point out that on input-output techniques the USSR has had considerable experience, where mathematical models have been used extensively in planning the Soviet economy both at national and regional level.[53]

SOCIAL ACCOUNTING

Social accounting is another example of a model found to be useful at national level, and which has been extended to the regional level. The application of the national model at regional level requires a comprehensive knowledge of the conceptual and technical problems involved in national accounting, which are focused mainly on the different ways in which wealth can be measured.

Social accounting is a term given to the statistical classification of the activities of human beings and social organizations involved in the process of producing scarce goods and services. The main function of regional accounting, known either as income accounting or social accounting, is to provide a better understanding of the state of a region's economy. Even where policy measures have had a social motivation, for example, unemployment, their effectiveness has often required changes in the economic development of the region.

Regional accounting requires the preparation of figures of gross domestic product for regions comparable to gross domestic product for nations. The national income accounts for the UK published annually in the National Income and Expenditure tables (Blue Book) published by the CSO, provide a detailed account of the performance of the national economy as a whole and each of the main component sectors. The national income is a measure of the money value of goods and services becoming available to the nation from economic activity.

The national income accounts provide a measurement of the nation's wealth, both at a point in time and its growth over time. The national income is important because it is the source of all expenditure to raise the standard of living, to increase investment, and to provide the government with revenue. The national accounts are of relevance not only because they measure national wealth, but because they also have important implications for preparing regional accounts. The use of Gross Domestic Product (i.e. the value of total domestic production) figures for regions comparable to the nation will enable an assessment to be made of the contribution of individual regions to the national economy. In addition, a set of figures of GDP for regions over a period of years would enable an assessment to be made of how rapidly regional economies were growing.

There are numerous ways in which an economy may be divided. The main elements of any economy are fourfold:

1 A personal or household sector to record transactions of people as consumers.
2 A productive sector to record the transactions of private and public enterprises.
3 A government sector to record the transactions of central and local government.
4 An overseas sector to record international transactions.

These constitutent sectors of any economy describe the way in which a system has and continues to function, and provides an insight into the interrelationships of economic and social processes. By studying the four main sectors which comprise an economy, the factors which determine the level of GDP can be assessed, and appropriate policies formulated.

An example of a set of national accounts for the UK in 1970 is illustrated in Figure 7.1. There are numerous technical difficulties involved in national income accounting which cannot be dealt with here. However, there are several excellent texts available on the process and problems of national income accounting.[54]

To measure the performance of a region's economy, a set of regional accounts is required; instead of the gross national product, estimates are needed of gross regional product. Unfortunately, one of the main statistical gaps in regional planning has been the absence of estimates corresponding to national income, gross national product or gross domestic product which will enable regional/national growth and interregional growth comparisons to be made in addition to an analysis of the economic structure of individual regions. As McCrone[55] has observed, while Britain was the first country in Western Europe to start a regional policy, it is surprising that it is not also ahead in the development of regional statistics. However, Italy, Belgium, West Germany, and

Expenditure	£ Million
1 Consumer's expenditure	31,238
2 Public authorities' current expenditure on goods and services	9,055
3 Gross domestic fixed capital formation	8,886
4 Value of physical increase in stocks and work in progress	454
5 Total domestic expenditure at market prices	49,633
6 Exports and property income from abroad	13,775
7 *less* Imports and property income paid abroad	−12,979
8 *less* Taxes on expenditure	− 8,458
9 Subsidies	848
10 Gross National Product at factor cost	42,819

Fig. 7.1   Gross National Product, UK 1970.
Source: *National Income and Expenditure,* Table 1 (HMSO, 1971).

to a lesser extent, France, are considerably further advanced than the UK. The only official statistics for regional GDP in the UK relate to Northern Ireland. Other work developed by private researchers includes the Welsh economic studies by Nevin and Tomkins,[56] and Woodward's regional accounts estimates for the UK.[57]

GRAVITY MODELS
The gravity model is a name given to those models concerned with spatial interaction.[58] The principle underlying gravity models is that the influence of an economic force at any point in space is directly related to the size of the force and inversely related to the distance between its source and the point in question. The use of gravity models in regional planning is made to assess how an aggregate quantity distributes itself across regional space. Use is made in these models of certain statistical relationships which can be given mathematical form and used for predictive purposes. These statistical relationships depend on the

premise that spatial interaction follows certain laws of statistical tendency and probability which can be best tested by an adequate information base.

In the use of gravity models the region is conceived as a mass, which is structured according to certain principles. These principles govern the range of behaviour of the individual component sections, both constraining and initiating their action. The first major developments in gravity model analysis were made by Stewart and Zipf.[59] The first major developments were made in the natural sciences based on those laws relating to density, pressure and temperature of gases, that were discovered only because matter was investigated as a mass. The measure of mass to be employed depends on the nature of the problem being studied and the availability of necessary information. The measures of mass may include items such as investment in particular facilities, number of families, number of jobs, gross regional product, or sales of newspapers. Similarly, distance may be measured in a number of ways, including those of mileage, travel time, and transport costs.

A conceptual analysis of the distance factor will help to explain the broad spatial patterns of, for example, retail activity. Reilly's Law of Retail Gravitation was one of the earliest applications of gravity models.[60] This law states that a city attracts retail trade from an individual customer located in its hinterland in proportion to its size (in terms of population) and in inverse proportion to the square of the distance separating the individual from the city centre.

The gravity shopping model is an attempt to illustrate the way in which consumers allocate their expenditure to different shopping centres.[61] Gravity models have been used to examine the spatial structure of a region in many different circumstances. Batty, for example, has applied a gravity model to measure the impact of a new town in central Lancashire.[62] On the other hand the Ministry of Transport in 1966 used a gravity model analysis in the examination of expansion proposals for a new dock at Portbury in Bristol.[63] The gravity model was used to produce a set of forecasts related to the flow of goods. In particular the model was used to test two hypotheses: that the share of export goods from a particular region sent through ports at a given distance away declines as a distance between region and port increases; and that, for a given exporting region, larger ports attract a larger share of exports than smaller ports at any given distance. The use of a gravity model in planning port development has also been made by Gwilliam in his study of the Haven Ports in East Anglia, especially to predict future traffic flows.[64]

SOCIAL AREA ANALYSIS

The technique of social area analysis has developed in response to the need for an analytical approach to the study of urban structure. As with many of the other analytical techniques, social area analysis was developed in the United States by Eshref Shevky and his colleagues in the late 1940s.[65] The Shevky urban typology has been analysed by Herbert in his review of social area analysis, and particularly his own study of Newcastle in 1961.[66] This technique is basically a classificatory device using standard census areas within an urban area and allocating scores on each of a number of indices which are selected to illustrate social differentiation between the census area populations. By dividing a town or city into a number of areas, and grouping those with similar scores, social area analysis offers an opportunity to identify and measure social needs and problems. The technique enables a close examination to be made of the relationship of spatial and social structure.

The technique of social area analysis has not been without its critics,[67] but empirical testing has shown it to be useful and meaningful. In recent years the technique has been placed on a more sophisticated statistical basis through the use of multivariate analysis, embracing both cluster and factor analysis. The first major study in Britain was, perhaps, that by Moser and Scott[68] in their survey of 157 towns in England and Wales, who used 60 variables to classify towns on the basis of their social, economic, and demographic characteristics. In their social area analysis, which used 1951 Census of Population as its main source of data, Moser and Scott used component analysis, which attempts a similar type of classification and the production of urban sub areas.[69] More recently a number of planning authorities have begun using social area analysis to form the basis of social malaise studies,[70] focused on specific urban areas rather than any corporate work between towns in a region, although the potential use of the technique for regional planning is considerable. However, Pahl has sounded a warning that research work on social area analysis may become too concerned with measurement and lose sight of meaningful sociological problems.[71] Indeed, a number of social malaise studies have perhaps become preoccupied with the collection and analysis of data for their own sake as a means of testing and refining the various quantitative techniques which are available.

The choice of indicators which represent social need is of central importance to social area analysis. The selection of indicators depends first, on conceptualizing problems which require measurement, and secondly, choosing an indicator(s) to represent the concept. One of the key problems in the development of both economic and social indicators is that it is often very difficult to measure the variables that are of direct interest, but rather surrogates must be selected to replace such values. In social area analysis, the vital element in the selection of indicators is the perception of people involved in the development process itself, i.e. measurement of the social reality of development. A considerable amount of literature has become available in recent years on 'social' indicators.[72]

As already noted, social area analysis has been an analytical technique used mainly in urban areas rather than for regions. One of the standard units for gathering data has been the enumeration district (ED), and this often presents problems. First, the indicators used in social area analysis are determined to a significant extent by the availability of data, and for smaller areas this availability is less than for larger areas. The Department of Employment, for example, is reluctant to issue employment data for small areas. Secondly, external agencies often have to be contacted to find out which households are to be allocated to individual EDs (e.g. DHSS on supplementary benefit dependency), and the process of consultation between the planner and a wide range of agencies can be quite lengthy. Finally, in the use of social, economic and environmental indicators, the degree of quantification varies substantially, and some balance has to be made between quantification and non quantifiable variables.

The potential use of social area analysis for regional planning is considerable. It has certainly been the case that regional planning has not engaged itself sufficiently with social problems, and this in itself has not encouraged the development of techniques for social analysis. The problems of data availability become fewer as the area studied increases in size, and with EDs these can be aggregated to ward level and beyond. While different agencies often have different administrative areas, amalgamation of EDs on to some common basis can ease the task. In addition, by aggregating EDs on to some larger area basis then the problem of allocating households to particular EDs for a wide range of variables can be lessened.

Social area analysis in regional planning might be applied in a wide variety of ways. For example, the technique could be used to analyse variations in social needs and deprivation (in both social and economic terms) between areas within a region. The, hitherto, broad classification of regions into either prosperous or poor (e.g. the South East and Midlands versus the periphery) is not very meaningful. Regional planning authorities will need to know with greater precision and sensitivity, of the nature and scope of social needs which people face.

SUMMARY OF MODEL BUILDING TECHNIQUES

As Ira Lowry has emphasized, the use of computer models as aids to regional planning has developed largely from the increased sophistication of planners and an awareness of the inadequacy of traditional techniques.[73] While the adequacy of such models is nearly always less than that required, the recent developments in model building and their application by computer have provided the tools for analysis and prediction of regional systems and sub systems. While major improvements might be expected in regional models in the future, without the present knowledge and expertise of model building techniques, the activity of planning at a regional level would have remained dependent on a much weaker information and knowledge base from which to tackle present problems and anticipate future situations.

Monitoring

To conclude this chapter some mention is made of the role of monitoring in the planning process. While the task of monitoring cannot be described as a specific technique, this activity does contain, as identified at the beginning of this chapter, elements of both analytical and procedural techniques. The nature and scope of monitoring enables the planner to use a range of methods and techniques, and provides some linkage between this chapter on analytical techniques and the one that follows on procedural techniques.

In relation to an analytical tool, monitoring may be used to assess the strengths and weaknesses of a region; as a procedural technique monitoring may be used as a review process. Planning involves some kind of controlling mechanism to achieve a community's goals. The effectiveness of the process can be assessed by various means, and the results fed back into it as an informational input. Thus the monitoring of change assumes an important role in the ongoing process of modification and improvement.

Monitoring has been defined as 'the periodic recording of selected information to show how a city (or area) is performing in the achievement of its stated intentions'.[74] Its purpose is to keep the development of the area within reasonable limits which allow the attainment of given objectives. A report commissioned by the Notts./Derby sub regional management committee saw the need for monitoring as a continuous planning process 'which will continuously review the changes in the sub region, update the forecasts and assumptions, improve understanding of the sub region and revise the recommendations for action. Continuous planning will ensure that the strategy remains appropriate and acceptable to the needs of the four local authorities'.[75]

References

1   For an attempt at producing a synthesis of analytical techniques, see Isard, W. *Methods of Regional Analysis*, Chapter 12 (MIT Press, 1960).

    An attempt to produce a synthesis of procedural techniques was made by the Planning Research Unit at Edinburgh. See Report 'Threshold Analysis and Optimisation', First Warsaw—Edinburgh Conference on Planning Research, May 1970.

2   Bickmore, D., Royal College of Art, *Automatic Cartography and Planning* (Architectural Press, 1971).

3   Willis, G., *Technological Forecasting* (Pelican, 1972).

4   op. cit. page 261.

5 For a more detailed examination of the various methods of population forecasting, see, for example, Isard, W., *Methods of Regional Analysis,* Chapter 1 (MIT Press, 1960).

6 See, for example, (a) *The Esk Valley Regional Study,* (Heriot-Watt University, 1969). (b) *Leicester & Leicestershire Sub Regional Planning Study* (Leicester City and County, 1969).

7 South East Joint Planning Team, *A Strategic Plan for the South East* (HMSO, 1970). See para 2.49 page 17 where conventional population forecasting is examined in a critical way.

8 *Notts./Derby Sub Regional Study 1969,* Page XI. Appendix 1.

9 Although very high response rates can be obtained, it was possible to obtain results from virtually all of the manufacturing firms in the steel town of Scunthorpe. See, Harris, D. F., Morgan, R. H., and Walker, L. G., *Scunthorpe, A Study of Potential Growth* (Scunthorpe MB, 1967).

10 *The National Plan,* Cmnd. 2765, 1965.

11 There are many useful textbooks which explain the use of standard statistical techniques in general, and regression analysis in particular: See for example, on regression analysis *Statistics* Ilersic, A. R. (HFL (Publishers) Ltd., 1964) 13th edition Chapter 9 or Reichmann, W. J., *Use and Abuse of Statistics* (Pelican, 1966) Appendix 3.

12 See especially, an article by Schultz, T. W., 'Investment in Human Capital'. *American Economic Review,* March 1961.

13 Based on work undertaken in an M.Sc. Thesis by J. Alden on *Regional Labour Markets in S.E. Scotland,* unpublished (Heriot-Watt University, 1969).

14 For a more detailed examination of the potential labour reserve of inactive females, see, Government Social Survey *A Survey of Women's Employment,* Two Volumes, March 1968. A. Hunt. 'Tabulations at National and Regional Level';

15 Wilson, A. G., *Entropy in Urban and Regional Modelling* (Pion, 1970).

16 A number of excellent texts are available on the use of model building in planning at a regional level. See, for example, Wilson, A. G., 'Some Problems in Urban and Regional Modelling' Colston Research Series. 1970; and Batty, M., 'Recent Developments in Land-Use Modelling: A Review of British Research', *Urban Studies,* June 1971.

17 Above cit.

18 See Wilson, A. G., 'Models in Urban Planning', *Urban Studies,* No. 5, 1968.

19 Isard, W., *Methods of Regional Analysis,* Chapter 7, 'Industrial Location Analysis'.

20 For a good example of the application of this technique, see Esk Valley Sub Regional Study. op. cit. Table 6.4. p. 68 in which the quotient is applied to each individual industry.

21 For a detailed illustration of specialization coefficients and curves, see Isard, W., Chapter 7, op. cit.

22 *Esk Valley Sub Regional Study,* Chapter 6 (Heriot-Watt University, 1969).

23 *A Report on the Economic Vitality of the SDA,* by J. Alden for the Glamorgan Community Development Project, 1971.

24 See Isard, W., op. cit., for a more detailed analysis.

25 Stillwell, F. J. B., 'Regional Growth & Structural Adaptation', *Urban Studies,* Vol. 6, 1969. Also see comments on shift and share analysis by Buck, T., Paris, J. and Stillwell, F. in *Journal of Regional Studies Association,* Vol. 4, No. 4, 1970.

26 Tiebout, C. M. 'The Community Economic Base Study', Supplementary Paper No. 16, Committee for Economic Development, New York, 1962.

27 Daly, M. C. 'An Approximation to a Geographical Multiplier' *Economic Journal,* 1940; and Hoyt, H. 'The Economic Base of the Brockton, Massachusetts Area, 1949.

28 Tiebout, C. ., 'Exports and Regional Economic Growth', *Journal of Political Economy,* Vol. 64, 1956. Also North, D. C. 'Exports & Regional Economic Growth: A Reply', *Journal of Political Economy,* Vol. 64, 1956.

29 SELNEC Transportation Study. Technical Working Paper No. 3. 1968, plus Report by Group 2 of the Working Party of the Planning Sub-Committee.

30 op. cit.

31 See, for example. Andrews, R. 'Comment Regarding Criticisms of the Economic Base Theory', *Journal of American Institute of Planners,* Vol. 24, 1958.

32 Isard, W., Chapter 6, *Regional Cycle and Multiplier Analysis,* especially pages 189 following. op. cit.

33 Blumenfeld, H., 'The Economic Base of the Metropolis', *Journal of the American Institute of Planners,* Vol. 21, 1955.

34 Pfouts, R. W., 'An Empirical Testing of the Economic Base Theory', *Journal of the American Institute of Planners,* Vol. 23, 1957.

35 On this latter point see, Anderson, R. J., 'A Note on Economic Base Studies & Regional Econometric Forecasting Models', *Journal of the Regional Science Association,* Vol. 10, No. 3, 1970.

36 For an explanation of these concepts in further detail see, for example, Samuelson's *Economics* Chapter 13 (McGraw-Hill, 1967) 7th Edition.

37 Brown, A. J. 'The "Green Paper" on the Development Areas', *National Institute Economic Review,* May 1967.

38 For a detailed account of leakages applied in a Scottish context, see Allen, K. J., Chapter 4, 'The Regional Multiplier', in *Regional and Urban Studies,* Orr, S. and Cullingworth, J. (eds) (Allen & Unwin, 1969).

39 op. cit.

40 See, for example, (a) 'Regional Multiplier Effects in the UK', Archibald, G. C., *Oxford Economic Papers,* March 1967. (b) Steele, D., 'Regional Multipliers in GB', *Oxford Economic Papers,* Vol. 21, 1969.

41 Allen, K. op. cit.

42 See, *The Future Shape of Local Government Finance,* Cmnd. 4741, Green Paper July 1971, in which the government examines the case for income tax, sales tax, payroll tax, motor fuel duty and motor vehicle duties, all being administered at local level.

43 Leontief, W., *Structure of the American Economy 1919-29,* (Oxford University Press, 1953).

44 Edwards, S. L. and Gordon, I. R., 'The Application of Input-Output Methods to Regional Forecasting: The British Experience', Colston Research Series 1970. op. cit. Also, in his book, *Input-Output Analysis and Regional Economics* (Weidenfeld and Nicolson, 1972), Harry W. Richardson examines the application of input-output techniques to regional economics, focusing upon both the theoretical problems and the practical value of input-output.

45 Czamanski. S., 'Applicability and Limitations in the Use of National Input-Output Tables for Regional Studies', *Journal of the Regional Science Association,* Vol. 23, 1969.

46 Hewings, G. J. D., 'Regional Input-Output Models in the UK: Some Problems and Prospects for the use of Non-Survey Techniques', *Journal of the Regional Studies Association,* Vol. 5, No. 1, 1971.

47 Studies in Official Statistics, No. 16, *Input-Output Tables for the UK 1963* (HMSO, 1970).

48 For a more detailed account of the construction and working of Input-Output Tables, see *Regional Input-Output Analysis'*, Thorne, E. Chapter 5, *Regional & Urban Studies,* Orr, S. and Cullingworth, J. B. (eds) (Allen & Unwin, 1969).

49 Nevin, E., *The Structure of the Welsh Economy* (University of Wales Press, 1966).

50 Blake, C. and McDowall, S., 'A Local Input-Output Table for St. Andrews', *Scottish Journal of Political Economy,* 1967.

51 Dolenc, M., 'Bucks County Inter-regional Input-Output Study', *Journal of the Regional Science Association,* Hague Congress, 1967.

52 Riefler, R. and Tiebout, C., 'California/Washington Input-Output Model', *Journal of the Regional Science Association,* August 1970.

53 Ellman, M. J., 'The Use of Input-Output in Regional Economic Planning: The Soviet Experience', *Economic Journal,* December 1968.

54 See especially *National Accounts Statistics: Sources and Methods,* (HMSO, 1963) Maurice, R. (ed) Pages 1–18, also, *National Income and Accounting,* Edey, H., Peacock, A. and Cooper, R. (Hutchinson University Library, 1967) 3rd Edition. For an examination of the conceptual and technical problems of regional income accounting, see also Chapter 4. Isard, W. *Methods of Regional Analysis* (MIT Press, 1960), and Leven, C. L. *Regional and Inter-regional Accounts in Perspective in Regional Analysis,* Needleman, L. (ed) (Penguin, 1968).

55 McCrone, G., 'The Application of Regional Accounting in the UK', *Journal of the Regional Studies Association,* Vol 1, No. 1, May 1967.

56 Nevin, E. & Associates, *The Structure of the Welsh Economy,* op. cit. and Tomkins, C. R. & Others. *Income & Expenditure Accounts for Wales 1965-68* (University College Bangor, Welsh Council 1971).

57 Woodward, V. H., 'Regional Social Accounts for the UK', *National Institute Economic Review,* Regional Papers. (Cambridge University Press, 1970).

58 A range of models in this field of analysis are covered by Isard, W. in Chapter 11 of his book. op. cit.

59 Stewart, J., 'Empirical Mathematical Rules Concerning the Distribution and Equilibrium of Population', *Geographical Review,* Vol. 37. 1947; and, Zipf, G. K. *Human Behaviour and the Principle of Least Effort,* 1949.

60 Reilly, W. J., Methods for the study of Retail Relationships, University of Texas, Bulletin Nó. 2944. 1929.

61 Eilon, S. Tilley, R. and Fowkes, T., 'Analysis of a Gravity Demand Model', *Journal of the Regional Studies Association*, Vol. 3, No. 2, 1969.

62 Batty, M., 'The Impact of a New Town: An Application of the Garin Lowry Model', *Journal of the Royal Town Planning Institute,* Vol. 55, 1969. Also, see his article in *Urban Studies* June 1972, 'Recent Developments in Land-Use Modelling: A Review of British Research'.

63 Ministry of Transport, *Portbury* (HMSO, 1966) see Annex 4.

64 Gwilliam, K. M., *A Pilot Study of the Haven Ports of Harwich, Felixstowe and Ipswich* (East Anglia Economic Planning Council, 1967).

65 Shevky, E. and Williams, M. *The Social Areas of Los Angeles: Analysis and Typology* (University of California, 1949). Also see, Shevky, E. and Bell, W. *Social Area Analysis: Theory, Illustrative Application and Computational Procedures* (Stanford University Press, 1955).

66 Herbert, D. T., 'Social Area Analysis: A British Study', *Urban Studies,* February 1967.

67 See, for example, Hawley, A. and Duncan, O. D., 'Social Area Analysis: A Critical Appraisal', *Land Economics,* Vol. 33, 1957.

68 Moser, C. and Scott, W., *British Towns: A Statistical Study of their Social and Economic Differences* (Oliver & Boyd, 1961).

69 For a comprehensive coverage of the statistical techniques of multivariate analysis including both cluster and factor analysis, see Van de Geer, J. P., *Introduction to Multivariate Analysis for the Social Sciences* (W. R. Freeman & Co., 1971).

70 See, for example, 'Liverpool Social Malaise Study, 1970'; 'South Hampshire Plan: Study Report Group D. No. 6'. 'Social and Community Life 1970; Methods of Analysing Needs'. Southwark 1970; and that undertaken by Glamorgan CC for the Rhondda 1971-73.

71 Pahl, R. A. *Readings in Urban Sociology,* 'Introduction', especially pages 6-8 on the testing of quantitative indices. (Pergamon Press, 1968).

72 See, for example. Bauer, R., *Social Indicators* (MIT, 1967), or Davies, B. *Social Needs and Resources in Local Services*, (Michael Joseph, 1969).

73 Lowry, I. S., 'A Short Course in Model Design', *Journal of the American Institute of Planners,* Vol. 31, 1965.

74 Milton Keynes Development Corporation, 'Notes on Monitoring and Evaluation', Technical Supplement No. 4. 1970.

75 'The Design of a Monitoring and Advisory System for Sub-Regional Planning: A Study by Iscol Ltd.' 1971. P. 3.3 Prepared for the Notts/Derby Sub-Regional Management Committee.

8 Procedural Techniques for Regional Planning

Introduction

Choice underlies the planning process regardless of which methods of plan making are adopted. The planner is faced with the difficult task of choosing between alternative courses of action in many different contexts and this problem is common to all methods of plan making. A number of techniques are available to assist the planner in his job of plan selection and choice of policy. Particular emphasis is given in this chapter to the role of threshold analysis, cost benefit analysis, goals achievement and techniques associated with these. As with the analytical techniques emphasis has been placed not only on the content of individual techniques but also on their function, including when and how to use them, together with some comments on their potential use. The evaluation techniques are not presented as obligatory; in practice the planner hopefully absorbs notions and elements of a number of the techniques and tackles problems with a suitable mixture of each.

While the procedural techniques have focused largely upon plan evaluation, the techniques of forecasting and monitoring also have an important role to play. Although both forecasting and monitoring were considered in the preceding chapter, and the strong link between analytical and procedural techniques recognized on these issues, one particular aspect of forecasting warrants emphasis at this stage. While the role of normative forecasting was discussed in Chapter 7, its implications for using procedural techniques are important. The majority of procedural techniques developed in recent years have focused upon the means of achieving certain goals and objectives, in the task of plan evaluation. However, one of the dangers of devoting so much time to quantifying the effects of adopting specific courses of action may be the neglect of formulating a wide range of alternative futures. Normative forecasting involves the exciting and demanding task of conceiving alternative futures and in the process of plan formulation and selection this aspect of forecasting may have an increasingly important role to play.[1]

Although plan selection techniques are considered here both individually and in combination, it must be recognized that the task of evaluation is increasingly seen to be dispersed throughout the planning process. Evaluation is not necessarily confined to one particular point in the process, although it has traditionally been seen to be so, following on after the identification of alternatives rather than also aiding their development.

Perhaps the best way of illustrating the problem of choice in the planning process at regional level and the use of techniques of plan selection, can be made by reference to some recent examples where major choices between alternative

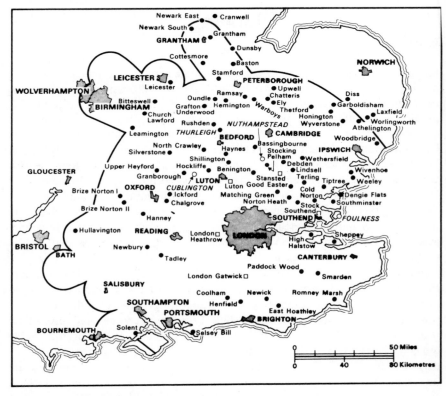

Fig. 8.1   The Third London Airport — alternative locations.
The rejected sites: At the start of its two year investigation to find a suitable site for a third London Airport, the Roskill Commission surveyed 78 possible sites The line shows their search area and the dots show areas of possibility. The four shortlisted sites are shown. Existing civil ariports are also indicated.

strategy plans at regional level have been made, and where techniques of plan selection were used in this process. Firstly, the Royal Commission on the Third London Airport (Roskill)[2] faced an immense task in choosing an optimum location from the four alternatives of Foulness, Nuthampstead, Cublington and Thurleigh (see Figure 8.1). While this case study is considered later in some depth, the conclusions of the Roskill Commission are of interest at this stage. The Royal Commission noted with some disappointment that while regional planning had been of greater concern than any aspect of the airport other than noise, it proved to be the one item on which the least tangible statements had been received. The Roskill Commission's research team undertook the most comprehensive cost benefit analysis yet undertaken in urban and regional planning in this country, in an attempt to provide a rational basis for choosing an optimum location site.

It is a common criticism that in the 1950s and 1960s planners attempted to achieve objectives by intuition and subjective analysis rather than through objectivity. This criticism of planning methodology is perhaps most applicable in plan selection, although some attempts have been made in recent years to achieve a more objective planning process. However, it must be recognized that there is no agreement amongst planners as to whether or not the use of quantitative techniques can make the activity of planning less subjective, or that it is possible through the use of objective techniques, especially evaluation techniques, for planning to move towards an objective approach resulting in better policies. However, there is general agreement that the evaluation techniques have considerable benefit in making values and choices more explicit, thereby permitting a more informed debate between planners, politicians and the public.

Secondly, the report of the South East Joint Planning Team (SEJPT) provided a regional strategy plan for the South East of England (illustrated in Figure 8.2) published in June 1970.[3] The aim of the study was the preparation of a strategic framework for decisions on longer term local development, public investment and policies within the region. The SEJPT formulated a number of provisional objectives and two hypothetical strategies at 1991. There were two main differences between the two alternative strategies 1991A and 1991B. Firstly, in 1991A it was assumed that Greater London's population would be stabilized at 7.3 million, while in 1991B it was assumed that the population would continue to fall to 7.0 million, and also that the number of jobs in Greater London would fall substantially. Secondly, although both strategies concentrated growth in a limited number of areas, 1991A tended to emphasize growth in the fringe of the region, while in 1991B more growth was concentrated in the Outer Metropolitan Area. An evaluation of the two strategies was made to assess both the extent to which they enabled the objectives to be achieved, and their feasibility. While the team sought to be

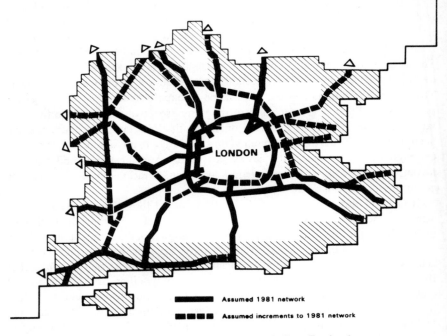

Fig. 8.2   Strategy plan for South East England.
Source: *Strategic Plan for the South East 1970*, map 35

systematic in its approach, it recognized that the methods of evaluation used
were experimental and tentative, since methodologies for analysing and
evaluating alternative strategies at regional level are in their infancy.

Techniques of plan evaluation have been developed only since the 1960s on
any scale, and such techniques as are available and relevant pose problems when
attempts are made to apply them to a regional plan. The SEJPT devised various
adaptations of cost benefit techniques to deal with the multiplicity of variable
factors at work in a regional system, and difficulties over quantification. A
different problem arose in the case of cost effectiveness, which is a method of
selecting the best way of achieving a given objective. In a regional plan there can
be no single objective but a number of objectives whose relationships one with
another inevitably change in the course of evaluation. The process of evaluation
eventually evolved by the SEJPT involved an assessment of how effectively the
provisional objectives were likely to be achieved in the two strategies.[4] Figure
8.3 illustrates the process.

Thirdly, the methodology of preparing a regional plan in the context of the
Nottinghamshire/Derbyshire sub region has been illustrated by Thorburn.[5] The

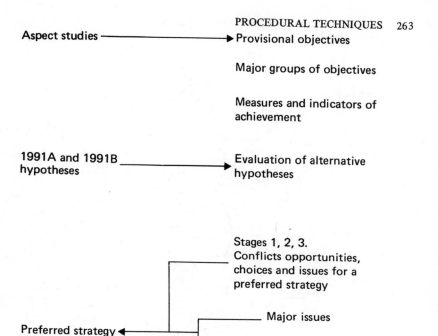

Aspect studies ⟶ Provisional objectives

Major groups of objectives

Measures and indicators of achievement

1991A and 1991B hypotheses ⟶ Evaluation of alternative hypotheses

Stages 1, 2, 3.
Conflicts opportunities, choices and issues for a preferred strategy

Major issues

Preferred strategy ◀

Final objectives

Fig. 8.3   Evaluation in regional planning.
Source: Report of the SEJPT, *Stretegic Plan for the South East,* June 1970, p. 66.

formulation of alternative strategies and testing of these formed a central task of the planning team. One of the important developments in the plan selection process undertaken by the planning team was the rejection of the formal adoption of the choice of a 'one-off' strategy. The strategy plan recommended in the study is shown in Figure 8.4, and this was based on a specific list of objectives.

As it has been emphasized with the techniques of forecasting, modelling and monitoring, it is unnecessary and perhaps even undesirable to attempt to allocate the use of evaluation techniques to any specific planning methodology. However, while the development of regional planning techniques has advanced at a rapid pace in recent years, many planners[6] have continued to question the framework of planning methodology in which planning techniques may be applied. There have been many cases, for example, where evaluation techniques have been used to provide a solution to a specific problem; the best example being, perhaps, the task of the Roskill Commission to find a third London airport. On the other hand, developments[7] have been made to use a combination of evaluation techniques focused upon strengthening the comprehensive rational model of planning. The development of new techniques has often reflected

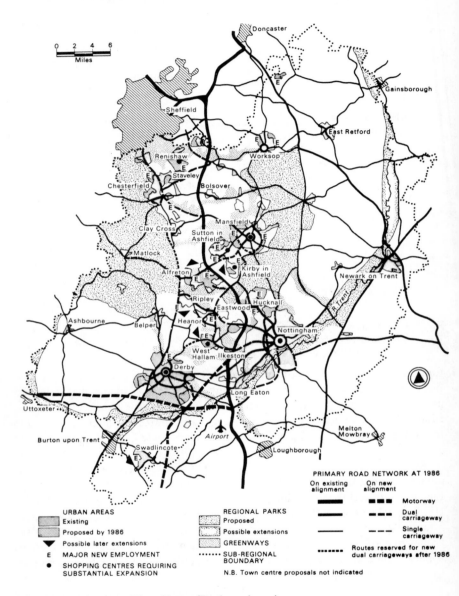

Fig. 8.4   Strategy Plan: Notts./Derby sub region.
            Source: Nottinghamshire and Derbyshire Sub Regional Study 1969.

either the search of the planner for better ways of doing his existing job, or a changing perception of what actually constitutes that job.

The development of techniques to assist in the formulation and evaluation of regional plans, as mentioned earlier, is still in its infancy; planning agencies have not adopted them in the routine process of planning, for a variety of reasons, not the least being that there are few people with expertise in the application of evaluation techniques. It would, however, be incorrect to assume that regional planning techniques are altogether a product only of recent years. The Greater London Plan of 1944 illustrated the use of physical planning techniques and the planner's perception of planning. In the post-war years, before the 1968 Town and Country Planning Act, local planning authorities have been statutorily obliged to prepare a Development Plan outlining future land use patterns within their area. Certain techniques of analysis were required by central government, and some quite sophisticated techniques were developed particularly to analyse population and employment trends. While Abercrombie's master plan for the Greater London region typifies the planner's approach to planning in the interwar and immediate post-war period, it also illustrates the use of techniques, both of forecasting and evaluation. On forecasting the Greater London regional plan projected a static population with no net natural increase and zero net migration, a situation similar to that forecast by the Barlow Report a few years earlier. However, while the Greater London Plan used limited techniques of analysis to forecast future needs, there was no explanation of any concept of alternative futures, or evaluation of any proposals. The preparation of regional plans 1943-49 was the first serious attempt in Britain to plan on a regional scale. These regional plans were to have been a useful guide for the newly established local planning authorities who under the 1947 Planning Act were required to prepare local development plans in a specific form and within a specific time period. As Brenikov has claimed,[8] this first series of regional plans failed partly because of the weak institutional framework, but also partly because of the inadequacy of techniques for planning at the regional scale. Twenty years after the first attempt to prepare regional plans, a second approach was made in the mid 1960s, which has developed in the 1970s on a similar line to those plans of the 1940s, in the sense that central government and local government, in conjunction with the Regional Economic Planning Councils, have worked together to prepare regional structure plans, within which local authorities are able to carry out their planning responsibilities, and for central government decisions on investment and economic and social policies related to the region's future development. As the Chief Planner to the Department of the Environment has emphasized,[9] a regional strategic plan will require the use of regional planning techniques to enable local authorities to prepare their structure plans, firstly, around a realistic population figure; secondly with a role that is clearly seen in relation to other areas; and thirdly, against a background of the availability of resources, constraints and opportunities that only a regional plan can indicate.

Requirements of an Evaluation Technique

In this section an attempt is made to identify some criteria by which evaluation techniques may be assessed for their usefulness. This assessment is followed by an examination of the individual techniques of evaluation available for planning at a regional scale. Lichfield has identified[10] ten criteria which a plan evaluation methodology should satisfy at a regional level before it is adopted for use. These ten criteria include the following:

1   Have regard to the objectives (ends, values) of the decision makers (which may not necessarily be the objectives of those for whom they are planning).
2   Cover all systems of urban and regional facilities in the plan.
3   Cover all sectors of the community which are affected.
4   Subdivide the sectors into producers/operators of the plan output, and its consumers, so that all the 'transactions' implicit in the plan are considered.
5   Take account of all costs to all sectors.
6   Take account of all benefits to all sectors.
7   Measure all the costs and benefits in money terms.
8   Facilitate the adoption of a satisfactory criterion for choice.
9   Show the incidence of the costs and benefits on all sectors of the community.
10   Be usable as an optimizing tool with a view to ensuring the best solution.

These ten criteria may be used as yardsticks to assess the range of evaluation techniques available. The nature and scope of these ten criteria in themselves demonstrate the movement towards stressing objectivity and rationality in the use of techniques. Lichfield has measured[11] the evaluation techniques against the ten criteria to assess the relative performance of individual techniques, and the results of this exercise are summarized in the form of a matrix in Table 8.1. The evaluation techniques have been listed in some order of ranking, starting with the least comprehensive techniques and ending with the most comprehensive. Each of the columns in Table 8.1 has been subdivided by Lichfield to show whether the methodology under review meets the criterion in either a partial (P) or full (F) sense, although no attempt is made to distinguish between degrees of achievement in which considerable variations exist. While the Planning Balance Sheet methodology most fully satisfies the ten criteria, it must be recognized that individual techniques need not necessarily be used in isolation. Indeed, there may be substantial advantages in combining two or more evaluation techniques in some form of integrated plan evaluation methodology. This potential development of plan evaluation techniques is considered later.

Table 8.1. *Evaluation Methodology of Regional Plans*

Techniques	1 Objectives P	F	2 Systems P	F	3 Sectors P	F	4 Producer/consumer P	F	5 Costs P	F	6 Benefits P	F	7 Measured P	F	8 Criterion P	F	9 Incidence P	F	10 Optimizing P	F
1 Checklist of criteria	X		X		X				X		X		X		X				X	
2 Cost minimization																				
(a) comparative cost	X		X		X				X				X		X		X		X	
(b) threshold analysis	X		X		X		X		X				X		X		X		X	
3 Cost effectiveness																				
(a) Planning, programming and budgeting	X		X		X						X		X		X		X		X	
4 Goal achievement matrix		X	X		X				X		X		X		X			X		X
5 Cost benefit analysis																				
(a) Cost benefit analysis			X		X					X		X		X		X	X			
(b) Warsaw optimization method	X		X		X				X		X		X		X		X		X	
6 Planning Balance Sheet		X		X		X		X		X		X				X		X		X

Source: Adapted from Table 1, 'Evaluation Methodology of Urban and Regional Plans: A Review', Lichfield, N., *Journal of RSA*, Vol. 4, No. 2, 1970.

The remainder of this chapter considers the nature and scope of each of the main groups of evaluation techniques, the use made of them in actual situations, and the use which might be made of them in the future.

Checklist of Criteria

This methodology is an early application of a cost-benefit technique, developed by physical planners. Until the present day, the checklist of criteria approach has been the most widely used as an evaluation technique. Its application requires no technical or statistical expertise; however, its simplicity gives the technique its main attraction. A good example of the use of the technique is that made by L.C. Kitching[12] in his selection of a planning strategy for the South East of England. Kitching attempted to prepare a balance sheet in general terms, of the advantages and disadvantages of five alternative strategies which could be adopted for the development of the South East. The three main assumptions underlying the analysis were, firstly, that the population increase in the South East 1964-81 would be between 2-4 million, and 1981-2000 between 4-8 million; secondly, overall town densities for new development between 13-20 persons per acre depending on town size; and thirdly, that the population of the Greater London Council area would remain stable.

The five patterns of possible development were, (a) unrestricted growth of London, (b) an intensification of population within the present pattern of development plans, (c) concentration of growth into one new city, (d) 6-12 new cities sited well away from London, and (e) expansion of London by corridors, the 'finger' or 'green wedge' plan. The South East Regional Economic Planning Council in their 1967 Report, and the SEJPT in theirs of 1970, followed closely Kitching's Number 4 and 5 strategies. The approach made by Kitching was largely subjective, with only implied references to objectives, costs and benefits, and no attempt was made at measurement, or consideration of the incidence of the advantages and disadvantages of the strategies on different sections of the community. However, despite this 'brainstorming' approach to strategy planning, it has a value in that the factors to be taken into account are clearly identified. In his analysis Kitching stated ten major items which were 'checked' against each of the five basic strategies for the growth of the South East.

This checklist of ten criteria included,

1   Comparative land costs of the different patterns of development.
2   Comparative costs of accommodating population growth in new towns and expanded towns.
3   Factors leading to economic and social success in town expansion schemes.
4   National factors likely to affect long term population distribution, e.g. Channel Tunnel or entry the EEC.

5   The minimum population required to attract office movement from London.
6   Social costs of new towns and town expansion schemes.
7   The feasibility of locating growth in one new city.
8   The best siting for up to 12 new cities.
9   The cost of extending basic facilities.
10 The changing pattern of traffic flows.

In recent years more objective approaches have been made in plan selection; for example, item 9 lends itself to threshold analysis, and on items number 2 and 7 Dr. P. Stone has examined[13] in some depth the cost of accommodating population growth. The checklist of criteria approach has been extended by Kitching in a more recent application to the four proposed sites selected by the Roskill Commission for the third London airport.[14] Kitching tested each of the four sites against seven criteria; communications, noise, growth potential, labour costs, amenity, agriculture and services. An advance on the 1963 approach was the ranking of the seven criteria for the four proposed sites. However, the approach was subjective, with no weightings attached to the items, because detailed costing, both in private and social terms had not been done.

The basic checklist of criteria approach was improved by the consultants[15] appointed by the Roskill Commission to find suitable locations for the associated urban development of each of the four alternative airport sites. The approach used in this situation included some costing of items, and uncosted criteria were examined to establish whether there were any factors which might outweigh the least cost. The main defect of introducing this dimension to the basic technique was that measured money costs could not be offset against items which could not be costed.

Quite clearly, although the checklist of criteria approach is a necessary step in plan selection, it is not sufficient in the sense that many questions are left unanswered. However, because increasing scepticism is held of the more sophisticated and comprehensive evaluation techniques, partly due to the resources required for application, and partly due to conceptual and technical difficulties, many planners have fallen back on the checklist of criteria approach as a basis for the task of plan selection. The North Gloucestershire sub regional study (1970) which evaluated the alternative feasible strategies by using a checklist of criteria linked to costs, is interesting because of the reasons why this technique was considered suitable. A series of strategies was 'evolved' to explore different possibilities of locating new development according to a number of policy options. These alternative strategy possibilities were evaluated against a number of performance criteria to choose a preferred solution. As the report explained, 'the purpose of the evaluation was essentially to enable the solution subjective basis. Clearly, the most comprehensive basis would have been to assess the total social costs against the total social benefits of each alternative strategy in final terms.' The planners found this task impossible because first, cost benefit techniques for application at sub regional level were not available; secondly the difficulty of reducing qualitative factors to monetary costs and benefits; and thirdly, a lack of expert staff. Therefore, the evaluation technique which the planners would liked to have used was not possible in the circumstances at the time.

A final example might be taken from the Severnside Feasibility Study; this report stated[16] that 'ideally a comparison of costs and benefits at alternative locations would assist the determination of policy on major expansion.' However, no attempt was made to do this work, although the resources available to the CUEP were substantial.

Cost Minimization

COMPARATIVE COST ANALYSIS

This technique seeks to identify and measure cost differentials between alternative strategies. The technique was used in 1967 by Shankland Cox and Associates in their supplementary evaluation for the expansion of Ipswich.[17] Just as the consultants' goal achievement evaluation was a benefit orientated approach, so comparative cost analysis is cost orientated. The two studies, one based on benefits and the other on costs, were undertaken separately, failing to take account of the incidence of the costs and benefits.

Ipswich was recommended in the 1964 South East Study for expansion to help accommodate the expected increase in population in South East England and overspill from London. In 1965 MHLG appointed Shankland Cox and Associates as planning consultants. In September 1966 the HMSO published the consultants' report on the expansion of Ipswich by 70,000 in 1981. The Ipswich sub region is shown in its regional setting in Figure 8.5. The report recommended that Ipswich should expand on the west and south west of the existing town, around the villages of Belstead and Bramford. This conclusion led to much controversy over the proposal to build on good agricultural land west of Ipswich rather than on poorer land to the east.

In Chapter 5 of the report the consultants considered various directions in which Ipswich might expand, and compared each of the alternatives with the social and economic objectives of expansion set out in Chapter 3, which included, (a) continuing economic growth; (b) choice of employment; (c) rational pattern of service centres; (d) compact urban form; (e) social integration; (f) local improvement; (g) efficient communications; (h) economic engineering services; (i) optimum use of land; (j) design. This methodology was,

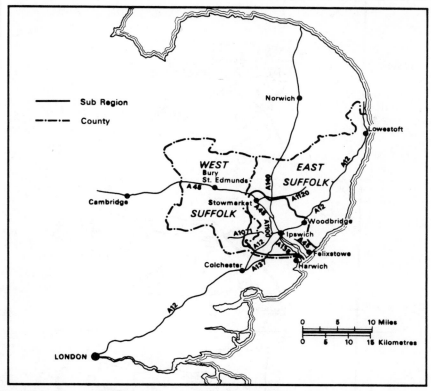

Fig. 8.5   The regional context of the Ipswich sub region.
Source: Lichfield, N. and Chapman, H., 'Cost Benefit Analysis in Urban Expansion. A Case Study of Ipswich,' *Urban Studies,* Fig. 1, August 1970.

essentially the checklist of criteria approach together with an element of goal achievement based on benefits.

Because of the controversy over the consultants' report, the MHLG commissioned the consultants to examine certain alternatives, with particular reference to their demands on agricultural land and their comparative costs. This second report was published in 1968. The first report, published in 1966, did not include estimates of the financial advantages of expansion on the west. The consultants in the second report attempted to assess the cost of agricultural land and loss of output, along with capital and recurrent costs of those items in the development which were likely to reveal major differentials. These major items

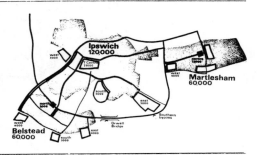

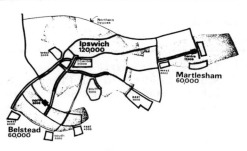

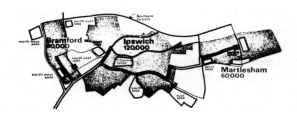

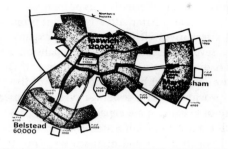

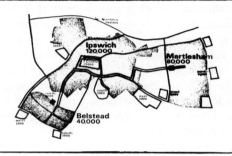

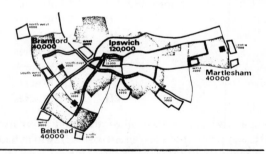

Key

☐ Employment zones
■ District centres
3000 Number of jobs

═══ Dual 3 lane road
━━━ Dual 2 lane road
━━━ Single 3 lane road
──── Single 2 lane road

Fig. 8.6   Alternative hypotheses for urban growth; Ipswich sub region
Source: 'Expansion of Ipswich, Comparative Costs,' Consultant's
supplementary report (HMSO, 1968).

were communications and drainage which could be costed with some precision. For this purpose, seven alternative hypothetical forms for the expansion of Ipswich were considered. Alternative I was that proposed in the first report, and the other six alternatives all included some expansion both east and west of Ipswich. These seven alternative forms of expansion are illustrated in Figure 8.6. The consultants did not consider the alternative of all expansion on the east of Ipswich because this would have led to a delay of five years before an expansion area could be provided with a sewerage system, whereas expansion on the west could make use of existing spare capacity.

Table 8.2 illustrates the capital items which were costed for each alternative. Costs for road construction and drainage were not the total cost of expansion since items common to all proposals were excluded; only major differentials were considered. Details of the estimates for road construction costs for each alternative were analysed in Appendix A to the report, and estimates for agricultural land acquisition costs in Appendix B. An additional £30 million common to all the alternatives to cover the cost of roads for travel with each district and Ipswich, and through traffic, was added to each scheme.

The same approach was applied to current costs as was made to capital costs; and these are illustrated in Table 8.3. The amount of agricultural land taken for each alternative was as follows:

Alternative	I	6,800 acres
	II	5,600 acres
	III	5,600 acres
	IV	5,600 acres
	V	5,900 acres
	VI	5,600 acres
	VII	5,800 acres

The comparative cost analysis illustrated that alternative I showed the lowest capital costs and recurrent costs; alternative VII, which had the next lowest costs would have required 1,200 acres less agricultural land but present some serious planning problems. The comparative cost analysis undertaken by the consultants confirmed their subjective judgement made in the first report on the expansion of Ipswich, and made a major contribution to justifying the selection of a particular scheme. Unfortunately not only does the comparative cost analysis ignore the incidence of costs and benefits, it only enables a choice to be made on the basis of cost, although it may not be desirable to choose the cheapest strategy. If the benefits are quantified then a more expensive scheme on cost grounds may be chosen rather than a cheaper one.

It must be recognized that while comparative cost analysis does assist the task of plan selection, this is made only on the basis of cost and therefore is partial in

Table 8.2. *Capital Cost of Each Alternative (Less Common Items) in Expansion of Ipswich*

	Capital Cost, £000s						
	1	2	3	4	5	6	7
Road construction	12,508	22,133	18,932	20,012	15,610	18,776	16,008
Drainage							
(a) Sewerage works	760	825	825	825	825	800	800
(b) Foul and surface water drainage	5,550	8,400	8,400	8,400	8,400	8,200	8,000
	18,818	31,358	28,157	29,237	24,835	27,776	24,808
Acquisition of agricultural land	2,040	1,634	1,634	1,634	1,670	1,538	1,684
Total	20,858	32,992	29,791	30,871	26,505	29,314	26,492

Source: Expansion of Ipswich, Comparative Costs, Consultants' Supplementary Report (HMSO, 1968).

Table 8.3. Recurrent Cost of Each Alternative in Expansion of Ipswich

	Recurrent Costs, £000s						
	1	2	3	4	5	6	7
Vehicular travel	4,354	5,984	6,198	6,060	5,363	5,919	5,268
Road maintenance	48	66	65	64	60	66	65
Accidents	234	289	327	309	305	309	297
Drainage							
(a) Sewerage works	55	70	70	70	70	73	70
(b) Foul and surface water drainage	100	165	165	165	165	155	150
	4,791	6,574	6,825	6,668	5,963	6,522	5,850
Plus annual gross value of lost agricultural output	408	281	281	281	281	251	306
Total	5,199	6,855	7,106	6,949	6,244	6,773	6,156

Source: Expansion of Ipswich, Comparative Costs, Consultants' Supplementary Report (HMSO, 1968).

coverage; other techniques are available, more comprehensive in scope, which improve the process of plan evaluation. In fact, in the case of Ipswich, the East Suffolk County Council were not satisfied with the consultants' comparative cost analysis and commissioned Lichfield and Associates to prepare a cost benefit analysis of the alternative proposals put forward in the consultants' comparative cost analysis. The results of this cost benefit analysis were published in 1970.[18]

The conclusion of the Ipswich cost benefit analysis was that, except for agricultural land considerations, the greatest net community advantage lay in developing to the west of Ipswich. The cost benefit analysis illustrated that the additional value of the land to the west compared to the east did not outweigh the additional resources required, and the additional disbenefits that would accrue, if expansion took place either all to the east or a mixture of east and west; for alternative I not only was the position one of least cost, but also greatest benefits.

THRESHOLD ANALYSIS

Threshold Theory

Threshold theory was evolved in Poland within the framework of a socialist planned economy, one of the chief goals of which is to 'eliminate irrational extremes in the development of different parts of the country'.[19] Such a policy has been implemented through long term economic plans of 15-20 years within which short term 5 year plans have then been worked out in detail. The Spatial Planning Act of 1961 introduced long term physical plans and short term stage plans to be correlated with the economic plans, so that in Poland, physical and economic planning are now very closely integrated. The physical planner tends to regard the distribution of resources as a spatial activity, and hence thresholds in relation to land. The economist, however, looks at the distribution of resources in a temporal fashion, and hence views thresholds in relation to output. Since thresholds can be defined as lines on a map or as peaks on a cost curve, Threshold analysis provides a useful common ground between physical and economic planners. However, although a particular economic plan may specify which towns are to be expanded, there was, until recently, no attempt to explore the alternative means of accommodating such expansion for a particular town.

It was to fill this gap that Threshold Theory and Analysis was evolved and developed by Professor Boleslaw Malisz, Director of the Polish Academy of Sciences in the early 1960s.[20] In Britain, Threshold Analysis has been developed almost exclusively by the Planning Research Unit of Edinburgh University, and by J. Kozlowski in particular.

The conceptual basis for the technique is the notion of thresholds of urban growth. The threshold is a well established concept in physics and biology where it denotes a limitation within which a variable does not change under the influence of a gradually increasing factor or stimulus. In a process of expansion, towns encounter limitations to their spatial growth, due to topography or to the technology of various public utility networks or to existing land uses. These limitations are therefore defined as the thresholds of urban growth. Of course, they can be overcome, but only at disproportionately high capital investment costs, which are defined as threshold costs. A threshold is not any limitation faced by urban growth (or decline); it is concerned with major limitations which have a significant effect on the costs per head of population. The nature of the thresholds will vary with town size; thresholds cannot be considered in abstract; a village will face different thresholds from a large town or city.

In general terms, the investment costs necessary to accommodate a given number of people in a particular area can be divided into two categories:

1 The costs proportioned to the number of inhabitants which are incurred irrespective of where the people are located, i.e. the non locational or fixed costs.
2 The costs which are incurred as a result of the characteristics of the area, i.e. the locational or variable costs. Thresholds theory focuses on these variable costs (which are in fact the threshold costs) using them as an index of efficiency in terms of the ratio of input to output.

The distinction between these two categories can be seen clearly when the investment costs are plotted on a per capita basis (Figure 8.7).

1 The fixed cost curve is logically a straight line since costs are directly proportional to numbers of people.
2 The threshold cost curve takes the form of a sine curve, with the peaks representing the thresholds. The per capita costs increase disproportionately in comparision with the fixed costs during the period when the threshold is being overcome, but this increase is compensated later by a disproportionate decrease in per capita threshold costs.

Clearly, as a town approaches a threshold, the expectation of high costs to overcome it will hold the town's spatial expansion within these boundaries as long as possible. If a town decides not to cross a threshold, future urban development can be accommodated, for example, by increasing densities or by stretching the capacity of services, but there is a limit to this process. Once the town decides to cross the threshold, then the quicker this is done the better, in order to minimize the time that expensive capital equipment is being underutilized. Thus, it is economically desirable that only one threshold area is developed at a time. Most communities will have exploited first the most

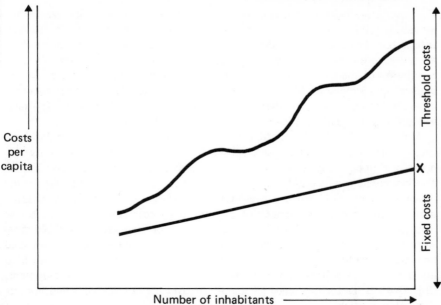

Fig. 8.7   Investment cost curves.

accessible and hence the cheapest areas, with the result that the subsequent threshold areas are more expensive to develop.[21]

Threshold Analysis

From these theoretical bases, Malisz has developed a practical method known as threshold analysis. The basic aim of threshold analysis is to identify the thresholds which can be plotted spatially or expressed in terms of quantity, and then to evaluate them in cost terms. In order to do so, Malisz[22] has suggested that three groups of studies need to be undertaken to reveal:

1 The physical thresholds — the suitability of land for urban purposes from the physiographic point of view.
2 The quantitative thresholds — the possibilities of extending the networks of public utilities.
3 The structural thresholds — the possibilities of changing the existing land use pattern.

The results are calculated quantitatively so that cost indices, for example for providing a water supply system or reclaiming land, can be deduced. All land within the area surveyed is then classified according to the investment costs needed before urban development can take place. In the case of a large city, full calculation of the costs cannot be made without the use of a computer, but in smaller areas simpler graphical methods can be adopted, classifying the area into three types: (a) land immediately suitable for urban development, (b) land needing improvement, and (c) land not suitable for building.

Malisz has claimed that until recently, each of these groups of studies have been carried out separately, and subsequently synthesized intuitively by the planner. Consequently this process of synthesis is subjective and unverifiable. The key element which helps in synthesizing these three groups of surveys is the concept of thresholds in urban growth. The process of synthesis enables the information from all the groups of surveys to be correlated, from which it is then possible to delimit threshold areas. For each of these areas, threshold costs are estimated, and thus it is possible to compare these areas in cost terms, and evaluate the various possibilities of town expansion, and the sequence in which threshold areas should be opened up to secure the optional path of development. Objectivity is maintained since all the alternatives are considered, and none is eliminated *a priori.*

Four main applications of threshold analysis may be identified:

1 It may be used in evaluating the relative effectiveness of particular alternative schemes for expansion which may be used to determine the growth potential of a single town.
2 It provides a tool for assessing the development possibilities of towns within regional or national space. If a regional planner gives a particular population projection for his region, threshold analysis can be used to define which towns can accept a portion of this growth, and hence to make decisions on the future regional strategy of development.
3 The technique provides guidelines for programming public investment during the course of the implementation of a plan, i.e. major thresholds are identified and therefore just when major public investments are required.
4 The rationalization of the planning process. In Poland, a new state plan used to be prepared every five years and the long term physical plan for each city was revised at the same time. Using threshold analysis, the long term economic sequence of development is known, and hence these revisions of the long term plan every five years are unnecessary.

Every plan evaluation technique has its drawbacks and limitations, and threshold analysis is no exception, as its ardent proponents have readily admitted.[23,24] The theoretical and practical difficulties of the technique may be summarized as follows:

1 Thresholds arise from many different types of constraints and it is unlikely that even two will be congruent in time or space. Hence it is necessary to simplify and systematize the available information in order to focus the study on just the major thresholds.
2 The importance, and therefore the costs, of certain thresholds may vary through time, and changes in technology may completely reduce the significance of a threshold considered crucial today.
3 Cost estimates for overcoming particular thresholds can be difficult to calculate or are subject to a margin of error.
4 Threshold analysis is primarily concerned with initial investment costs. There is no consideration of frozen assets or running costs which might easily change the final conclusions, and, more importantly, there is no consideration of the likely benefits which each alternative would bring.

Validity of the Technique

Despite these recognized limitations, there have been much more fundamental doubts raised about the actual validity of threshold theory and analysis. These are discussed here in some detail in order to further clarify in what situations the technique can, and cannot, be used. W. Lean[25,26] has argued that, for a variety of reasons, the economic significance of thresholds is nowhere near as great as that put forward by the theory. Firstly, since the high costs of overcoming a threshold are followed by lower development costs, the overall significance of the threshold is reduced. Secondly, even though it is possible that in isolation a particular threshold may be of significance and be reflected in fluctuating per capita threshold costs, over a long period there will be a myriad of different thresholds occurring at different times. Hence, in the long term, these fluctuations are likely to even out, and aggregate per capita costs will remain relatively stable. And from a planning point of view it is total, not per capita, costs which are important anyway. Thirdly, where cases do occur of large fluctuations in the costs of town expansion, admittedly these will be caused by the bunching of thresholds. But this is only likely to occur in planned towns where all facilities will have been provided for a given population size and hence many thresholds will occur at the same point in time. Fourthly, the fact that thresholds can be postponed, for example by increasing densities, implies a certain flexibility which again reduces their significance. Fifthly, many towns have continued to grow over the centuries in spite of the presence of physical limitations. The response to being confronted with a threshold is likely to be a partial adaptation through a more efficient use of resources rather than a full stop.

However, Lean's most serious criticism of threshold analysis is that it is simply a cost minimizing technique. The assessment of urban development possibilities may not be made on a basis of the cheapest alternative because extra costs above the minimum may bring a more than proportionate increase in the benefits. Lean has been supported in this line of argument by W. Wright[27] who draws a comparison between cost effectiveness analysis (of which he considers cost benefit analysis and the planning balance sheet are special cases) and threshold analysis. Threshold analysis, he noted, concentrates exclusively on the capital costs of urban expansion and ignores the benefit side of the equation, while in contrast, cost effectiveness analysis enumerates and evaluates all the factors involved. Another serious deficiency identified by Wright is that the results of threshold analysis are simple market costs. There is no attempt to weight the analysis according to non-market factors, social costs and benefits etc, as cost effectiveness analysis does. Wright concludes that cost effectiveness analysis possesses all the advantages claimed by threshold analysis, plus many additional ones, yet has none of its disadvantages.

However, there have been attempts to answer these challenges to the validity of threshold theory and analysis, particularly by N. Famelis.[28] In reply to Lean's criticisms, Famelis has claimed that only when thresholds are of approximately the same magnitude and occur at equal time intervals will per capita costs be stabilized. At any given moment, therefore, costs incurred in overcoming a threshold will be exactly balanced by declining costs from the overcoming of the previous threshold. But this, of course, is a very idealized case, and the evidence suggests that in fact there is great diversity in the magnitude and frequency of thresholds encountered by expanding towns. Famelis has also contradicted Lean's view of the process of partial adaptations in urban development by pointing to the subdivision of threshold costs into 'initial' and 'gradual' elements. Initial threshold costs are those necessary before development can begin, and represent substantial lumps of capital. Hence they can be described as stepped, discrete or discontinuous. Grade threshold costs are those spread over the whole period of development, and thus they can be called grade or continuous costs. But because gradual costs appear jointly with the normal costs, it is difficult to distinguish between them. Partial adaptations are not a way of avoiding thresholds, therefore, but are seen instead as grade thresholds. Because grade threshold costs are spread over the whole period of implementation, partial adaptation is inherent in the threshold being overcome. In addition, threshold analysis is not simply a cost minimizing technique because it works within the constraints imposed by the requirements of an acceptable urban environment, and hence environmental objectives are implicit in the results.

While cost effectiveness analysis may help to evaluate development options, threshold analysis can be used to precede it by contributing toward the rational, formulation of these options. By definition, it cannot analyse the benefits of such options since they do not yet exist at the initial stage of the planning process. Threshold analysis may be used, therefore, for both plan formulation as well as plan evaluation. This latter point has been developed by Malisz[29] the originator of the technique. Threshold analysis does not attempt to decide benefits inherent in alternative spatial solutions, but merely aims to show what are the cost consequences of developing different areas, and in what sequence they should be developed. Having identified the threshold, it seems logical to use cost effectiveness analysis as a complementary tool to investigate possible ways of overcoming it. By doing this, some of the other costs, such as running costs, not so far considered by threshold analysis, could be examined. Threshold analysis and cost effectiveness analysis are not alternatives to one another, and just as threshold analysis has it limitations so the comprehensiveness of cost effectiveness analysis can be questioned. There is no guarantee in using cost effectiveness analysis that all possible solutions will be evaluated, or that the benefits, many of which are immeasurable, are being evaluated correctly.[30]

Threshold analysis, is a valuable developmental tool, with acknowledged shortcomings as well as advantages, and which can perform a useful function in both plan formulation and plan evaluation.

Application of Threshold Analysis

The debate that has taken place over threshold analysis has been confined largely to theoretical terms because of the very few examples of the technique in practice. If there had been more case studies to provide evidence, then perhaps several of the misunderstandings and arguments would not have arisen. According to Malisz,[31] threshold analysis is a widely practised technique in Polish planning and has been applied to at least 600 towns, so by comparison its use outside Poland has been negligible. However, in Italy, B. Secchi[32] has investigated the initial investment costs or urban development along similar lines to threshold theory. He postulated a sine curve of investment costs for a variable population size with the assumption of a constant level of services. This curve was then tested against the costs of investment and other variables, such as the rate of industrialization and population density, in large Italian cities during the period 1953-1958. The results he obtained are theoretically and empirically very near to those found by Malisz.[33]

In Britain, there have been only two major published studies using threshold analysis; both are studies of sub regions of Scotland undertaken by the Planning Research Unit of Edinburgh University. In the Central Borders Study,[34] threshold analysis was applied to a group of small towns in a fairly simple way, identifying the consecutive thresholds for each town, and then the overall regional threshold within which the total urban growth potential was calculated. The areas contained within the consecutive thresholds for each town were then defined on a map and the main costs investigated on a per capita basis. A much more detailed version of threshold analysis was used in the Grangemouth/Falkirk Regional Survey and Plan.[35] The Planning Research Unit attempted to build a model method for a typical physical planning process, within which threshold analysis was integrated with several other analytical studies and models of urban structure in order to formulate a final solution.[36] Few other studies which have used threshold analysis have applied it in as much detail.[37] In the Esk Valley Study,[38] threshold analysis was used in its purely physical form, i.e. without the calculation of cost indices. The threshold analysis developed into a series of sieves indicating the availability and suitability of land for urban development in the region relative to goals determined from earlier economic and social studies. The potential development indicated in the study is shown in Figure 8.8. From these results, alternative plans were then evaluated. However, the quantification of the various thresholds in cost terms was extremely limited and the analysis was based largely on physical data.

The Potential of Threshold Analysis

The basic threshold analysis has been developed to consider not only minimization of costs but also maximization of effects. This development has been made in relation to a technique known as Warsaw Optimization Method, evolved in Poland, which as been described by Kozlowski,[39] and in much greater detail by S. Broniewski and B. Jastrzebski.[40] There are three main stages involved with the technique:

Stage 1:   Map of costs: this is essentially a quantified subdivision of areas delimited by a threshold analysis according to various degrees of land suitability for alternative types and intensity of urban land uses. In theory, it would be desirable to calculate the costs of land adaptation for all possible types and distributions of land uses, but this would require the analysis of millions of possibilities. In practice, therefore, only two types of land uses have been considered so far, residential and industrial, and an appropriate average intensity of development for each is assured. The land uses and their distributions are evaluated in terms of the costs associated with topographical factors, infrastructure, roads, interrelations with surrounding areas, and existing land uses. The results are further modified by introducing intangible or non-quantifiable factors, such as areas of cultural and historical associations. The final product from this phase is then an integrated map of costs.

Stage 2:   The land uses and urban functions for which the plan has to cater are next distributed throughout the area in accordance with basic planning criteria and in the light of the map of costs. A much larger

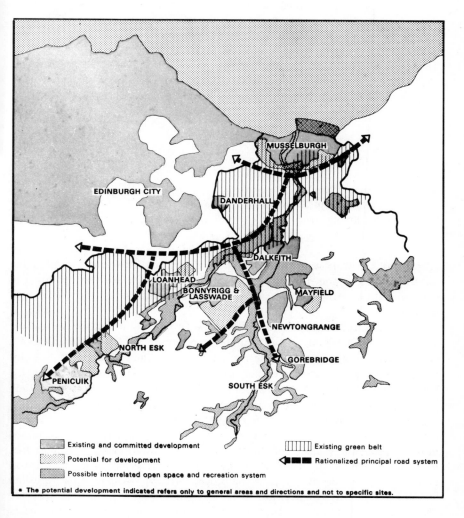

Fig. 8.8   Development potential in the Esk Valley sub region.
Source: The Esk Valley Sub Regional Study, Map 14.2 (Heriot Watt University, 1969).

number of land uses and functions are considered than will actually be required.

Stage 3:   A computer then classifies all the possible combinations of urban land uses in accordance with the map of costs to select the optimum set which together fulfil the planning brief.

The Warsaw Optimization Method, therefore, goes further than threshold analysis since it considers not only minimization of costs but also maximization of effects, and hence begins to answer some of the criticisms of threshold analysis. An 'index of efficiency' can be calculated as a yardstick of optimization:

$$E = \frac{L + K}{P}$$

where E = effectiveness
L = initial capital investment
K = running costs
P = effects

At present, the Warsaw Optimization Method only partially treats sectors, costs, benefits, criteria and incidence; either more research will be required to overcome these deficiencies, or other techniques, such as cost benefit, will be required.

Both threshold analysis and the Warsaw Optimization Method are closely related. With threshold analysis, there is no need to formulate initially a development programme since the analysis evaluates the various possibilities for urban growth from the implications of existing physical conditions. With the Warsaw Optimization Method, an outline of the policies (such as population projections) must be defined as a prerequisite since this method is not oriented toward defining thresholds, but works within the scope of those delimited by the threshold analysis. Threshold analysis is thus an input (among several others) into the preliminary stages of the Warsaw Optimization Method. A start has, therefore, been made to incorporate threshold analysis with other plan evaluation techniques in the planning process. This was perhaps first suggested by J. Forbes[41] in connection with a technique developed by her for quantitatively analysing the supply of potentially developable land in terms. of physical and socio-economic factors. However, Kozlowski,[42] a firm advocate of the rational model, has taken this much further. He has defined the rational planning process as one divided into sequential parts so that each conclusion leads logically to the next. The process begins with the formulation of goals which provide an essential framework for the effective application of quantitative methods. Threshold analysis can be used to provide the necessary information for the verification of goals, and will become an input to optimization. The planning balance sheet can then be used to analyse the alternative models resulting from the threshold analysis and the Warsaw Optimization Method. Additionally, the goals achievement matrix may serve as a complementary tool in various stages of the planning process, but particularly in the final choice in cases where no satisfactory answers were obtained from the planning balance sheet.

Nevertheless, it would be unfortunate if the use of these techniques, whether used singly or in combination, were seen to point exclusively towards the rational comprehensive form of planning; they may be equally appropriate to other planning approaches.

Cost Effectiveness Analysis: Planning, Programming and Budgeting

While planning, programming and budgeting (PPB, or PPBS as it is sometimes called) has not, hitherto, been used as an evaluation technique in regional planning, it warrants consideration because of its potentiality in this dimension of planning. The technique of PPB has been developed to assist choice in the planning of public expenditure and in making resource use more effective. As with all evaluation techniques the purpose of PPB is to provide in a systematic way information and analysis which will allow better decisions to be made. In principle there is nothing that can be done within the framework of a PPB system that could not be done without it; PPB does not make decisions, although it should make for better decisions.

The PPB approach was first developed in any comprehensive way in the United States Federal Government in the mid 1960s, and R. Millward has illustrated[43] the extent to which the PPB was the brainchild of the Rand Corporation in California, and first used in the Department of Defense by the Secretary McNamara. Since then other governments and public authorities have examined the technique relating to policy formulation.[44] In Britain the PPB approach has been adopted by a number of public authorities, mainly at the city level, including for example, Liverpool, Coventry and Lincoln.[45] At the national level three particularly significant applications of the PPB approach have been made by the Department of Education and Science,[46] the Ministry of Defence, and the Home Office[47] in relation to the police force taking decisions about resources. In relation to the PPB undertaken by the Home Office, the technique provided information about expenditure not only in terms of the conventional accounting symbols of salaries, petrol, debt charges etc., but also by programme or activity, e.g. traffic control, patrolling, crime investigation etc.

Underlying the PPB approach is the belief that decisions will be better if the following dimensions of expenditure are known:

1 Formulation and definition of objectives.
2 Information available on how resources are being used now in relation to the objectives they are intended to attain.
3 Information available on how effective the programmes are in meeting their declared objectives.
4 Alternative ways of achieving the same objectives are considered and evaluated.
5 Plans are made which relate the consequences of present decisions to future needs.
6 A systematic procedure for reviewing plans and programmes in light of new situations, new evaluations, and new analysis.

The purpose of PPB is to find more effective ways of using resources to promote an authority's objectives. While cost benefit analysis has been applied in this context to many questions of a similar nature, to many people the cost benefit analysis appears too rigid in its approach, and too dependent on market prices being used as a yardstick of costs and benefits. While some of the disadvantages of cost benefit analysis have been overcome with the planning balance sheet approach, the technique of PPB has been developed within a more liberal framework.[48] The PPB approach is flexible to the extent that information inputs may be quantitative or qualitative.

While the strength of the PPB technique is drawn from its formulation of objectives, as is the goal achievement matrix, the difficulties have focused upon the measurement of effectiveness. The use of economic and social indicators in measuring community development were considered in relation to the role of monitoring at the end of Chapter 7. While some progress has been made in the use of techniques to measure community development, this remains a relatively unknown and underdeveloped field of study.

Although the PPB technique is strongly objective-orientated it must be recognized that considerable conceptual problems arise.[49] These have been identified earlier in the discussion of the rational comprehensive model. PPBS is the most recently developed operation in government's quest to realize this ideal model. While the PPB approach has potential in the formulation and implementation of regional plans, there have been no formal applications made at the present time, due to the nature of the regional institution framework.

Goal Achievement

This method of evaluating alternative strategies is similar in application to two of the techniques considered earlier. Firstly, the goal achievement approach to plan evaluation forms a central element of the PPB which is strong on the formulation of objectives by which output is measured; secondly, the goal achievement approach is similar to the checklist of criteria technique except the criteria against which performance is judged are expressed in terms of the original goals of the plan. Shankland Cox in selecting a strategy for the expansion of Ipswich[50] tested expansion options against generalized social and economic goals derived independently in an earlier stage of the process as representing the goals and objectives which their proposals should seek to achieve. Opportunities and constraints may be included in these criteria by expressing them in terms of achievable goals.

The re-introduction of the original goals at the evaluation stage, as criteria for selection, brings this approach towards the rational model, but it does not appreciably reduce subjectivity as the planner must intuitively derive overall goals for society and also judge the comparative extent to which plans move towards achievement of those goals.

GOALS ACHIEVEMENT MATRIX

The goals achievement matrix (GAM) technique has developed the goals achievement approach with greater sophistication; it seeks to allocate benefits (i.e. movement towards achieving a goal) to groups within society and by looking at the different mixes of goal satisfaction and full achievement within each strategy. The approach remains essentially benefit orientated and does not fully take into account the social incidence of costs consequent upon moving towards a goal. Even if some cost element were to be introduced, the technique remains essentially subjective as, just as 'benefit' implies movement towards a goal, so 'cost' would be measured in terms of divergence from goals. The GAM defines both costs and benefits in terms of goal achievement. Each objective has its costs and benefits measured in the same terms as the objectives. The preferred strategy is determined on the basis of a GAM by weighted indices of goals achievement; the final outcome is to a large extent dependent on the validity of the weighting system used and the measurement scales adopted.

The GAM approach was developed by M. Hill, and illustrated in an article[51] which has become a standard reference for this technique. In his review of plan evaluation methodology, Hill criticized Lichfield's planning balance sheet approach on the grounds that traditional cost benefit analysis and the PBS approach have meaning only in relation to a well defined objective.

For the purposes of the GAM, the first stage of the exercise requires that goals should, as far as possible, be defined operationally, i.e. they should be expressed as objectives. In this way the degree of achievement of the various objectives can be measured directly from the costs and benefits that have been identified; for example, the ideal of greater economic welfare can be defined in terms of objectives related to the rate of growth in Gross Regional Product; or the ideal of an attractive environment in terms of objectives related to environmental improvement.

Secondly, it is necessary to identify different groups within the community who are affected by the consequences of a particular course of action since the consequences are unlikely to affect all groups of the community to an equal extent. The weighting of goals is one of the most crucial and controversial aspects in preparing a GAM. As Hill says 'The weightings should reflect the community's valuation of the various objectives and its valuation of appropriate incidence of benefits and costs'.

Thirdly, the time dimension of costs and benefits is important because costs and benefits are not of equal weight. The problem of discounting costs and benefits to take account of the timing of costs and benefits is a key problem central to all the more sophisticated methods of plan evaluation.

The form of the GAM for any particular plan is illustrated in Table 8.4 with costs and benefits always being defined in terms of goal achievement. The goals, a, P, Y, S, have relative weights of 2, 3, 5 and 4 respectively; these having been determined by an assessment of the community's problems and values. Different groups within the community are shown on the vertical axis, a, b, c, d and e, and their goals are given different weights to reflect their degree of adoption of the various goals. The letters, A, H, L, K etc are the costs and benefits expressed in the relevant terms; in some cases these will be monetary, and in others qualitative. In situations where all the costs and benefits for any goals can be expressed in the same quantitative terms these can be aggregated (illustrated by the Σ sign) to give the total product of the GAM. As Hill himself has noted, it is unlikely that all the costs and benefits of all the goals can be expressed in the same units, and therefore a grand cost benefit summation will be an exception rather than a rule.

A situation where quantitatively defined objectives must be compared with qualitatively defined objectives poses another problem for the GAM. However, this difficulty has been overcome partially by using a hierarchy of classes of scales of measurement, defined as the nominal, ordinal, internal and ratio scales. In particular, the nominal scale which classifies and numbers entities, and the ordinal scale which ranks entities, may be employed for the measurement of the achievement of qualitatively defined objectives.

As mentioned earlier, the validity of plan evaluation by means of a GAM rests largely with the weights used in weighting objectives, activities, groups, or sectors within the region. As Hill has emphasized, ideally the goals and their relative weights should be determined iteratively as a result of a complex process of interaction among elected representatives, administrators, planners and the various formal and informal groups reaching to explicitly stated goals and alternative courses of action proposed to meet these goals. However, in practice it may be difficult to avoid being arbitrary in the weighting of goals in the absence of such interaction between groups.

Table 8.4. The Goals Achievement Matrix

Goal description:	a 2			P 3			Y 5			S 4		
Incidence	Relative weight	Costs	Ben.	Relative weight	Costs	Ben.	Relative weight	Costs	Ben.	Relative weight	Costs	Ben.
Group a	1	A	D	5	E	—	1)		N	1	Q	R
Group b	3	H)		4	—	R	2)		—	2	S	T
Group c	1	L)	J	3	—	S	3)	M	—	1	V	W
Group d	2	—)		2)	T	—	4)		—	2	—	—
Group e	1	—	K	1)	—	U	5)		P	1	—	—
		Σ	Σ					Σ	Σ			

Source: Hill, M., JAIP, No. 34, 1968, Table 2.

The approach used for the GAM may be summarized as comprising the following phases:

1 The establishment and ordering of goals; for this purpose a goals achievement tree may be prepared which distinguishes between primary (e.g. to establish for an underdeveloped region, such as Mid-Wales, a policy catering for its present and future needs), secondary (in the case of Mid-Wales, e.g. to achieve self generating economic growth, or to maintain/enhance the quality of the environment), and tertiary (in relation to generating economic growth a tertiary goal may be to provide a variety of choice of jobs or provide adequate educational opportunities) goals and place tertiary goals in the context of wider goals. A goals achievement tree, in the context of a region like Mid-Wales, is illustrated in Figure 8.9.

2 A goals compatability matrix must be prepared to identify basic areas of conflict between goals.

3 Preparation of a matrix with unweighted goals and the selected strategies.

4 Preparation of a matrix with weighted goals.

5 Formulation final matrices with weighted goals versus strategies for each system.

6 The simplest approach in the presentation of a GAM has been demonstrated by Hill, whereby costs and benefits are measured on the ordinal scale +1: where progress toward the objective is made a score of +1 is awarded; where there is no effect 0, and where goal achievement is decreased a score of −1 is awarded. The weights of the individual objectives are then introduced and an index goal achievement determined for the complete strategy plan. The example used by Hill is illustrated in Table 8.5.

Table 8.5   Goals Achievement by Measurement on Ordinal Scale − Summary

		Weighted accessibility			Weighted community disruption	
		Weight (Community wt. = 2)			*Weight (Community wt. = 1)*	
		Plan A	*Plan B*		*Plan A*	*Plan B*
Group a	3	+6	−6	3	−3	0
Group b	1	−2	+2	2	0	−2
		+4	−4		−3	−2

Result: Weighted index of goals achievement

$$\text{Plan A} = +1 \, (+4-3)$$
$$\text{Plan B} = -6 \, (-4-2)$$

Plan A is thus preferable to plan B.

Source: Hill, M., *JAIP*, No. 34, 1968, Table 3.

As with any relatively sophisticated technique, the preparation of the GAM is complex and expensive in the resources required. However, the conceptual framework does contribute towards providing a more rational basis for decision making in plan selection. The GAM has not, hitherto, been applied in any comprehensive manner in regional planning,[52] although potentially it is a very useful technique. Some concern arises over the problem of attaching weights to the goals and to different groups in the community, and also to the preparation of a goals achievement approach in static terms whereby goals identified and expressed at a given point in time may change substantially over a period of time. The GAM compares and ranks alternative strategies rather than tests for absolute desirability, which may be inevitable in view of the difficulties of measurement associated with evaluation. The methodology of the GAM relies heavily on the planner's resources of intuition and experience in the estimation of the matrix parameters. However, despite the lack of quantitative accuracy, the attractiveness of the technique in regional planning for many people may be that, unlike cost benefit analysis or the planning balance sheet methods of evaluation, no 'spurious' impression of mathematical accuracy is given. The use and abuse of cost benefit analysis and the planning balance sheet in plan selection occupy the remainder of this chapter.

Cost Benefit Analysis

The purpose of this section on cost benefit analysis (CBA) is to provide an introduction to the nature and role of CBA as a regional planning technique; as some excellent texts are available[53] on the conceptual and operational dimensions of CBA as an evaluation technique, the coverage of the technique here is focused upon its usefulness and potential in regional planning.

The cost benefit technique attempts to enumerate and value the costs and benefits to the various interests affected in alternative schemes, and then to maximize the value of all benefits minus all costs, discounted to present value, subject to certain constraints. CBA, therefore, provides guidelines as to which of a number of alternative schemes will bring the greater margin of benefits over costs. CBA analysis is similar to the methods of investment project appraisal used by businessmen. The methods of investment appraisal (e.g. discounted cash flow) are aimed to show the size and timing of proceeds expected to be received from an initial outlay. The businessman is concerned primarily with his own objectives and therefore a limited range of private costs and benefits which can normally be measured by market prices. In contrast, in the public sector, community objectives must be met, the range of costs and benefits are wider, and many benefits being public goods have no market price as a guide to their value. The main difference between a social cost benefit analysis and a financial comparative cost analysis is that CBA takes into account social as well as private costs and benefits.

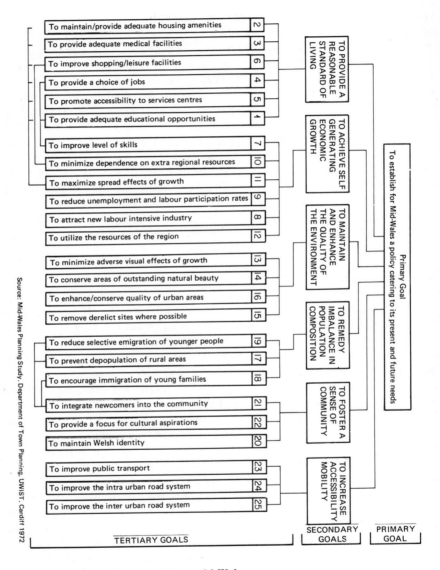

Fig. 8.9   Goals achievement tree-mid Wales.
Source: Mid Wales Planning Study, Department of Town Planning,
UWIST, Cardiff, 1972.

CBA is particularly suitable firstly, where there are a number of alternatives to be considered; secondly, where repercussions are likely to extend a considerable way into the future; thirdly, where the repercussions affect many individuals and institutions; and finally, where there are a number of constraints to be met.

It is in the public sector that CBA has been receiving growing attention, particularly for public investment decisions. One of the objectives of planning is to remedy the market inadequacies by setting out a framework within which individual decisions can be influenced so that the resultant whole is better than what would otherwise have occurred. Such a plan, being an investment framework, may lend itself to CBA. Although CBA as a subject has come into prominence only in recent years, it has a long history, with Dupuit's paper on the utility of public works being published in 1844.[54] In the present century, CBA first came into prominence in the USA (as with many other techniques), where it was originally applied to the improvement of navigation and water resources projects, and has since been extended to other subjects. A conference was held at the Brookings Institution in the USA in November 1963 to explore the problems of appraising the benefits that were likely to accrue from proposed public investment projects. At the conference, papers were submitted dealing with CBA in seven contexts; research and development, outdoor recreation, education, aviation, highways, urban renewal, and public health. While the application of CBA has been developed mainly for physical projects of this nature little work has been undertaken in the application of CBA to urban and regional planning.

It must be recognized that CBA is a method which can be used inappropriately as well as appropriately. There are two general limitations of principle (apart from many of practice) which must be recognized. Firstly, CBA is only a technique for taking decisions within a framework which has to be decided upon in advance, and which involves a wide range of considerations, many of them of a political or social character. CBA helps to choose between means, but is no guide to the desirability of ends; it is, therefore, an appropriate tool for plan selection. Secondly, CBA techniques so far developed are least serviceable for large size investment decisions. If investment decisions are so large (third London Airport?) relatively to the region, or sub region, that they are likely to have very widespread repercussions on the economy, the standard technique will be limited in use. As R. Turvey has illustrated,[55] the general principles of CBA might be stated as:

1 Which costs and benefits are to be included?
2 How are they to be valued?
3 At what interest rate are they to be discounted?
4 What are the relevant constraints?

A situation may arise where, although the direct costs and benefits could be estimated, the indirect costs and benefits could not be estimated reliably enough to justify the trouble and effort involved in a cost benefit calculation, although the planning balance sheet approach (considered later) has been developed to extend the scope of traditional CBA, which is based on mathematical neatness. C. D. Foster has described a full social CBA, in which *all* the costs and benefits are included as unfeasible, 'a piece of utopianism'.[56]

The application of CBA was first made in Britain in relation to transport problems, notably the London–Birmingham Motorway (M1) in 1960, and the Victoria Line extension to the London Underground network in 1963. The application of CBA to both these studies, and others, has been analysed by G. Peters in a useful review of CBA in relation to public expenditure.[57] At the time Peters was writing, in 1966, he noted that 'regional planning problems have not so far been tackled rigorously in terms of cost benefit'. Indeed, he was not optimistic of its developmental potential but rather emphasized the advantages of the 'checklist of criteria' approach in preparing a balance of advantages and disadvantages of alternative strategies, developed earlier by L. Kitching.[58]

The Victoria Line Study[59] illustrated the importance of the choice of the discount rate (6 per cent in this case). Why must the value of costs and benefits be discounted? Of all the current issues in CBA, none is more complex than the choice of a suitable discount rate. The application of a discount rate implies that the community values benefits and costs falling at different times differently; a positive discount rate implies that the community prefers consumption today to consumption tomorrow. Money in the hand today is worth more than the same sum in 50 years time. If the money is not invested in a particular scheme then it could be invested in alternative projects; the rate of interest is a measure of the community's value of particular projects. The rate of return expected on a project is the social opportunity cost, for which the rate of interest is a comparable measure. Discounting is similar to calculating compound interest. In the Victoria Line Study, for example, the value of capital expenditure was compared with the discounted value of benefits occurring through an assumed life of 50 years for the project. If the interest rate is 3 per cent, then £100 is worth £100 × 1.03 = £103 in one year's time; £100 × 1.03^2 = £106.09 in two years time etc. Similarly, £106.09 available in two years time discounted at 3 per cent is worth £100 today i.e. present value. In February 1970 N. Lichfield published[60] two volumes on CBA applied to the growth of Stevenage. Lichfield used a discount rate of 8 per cent, being the rate then quoted by the government for the nationalized industries as their yardstick of the average rate of return to be achieved. Lichfield estimated the present discounted value of costs over the life of the project, namely 54 years. To test the effect of the discount rate on the end result rates of 4 and 10 per cent were also chosen. Any CBA must base its analysis on a range of discount rates.

THIRD LONDON AIRPORT

The CBA for the Third London Airport produced by the Roskill Commission's Research Team is the most comprehensive CBA undertaken in urban and regional planning so far in Britain, and therefore justifies at least some examination. The issue involved was a simple one; which of four sites would be best suited for a new international airport (London's third)? By adopting a 'scientific' basis for decision making the Royal Commission sought to make an objective decision. It is worth noting the Commission's comments on this subject in paragraph 4 of the Report;[61] 'it is assumed by some that subjective judgement properly exercised, is a substitute for quantitative analysis and assessment. On this hypothesis, judgement takes over when quantitative analysis begins to weaken, and it is unwise to push quantitative analysis into the area more appropriate to pure judgement. However, it is preferable to consider judgement as something which both informs and is applied to quantitative analysis. It informs such analysis in the sense of defining objectives and determining the most effective ways of throwing light on the points at issue. It is an obvious prerequisite in the interpretation of the results of analysis, and in drawing up conclusions and recommendations for action. Judgement cannot, therefore, act *in vacuo*, unless it is to be debased into at best mere intuition or at worst mere prejudice'.

The papers and proceedings of the Roskill Commission run to seventeen volumes; Volume VII, over 500 pages, examines the work of the research team on CBA in relation to both the method of approach and the quantitative assessment. The CBA on the third London airport in being such a complex project illustrates some of the major limitations of CBA.

A CBA measures in money terms all the costs and benefits to be expected over the future of a project, and the project is accepted if the sum of benefits exceeds the sum of costs by a sufficient margin. However, a CBA does not require that everyone shall be made better off, or even that some people shall be made better off while no others are made worse off. It is quite compatible with CBA that some people will be made worse off. As Mishan has emphasized[62] a project admitted on a CBA is, therefore, consistent with an economic arrangement which makes the rich richer and the poor poorer. In order, then, for a project to be socially acceptable, it is not sufficient to show that the outcome of a CBA is positive; it must be established that the resulting redistributional effects are not unduly regressive.

The key tables in the CBA on the third London airport relate to Table 29.1 of Volume VII (pages 490/491) summarizing the estimates of costs and benefits at 1968 prices, discounted to 1975 and 1982. At the start of its two year study the Roskill Commission looked at 78 possible sites, ranging from Grantham in the north, Bath in the west, Diss in the east, and Portsmouth in the south. From the initial list of sites a short list of four was prepared. A comparison of the four sites, discounted to 1982 is illustrated in Table 8.6.

Table 8.6   Summary of Estimates of Costs and Benefits Discounted to 1982

1	Cublington	£4,416 million (0)	
2	Thurleigh	£4,419 million (3)	Excess of cost over lowest
3	Nuthampstead	£4,434 million (18)	site: £millions
4	Foulness	£4,651 million (235)	

Source: Table 29.1, p. 490/491, Vol. VII, Roskill Commission's Report (HMSO, 1970).

The differences between the first three sites were too slight in proportion to likely errors to be taken seriously. Foulness was clearly the most costly site, the major reason being that a loss of potential benefit amounting to £44 million was made against Foulness because of the smaller air traffic it was expected to generate as compared with the three inland airports, all of which happened to be on the right side of London to attract traffic from the North and Midlands. In the year 2000, the total number of air passengers was expected to be between 6—10 million less if Foulness had been chosen rather than one of the others.

Another relevant item in Table 29.1. of Volume VII was the cost of airport construction (Table 8.7).

Table 8.7   The Cost of Construction of a Third London Airport Discounted to 1975

1	Cublington	£184 million
2	Foulness	£179 million
3	Nuthampstead	£178 million
4	Thurleigh	£166 million

Source: Table 29.1, p.490/491, Vol. VII, Roskill Commission's Report (HMSO, 1970).

Foulness was actually more favourable than Cublington on construction costs. In January 1971 the Roskill Commission published its full report, which again recommended Cublington as the site for a third London airport; the Commission stated in their report that the choice of Cublington versus Thurleigh had been a difficult one, but the former chosen because of better access to main airlanes, less environmental loss and less interference to scientific establishments. Although the choice of Cublington involved disruption of the plans for Milton Keynes, the cost was seen to be small in relation to the total cost of the new town's programme.

Table 29.1 of the Royal Commission's report illustrates all the factors considered in the CBA; the costs and benefits of two key items, noise and recreation, are illustrated in Table 8.8.

The recreational item included outdoor recreation, churches, historic buildings and sites of scientific interest. The placement of values on those items, analysed in Chapter 24 of the Royal Commission's report, have been a matter of

Table 8.8 Summary of Estimates of Costs and Benefits of Noise and Recreation, Discounted to 1975 (£millions)

		Noise	Recreation
1	Cublington	14.3	6.7
2	Foulness	11.1	0.3
3	Nuthampstead	23.9	3.6
4	Thurleigh	14.4	3.8

Source: Roskill Commission's Report above cit.

controversy, especially, a free amenity deemed to have no cast value, and costing of historic churches by their insurance premiums. Some valuable work has been undertaken by the Highway Economics Unit in the Department of the Environment in London in estimating benefits from recreation sites and the provision of a new recreation facility.[63] On January 14th 1971 the Civic Trust, the Royal Institute of British Architects, the Royal Town Planning Institute and Institute of Landscape Architects signed a joint letter to *The Times* expressing concern on the Roskill Commission's low priority given to the protection of the environment. In the event, the environmental issue persuaded the government to reject the recommendation of the Royal Commission and, for the time being, to accept Foulness as the potential site for the third London Airport.

The two largest items in the CBA were, airspace movement, and passenger user cost; they accounted for over 80 per cent of the total costs, and both depended heavily on the value placed on passengers' time. In particular, it was the additional time and the cost of reaching the Foulness site that forced the figure for 'Passenger User Cost' to £152 million more than the figure for the next most costly site in this respect, namely Thurleigh. The values attributed to travel time have been hotly contested: 46 shillings (£2.30p) per hour placed on business travel in 1968 (rising to 72 shillings in 2000) but only 4/7d (0.23p) per hour allocated for 'leisure passengers'. The time values had been based on a person's earnings, although this implied that a person valued his leisure very little in comparison with work.

The CBA on the Third London airport reached a new level of sophistication in applying the technique. However, it also illustrated its weakness. These weaknesses were examined critically in a special issue[64] of the Journal of the Regional Studies Association in September 1971, devoted to the report of the Roskill Commission. Lichfield believed that had the Commission made better use of the CBA as a framework for arriving at its decision it was possible that an alternative conclusion would have been reached, namely the one subsequently reached by the government, Foulness. Among the limitations of the technique three in particular might be mentioned; first, the number of variables to be considered for a large scale project; secondly, the basis on which values are measured; thirdly, the exclusion of equity or incidence in economic calculations. The businessman and holidaymakers were shown to benefit to such an extent that they more than compensated for the victims of the project, and this was consistent with CBA, although compensation was not to be paid to the victims.

CBA must be judged for what it is, as with other techniques, a substantial and valuable device for gathering information about preferences, but one which still has many defects and loopholes.

Planning Balance Sheet

The planning balance sheet (PBS) technique has been developed to extend the scope and comprehensiveness of CBA. The methodology underlying the PBS has been pioneered by N. Lichfield and described fully in the literature.[65] The PBS has been applied to a number of case studies[66] in urban planning which have demonstrated the potential of the technique. However, the application of PBS in regional planning has been a relatively recent development.

Although ideally plan selection should evaluate the costs and benefits of alternative strategies for every individual in the community, this is not possible, although plan evaluation is most meaningful and has its reality in relation to the individual. The PBS attempts a second best in grouping the community into homogeneous sectors distinguished by their main form of operation. The PBS evaluates alternatives on the basis of balancing the advantages (benefits) and disadvantages (costs) to assess which strategy yields the maximum net advantage (benefits). The PBS does not seek to provide a measurement of alternatives wholly in money terms, but rather attempts to widen the scope of the traditional CBA, and approaches plan evaluation in assessing the implications of alternative strategies for both the community as a whole and various groups within the community.

The applications of the PBS to plan selection illustrate the approach to CBA, whereby social costs and benefits are divided into the *measured* analysis in money terms, and the *unmeasured* analysis of intangibles, which are assessed on a points system. Clearly, the intangibles cannot be measured as precisely as the tangibles. However, the PBS approach has its value in identifying all those factors which must be taken into account when choosing between alternative projects. Some information on general orders of magnitude for intangibles enables a more informed decision to be made than no knowledge at all.

In the PBS approach the community is not considered merely as a whole but also by main sectors; the most commonly used approach has been to distinguish between, (a) producers and operators, and (b) consumers. A classification of this type is useful in so far as the incidence of costs and benefits will vary significantly between sectors, and equity between sectors is as important as overall efficiency. Table 8.9 illustrates the PBS approach to CBA with particular reference to distinguishing between the main sectors upon whom the incidence of costs and benefits is borne. The example used in this context has been taken from Lichfield's application of the PBS to the expansion of Ipswich (mentioned earlier in this chapter in relation to techniques of cost minimization).

The essence of the PBS method is to clarify to the planner the balance between monetary and physical costs with intangibles, and at the same time to identify their incidence on different groups in the community. The strength of the PBS lies in that it takes all envisaged factors into account. While the technique faces many of the problems encountered in CBA in making numerous assumptions, its chief advantage is the thoroughness in which it rationalizes a situation where even though the intangibles defy measurement, the acknowledgement of their existence as intangibles can lead to a decision which takes all these facets into account. Therefore, the PBS approach rationalizes what may normally be done as an intuitive thought process when a decision is made. However, it must be recognized that while the PBS produces a series of net advantages to alternative strategies, the relative importance attached to the distribution of net advantage in respect of a number of alternative strategies must itself be to a large extent subjective. If the PBS technique is to make a substantial contribution to plan selection in regional planning it will require some concensus as to the goals which need to be achieved. The technique may, therefore, be used for comparing strategies already derived by other means; for example, the GAM may identify basic goals and their relative importance, and threshold analysis may be used to illustrate the physically, economic strategies leading to the fulfilment of these goals.

Conclusion on the Evaluation Techniques

Despite the search for more objective techniques to assist decision making in plan selection, the techniques of regional planning are not yet sufficiently developed to be able to put forward basic decisions other than on a largely subjective basis. The variety of new methods of evaluating alternative plans which have been developed in recent years is an indication of the need to establish more acceptable procedural techniques and the dissatisfaction with present ones.[67] As many regional investment projects are large scale in size, their impact, both direct and indirect, tends to be made in an infinite number of ways. One of the major obstacles to the development of acceptable procedural techniques has been the large number of unquantifiable issues which arise in comprehensive planning studies at the sub regional and regional level. However, the increasing sophistication of evaluation techniques in plan selection cannot, and does not, seek to eliminate the subjective element from planning. The approach to plan making in the formulation of regional plans of the 1960s and 1970s has been different to that undertaken in the early post-war years. The

Table 8.9. *The Planning Balance Sheet Approach to Cost Benefit Analysis. Expansion of Ipswich*

Item No.	Sector	Proposal				
		1 (W)	2 (Bel/M)	4 (Br/M)	7 (Bel/Br/M)	8 (E)
	PRODUCERS/OPERATORS					
1.0	DEVELOPMENT AGENCY	0	−4	−4	−5	−7
3.0	CURRENT LANDOWNERS					
3.1	Displaced					
3.1.1	In Urban and Village Areas	0	0	0	0	0
3.1.2	Agricultural Landowners/Farmers	0	+3	+1	+2	+4
3.3	Not displaced					
3.3.1	In Urban and Village Areas	0	−1	−1	−1	−2
3.3.2	Farmers	0	+2	+2	+1	+3
5.0	LOCAL AUTHORITIES AND RATEPAYERS	0	−4	−2	−1	−3
	PRODUCERS/OPERATORS OVERALL REDUCTION	0	−4	−4	−4	−5
	CONSUMERS					
2.0	THE PUBLIC IN THE EXPANDED TOWN					
2.2	In Town and District Centres: Commercial Occupiers	0	−4	−4	−7	−7
2.4	In Residential Areas: Remaining or New Occupiers	0	−4	−4	−4	−5
2.6	In Principal Industrial Areas: Industrialists and Workers	0	0	0	0	0
2.8	Users of Regional Open Space and Countryside	0	−1	−1	−1	−1
2.10	On Principal Communications System:					
2.10.1	Vehicle Users: Internal Traffic	0	−2	−6	−4	−3
	External Traffic	0	+1	0	−1	+2
	Through Traffic	0	+1	−1	0	0
2.10.2	Public Transport: External	0	0	0	0	0
2.10.3	Pedestrians	0	0	0	0	0

Item No.	Sector	Proposal				
		1 (W)	2 (Bel/M)	4 (Br/M)	7 (Bel/Br/M)	8 (E)
4.0	CURRENT OCCUPIERS					
4.2	Displaced					
4.2.1	In Urban and Village Areas	0	−1	−1	−1	−2
4.2.2	Agricultural Occupiers			Not certain		
4.4	Not Displaced					
4.4.1	In Urban and Village Areas	0	−1	−1	−1	−2
4.4.2	Agricultural Occupiers	0	+2	+2	+1	+3
	CONSUMERS OVERALL REDUCTION	0	−9	−16	−18	−15
	PRODUCERS/OPERATORS AND CONSUMERS OVERALL REDUCTION	0	−13	−20	−22	−20

Source: Lichfield, N., and Chapman, H., 'Cost Benefit Analysis in Urban Expansion, A Case Study of Ipswich', *Urban Studies*, August 1970, Table B.

planner no longer faces the problems and issues in hand with his own personal assessment of a solution in mind. There is now a much more conscious and explicit exploration of alternatives, and an obligation upon the decision makers to consider different ways of shaping the future of a community. However, in the assessment of alternatives in plan selection the planner must still use subjective criteria. Each of the evaluation techniques examined in this chapter requires the planner to make some subjective assessment either of criteria against which to judge strategies, or of the extent to which a strategy satisfies criteria, or is to the benefit or detriment of the community. Hill and Tzamir have recently developed multidimensional scalogram analysis (MSA), a form of multivariate analysis, as a method of evaluation for regional plans serving multiple objectives. While the method is still in an experimental stage, the technique enables the logic of decision making to be constantly tested while value preferences can be explicitly incorporated.[68]

Further attention must be given to the integrated use of evaluation techniques in plan selection. While in isolation an evaluation technique may be found to be lacking, used in combination with others a more suitable evaluation system may be evolved. In evaluating regional plans, for example, the checklist of criteria and GAM approaches may be used as a sieving device in the preliminary testing of alternative strategies; threshold analysis may be used in the formulation of fully worked out alternative strategies; and finally, CBA and PBS may be used as a guide to final decision making.

References

1 See, for example, Jantsch, E. *Technological Planning and Social Futures* (Cassell/Associated Business Programmes).

2 Chapter 26, vol. 7. op. cit.

3 *Strategic Plan for the South East*, SEJPT, June (HMSO, 1970).

4 See Report of the SEJPT op. cit. Chapter 9.

5 Thorburn, A., 'Preparing a Regional Plan: How We Set About The Task in Notts/Derby', *JTPI*, May 1971.

6 See, for example, Needham, B., 'Concrete Problems not Abstract Goals', *JRTPI*, July/August 1971.

7 Kozlowski, J., Planning Research Unit, Edinburgh University, 'Analytical Techniques in the Urban & Regional Planning Process', first Warsaw—Edinburgh Conference on Planning Research, May 1970.

8 Brenikov, P., 'Regional Planning in Practice', *Planning Outlook*, Spring 1967.

9 Burns. W., 'National and Regional Planning Policies in England', paper presented to Annual Conference of the RTPI Edinburgh, May 1971. Published in *JRTPI*, July/August 1971.

10 Lichfield, N., 'Evaluation Methodology of Urban and Regional Plans: A Review', *Journal of Regional Studies Association*, Vol. 4, No. 2, August 1970.

11 op. cit.

12 Kitching, L.C., 'Conurbation into City Region – How Should London Grow?', *JTPI* November 1963.

13 Stone, P.A., 'Urban Development in Britain: Standards, Costs and Resources 1964–2004' (Cambridge University Press, 1970).

14 Kitching, L.C., *Regional Planning Considerations: Evidence Submitted to Roskill Commission on the Third London Airport*, 1969.

15 Llewelyn Davies *et al.*, *Airport City: Urbanisation Studies for the Third London Airport* (HMSO, 1970).

16 Central Unit for Environmental Planning, *Severnside Study* (HMSO, 1971).

17 *Expansion of Ipswich. Comparative Costs*, Supplementary Report. MHLG (HMSO, 1968).

18 Lichfield, N., 'Cost Benefit Analysis Applied to the Expansion of Ipswich', *Urban Studies*, August 1970.

19 Malisz, B., 'Urban Planning Theory: Methods and Results', in *City and Regional Planning in Poland*, Fisher, J. (ed) (Cornell University Press, 1966).

20 Malisz, B., 'Physical Planning for the Development of Satellite and New Towns', in *The Analysis of Urban Development Possibilities*, Papers of the Institute of Town Planning and Architecture, Book 78, Warsaw, 1963.

21 Kozlowski, J. and Hughes, J., 'Urban Threshold Theory and Analysis', *JTPI*, February 1967.

22 Malisz, B., 1963, op. cit.

23 Hughes, J. and Kozlowski, J., 'Threshold Analysis – An Economic Tool for Town & Regional Planning', *Urban Studies*, June 1968.

24 Kozlowski, J., 'Threshold Theory and the Sub-Regional Plan', *TPR* July 1968.

25 Lean, W., 'An Economist's Note on the Validity of Urban Threshold Theory', *JTPI*, July/August 1969.

26 Lean, W., 'On the Validity of Urban Threshold Theory: A Rejoinder', *JTPI*, March 1970.

27 Wright, W., 'A comparison between Cost-Effectiveness and Threshold Analysis', *JTPI*, April 1970.

28 Famelis, N., 'On the Validity of Urban Threshold Theory: Further Comment', *JTPI*, January 1970.

29 Malisz, B., 'Validity of Urban Threshold Analysis – But What For?', *JTPI*, September/October 1970.

30 Mishan, E., 'What is wrong with Roskill?', *Journal of Transport Economics and Policy*, September 1970.

31 Malisz, B., 1969, op. cit.

32 Secchi, B., 'The Costs of Establishment in the Big Italian Cities', *Urbanistica*, 41, August 1964.

33 Malisz, B., 1963, op. cit.

34 Scottish Development Department, *The Central Borders – a Plan for Expansion*, 2 Vols. (HMSO, 1968).

35 Scottish Development Department, *The Grangemouth/Falkirk Regional Survey and Plan*, 2 Vols. (HMSO, 1968).

36 Kozlowski, J., 1968, op. cit.

37 For a detailed application of threshold analysis of a single town, Thetford in East Anglia, see 'Threshold Theory and Analysis', Hudson, P., Unpublished Thesis, UWIST, Department of Town Planning, 1971.

38 Heriot-Watt University and Midlothian County Council, *The Esk Valley Study*, 1969.

39 Kozlowski, J., 'Optimisation Method – A Case for Research', *JTPI*, April 1970 (b).

40 Broniewski, S. and Jastrzebski, B., 'Optimisation Method', in *Threshold Analysis Optimisation*, Planning Research Unit, (University of Edinburgh, 1970).

41 Forbes, J., 'A Map Analysis of Potentially Developable Land', *Journal of Regional Studies Association*, September 1969.

42 Kozlowski, J., 'Towards an Integrated Planning Process', in *Threshold Analysis Optimisation*, Planning Research Unit, (University of Edinburgh, 1970).

43   Millward, R.S., 'PPBS: Problems of Implementation', *Journal of American Institute of Planners*, March 1968. For a fuller account of the nature of PPB, see, Leyder, F. and Miller, E., *A Systems Approach to Management*, (Markham Publishing Co., 1970).

44   Rose, K., 'Programme Budgeting with Particular Reference to the USA', *Institute of Municipal Treasurers & Accountants*, September 1969.

45   See, for example, the use of PPB by Liverpool in (a) City Centre Review 1970, and (b) Inner Areas Plan 1970. See, too, Rose, K., Planning and PPBS. With Particular Reference to Local Government, *Environment & Planning*, Vol. 2, 1970.

46   'A Study of the Feasibility of Introducing Output-Budgeting in the DES', Education Planning Paper No. 1, April 1970, HMSO.

47   See Treasury Economic Progress Report, October 1970, for description of the work on PPB by the Ministry of Defence and the Home Office.

48   Hinriche, H. and Taylor, G.M., *Programme Budgeting and Benefit Cost Analysis* (Goodyear Publishing Co. Inc. California, 1969).

49   The nature and extent of the challenge of decision-making at the city level within a PPB framework has been well defined in the case of Liverpool by H. Steward. 'Decision Making at the City Level', Unpublished paper to Regional Studies Association Conference on Politics and Planning, held at Imperial College, October 1971.

50   See first report. op. cit.

51   Hill, M., 'A GAM for Evaluating Alternative Plans', *Journal of American Institute of Planners'*, No. 34, 1968.

52   While the technique has not been used in published studies in the regional planning field in Britain, a considerable amount of work on this technique has been done in the Department of Town Planning, UWIST, Cardiff, in relation to South Wales and Mid Wales.

53   See, for example (a) Mishan, E.J., *Cost Benefit Analysis*, (Allen & Unwin, 1971). The book contains 125 further references on this technique. (b) Walsh, H.G. and Williams, A., 'Current Issues in Cost Benefit Analysis', C.A.S. Occasional Papers (HMSO, 1969). (c) 'Cost Benefit Analysis in Local Government', Institute of Municipal Treasurers & Accountants, 1969.

54   Dupuit, J., 'On the Measurement of the Utility of Public Works, 1844', Translated from the French, in *International Economic Papers*, No. 2, London, 1952.

55 Turvey, R., 'Cost Benefit Analysis: A Survey', *Economic Journal*, Vol. 75, December 1965.

56 Foster, C.D., *The Transport Problem* (Blackie, 1963).

57 Peters, G.H., 'Cost-Benefit Analysis and Public Expenditure', Eaton Paper No. 8, Institute of Economic Affairs, 1966.

58 op. cit.

59 Foster, C.D. and Beesley, M.E., 'Victoria Line Study', *Journal of Royal Statistical Society*, Series A, Vol. 126, 1963.

60 Lichfield, N. & Associates, *Stevenage Public Transport: CBA*. 2 Vols. (Stevenage Development Corporation, February 1970).

61 *Royal Commission on the Third London Airport*, Volume 7, of the Report. Para 4, page 6, Chapter 1 (HMSO, 1970).

62 Mishan, E.J., 'What is Wrong with Roskill?', *Journal of Transport Economics and Policy*, September 1970.

63 'The Estimation of Benefits from Recreation Sites and the Provision of a New Recreation Facility', Highway Economics Unit, Department of the Environment, *Journal of Regional Studies Association* Vol. 5, No. 2, July 1971.

64 Special issues of the *Journal of Regional Studies Association*, Vol. 5, No. 3, 1971. Contributions by Sharman, Parry Lewis, Lichfield, Carruthers and Dale. Also, see, Dasqupta, A.K. and Pearce, D.W., *Cost-Benefit Analysis: Theory and Practice*, Chapter 9, 'A Case Study of the Siting of London's Third Airport', (Macmillan, 1972).

65 See, for example, Lichfield, N., 'CBA in City Planning', *JAIP*, No. 26, 1960, or 'CBA in Plan Evaluation', *Town Planning Review*, No. 35, 1964.

66 Application of PBS in case studies by Lichfield & Others, on
    (a) Swanley, *Urban Studies*, November 1966.
    (b) Peterborough. *Journal of Regional Studies Association*, Vol. 3, No. 2, September 1969.
    (c) Ipswich, *Urban Studies*, June 1970.
    (d) Stevenage, Stevenage Development Corporation, February 1970.

67 Holmes, J.C., 'An Ordinal Method of Evaluation', *Urban Studies*, June 1972.

68 Hill, M. and Tzamir, Y., 'Multidimensional Evaluation of Regional Plans Serving Multiple Objectives', Eleventh European Congress of the Regional Science Association, Vol. 29, 1972.

9 Problems and Prospects of Regional Planning

Introduction

In this concluding chapter the major issues and problems that appear to confront regional planning are identifed and discussed. These are broadly categorized into issues concerning its identity, its institutional base, its operational procedures and its relevance. In discussing these issues the underlying concern is to make suggestions and recommendations for their confrontation and resolution. The chapter concludes with a set of recommendations in the form of an outline strategy which it is contended will help to maximize the capability and contribution of regional planning as a planning tool.

ISSUES OF IDENTITY
The first and most fundamental problem of regional planning is that it lacks any precise and generally accepted identity. In the first place this is a matter of definition. There are many definitions of the subject but almost all of them are partial and many positively unhelpful. Unless some form of definition is forthcoming and generally acknowledged, however broad its form, then communication and discussion must be inhibited and concerted focus on the immediate and longer term problems of the subject will not be forthcoming.

The current array of half formed and competing definitions of regional planning stems in part from the history of the subject. It was suggested in Chapter 2 that the history of regional planning comprises several distinct strands. Each of these strands can be seen as a response to a particular pressure or problem within society. Each involved the conceptualization of a problem by powerful intellectual groups who saw solutions in terms of some form of regional planning.

Thus for the town planning profession regional planning has been seen as a means of embracing, ordering and thus combating the problem of the exploding urban area. Regional planning is thus large scale physical planning. It is seen by virtue of its spatial scope to be able to encompass the movement patterns of increasingly mobile populations and thus, too, to provide terms of reference for the planning of more territorially circumscribed local planning agencies.

The interest of the economist in regional planning has grown out of the problem of how to maximize national economic growth rates. The answer has been seen in part to depend upon the possibility of devising spatially disaggregated policies for the different parts or regions of the country. Through a comprehensive system of regions it may be possible to achieve a more balanced disposition of resources and thus a more efficient economy. At the same time it may be possible to secure the better use of all the nation's resources. Relatively immobile resources, for example in the form of unemployed men and women, may be articulated through the regional measures of national government. These considerations have led to the development of that form of planning termed national regional policy. This concern to disaggregate national policy measures by regions has in turn stimulated regional planning. This is so because in so far as regional policy involves a withdrawal of resources from or allocation of resources to regions as a whole, then some form of action is required to channel this movement of resources within regions, to ensure that resources are effectively allocated and articulated. Resources will be most effectively deployed and developed where regard is paid not simply to the different regions of the nation but also to the different parts of each region. Regional planning thus appears to be viewed by the economist as an institutional means at the lower or finer level of an hierarchical arrangement through which the economic system may be articulated.

Regional planning may, therefore, be defined either in terms of large scale physical planning or intra national economic planning, as a means of achieving the aesthetic and economic arrangement of societal forms whether settlements or industries, through a new level in the hierarchy of the planning system. Regional planning has, however, come to be seen not simply in terms of physical or economic planning but more particularly as an amalgam of these, and it is now perhaps most commonly defined as a unique synthesis of physical and economic planning.

This view of regional planning is rejected here for its narrowness and aridity. It may well be the case that the main problems which have initiated regional planning have been physical and economic ones, but it would seem excessively myopic and circumscribing to suggest that these are the only problems which it can tackle. For example, social issues such as those of deprivation and access to social opportunities and more embracing issues such as participation in political affairs and the quality of life may equally be and need to be confronted by regional planning actions. At the same time it may well be the case that the profession of physical planning and discipline of economic planning have been the main intellectual interests informing the subject but to suggest they comprise an adequate intellectual base for the full development of the subject would seem excessively crabbing, making it dependent upon subjects which are themselves searching for a more substantial intellectual foundation; they provide an opportunistic basis — the fact that regional planning has grown up historically in this way — rather than a fundamental basis for the development of the subject.

It is suggested that regional planning should not be defined in terms of the traditional concerns of established interests nor as an area within which the expertise of these interests may be practised. Regional planning is not, by definition, economic or physical planning or economic fused with physical planning. Regional planning may be defined quite simply as a particular type of public planning. This definition is at once more open and less circumscribing than those noted above. It identifies the central issue of regional planning which is how to develop itself as a form of planning and decision making rather than how to develop and synthesize a given set of interests and skills. It is a definition which locates regional planning within the newer but broader based discipline of public planning. It is a definition which does not limit *a priori* the problems which regional planning can address. It is a definition, too, which provides for the possibility of substitution and replacement of regional planning by other types of public planning and vice versa; it is only one tool in the total public planning process. It underlines the point that what is at stake is the need for society to be served by an efficient and effective public planning process and not the development and implantation of a particular type of planning at all costs; that the subject needs to develop with sensitivity to its limitations and with a concern for its specific contribution *vis-a-vis* other types of public planning.

Given that the definition of regional planning as a particular type of public planning is the most fruitful one on which to proceed, the next issues revolve around the distinctive characteristics of this type of public planning. It has been suggested that the most appropriate definition of a region is that it is a supra urban space. It follows that regional planning may be more fully defined as a type of public planning which is supra urban in scale.

It must be admitted that this definition is not altogether satisfactory. In the first place it implies that regional planning is urban in focus whereas this is not necessarily the case. It also begs the question of how urban is to be defined. Urban is perhaps best viewed as equivalent to terms such as city region and sub region, namely as an area of relatively dense population clustering embracing intense daily activity flows and possessed usually with a marked degree of self government. There is a question here regarding the nature of metropolitan planning and its relationship with regional planning. In the foregoing chapters the two terms have been treated as synonymous but it may be that metropolitan planning is a distinct sub type. As has been noted, Harris[1] has suggested that metropolitan planning and regional planning are different in terms of the availability of space and that the latter is granted a much greater freedom for allocating activities to space. This in turn raises questions about the point at which space can be said to be readily available, a dilemma which is probably best resolved by accepting that metropolitan and regional planning overlap with one another; nevertheless Harris does raise a useful point about the distinctive problems and skills of each of them and it is one worth noting.

Regional planning, then, is a type of public planning which is supra urban in scale. As such it embraces spaces from the larger than urban right up to but not including the nation as a whole; a range which might be held to imply vagueness and confusion, or more positively a supremely flexible capability.

One further final defining characteristic of the type follows on from this point about the range over which it might apply.

It is extremely common to refer to regional planning as a particular level of planning. This tends to imply that it is a part of a hierarchy of levels and it also tends to imply the existence of a systematic and coherent set of regions – a level throughout the planning system. Both implications are questionable. Some regional planning may conceivably go on with little regard or reference to other levels and more certainly regional planning may be undertaken at only one or two places in national space – at a number of innovative regional institutions for instance. It may thus be misleading to characterize regional planning as a level of decision making and preferable to characterize it as decision making at a particular scale.

A final point that deserves considerable emphasis is that regional planning does involve decision making actually within the region. It is a form of planning and decision making at a particular scale and not for example decision making by national government in which action is applied to a region or regions. The latter, it has been emphasized, is central government regional policy making and not regional planning. The point deserves emphasis because these two types of planning are sometimes confused. Hall, for example, has recently suggested that regional planning consists of two components, namely national-regional and regional-local decision making. This is clearly not the case for the first of these is indeed regional policy not regional planning.[2]

It is necessary to acknowledge that here as with metropolitan planning regional planning merges with regional policy rather than having a sharp boundary with it. This is so because it may in practice be difficult to locate the exact source of decisions and it may well be that certain elements of a decision are made regionally, other elements nationally. Nevertheless this does not invalidate the point that regional policy and regional planning are fundamentally different types of public planning. A point which will hopefully become accepted as regional planning and regional policy too become more systematically developed.

At this stage then issues revolving around the definition of regional planning may best be resolved by defining it as a type of public planning which involves decision making within a region which is a scale rather than a level of operation and which is supra urban and sub national in dimensions.

Given these defining structural characteristics of regional planning the next issues that must be confronted are more complex and less easily resolved. If regional planning is a particular type of public planning then these issues are: in what ways is it distinctive and what is the degree of this distinctiveness? Is regional planning simply a minor variation of public planning or a substantial variation demanding concerted intellectual effort and specific skills to realize its effective operation?

There would appear to be at least four sources of its distinctiveness. In the first place regional planning operates in a distinctive environmental setting; it works between national government and local government and typically in an immediate institutional environment of relatively strong but few institutions. In the second place the institutional base of regional planning tends to be distinctive in so far as it typically lacks the executive power and control over a wide range of government functions, as is for example the case of urban and national planning.

In the third place regional planning is distinctive because of the scale over which it applies action; this means in ways which are not yet clear that the regional planning act will be without the detail of local acts and without the abstractness and generality of national planning acts, and that distinctive means are required through which regional phenomena can be measured and evaluated and the impact of actions fed back. And finally regional planning is differentiated from other forms of planning because it needs to draw on a particular body of knowledge, knowledge about how society works in supra urban space in order to deliver its actions. This in itself does not mean that regional planning actions are different from other types of public planning actions; it does mean that the act needs a specialized and distinctive input.

It is suggested that regional planning is distinctive in each of these dimensions and in the combination of these, and that, although the full implications of these differences are not yet clear, they do comprise grounds for viewing regional planning as a significant variant of public planning. How significant it is impossible to say at this stage, not least because public planning is itself undeveloped. The issue of the degree of its variation is taken a little further below.

INSTITUTIONAL ISSUES

A fundamental question mark which has always plagued regional planning is the lack of and difficulty of realizing an adequate institutional structure for delivering significant regional planning actions. In unitary states such as Great

Britain the capabilities for public action are concentrated in the organs of central and local government; the regional organs where they exist, have, generally speaking, a limited capability.

The implementation of some form of provincial government offers the first and most obvious solution to this issue. This has been a continuing theme in the history of regional planning and one which took a notable step forward recently in Great Britain with the creation and subsequent reporting of a Royal Commission charged to look at this very issue. Unfortunately the report has not been enthusiastically received, and popular debate has been very muted. The work of the Commission has brought into being a very useful addition to a limited stock of knowledge critical to regional institutional reform, and has added to the limited range of authoritative alternative proposals. It may help to induce a strengthening of the existing regional machinery in England and to encourage the realization of provincial government in Scotland and Wales but these are optimistic assessments and overall it would seem unlikely that radical changes will be immediately forthcoming as a result of the Commission's work. Basically it would seem that regional identities are weak, the relevance of a provincial government not proved and the interests of national government opposed. It might be noted too that the methodology of such large scale administrative reform is completely undeveloped.

With the possible exception of Scotland and Wales it does seem then that the provincial government formula is unlikely to provide the solution to the institutional dilemma of regional planning. However other institutional formulas do exist including *ad hoc* institutions, inter local authority associations and administrative decentralization by central government. All of these exist in most countries and they thus offer the supreme advantage of a base on which to build; further it is not difficult to envisage means by which each could be improved significantly. It may well be that a broad open ended strategy of improvement on existing institutions offers one of the most appropriate ways forward.

Common to these improvements is the need not only to seek internal improvements but also to build outward links with other institutions thus devising and promoting inter institutional systems of action. Such an approach to the solution of the institutional problem of regional planning implies an abandonment of a particular institutional ideal, such as provincial government, but more positively it implies that the problem is to be resolved through the adoption and development of planning skills and styles by the regional planner himself. It is suggested that it is the need for these skills and styles which constitutes one of the distinctive features of regional planning.

The prospects for this approach have improved in Great Britain with the recent implementation of significant institutional reforms in services such as water and health; reforms which inform these institutions with a concern for planning method. They have improved too with recent attempts to conceptualize and understand the type of planning institutional skills that are involved[3]

Finally one other approach to the institutional problem may be identified. This side steps the issue by emphasizing the need for regional planning to consider and contribute in ways other than through direct action. Regional planning institutions might concentrate rather on the output of information analysis and diagnosis for action by others. There would seem to be very considerable potential for this role. The Northern Economic Planning Council could for example, given staff resources, provide fresh thorough diagnosis of the region's problems rather than relying as it does on the now dated diagnosis of the Durham County Council;[4] diagnosis which might inform a whole range of institutional actions.

This type of approach might well be bolstered in the future through the advantage that the region offers to institution building by virtue of its economies of scale. Institutes for futures studies, for independent planning information and advice are readily conceivable at the regional scale. The Glasgow based Planning Exchange is a possible forerunner of future developments in this sphere.[5] Such institutes could well provide at the same time independent voices on the region's future and its planning and thus offer a partial surrogate for individual citizen participation.

In conclusion it seems that there is no single leading solution to the institutional issues of regional planning, but that on the other hand no fundamental reason for assuming that headway cannot be made and that regional planning must inevitably remain moribund. A number of alternative strategies and tactics have been identified and it is suggested that the scope can and should be found for each of them.

These imply that the regional planner must be intimately involved in institution and inter institution building and this is a further aspect of the distinctiveness of regional planning. Ultimately however the success of developments in this sphere and the energies with which they are informed will depend not so much on the regional planner and his capabilities but on the degree to which society views regional planning as relevant. This issue is taken up further below.

OPERATIONAL ISSUES

There are a host of issues which revolve around the current state of ability to undertake regional planning processes and the possibilities for the development of this ability. These issues are in the first place methodological. The problem that must be confronted here is the need to elaborate methods for conducting the regional planning process. It has only very recently become possible to conceptualize a number of alternative public planning methodologies, and it is apparent that a great deal of developmental work is needed on these, much of which can only be achieved through experience gained from their actual practice. It is possible tentatively to point to those which might be most relevant to regional planning and how they might need modification in order to work in the regional context, but the discussion (see Chapter 6) is too *a priori* and cannot yet be sufficiently *a posteriori*. Much more practical experience is needed, experience which is carefully evaluated in terms of its methodological implications. This means looking not only at the performance of different methods but teasing out the relevant critical dimensions of the environment of regional planning and how these impact upon methods and their operation.

Similar points may be made regarding the use of techniques in the regional planning process. Although the technological sophistication of public planning has increased rapidly within the last few years and a range of techniques have been developed for various critical points in the process, there is as yet too little practical experience of their actual operation: how they need to be elaborated and modified, if at all, to fit the regional context; how the very scale of the region for example affects information gathering or post plan evaluation. Hopefully one danger can be avoided, namely that of stringing together a number of techniques into a 'planning process'. In effect the underlying methodology then remains implicit and thus uncriticized. The critical point is that there is no one method of planning implicit or explicit, and that there is a conscious choice to be made in each regional planning situation.

One further issue in this context is that a decision to use certain types of techniques and thus technical skills may pre-empt wider more basic decisions on methods. There is a need to be conscious of this interplay and more fundamentally to understand the relationships between various techniques and technical skills, and between various methods and methodological skills in terms of their compatibility and incompatibility. It is for these reasons and because regional planning has sometimes been seen as a means for operating certain types of statistical techniques that Chapters 7 and 8 have emphasized the need to put techniques in their place and to show where and when they may be appropriate.

These issues regarding method and technique call for direct confrontation in the sense that they call for the regional planner to be conscious of the choices that are likely to be present in a given situation. But in terms of their ultimate resolution they indicate the need for stringent evaluation work. However, the number of regional planning processes going on at any one time may most likely always be much fewer than, say, urban planning processes. The onus is therefore on the regional planner to learn as much as possible from each and every one of them. They may be all too few, particularly in the short term. One particular step that can be taken to widen the universe of experience is to develop a commitment to learn from experiences in other countries. It is significant and encouraging in this respect that the United Nations is already beginning to play a role which will allow the experiences of different countries to be exchanged.[6]

A second step that can be taken to widen the empirical base of regional planning is to ensure that the maximum is learned from every public institution that does develop regionally. Thus the new regional health and water authorities are not only critical to any comprehensive multi-agency regional planning operation, but they are each in themselves regional public planning institutions and as such offer a basis for understanding regional public planning and decision making. They in turn may need to be conscious of the fact that the problems that they confront in making decisions of a regional nature are shared by other institutions; problems that are systematically confronted in the developing field of regional planning. It may be that a similar learning can be gained from and contributed to institutions in the private sector.

A more fundamental and more difficult operational issue underlies those already noted. The point here is the need for a clearer understanding of the capability of regional planning, of the types and problems it can and cannot confront and linked with this there is a need for a clearer understanding of the costs, latent and otherwise, which attend its practice.

This means that regional planners will need constantly to evaluate regional planning itself and to derive the criteria for this evaluation from very wide perspectives. In effect it means that the evaluation of the appropriateness of methods as previously suggested needs to be informed not simply on the question whether or not one method is preferable to another in a given situation but whether indeed regional planning is itself appropriate in that situation and that this needs to be answered not only in terms of effectiveness in realizing intended aims but in terms of effect upon a wider universe of societal values. The impact of a regional planning operation orientated to certain social and economic aims, for example, might need to be considered in terms of its effect on the quality of political life including the degree to which it inhibits local initiative.

Fortunately regional planning is new and, if care is taken by its proponents, wide ranging and deeply penetrating criteria of evaluation can be built into its development, unlike urban planning for example where traditions of evaluation are now having to be created.

The degree to which regional planning is evaluated in these terms by regional planners will reflect both their ethical standing and also too their commitment to a more embracing public planning process. This in turn suggests the need for caution in the way in which regional planning separates itself off as a distinct type of planning in terms of those forms of organization and individual investment which inhibit evaluation. It also tends to imply that regional planning is best taught in schools of public planning alongside other types of planning and in schools which are prepared to confront ethical and philosophical issues.

Given internal evaluation by regional planners and external evaluation by other interests, it should be possible to gain a clearer understanding of the capabilities, limitations and implications of regional planning practice. Given, too, similar disciplined thinking within other types of planning, it should be possible for society to judge the relative merits of these and to make where possible the appropriate substitutions.

As far as regional planning is concerned, there is a very clear need for more evaluation to be given to national regional policy which is a partial but by no means complete substitute for it. Although regional policy is a field to which more intensive thought is now being given, it is apparent that most of the effort so far as has been devoted to an elaboration of economic policy measures, elucidation of the basic nature of regional policy making has not proceeded very far. It is desirable to recognize this as a particular type of planning and for its basic methods and problems to be elaborated. Part of this process may involve a redefinition of the term, for regional policy is a misnomer and might preferably be termed national spatial policy. Given an elaboration of this, it will become possible to consider its relationship with regional planning to better effect. In particular through an appreciation of its costs and constraints, it will be possible to consider to what extent it is a substitute for and can be substituted by regional planning.

A final operational issue concerns the development of adequate knowledge of how regions work, how society operates in supra urban space. This is a rich and developing field of knowledge but one where more work is needed in testing and filling out existing hypotheses and models and in developing what is virtually total ignorance in other sectors of the field. A major need is for more work on the phenomenon of polarization. Generally the empirical evidence on growth poles is very limited and certainly does not seem to warrant the confidence which regional planners place in it. The testing needs too to be undertaken from a wider perspective than that apparent until now. The social and especially the political dimensions of pole development are only now beginning to be examined by social scientists, and in pointing towards the imperialist dimensions of the phenomenon are adding further criticisms to pole development policy and to further appreciation of the working of society in supra urban space.[7] Equally there may be a need to extend the territorial horizons over which core periphery phenomena are observed and measured. Frank[8] for example has argued that there are international dimensions to this phenomenon, the corollary of which is supra national planning which may be a necessary complement to national regional policy and regional planning operations. Economic polarization apart, there is a need to improve the lack of knowledge in the social and political dimensions of regional life, and in particular to discover how life chances and political leverage are distributed across regions and influenced by their spatial structures.

This state of affairs in the substantive sphere of regional planning knowledge is possibly an interesting reflection of the influence of the weak institutional structure of regional planning. The knowledge that has developed has reflected national economic interests; pole theory, developed as a result of these interests, is then imposed upon the regions perhaps further embracing them in a set of dependency relationships. Given more autonomous institutions it might have been expected that more knowledge would have been built up from below, inductively. Valid or not the hypothesis points towards the underlying interrelationships between institutional, substantive knowledge and operational issues.

There are further dimensions to this interrelationship between regional planning institutions, procedural theory and substantive theory. For example, developing knowledge of political-institutional performance in supra urban space may feed back to help in the design of regional planning institutions. More fundamentally the whole problem of the design of public institutions needs to be embraced into the discipline of public planning thus giving institutional reform the base which it lacks and giving public planning a simultaneous concern for the planning process and the institution delivering this process: the planning of institutions and the planning of acts by those institutions need to be seen as part of a total process of societal self articulation. Friedmann has emphasized this as a general argument[9] and has given particular expression to it in the idea of innovative planning.

In addition to these interrelationships it may also be noted that developing knowledge of the way regions work — substantive knowledge may feed back to effect procedural knowledge — and implementing planning actions may in turn add to substantive understanding. Posing questions about how these dimensions affect one another needs to be followed up by some hard empirical work. In particular, for example, it is necessary to probe into the way substantive theory might imply some methods rather than others and the way in which choice of certain methods leads substantive theory to be developed in certain directions.

These are difficult questions — questions which might need rephrasing and reorientation with the development of the subject. However the prospects for their resolution and for significant strides in the intellectual foundations of regional planning are increasing as public planning theory itself develops which it is now clearly doing.[10] Finally and equally importantly it must be emphasized that this latter group of questions and issues underlines the need to view the subject as a whole and to treat it as such and not as a set of discrete facets and issues.

FUTURE PROSPECTS: ISSUES OF RELEVANCE

The final question for regional planning is whether or not it is likely to become more or less relevant to future societies. It is this which will ultimately determine the degree of effort that is applied to improving regional planning and to the resolution of the issues noted above.

It has been suggested (Chapter 1) that regional planning has three critical contributions to make, although of course others may be invented. In the first place regional planning is a device for giving a concerted attack on certain types of problems that occur in society; problems which are outside the power and territorial scope of urban government. It is difficult to envisage these decreasing in significance in the future: patterns of human habitation are likely to continue to mean the incidence of regional problems. These indeed may be added to as personal mobility from a central node occupies not settlement space but regional spaces, so that pressures for recreation for example may require regional solutions. At the same time as society increases the quality of information about itself and devises more flexible means of recording that data untied to pre-existing statistical areas, so may the incidence of regional problems be more readily perceived and acted upon.

Regional planning is also a supportive device to other types of planning, particularly local and national planning, and therefore to the extent that these increase in significance in the future so too will regional planning. What seems particularly likely in this context is the continuation and possible intensification of national planning and thus too regional planning in the Eastern Bloc and especially the Third World. In Britain the pattern for the future is already set in the local context where it is apparent that the corollary of current local government reform is the need for a regional strategy context.

Finally regional planning is also a function of regional or provincial government and here the pattern of change is more difficult to assess. In the British context and weighed against the points noted earlier are factors such as the movement to achieve greater participation in and democratization of government, a movement which might be intensified given the formation of supra national blocs such as the European Community; and given the likelihood of an increasing role for government in societal affairs, an increase which may induce congestion of central government and force devolution to regions.

At the least it appears from these few points that regional planning is unlikely to decrease in significance and may well increase considerably. Whatever the actual future within this arc of possibilities, and an historical view of the subject's development pushes it to the less significant, commitment and effort to its improvement and development seem warranted.

A Strategy for Development

It is possible to bring out the critical points that have been made above and to express these in a set of recommendations for the future development of the subject.

The strategy is addressed to those interested in, concerned about, and committed to the development of regional planning.

1 View regional planning as a particular type of public planning: the historical view of regional planning which searches for its identity in uniting the strands of its history is not a fruitful base for its development.

2 Develop regional planning within a public planning context drawing on and contributing to this emerging discipline. There are in principle a number of quite logical but sophisticated questions one could pose about regional planning, for example: the distinctive characteristics of regional planners, their influence and effect on the planning process compared to planners at other levels. But it is important to ask the basic questions not only for the obvious logical reasons, but because these finer more detailed questions are only likely to become meaningful against a more fully elaborated portrait of public planning. This does not mean that regional planning must await on the development of public planning, but it does mean that its development has to be sensitive to the state of the subject as a whole and that it must weigh up the relative returns of additional investment in its own problems compared to those derived from improving its ultimate base, namely public planning.

3 Develop regional planning with an awareness of its limitations and with a concern to elucidate its specific contribution to the public planning process.

4 Develop regional planning with a sensitivity to the degree to which it is a substitute for and can be substituted by other types of public planning.

5 Develop regional planning without those forms of organizational and individual commitment which inhibit deeply penetrating evaluations of its usefulness.

6 Secure the teaching of regional planning in schools of public planning alongside other types of public planning and in a way which explicitly confronts ethical questions.

7 Take extra care to ensure that the maximum is learned from each regional planning operation.

8 Develop an international orientation in order to maximize the universe of the experiences of regional planning.

9 Develop regional planning with a rounded concern for each facet of its subject matter: regional planning needs to be treated as a whole.

10 Ensure that there is an awareness and understanding of the capabilities of regional planning in wider society; do this not as a public relations exercise or to secure the status of regional planning or to inveigle it into society, but in a way which will allow society to grasp the maximum advantage from regional planning.

References

1 Harris, B., Comments on Friedmann, 'Regional Planning as a Field of Study', *AIP*, August 1963.

2 Hall, P., *Theory and Practise of Regional Planning*, (Pemberton Books, 1970).

3 See the works of Friend, Yewlett and Power, op. cit.

4 Northern Economic Planning Council, 'Outline Strategy for the North, 1969;' and Durham County Council, 'County Development Plan, Written Analysis,' 1951.

5 Cullingworth, J. B., 'Why are we Floating the Planning Exchange?', *Built Environment*, April 1972.

6 See for example the research and publication programme of the United Nations Research Institute for Social Development, Geneva, and more particularly Dunham, D. and Hilhorst, J, *Issues in Regional Planning,* (Mouton, 1971).

7 See for example Durston, J., 'Regional Socio-Economic Development: a Conceptual Framework,' *International Social Development Review*, No. 4, 1972.

8 Frank, A., *Capitalism and Underdevelopment in Latin America,* (Penguin, 1971).

9 Friedmann, J., 'Notes on Societal Action', *AIP*, September 1969.

10 See especially Faludi, A., *Planning Theory,* (Pergamon, 1973).

Appendix 1 Regional Differentials in Economic and Social Performance in Britain and EEC Countries 1968

APPENDIX 1. Regional Differentials in Economic and Social Performance in Britain and EEC Countries: 1968

Region	Income per head relative to national average	Activity rates		Rate of unemployment	Net migration balance (thousands)	Percentage of labour force in Agriculture
		Male	Female			
Germany						
Schleswig-Holstein	84	83.2	35.5	1.2	+ 13.3	12.0
Hamburg	180	83.8	44.6	0.3	− 11.1	2.1
Niedersachsen	88	83.1	37.4	1.1	− 7.2	14.5
Bremen	125	84.6	35.4	0.9		1.1
Nordrhein-Westfalen	104	83.4	33.6	0.9	− 38.8	4.5
Hessen	107	83.1	39.4	0.4	+ 18.5	7.1
Rheinland-Pfalz	85	81.8	38.1	0.7	− 0.8	14.6
Baden-Wurtemberg	100	84.0	46.3	0.4	+ 18.4	9.6
Bayern	92	83.8	49.6	1.0	+ 21.4	16.3
Saarland	81	76.2	25.0	1.5	− 4.5	2.3
Berlin (W)	108	83.1	51.6	0.9	− 9.2	0.5
					(all 1967 figures)	
France						
Region Parisienne	147	84.9	56.6	1.9	+ 67.5	1.1
Basin Parisienne	90	84.8	46.7	1.1	+ 0.8	18.4
Nord	87	79.6	38.1	1.8	− 80.0	8.3
Ouest	85	83.7	47.8	1.2	− 75.9	29.5
Est	91	83.8	41.1	1.1	+ 9.8	11.9
Sud − Ouest	84	93.1	45.2	1.8	− 50.1	25.2
Centre − Est	94	84.3	46.6	1.3	+ 42.5	14.2
Mediterranee	92	81.0	37.4	3.2	+ 88.5	13.7
					(total 1962−68)	
Italy						
Nord-Ouest	134	85.5	33.2	2.2	+ 54.0	16.5
Lombardia	148	85.3	36.1	1.9	+ 52.1	7.3

...	...	...	...	2.7	...	26.8
Emila-Romagna	117	85.7	39.4	2.7	+ 10.3	26.8
Centre	101	83.2	31.7	2.9	+ 7.0	23.3
Lazio	107	80.1	24.0	4.2	+ 23.7	14.7
Compania	66	80.5	25.7	4.3	− 28.0	27.4
Abruzzi-Molise	64	79.9	31.5	4.3	− 7.8	42.2
Sund	59	80.6	29.3	5.1	− 59.3	41.7
Sicilia	66	82.9	15.5	3.7	− 44.2	31.5
Sardenga	68	79.6	19.1	4.8	− 10.0	32.7
Netherlands						
Noord	87	81.7	22.7	2.9	+ 0.3	17.0
Oost	88	83.8	25.7	1.4	− 4.1	11.0
West	114	83.7	27.8	0.7	+ 2.7	4.6
Zuid	92	82.8	25.2	2.0	+ 1.0	9.0
					(all 1967 figures)	
Belgium						
Flamande	93	81.2	32.8	2.5	− 0.4	7.0
Wallone	91	78.8	30.6	3.3	− 4.7	7.0
Bruxel	126	82.0	41.5	1.8	+ 5.1	2.6
					(all 1967 figures)	
Great Britain						
Northern	94	70.0	34.8	4.7	− 1.6	1.7
Yorkshire – Humberside	96	74.7	38.8	2.6	− 7.9	1.5
East Midlands	99	74.1	39.3	1.9	+ 10.1	2.4
East Anglia	94	64.6	33.1	2.0	+ 19.0	9.4
South East	109	77.9	43.4	1.6	+ 15.2	1.3
South West	98	63.5	32.2	2.5	+ 20.8	3.6
West Midlands	101	78.4	42.6	2.2	− 1.0	1.3
North West	95	75.9	42.1	2.5	− 9.5	0.6
Wales	95	65.6	30.1	4.0	− 0.1	1.5
Scotland	94	74.5	40.4	3.8	− 33.0	3.1

Sources: (a) *Regional Statistics:* 1971 Yearbook, Statistical Office of the European Commission.

(b) For Great Britain: *Abstract of Regional Statistics*, No. 5 and No. 6, (HMSO, 1970).

Appendix 2   A Summary Bibliography on Regional Planning Techniques

Industrial Location Analysis

Brown, H.J., 'Shift and Share Projections of Regional Economic Growth: an Empirical Test, *Journal of Regional Science Association*, April 1969.

Buck, T, Paris, J. and Stillwell, F., 'Shift and Share Analysis', *Journal of Regional Studies Association*, Vol. 4, No. 4, 1970.

Clark, C., Wilson, F. and Bradley, J., 'Industrial Location and Economic Potential in Western Europe', *Journal of Regional Studies Association*, Vol. 3, No. 2, 1969.

Goddard, J., 'Multivariate Analysis of Office Location Patterns in The City Centre: A London Example', *Journal of Regional Studies Association*, Vol. 2, No. 1, 1968.

Isard, W., *Methods of Regional Analysis*, Chapters 7 and 9. (MIT Press, 1960).

McKay, D.I., 'Industrial Structure and Regional Growth: A Methodological Problem', *Scottish Journal of Political Economy*, Vol. 15, June 1968.

Richardson, H.W., *Regional Economics*, Chapters 7 and 13. (Weidenfeld and Nicolson, 1969).

Stillwell, F.J.B., 'Regional Growth and Structural Adaptation', *Urban Studies*, Vol. 6, 1969.

Townrowe, P.M., 'Industrial Structure and Regional Growth: A Comment', *Scottish Journal of Political Economy*, February 1969.

Economic Base Analysis

Anderson, R.J., 'A Note on Economic Base Studies and Regional Economic Forecasting Models', *Journal of the Regional Science Association*, 1970.

Andrews, R., 'Comment Regarding Criticisms of the Economic Base Theory', *Journal of American Institute of Planners*, Vol. 24, 1968.

Blumenfeld, H., 'The Economic Base of the Metropolis', *Journal of American Institute of Planners*, Vol. 21, 1955.

Daly, M.C., 'An Approximation to a Geographical Multiplier', *Economic Journal*, 1940.

Hoyt, H., 'The Economic Base of the Brocktown, Massachusetts Area', 1949.

Isard, W., *Methods of Regional Analysis*, Chapter 6 (MIT Press, 1960).

Kazimierz, D., 'The Concept of the Urban Economic Base: Overlooked Aspects', *Journal of Regional Science Association*, Vienna Congress, 1966.

Pfouts, R.W., 'An Empirical Testing of the Economic Base Theory', *Journal of American Institute of Planners*, Vol. 23, 1957.

Richardson, H.W., *Regional Economics*, Chapter 10. (Weidenfeld and Nicolson, 1969).

'SELNEC Transportation Study', Technical Working Paper, No. 3, 1968.

Tiebout, C.M. and North, D.C., 'Exports and Regional Growth', *Journal of Political Economy*, Vol. 64, 1956.

Tiebout, C.M., 'The Community Economic Base Study', Supplementary Paper, No. 16, Committee for Economic Development, USA, 1962.

Regional Multiplier Analysis

Allen, K., 'Regional Multiplier Analysis', *Regional and Urban Studies*, S. Orr and B. Cullingworth (eds) (Allen and Unwin, 1969).

Archer, B.H. and Owen, Christine B., 'Towards a Tourist Regional Multiplier', *Journal of Regional Studies Association*, Vol. 5, No. 4, December 1971.

Archibald, G., 'Regional Multiplier Effects in the UK', *Oxford Economic Papers*, March 1967.

Brown, A.J., 'Regional Multipliers', *National Institute Economic Review*, May 1967.

Isard, W., *Methods of Regional Analysis*, Chapter 6 (MIT Press, 1960).

Richardson, H.W., *Regional Economics*, Chapters 10 and 13. (Weidenfeld and Nicolson, 1969).

Steele, D.B., 'Regional Multipliers in Great Britain', *Oxford Economic Papers*, Vol. 21, 1969.

Steele, D.B., 'A Numbers Game (or the return of regional multipliers)', *Journal of Regional Studies Association*, Vol. 6, No. 2, June 1972.

Wilson, T., 'The Regional Multiplier: A Critique', *Oxford Economic Papers*, November 1968.

Input – Output Analysis

Blake, C. and McDowall, S., 'A Local Input–Output Table', *Scottish Journal of Political Economy*, November 1967.

Input–Output Tables for the U.K. 1963, *CSO Studies in Official Statistics*, No. 16, 1970.

Czamanski, S. and Malizia, E.E., 'Applicability and Limitations in The Use of National Input—Output Tables for Regional Studies', *Journal of Regional Science Association*, Vol. 23, 1969.

Dolenc, M., 'The Bucks County Inter-regional Input—Output Study', *Journal of Regional Science Association*, Hague Congress, 1967.

Edwards, S.L. and Gordon, I.R., 'The Application of Input—Output Methods to Regional Forecasting: The British Experience', *Colston Research Series*, 1970.

Ellman, E.J., 'The Use of Input—Output in Regional Economic Planning: The Soviet Experience', *Economic Journal*, December 1968.

Greytak, D., 'Regional Impact of Inter-regional Trade in Input—Output Analysis', *Journal of Regional Science Association*, Vol. 25, 1970.

Hewings, G.J.D., 'Regional Input—Output Models in the U.K. Some Problems and Prospects for the Use of Nonsurvey Techniques', *Journal of Regional Studies Association*, Vol. 5, No. 1, April 1971.

Isard, W., *Methods of Regional Analysis*, Chapters 5 and 8 (MIT Press, 1960).

Leontief, W., 'Inter-regional Theory', in *Studies in the Structure of the American Economy, 1919—29* (Oxford University Press, 1953).

Miernyk, W.H., *Elements of Input—Output Analysis*, (Random House, New York 1966).

Nevin, E.T., Roe, A.R. and Round, J.I., *The Structure of the Welsh Economy* (University of Wales Press, 1966).

Peacock, A.T. and Dosser, D.G.M., 'Regional Input—Output Analysis and Government Spending', *Scottish Journal of Political Economy*, Vol. 6, 1959.

Piefler, R. and Tiebout, C.M., 'Inter-regional Input—Output: An Empirical California—Washington Model', *Journal of Regional Science Association*, Vol. 10, August 1970.

Richardson, H.W., *Input—Output and Regional Economics* (Weidenfeld and Nicolson, 1972).

Round, J.I., 'Regional Input—Output Models in the U.K. A Re-appraisal of Some Techniques', *Journal of Regional Studies Association*, Vol. 6, No. 1, March 1972.

Thorne, E., 'Regional Input—Output Analysis', in *Regional and Urban Studies*, S. Orr and B. Cullingworth (eds) (Allen and Unwin, 1969).

Social Accounting

Beckerman, W., *An Introduction to National Income Analysis* (Weidenfeld and Nicolson, 1968).

Edey, H., Peacock, A. and Cooper, R., *National Income and Accounting* (Hutchinson University Library, 1967).

Hirsch, W.Z. (ed), *Regional Accounts for Policy Decisions* (Johns Hopkins Press, Baltimore, 1966).

Isard, W., *Methods of Regional Analysis*, Chapter 4 (MIT Press, 1960).

Leven, C.L., 'Regional and Inter-regional Accounts in Perspective', in *Regional Analysis*, L. Needleman (ed) (Penguin, 1968).

Maurice, R., *National Accounts Statistics: Sources and Methods* (HMSO, 1968).

McCrone, G., 'The Application of Regional Accounting in the UK', *Journal of Regional Studies Association*, Vol. 1, No. 1, May 1967.

Nevin, E. and Associates, *The Structure of the Welsh Economy* (University of Wales Press, 1966).

Richardson, H.W., *Regional Economics*, Chapters 9 and 10 (Weidenfeld and Nicolson, 1969).

Tomkins, C.R., *et al.* 'Income and Expenditure Accounts for Wales 1965–1968', University College, Bangor; Welsh Council 1971.

Woodward, V.H., 'Regional Social Accounts for the UK', National Institute of Economic and Social Research Regional Papers 1 (Cambridge University Press, 1970).

Gravity Models

Batty, M., 'The Impact of a New Town: An Application of the Garin Lowry Model', *Journal of Royal Town Planning Institute*, Vol. 55, 1969.

Batty, M., 'Recent Developments in Land-Use Modelling: A Review of British Research', *Urban Studies*, June 1972.

Carrothers, G.A.P., 'An Historical Review of the Gravity and Potential Concepts of Human Interaction, *Journal of American Institute of Planners*, Vol. 22, 1956.

Eilon, S., Tilley, R. and Fowkes, T., 'Analysis of a Gravity Demand Model', *Journal of Regional Studies Association*, Vol. 3, No. 2, 1969.

Gillespie, J. and Hall, D., 'An Application of the Lowry Model to County-Scale Planning in Cheshire', in Masser, I. (ed) *An Introduction to the Use of Models in Planning* (University of Liverpool).

Gwilliam, K.M., 'A Pilot Study of the Haven Ports; East Anglia', Regional Economic Council, 1967.

Hill, D.M., 'A Growth Allocation Model for the Boston Region', *Journal of American Institute of Planners*, Vol. 31, 1965.

Isard, W., *Methods of Regional Analysis*, Chapter 11 (MIT Press, 1960).

Lowry, I.S., 'A Short Course in Model Design', *Journal of American Institute of Planners*, Vol. 31, 1965.

Ministry of Transport, Portbury, *Construction of a New Dock at Portbury*, Bristol (HMSO, 1966).

Reilly, W.J., 'Methods for the Study of Retail Relationships', University of Texas, Bulletin No. 2944, 1929.

Steeley, G., 'Analysis by the Garin—Lowry Model', Papers from the Seminar on the Notts/Derby Sub-Regional Study, Centre for Environmental Studies, 1970.

Wilson, A.G., 'Models in Urban Planning: A Synoptic Review of Recent Literature, *Urban Studies*, Vol. 5, 1968.

Wilson, A.G., *Entropy in Urban and Regional Modelling*, (Pion Limited, London, 1970).

Social Area Analysis

Busby, D., 'Research on Social Needs — An Examination of the Liverpool Study', in *Clearing House for Local Authority Social Services Research*, Vol. 1; Institute of Local Government Studies, University of Birmingham, 1972.

Centre for Urban and Regional Studies, Birmingham, *Social Patterns in Birmingham, 1966*, 1970.

Hawley, A. and Duncan, O.D., 'Social Area Analysis: A Critical Appraisal', *Land Economics*, Vol. 33, November 1957.

Herbert, D.T., 'Social Area Analysis: A British Study', *Urban Studies*, February 1967.

Liverpool Social Malaise Study, 1970.

Moser, C. and Scott, W., *British Towns: A Statistical Study of their Social and Economic Differences* (Oliver and Boyd, 1961).

Pahl, R.W., *Readings in Urban Sociology*, Introduction (Pergamon Press, 1968).

Shevky, E. and Bell, W., *Social Area Analysis: Theory, Illustrative Application and Computational Procedure* (Stanford University Press, 1955).

South Hampshire Plan, Study Report Group D. No. 6, Social and Community Life, 1970

Van de Geer, J.P., *Introduction to Multivariate Analysis for the Social Sciences* (W.H. Freeman & Co., 1971).

Threshold Analysis

Edinburgh Planning Research Unit on Threshold Analysis and Optimisation, Proceedings of first Warsaw — Edinburgh Conference on Planning Research, May 1970.

Famelis, N., 'The Validity of Urban Threshold Analysis', *Journal of Town Planning Institute*, January 1970.

Grangemouth/Falkirk Regional Survey (HMSO, 1968).

The Central Borders: A Plan for Expansion (HMSO, 1968).

Kozlowski, J., 'Optimisation Method', *Journal of Town Planning Institute*, April 1970.

Kozlowski, J., 'Threshold Theory and the Sub-Regional Plan', *Town Planning Review*, July 1968.

Kozlowski, J. and Hughes, J., 'Threshold Analysis: An Economic Tool for Town and Regional Planning', *Urban Studies*, June 1968.

Kozlowski, J. and Hughes, J., 'Urban Threshold Theory and Analysis', *Journal of Town Planning Institute*, February 1967.

Lean, W., 'The Validity of Urban Threshold Analysis', *Journal of Town Planning Institute*, August 1969.

Lichfield, 'Evaluation Methodology of Urban and Regional Plans', *Journal of Regional Studies Association*, Vol. 4, No. 2, 1970.

Malisz, B., 'Implications of Threshold Theory for Urban and Regional Planning', *Journal of Town Planning Institute*, March 1969.

Malisz, B., 'Urban Planning Theory: Methods and Results', in Fisher, J. (ed) *City and Regional Planning in Poland*, (Cornell University Press, 1966).

Mishan, E.J., 'What is Wrong with Roskill?', *Journal of Transport Economics and Policy*, September 1970.

Shankland Cox and Associates, 'Expansion of Ipswich, Comparative Costs Analysis, Supplementary Report (HMSO, 1968).

Wright, W., 'Cost Effectiveness and Threshold Theory', *Journal of Town Planning Institute*, April 1970.

Planning, Programming and Budgeting Systems. PPBS

Bridgeman, J.M., 'O & M Bulletins on PPBS', published by Civil Service Dept. November 1969 and February 1970.

Department of Education and Science, Education Planning Paper No. 1, April 1970, HMSO.

Hinriche, H. and Taylor, G.M., *Programme Budgeting and Benefit—Cost Analysis* (Goodyear Publishing Co. Inc., California, 1969).

Lyden, F. and Miller, E. (ed), *A Systems Approach to Management*, (Markham Publishing Co., Chicago, 1970).

Liverpool Corporation, 'Use of PPBS in City Centre Review and Inner Areas Plan', 1970.

Department of Education and Science, Education Planning Paper No. 1, April 1970, HMSO.

Novick (ed), *Programming Budgeting – Programme Analysis and the Federal Budget* (Harvard UP, 1965).

Novick, D., *New Tools for Planners and Programmers* (The Rand Corporation, 1961).

Rose, K.E., Programme Budgeting with special reference to the USA', *Institute of Municipal Treasurers and Accountants*, 1969.

Rose, K., 'Planning and PPBS, with Particular Reference to Local Government', *Environment and Planning*, Vol. 2, 1970.

Stewart, J.D., 'The Case for Local Authority Policy Planning', *Town Planning Institute*, Summer School, Nottingham, 1969.

Cost Benefit Analysis (including the Goals Achievement Matrix and Planning Balance Sheet)

Dasqupta, A.K. and Pearce, D.W., *Cost Benefit Analysis: Theory and Practice* (MacMillan, 1972).

Dorfman, R. (ed), *Measuring Benefits of Government Investments* (Brooking Institution, Washington D.C., 1965).

Goss, A. and Alden, J.D., 'Cost Benefit Analysis Applied to Expansion of Stevenage', *Journal of Traffic, Engineering and Control*, June 1970.

Highway Economics Unit. Department of the Environment, 'The Estimation of Benefits from Recreation Sites and the Provision of a New Recreation Facility', *Journal of Regional Studies Association*, Vol. 5, No. 2, July 1971.

Haveman, R.H. and Krutilla, J.V., *Unemployment, Idle Capacity and the Evaluation of Public Expenditures, National and Regional Analyses*, (Johns Hopkins Press, October 1969).

Hill, M., 'A Goals Achievement Matrix for Evaluating Alternative Plans', *Journal of American Institute of Planners*, No. 34, 1968.

Holmes, H.C., 'An Ordinal Method of Evaluation', *Urban Studies*, June 1972.

Institute of Municipal Treasurers and Accountants, 'Cost Benefit Analysis in Local Government', 1969.

Kitching, L.C., 'Conurbation into City Region: How Should London Grow?' *Journal of Town Planning Institute*, November 1963.

Kitching, L.C., 'Regional Planning Considerations: Evidence Submitted to Roskill Commission on the Third London Airport', 1969.

Lichfield, N., 'Evaluation Methodology of Urban and Regional Plans: A Review', *Journal of Regional Studies Association*, Vol. 4, No. 2, August 1970.

Lichfield, N., 'Cost-Benefit Analysis in Planning', *Journal of Regional Studies Association*, Vol. 5, No. 3, September 1971.

Lichfield, N., 'Application of Planning Balance Sheet to Urban Growth':
(a) Swanley, in *Urban Studies*, No. V, 1966.
(b) Peterborough in *Journal of Regional Studies Association*, Vol. 3, No. 2, Sept. 1969.
(c) Ipswich, in *Urban Studies*, June 1970.
(d) Stevenage, for Stevenage Development Corporation, February 1970.

Llewelyn, Davis *et al.*, *Airport City: Urbanisation Studies for the Third London Airport* (HMSO, 1970).

Mishan, E.J., *Cost Benefit Analysis* (Allen and Unwin, 1971).

Mishan, E.J., 'What is Wrong with Roskill?', *Journal of Transport Economics and Policy*, September 1970.

Peters, G.H., 'Cost Benefit Analysis and Public Expenditure', Eaton Paper No. 8, Institute of Economic Affairs, 1966.

Roskill Commission on the Third London Airport. Papers and Proceedings, especially Vol. 7, Parts 1 and 2 (HMSO, 1970).

Stone, P.A., *Urban Development in Britain: Standards, Costs and Resources 1964–2004* (Cambridge University Press, 1970).

Turvey, R., 'Cost Benefit Analysis: A Survey', *Economic Journal*, Vol. 75, December 1965.

Walsh, H.G. and Williams, A., 'Current Issues in Cost Benefit Analysis', C.A.S. Occasional Paper (HMSO, 1969).

Special Issue of *Journal of Regional Studies*, on Cost Benefit Analysis and the Third London Airport, Vol. 5, No. 3, 1971. Contributions by Sharman, Parry Lewis, Lichfield, Carruthers and Dale.

Appendix 3   An Introduction to Published Sources Containing Regional Data on Regular Time Series

The purpose of this Appendix is to provide an introduction to the main sources of published data at the regional level. Although developments are continually occurring in this aspect of planning, providing better access to existing data, new data sources being tapped, and improved methods of data collection, organization, and analysis, and despite the tendency for any list of data availability to become rapidly dated, some statement on the existing stock and flow of data is essential.

The Appendix has been arranged to illustrate the main sources of regional data in Britain, a description of the statistics, the frequency of publication, the date when data become available, and supplementary remarks on the nature and extent of the series. The availability of regional data in Common Market countries is considered at the end of the Appendix in Section N; with British membership of the EEC it can be expected that regional data needs in Britain will be seen increasingly within an EEC context.

While this Appendix focuses on published sources of regional data, mainly from central government, it is recognized that other sources of data do exist and may in certain cases assume substantial significance; for example, data collected from local firms, or from household surveys. However, this list of published sources of regional data may provide a useful starting point on data availability and lead to an appreciation of the gaps that remain to be filled.

SUMMARY LIST OF PUBLISHED SOURCES CONTAINING REGIONAL DATA ON REGULAR TIME SERIES

Primary Sources	Title of publication	Source	Frequency of publication
1	*Housing Statistics (GB)*	MHLG	Quarterly
2	*Local Housing Statistics (England and Wales)*	MHLG	Quarterly
3	*Rates and Rateable Values (E & W)*	MHLG	Quarterly
4	*Occasional Bulletin*	Nationwide Building Society	
5	*Statistics for Town & Country Planning, Series II (Floorspace)*	MHLG	Quarterly
	Annual Reports on:		
6	*Control of Office Development (ODP)*	DTI	Annually
7	*Control of Local Employment (IDC)*		
8	*Investment Grants*		
9	*Agricultural Statistics (E & W)*	MAFF	Annually
10	*Results of Derelict Land Survey Circular No. 57/69*	MHLG	Annually
11	*Annual Estimates of Population (E & W)*	GRO	Annually
12	*Quarterly Return for E & W*	GRO	Quarterly
13	*Employment Gazette*	DE	Monthly
14	*Highway Statistics*	M of T	Annually
15	*Roads in England*	M of T	Annually
16	*British Airports Authority Report*	BAA	Annually
17	*Digest of Port Statistics*	National Ports Council	Annually
18	*County Councils Gazette*	CCA Council	Monthly
19	*Local Government Financial Statistics (E & W)*	MHLG	Annually
20	*Bulletin of Construction Statistics*	MPBW	Monthly & Annually
21	*Sand and Gravel Production*	MPBW	Annually
22	*Family Expenditure Survey*	DE	Annually
23	*Report of Commissioners of Inland Revenue*	IRB	Annually
24	*Report of Commissioners of Inland Revenue*	IRB	Quinquennially
25	*Digest of Energy Statistics*	DTI	Annually
26	*Statistics of Education*	DES	Annually
27	*Statistics on Activities of Nationalised Industries*	see Individual Reports	Annually

Secondary Sources

28	Abstract of Regional Statistics*	CSO	Annually 1965 and 1968
29	Analysis of Regional Economic and Social Statistics	E. Hammond Durham University	
30	Statistical News	CSO	Quarterly
31	Social Trends	CSO	Annually

Irregular time series

32	Census of Population	GRO	Quinquennial (sample) and Decennial (full)
33	Census of Production	DTI	Quinquennial (Annual from 1970)
34	Census of Distribution	DTI	Quinquennial (sample) and Decennial (full)

N.B. MHLG, MPBW and M of T now in Department of the Environment.

*N.B. A separate Digest of Statistics is published annually for Wales and Scotland in addition to data for these regions in the ARS.

THE AVAILABILITY OF STATISTICS FOR REGIONAL PLANNING (ECONOMIC PLANNING REGION AND SUB-REGIONS)

Department collecting the statistics	Description 1 Statistics	Frequency	Date when data available	Remarks
A General Register Office (Now OPCS)	1 Population Estimates (persons only)	Annual	Appears Jan/Feb each year for previous mid-year	Home population by region, county and local authority area. Coresponding civilian populations (and change components) supplied to the Ministry of Housing and Local Governemnt
	2 Population by age and sex	Annual	Available each Feb/March for previous mid-year	For region as a whole only, back to 1961 mid-year figures published in RGs Quarterly Return
	3 Children under 15 (not by sex)	Annual	Available each Feb/March for previous mid-year	Counties and CBs only published in RGs Quarterly Return, as above
	4 Persons 65 & over	Annual	Available each Feb/March for previous mid-year	Local Authority areas. Unpublished
	5 Births and deaths	Annual	Available each Feb/March for previous mid-year	By region, county and local authority area. Published in RGs Annual Statistical Review Totals and Rates only for region as a whole
	Births and deaths	Quarterly	End of following quarter	
	Births and deaths	Weekly	End of following week	Published in RGs Weekly Returns

6 1961 Population Census		All county and national subject volumes are published	Regional statistics relate to old standard regions but county figures can be aggregated for new regions. Rates have to be re-calculated of course, and migration/journey to work data cannot be readily aggregated
7 1966 Population Census (sample)		National Summary Table, County volumes and subject volumes, all published	Volumes cover population by age, sex, marital condition, birth place, housing density, households by size, tenure and amenities. Subject volumes include economic activity, workplace and migration
8 1971 Population Census (Full)		Some volumes published; others forthcoming	Preliminary Report and County Volumes already published. Main subject volumes available in 1973/74. Ward Library data available Spring 1973
B Department of Employment			
9 Register of major employer (employing 5+) name, date of establishment. IC, MLH, sex	Kept up to date on a continuous basis	Continuous basis	Data from Employer's Record I and II – available to local planning authorities. Data based on employment exchanges
10 Numbers employed by SIC, MLH, sex, age	Annual	Annual data based on June are published in Autumn of following year	Available for previous years DE employment figures will be influenced in the future by (a) a yearly employment census based on PAYE and (b) employment figures

11 Estimates of employees in employment, employers, and self employed	Quarterly	Data published in *DE Gazette*	collected by the BSO in its annual survey of firms. (c) employment figures collected by DTI in the New Censuses
12 Employee activity rates 5 year age groups males/females	Annual	Data published in *DE Gazette*	Production Employment figures of DE now available in format of 1968 and 1958 SIC
13 Young persons entering employment boys/girls	Annual	Data published in *DE Gazette*	
14 Unemployment and vacancy statistics by MLH, SIC, and sex	Monthly	Available from April 1968 for regions	Totals available usually on the third Thursday of each month. Industrial analysis available three weeks later
15 Placing of work and unfilled vacancies. Males/females/youths	Monthly	Data published in *DE Gazette*	
16 Occupational and SIC analysis of unemployment and vacancies, by sex	Quarterly	Data published in *DE Gazette*	
17 Family expenditure Annual survey weekly income by household and average weekly household expenditure on 10 commodities	Annual	Some details of the 1965 survey were published for regions in Sept. 1966. Surveys have been published annually since 1966	Old standard regions have been discontinued. Survey based on sample of 10,000 households nationally

18 New earnings survey by DE. Distribution of earnings by sex, industry, occupation manual/non manual by level of skill. Also age analysis, make-up of pay and reasons for loss of pay	Annual	Results published in *DE Gazette*. The first survey undertaken in September 1968 available in *DE Gazette* May–October 1969	Survey based on one per cent sample nationally. Most detailed survey ever undertaken on earnings. However, much data available in 1968 pilot surveys
C Department of Trade and Industry			
19 IDC control details of number of permits and areas refused, approved and completed. Also data on employment	Quarterly	Data available in DTI Annual Reports and on request	Some limitations on the data as only development above a certain size are included, and these size limits have not been consistent through the years
20 Industrial progress of overspill towns jobs provided	Quarterly	Data available can be brought up to date on request	
21 Industrial analysis of IDCs for manufacturing industry approved for overspill towns	Quarterly	Data available can be brought up to date on request	
22 Industrial building (million sq.feet)	Quarterly	Data available Annually	Figures can be brought up to date on request

23 Movement of firms into and out of the region also intra-regional moves	Data held by BSO in the Central Register of Business	Some information available now – and further material becoming available	The BSO is improving data in this field. Data available on request
24 Office development control		Information available on request	A limited amount of information on ODPs since Regions concerned covered only since July 1966. Problems of coverage as with IDCs
25 Census of production gross and net output, and employment in manufacturing industry	Every five years until 1970. From 1970 Annually	1958 Census data available for old standard regions to be published. 1963 Census data for old standard regions available end 1970 for new standard regions published in *Abstract of Regional Statistics*, No. 6, 1970	
26 Census of Distribution of establishments, turnover and employees	Every five years	Some 1971 Census data available end 1972. Final reports in 1973 and 1974	Information of earlier censuses available only for old standard regions. In 1966 Census some information for new standard regions. Availability of data for sub-regions on request. Full Censuses in 1950, 1961 and 1971. Sample Censuses in 1957 and 1966

D Department of the Environment: MHLG			
27 Existing housing stock	Twice yearly	Published in *Housing Statistics*	
28 Dwellings in tenders approved (public only) dwellings started, under construction, completed. Public/private	Quarterly	Published in *Local Housing Statistics*	Data available for local authority areas
29 Rating and valuation	Annual	Data available on request	
30 Storey heights of public dwellings in tenders approved	Quarterly	Published in *Housing Statistics*	Data available for local authority areas
31 Industrialized dwellings (public sector) in approved tenders, started under construction and completed	Quarterly	Published in *Housing Statistics*	
32 Houses demolished in clearance areas and unfit houses demolished or cleared elsewhere	Quarterly	Published in *Housing Statistics*	Data available for local authority areas

	33 Acreage and dwellings granted planning permission (public/private)	Annual	Published in *Housing Statistics*
	34 Dwellings with improvement grants (public/private)	Annual	Published in *Housing Statistics*	Survey undertaken as a result of MHLG Circular 57/68
	35 Derelict land (a) acreage in spoil heaps, pits and other and the proportion justifying treatment (b) acreage restored (3 categories) in past year (c) acreage proposed for treatment in coming year (3 categories)	Annual	Results of the Derelict Land Survey
		Annual	Results of the Derelict Land Survey
		Annual	Results of the Derelict Land Survey
E Ministry of Transport	36 Vehicles currently licensed	Annual	Published in *Highway Statistics*	*Highway Statistics* has been published annually since 1963
	37 Newly registered	Annual – available unpublished on quarterly basis	Published in *Abstract of Regional Statistics*
	38 Mileage of roads	Annual	Published in *Highway Statistics*

39 Expenditure on roads new construction, maintenance, administration	Annual		
40 Future estimates of expenditure on trunk roads, principal roads and motorways, showing those completed or in progress, in formal programmes and being prepared	Annual	Published in *Roads in England and Wales*	
41 General Traffic Census surveys of road goods transport	At irregular intervals	Data available on request. The 1967/68 Survey published 1972	Data are available for about 2000 census points in Great Britain
42 Rail commuting — numbers arriving at main line termini, with train capacities and loadings	Annual	Surveys undertaken in October each year	Data unpublished but available from British Rail on request
43 Miscellaneous information relating to transport in London	Quarterly		Data unpublished but available from LTB on request

Additional Data on Transport

44 Aircraft movements, passengers handled, cargo tonnage	Monthly figures available, published annually	Data published in *BAA Annual Report*	

45 Activity at 36 principal airports, showing all movements, passengers and freight	Irregular publications, for example, 1961 and 1965	Data available irregularly for example, 1961 and 1965	Based on figures supplied by DTI Civil Aviation Division
46 Ports: Tonnage of foreign trade imports and exports coastwise trade, inward and outward. All by categories	Annual	Data published in Autumn by National Ports Council	
47 Ports: Foreign and Coastal Trade, arrivals and departures (tonnage)	Annual	Data published in *DTI Journal*	
F Commissioners of Inland Revenue 48 Floorspace data: (a) income from self employment (b) income from employee employment (c) income from unearned investment	Quinquennial surveys for county data, but annual for regions. In addition to the quinquennial and annual surveys – special publication Inland Revenue Statistics published annually	The Quinquennial surveys for 1959/60 and 1964/65 published. The 1969/70 survey published in 1972	The Inland Revenue data are based on a larger sample than that of the DHSS. Note that data refer to tax cases not individuals; persons only covered if above the tax exemption limit; analysis is by place of work; civil servants and members of armed forces excluded because assessed centrally

G Department of Health and Social Security	49 Data on Earnings – analysis by sex and level of earnings – figures relate to place of residence – figures based on small sample: one half per cent	Annual	Data published in *Abstract of Regional Statistics* for years 1964/65 to 1968/69	Some data available for counties and county boroughs. The DHSS data refer to average gross annual earnings. The figures for standard regions relate to persons between age 18-64, 18-59 (men/women), whereas county data include men aged 65/69 and women 60/65 who because they continued to work were not entitled to retirement pensions
	50 Statistics on Health and Welfare. Data supplied by Home Office as well as DHSS	Data available on regular basis	Most of the data available on request or published in annual report of DHSS	This information is not collected on a standard region basis but data are available which can be aggregated to regional level
	D Data available on sickness and injury sick pay schemes, prescriptions, patients per doctor and dentists, hospitals Also social characteristics of social class, family size, illegitimacy, betting, drunkenness, crime, mental illness, and voting		*N.B.* From 1969 annual publication of Digest of Health Statistics	Information on social security benefits and hospital facilities published for first time in *Abstract of Regional Statistics*, No. 6, 1970

Organisation	Series	Frequency		
H Central Statistical Office	51 Social Statistics	Annual	New publication *Social Trends*	First publication in 1970. The 1971 issue (No. 2) contains enlarged section giving regional tables
I Department of Education and Science	52 School population, type of school, staff, finance	Annual	Published in Part 1 of *Statistics of Education*	*Statistics of Education*, published annually since 1962 contains data for counties. From 1966 a separate volume published on each of the 3 parts. Data not available on a standard region basis but country data can be aggregated to a regional level
	53 Education building, examination successes, scholarship awards, school leavers etc. Also data on technical education and universities		Published in Parts II and III of *Statistics of Education*	
J Ministry of Agriculture, Fisheries and Food	54 June Agricultural Census acreage of crops and gross number of workers, size of holding etc.	Annual	Annual data for June of each year published in Autumn of following year	Available for previous years. Available for counties. Parish results available
	55 Glasshouse Censuses area of glasshouses and acreage of crops	Annual January and July		Available for previous years. Available for counties

56 Machinery Censuses estimated number of certain machines and implements owned by occupiers of agricultural bodies holdings and agricultural contractors	Annual March, September, December		Available for previous years. Available for counties
57 Vegetable Censuses – acreage of vegetables for human consumption	Annual September and December		Available for previous years. Available for counties
58 Orchard Fruit Census	Quinquennial	Census in November 1962, 1967 and 1972	Mostly in counties but some by special Orchard areas
59 A variety of statistics and analyses are produced and published as a by-product of the above censuses			
60 Agricultural wages and employment inquiry	Annual		One table for regions
61 National Food Survey household characteristics, food consumption etc.	Annual		Data published for regions and type of area (urban/rural)

K Ministry of Power	62 Fuel consumption – by type of consumer	Annual	All energy statistics published in Digests of Energy Statistics
	63 Petroleum inland deliveries by product	Annual	
	64 Petroleum: use of fuels by industry groups	Annual	Figures for earlier years are available
	65 Coal consumption by main industrial groups	Annual	Figures for earlier years are available
	66 Coal distribution – to domestic market. Sub-regional data not available	Monthly	Figures for earlier years are available (back to 1950)
			Data available on request

Statistics on the construction industries by region in which work is carried out

L Ministry of Public Building and Works	67 Value of new orders	Quarterly	Statistics for new Standard region available from first quarter 1966 subject to three month lag
	68 Building materials: Bricks – production delivery and stocks cement deliveries	Monthly	Statistics available from first quarter 1966 subject to one month lag
	69 Sand and gravel production	Quarterly	Statistics available from first quarter 1966 subject to three month lag

By region of registration of firm

	70 Operatives, output and number of firms	Quarterly	Statistics available from first quarter 1966 subject to three month lag	
	71 More detailed analysis of employment structure	Annual	Statistics available each September from 1966	
	72 Local authorities – number of authorities operative	Quarterly	Statistics available from first quarter 1966	
	73 Public and private investment in new construction		Published in *Abstract of Regional Statistics*	Based on unpublished data prepared by the CSO
M Additional information on Investment	74 Local authority finances	Annual	Published in *County Councils Gazette*, and *Journal of Institute of Municipal Treasurers*	
	75 Investment grants paid to regions 1966–1970		Published in *Abstract of Regional Statistics*	These figures first published in No. 5. 1969

N Regional Statistics in Common Market Countries

The main publication containing regional Data in EEC countries is *Regional Statistics 1971 Yearbook*. In this publication, the first of its kind by the Statistical Office of the European Communities, series of social and economic phenomena are given to enable some assessment to be made of the regional economies of the Community countries. The main subjects included in this volume cover population and manpower, regional product, foreign trade, agriculture, manufacturing, service industries, transport, credit institutions, income, consumption and investment. The publication is of a considerable size, covering 270 pages. There are some gaps in the statistical information; partly because the Statistical Office was not able to make use of all sources at present available for the first issue and partly because facilities for the collection of regional data are less extensively developed in certain countries. The number of series adopted will be increased in future issues of the yearbook and their comparability improved. Other regional information may be found in specialized publications (agricultural statistics, social statistics, etc.) obtainable from the Statistical Office of the European Communities.

The regions of the EEC and Great Britain are distributed as follows:

Community	Regions	
Germany	Lander	11
France	ZEAT*	8
Italy	Regions	11
Netherlands	Geographical Zones	4
Belgium	Linguistic Regions	3
Luxembourg	Grand Duchy	1
Great Britain	Economic Planning Regions	10

*Zones d'etudes et d'Amenagement du territoire.

Index

Subject Index

Abstract of Regional Statistics, 109
Activity rates, 223–226
Adaptive planning, 196–197
Ad hoc regional planning institutions, 133–137
   The Highlands and Islands Development Board, 134, 136–137
   The Cassa per il Mezzogiorno, 134–135
   The Corporacion Venezolana de Guyana, 134–135
   The Tennessee Valley Authority, 134, 136
   The Appalachian Regional Commission, 135
Adjunctive planning, 177
Administrative decentralization, 124–132
Administrative devolution, 132–133
Advocacy planning – *see* Procedural theory
Analytical techniques, 211, for individual techniques *see* industrial location analysis, economic base analysis, input-output analysis, multiplier analysis, gravity models, social area analysis, social accounts, monitoring
Appalachian Regional Commission, 135

Barlow Report (Royal Commission on the Distribution of the Industrial Population 1940), 25–26, 53
Buchanan Report (Traffic in Towns 1963), 54

Cassa per il Mezzogiorno, 48, 50, 134–135
Central place theory, 67–70
Central Unit for Environmental Planning, 270, 305
Checklist of criteria approach, 268–270
Clyde Valley Regional Plan – *see* Regional Plans
Coders, 32
Community Development Projects, 87, 110–115
Community planning, 182–183
Comprehensive planning, 178–180
Computerized cartography, 214–215
Confederation of British Industry, 87, 119
Core-periphery model – *see* substantive theory, 65–67
Corporate planning, 180–184
Corporacion Venezolana de Guyana, 134–135
Cost Benefit Analysis, 293–302 (and the associated Planning Balance

Sheet, 302–303)
Cost minimization techniques, comparative cost analysis, 270–277, threshold analysis, 277–287
Counter planning, 196–197

Department of Economic Affairs, 23–24
Depressed areas, 16–20
Development areas, 90–97, 102–106
Development planning, 196–197
Dispirited incrementalism, 173–176
Drift to the South (myth of), 99

Economic development and regional planning – *see* Substantive regional planning theory
Economic base analysis, 235–237
Economic growth, 20–24, 57
Education for regional planning, 50–51
Esk Valley Sub Regional Study, 221, 222, 233, 234, 252, 285
European Economic Community, regional policy and planning, 116–118
    supra-national government, 158–159
    regional differentials: Appendix I

Filtering-down theory of industrial location – *see* substantive theory, 70–71
Forecasting techniques,
    general, 215–216
    population, 217–218
    manpower, 218–227
French regional planning, 48–49, 130–131
Future strategy (of regional planning), 320–321

Goal achievement, 289–294
Gravity models, 247–248
Greater London Council, 98–99
Greater London Plan 1944, *et seq., see* Regional plans, 28–33
Growth points, 84, 113

Growth poles, 61–65

Highlands and Islands Development Board, 134, 136–137, 194–195
Hunt Report on Intermediate Areas (1969), 102–103

Industrial Development: White Papers
Industrial and Regional Development 1972, 94
Industry Act 1972, 94
Industrial Development Associations, 151–152
Industrial Development Certificates, 93–96
Industrial Development Executive, 107–108, 130
Industrialized countries, regional planning in, 48–50
Industrial Location,
    Analysis, 229
    Location quotient, 230–231
    Co-efficient of specialization, 231–232
    shift ratio, 232–234
    relative growth charts, 234–235
Innovation and economic development, 61, 63–64, 70
Innovative planning, *see* procedural theory, 193–196
Innovative regional planning institutions – *see ad hoc* regional planning institutions
Input-output analysis,
    introduction, 240–241
    national analysis, 242
    input-output tables, 242–244
    applications, 244–245
Institute of Municipal Treasurers, 307
Institutions for regional planning,
    alternative models discussed, 124, 153–154, 313–314
    institutional environments of regional planning, 154–158
    European Economic Community, 158–159
    future prospects, 313–315, 317

Inter corporate planning, 193–202
Inter local authority institutions, 151–153
Investment incentives, 94–96, 106–107, 109–110
Investment incentives, 1970, 94–96

Kilbrandon, Royal Commission on the Constitution, 1969–73, 114, 144–150

Leicester and Leicestershire Sub Regional Planning Study, 32, 252
Local authority policy planning, *see* corporate planning
Local Government Act 1972, 37, 41
Local Government finance,
   Green paper on reorganization 1971, 254
Location quotient – *see* Industrial location analysis

Manpower forecasting, *see* forecasting techniques
Marginal areas, 111–114
Methods of regional planning, *see* procedural theory
Milton Keynes Development Corporation (monitoring), 257
Mixed scanning, 190–191
Model-building, 227–229
Monitoring, 251
Multiplier analysis, 237–240

National Plan, 22, 24, 118, 219
National regional policy, *see* Regional policy
New Towns, 101
New York Metropolitan Region, 13–14
Normative planning, *see* procedural theory
North East Development Council, 121 152
Northern Regional Economic Planning Council, 218
Nottinghamshire/Derbyshire Sub Regional Study, 32, 219, 251

Organization for Economic Co-operation and Development (OECD), 97–98, 119, 120
Office Development Permits, 94–95

Planning: definition, 1–2, 310–311
Planning Advisory Group, 28
Planning Balance Sheet, *see* Cost benefit analysis
Planning, programming, budgeting systems (PPBS) *see*
Procedural theory, 181–184, 287–288
Planning theory and the planner, 197–200
Political development and regional planning, *see*
Substantive regional planning theory
Population forecasting, *see* forecasting techniques
Population growth, 34–35
Portbury, Ministry of Transport, 256
Problems and Prospects of regional planning, 309 *et seq.*
Procedural techniques,
   role of, 211–212, 259–269
   for individual techniques *see* under checklist of criteria, cost minimization (covering comparative cost analysis and threshold analysis); goal achievement; PPBS cost benefit analysis and planning balance sheet
Procedural regional planning theory,
   the main elements distinguished and discussed, 200–203
   the methods,
      a choice theory of planning, 170–171
      holistic social engineering, 172
      disjointed incrementalism, 173–176
      probabalistic programming strategy, 175
      adjunctive planning, 177
      comprehensive policies planning, 178–180

corporate planning, 180–184
community planning, 182–183
spatial policy planning,
    a systems approach, 184–189
systematic planning, 188
mixed scanning, 190–191
advocacy planning, 192–193
innovative planning, 193–196
adaptive planning, 196–197
developmental planning, 196-197
counter planning, 196–197
inter corporate planning, 193–202
Propellent industries, 62–64
Provincial government, 137–151
    the Greater London Council,
        139–140
    in Northern Ireland, 140–141
    the proposals of,
        Redcliffe Maud,
        Royal Commission Local Govern-
            ment (1969), 141–142
    the proposals of J.P. Mackintosh, 143
    the report of the Royal Commission
        on the Constitution (Kilbrandon),
        114, 144–150

Rational paradigm in planning, 169
Rational model of decision making,
    169 et seq.
Region: definition, 2, 310–311
Regional Boards for Industry, 36
Regional Commissioners, 125
Regional Conferences of Local
    Authorities, 152–153
Regional Economic Planning Councils
    and Boards, 22, 36, 127–130
Regional Employment Premium, 53
Regional Government, see Provincial
    government
Regionalism, 35–36, 45–46
Regional planning:
    defined, 1–2, 310–312
    characteristics of, 313
    evaluation of, 317–318
    distinguished from metropolitan
        planning, 203
    and national planning, 4, 313, 318,

    and Chapter 4, National Regional
        Policy and Regional Planning
Regional Planning Theory
    substantive and procedural theory
        distinguished, 57, 167
    see substantive theory
    see procedural theory
Regional planning techniques,
    analytical and procedural techniques
        distinguished, 211–212, 259–260
    see analytical techniques
    see procedural techniques
Regional plans, some early examples,
    Doncaster Regional Planning Scheme
        1922, 11-12, 14
    South Wales Regional Survey 1920,
        11–12
    New York Regional Plan 1927,
        13–14
    Siedlungsverband Ruhrkohlenbezirk
        (SVR) 1920, 14–16
    Clyde Valley 1946, 27–28
    North East Development Area
        Outline Plan, 27–28
    Plans for London and South East
        England 1944–71, 28–33
Regional plans, some recent examples,
    East Anglia Regional strategy, 189
    Highlands and Islands Development
        Board, 134, 136–137, 194–195
    Region Nord, Strategy, 202
Regional Economic Planning,
    Council's approach to regional
        planning, 191
    Lerma-Santiago Regional Plan,
        178–179
    Yorkshire and Humberside regional
        strategy, 178
Regional Policy (National),
    definition, 83–85
    aims of, 85–89
    effectiveness, 89–91
    measures of, 92–96
    evaluation of, 94, 96–99
    expenditure on, 97–98
    designation of areas, 102–106
    inflexibility of, 105–110

societal needs, 110–115
regional planning and the EEC, 116–118
Regional problems – local experience, 110–115
Regional Science Association, 11
Rome Treaty, 116–117
Royal Commission on Local Government in England (Redcliffe-Maud) 141–142
Royal Commission on the Constitution, see Kilbrandon
Royal Commission on Third London Airport (Roskill), see Third London Airport
Ruhr Regional Planning Authority, 14–16, 134, 153

Scottish Council (Development and Industry), 22, 152
SELNEC, 37, 39–40, 236
Services (regional provision),
    administration, 35–36
    health, 37–38
    transport, 37, 39–41
    water, 42–44
    recreation, 42, 45
South East Joint Planning Team, 32, 218
Social Accounting, 245–247
Social Area Analysis, 248–250
Social context of regional planning, 10
Social development and regional planning, see substantive regional planning theory
Social and Economic policies, 87–89
Social, Economic and Physical policies planning, see Procedural theory, 178–180
Societal action, see Procedural theory, 196–197
Spatial interaction models, see Gravity Models
Spatial policy planning, a systems approach, 184–189
Spatial structure,
    economic development, 59–71

social development, 72–74
political development, 75–77
Special areas, 17–19
Standard regions, 125
Standing Conferences of Local Authorities, 28, 30
Stormont, 140–141
Strategy of muddling through, 173–17[
Strategy of maximizing bounded rationality, 177 et seq.
Strategy of modified rationality, 190 et seq.
Sub-regional planning, 32
Substantive regional planning theory,
    core-periphery model, 65–67
    defined, 57–58
    syntheses, 77–78
    economic development and concentration, 59–60
    economic development and urbanization, 60
    filtering down theory of industrial location, 70
    growth poles (Perroux's theory of), 61–64
    economic development and integration of the space economy, 71
    economic development and the hinterland of cities, 69–70
    economic development and the diffusion of innovation, 70
    economic development and political spatial structure, 76–77
    economic development and the system of cities, 67–71
    information model of urbanization, 61
    key industry, 62
    propellent industry, 62–64
    political development and spatial structure, 75–77
    political development and the role of the capital, 75–76
    political development and the law o[peripheral neglect, 76
    political development and settlemen[size, 75

social development and spatial
structure, 72–74
social development and optimum
city size, 73–74
social development and spatial
democratization, 73
spread effects and backwash effects,
66
society and supra-urban space,
58–59
udene, 134
ystems Method, *see* procedural theory

echniques of regional planning, *see*
analytical and procedural;
also *see* – future prospects, 316
– appendix 2 for summary
bibliography
ennessee Valley Authority, 134, 136
heories of regional planning, *see* under
substantive and procedural
hird London Airport, 297–302

Threshold analysis, *see* cost minimiza-
tion techniques (plus Warsaw
Optimization Method)
Toothill Report 1961, 22
Trade Union Congress Economic
Review, 110
Training Opportunities Scheme,
92–93
Transport Act 1968, 41
Transportation Studies, 37, 39–41

Urban growth, 24–35

Victoria Line Study, 296

Warsaw Optimization Method, *see* cost
minimization techniques
Welsh Council, 101, 107, 110
West Midland Group, 160
White papers, *see* subject e.g. industrial
development

uthor Index

bercrombie, Sir, P., 52
lden, J.D., 252, 253
llen, K.J., 81, 119, 254
nderson, R.J., 254
ndrews, R., 253
rchibald, G.C., 254

anks, J.C., 162
anfield, E. and Myerson, M., 204
annerman, J.E., 56
atty, M., 252, 256
auer, R., 256
elassa, B., 81
erry, B.J.L., 80
erry, B.J.L. and Neils, E., 79, 80
icanic, R., 204
ickmore, D., 251
ake, C. and McDowall, S., 255
umerfeld, H., 253
olan, R., 208

Boudeville, J.R., 8
Boyce, D.E., Day, N.B. and McDonald,
C., 207
Braybrooke, D. and Lindblom, C.E., 204
Brenikov, P., 304
Broady, M., 121, 205, 209
Broniewski, S. and Jastrzebski, B., 306
Brown, A.J., 119, 254
Brown, G., 160
Buck, T., Paris, J., and Stillwell, F., 253
Burby, R., 208
Burns, W., 305

Camerson, G.C., 119
Cassett, J., 206
Catanese, A.J. and Steiss, A.W., 207
Chadwick, G., 207
Chester, T.E. and Gough, I.R., 160
Churchman, R., 207
Clarke, R., 163

Cole, G.D.H., 54, 163
Cross, J.A., 160
Cullingworth, J.B., 56
Czamanski, S., 254

Dahl, R.A. and Lindblom, C.E., 204
Daly, M.C., 253
Dasqupta, A.K., and Pearce, D.W., 308
Davidoff, P., 207
Davidoff, P. and Gold, 207
Davidoff, P. and Reiner, T.A., 204
Davies, B., 256
Denison, S.R., 52
Deutsch, K., 207
Dimitriou, B., 207
Dinkelspiel, J., 161
Dolenc, M., 255
Donnison, D., 163
Donnison, D. and Eversley, D., 163
Dower, M., 56
Drewnowski, J., 80
Dror, Y., 204
Duncan, O.P., 81
Dunham, D. and Hilhorst, J., 322
Dunn, E.S., 207
Dupuit, J., 307
Durston, J., 322

Eddison, T., 206
Edwards, J.A., 162
Edwards, S.L. and Gordon, I.R., 254
Eilon, S., Tilley, R. and Fowkes, T., 256
Etzioni, A., 207, 208

Fagin, H., 206
Fainstein, S.S. and N.I., 205
Faludi, A., 205, 208
Famelis, N., 306
Fawcett, C.B., 54
Fisk, T.A. and Jones, T.K., 165
Fogarty, M.P., 164
Foley, D., 205
Forbes, T.A., 306
Foster, C.D., 308
Foster, C.D. and Beesley, M.E., 30
  et seq.

Frank, A., 322
Fried, R.C., 163
Friedmann, J., 8, 52, 55, 78, 79, 81,
  162, 204, 207, 208, 209, 322
Friedmann, J. and Alonso, W., 52
Friend, J.W., Power, J.M. and
  Yewlett, C., 209

Grakenheimer, R., 55
Gans, H.J., 205
Geddes, P., 54
Gilmore, D., 164
Gremion, P., 161
Grieve, R., 162, 208
Gwilliam, K.M., 256

Haddad, P.R., 55
Hagerstrand, T., 80
Hall, P., 52, 53, 56, 322
Hallett, G., Randall, P. and West, E.G.,
  118
Hansen, N.M., 56, 79, 205
Hanson, A.H. and Walles, M., 163
Harris, B., 209, 322
Harris, D.F., Morgan, R.H. and Walter,
  L.G., 252
Howley, A. and Duncan, O.D., 256
Hedges, J., 56
Henriche, H. and Taylor, G.M., 307
Herand, B., 208
Herbert, D.T., 256
Hermansen, 80, 81
Hewings, G.J.D., 254
Hightower, H., 78
Hilhorst, J., 79
Hill, M., 307
Hill, M. and Tzamir, Y., 308
Hirschman, A., 79, 81
Hirschman, A. and Lindblom, C.E., 204
Holmans, A.E., 120
Holmes, J.C., 308
Hudson, P., 306
Hufschmidt, M.M., 52
Hughes, J. and Kolzlowski, J., 205
Hunt, A., 252
Huxley, J., 161

ersic, A.R., 252
sard, W., 251, 252, 253, 255

ames, P.M.B., 161
antsch, E., 304

aldor, N., 119
alk, E., 161
aspersen, R.E. amd Minghi, J.V., 81
itching, L.C., 305, 308
leinpenning, J., 162
orh, L. (see Kohr's Law of peripheral
    neglect), 81
ozlowski, J., 304, 305, 306
ozlowski, J., and Hughes, J., 305
uklinski, A.R., 56
utty, M.G., 56

ampard, E.L., 78
ansen, J.R., 79
awrence, R.J., 163
ean, W., 305, 306
eontief, W., 254
enin, M., 162
eyden, F. and Miller, E., 206, 307
eys, C., 205
eys, C. and Morris, P., 206
ichfield, N., 78, 305, 308
indblom, C.E., 204, 205
loyd, A. and Jackson, H., 27
lewelyn Davies, *et al*, 305
omas, G., 205
owry, I., 256
uttrell, W.F., 161

aas, M., 163
ackay, G.A., 162
cMurray, T., 162, 208
ackintosh, J., 160, 161, 163
acmillan, A., 164
alisz, B., 305, 306
cCrone, G., 53, 79, 162
cGuiness, J., 161
cLoughlin, J.B., 207
illward, R.B., 206, 307
ishan, E.J., 53, 307, 308
isra, R.P., 80

Morgan, R.H. and Hockaday, M.J., 164
Morsink, H., 165
Moseley, M.J., 80
Moser, C., and Scott, W., 256
Myerson, M., 204
Myrdal, G., 79

Needham, B., 304
Nevin, E., 121, 255
North, D.C., 253

Odum, H.W. and Moore, E., 52
Oliver, J.A., 163

Pahl, R.E., 80, 251
Painter, C., 161, 164
Pajic, R., 165
Pastore, J.M.D., 162
Pepler, G. and Macfarlane, P.W., 27
Perloff, H., 8, 209
Perroux, F., 78
Peters, G.H., 308
Pfouts, R.W., 254
Popper, K., 204
Pounds, N. and Bell. S., 81
Powell, A.G., 209
Pred, A., 78

Rath, R.A., 208
Ray, D.M., 80
Reade, E., 208
Rees, J., 165
Reichmann, W.J., 252
Reifler, R. and Tiebout, C., 255
Reilly, W.J., 256
Richardson, H., 254
Robertson, D.J., 78
Rodgers, W., 161
Rodwin, L., 55, 162
Roll, Sir, E., 53
Rondinelli, D., 205, 209
Rose, K., 307
Rouvre de, J.B., 209
Rowlands, E., 161

Samuelson, P., 254
Schultz, T.W., 252

Secchi, B., 306
Seeley, J., 204, 205
Self, P., 160
Selznick, P., 161
Shachar, A.S., 79
Sheuky, E. and Williams, M., 256
Shibli, K., 56
Shindman, B., 81
Slesser, M., 55
Smith, B.C., 160, 161, 164
Steele, D., 254
Steward, H., 307
Stewart, J., 255
Stewart, J.D., 206
Stewart, J.D. and Eddison, T., 206
Stillwell, F.J.B., 120, 253
Stone, P.A., 54, 305
Stuart, D.G., 206

Thomas, R., 120
Thompson, J., 54
Thompson, W.R., 80
Thorburn, A., 78, 161, 304
Thorne, E., 255
Thornhill, W., 160, 163
Tiebout, C.M., 253
Tomkins, C.R., *et al*, 255
Townroe, P., 207
Turnbull, P., 160

Turvey, R., 308

Ullman, E.L., 78, 81

Vance, R., 52
Viney, M., 160
Van de Geer, J.P., 256

Walsh, H.G. and Williams, A., 307
Waterston, A., 55
Watson, M.M., 56, 161, 162
Webber, M., 204, 205
Wheaton, W., 204
Wiesling, L., 164
Wildmer, R., 162
Williams, G., 161
Williamson, J.G., 79
Willis, G., 251
Wilson, A.G., 252, 253
Wingo, L., 208
Woodcock, G., 164
Woodward, V.H., 255
Wright, W., 306

Yeates, M.H. and Garner, B.J., 52
Young, M. and Willmott, P., 53

Ziolkowski, J., 80
Zipf, G.K., 255